Revolutionary Legacies

SUNY series in Feminist Criticism and Theory
―――――――
Michelle A. Massé, editor

SUNY series in Contemporary Jewish Thought
―――――――
Richard A. Cohen, editor

Revolutionary Legacies

Jewish Feminist Political Thinking
with Jamaica Kincaid, Golda Meir,
Hannah Arendt, Frida Kahlo,
Gertrude Stein, and Emma Goldman

MARLA BRETTSCHNEIDER

Cover credit: *Protest Against Child Labor in a Labor Parade*. New York, 1909. Photograph. https://www.loc.gov/item/97519062/.

Published by State University of New York Press, Albany

© 2025 State University of New York

All rights reserved

Printed in the United States of America

No part of this book may be used or reproduced in any manner whatsoever without written permission. No part of this book may be stored in a retrieval system or transmitted in any form or by any means including electronic, electrostatic, magnetic tape, mechanical, photocopying, recording, or otherwise without the prior permission in writing of the publisher.

Links to third-party websites are provided as a convenience and for informational purposes only. They do not constitute an endorsement or an approval of any of the products, services, or opinions of the organization, companies, or individuals. SUNY Press bears no responsibility for the accuracy, legality, or content of a URL, the external website, or for that of subsequent websites.

For information, contact State University of New York Press, Albany, NY www.sunypress.edu

Library of Congress Cataloging-in-Publication Data

Name: Brettschneider, Marla, author.
Title: Revolutionary legacies : Jewish feminist political thinking with Jamaica Kincaid, Golda Meir, Hannah Arendt, Frida Kahlo, Gertrude Stein, and Emma Goldman / Marla Brettschneider.
Description: Albany : State University of New York Press, [2025] | Series: SUNY series in contemporary Jewish thought | Includes bibliographical references and index.
Identifiers: LCCN 2024022287 | ISBN 9798855800609 (hardcover alk. paper) | ISBN 9798855800616 (ebook) | ISBN 9798855800593 (pbk. : alk. paper)
Subjects: LCSH: Women in Judaism. | Jewish women—Political activity. | Feminism—Political aspects. | Feminist theory—Political aspects.
Classification: LCC BM729.W6 B7467 2025 | DDC 305.48/8924—dc23/eng/20241011
LC record available at https://lccn.loc.gov/2024022287

This book is dedicated to Martha Ackelsberg

For all the reasons

Contents

Acknowledgments		ix
Chapter 1	Introduction	1
Chapter 2	Jamaica Kincaid: Diasporic and De-colonial Interstices	27
Chapter 3	Golda Meir: Smashing Binaries of Gender, Diaspora, and Anticolonialism	47
Chapter 4	Hannah Arendt: *Rahel Varnhagen* and Diasporic De-colonial Justice Theorizing: On Pariahs and Parvenu?e.s	89
Chapter 5	Frida Kahlo: On Creating Vibrant, Transnational Jewish Networks	115
Chapter 6	Gertrude Stein: A Queer Feminist Jew-ing: Constraints and Possibilities for Post-Emancipation Jewish Lives	145
Chapter 7	Emma Goldman: Anarchist Feminism, a New Frame for Diasporic Longings and Jewish Studies?	175
Notes		211
References		253
Index		277

Acknowledgments

This book has been decades in the making. So many people and groups have helped me along the way. Of course, all of its shortcomings are mine alone.

This book is dedicated to Martha Ackelsberg, for the long haul. And with gratitude for her friendship, for walking the path with me, for reading drafts of the whole manuscript, and for our many conversations.

Sincerest thank-yous to:

SUNY Press and its board and staff, James Peltz, the Contemporary Jewish Thought and Feminist Theory and Criticism series editors, and the anonymous external reviewers.

The organizers and participants in the following associations and academic conferences where I gave papers on aspects of this project over time: the Association for Jewish Studies; the Jewish Women's Archive; the International Society for the Study of African Jewry; the Western Political Science Association; Delia Konzett and the Black New England Conference; Ruach HaYam; Federica Francesconi, Elissa Bemporad as discussant, and participants at the New York State Working Group on Jewish Women and Gender in Global Perspective (supported by a grant from the American Academy for Jewish Research); the Jewish Women Thinkers sourcebook working group; the Hadassah-Brandeis Institute; the Brandeis University Seminar on Contemporary Jewish Life; Sabrina Sojourner and Theater J's Expanding the Canon; the Costa Rica—United Nations-mandated University for Peace; Sir Martin Gilbert Learning Centre, London; Edward Waters University; the University of North Florida; the Center for Jewish History; the Academy for Jewish Religion; the Jewish Museum of Florida-FIU; the American Jewish Historical Society Biennial Scholars Conference; Ferry Beach Conference Center; and numerous synagogues and community organizations across the US.

Richard Cohen and the Department of Jewish Thought at the University at Buffalo, SUNY; Rebecca Epstein-Levi, Alexander Joskowicz, and those in the Departments of Jewish Studies and Gender and Sexuality Studies at Vanderbilt University during that fateful week of October 7, 2023; Lewis and Jane Gordon and the Women's, Gender, and Sexuality Studies and Judaic Studies Programs at the University of Connecticut; Jonathan Branfman and the College of William and Mary; and FZA members' support and Annette Miller for having me do a talkback at the 2024 Boston run of the revival for the play *Golda's Balcony*.

During a solid period of the time in which I have worked on this book, I had the good fortune to have held the University of New Hampshire (UNH) Pamela Shulman Holocaust Studies Chair and been supported by the Hans Heilbronner Fund for Holocaust Education. I am very grateful for this. It was good timing to be called into engagement in Holocaust studies in many ways. At the start, I asked myself, What might be a "Marla-type," more formal entry into Holocaust studies and communal work? I knew I would operate with the co-constitutive theoretical orientations of Jewish, feminist, queer, antiracist, and class-based analysis. Along with my work on the Jewish phenomenon in Sub-Saharan Africa that developed over this period, this project also brought me into de-colonial critical theory more explicitly than had my previous work. Holocaust (and still, largely, Jewish) studies within de-colonial studies remains rare. It has been important and productive for me.

At UNH more broadly: the Department of Women's and Gender Studies; Joelle Ruby Ryan, Melissa Day, and the WGS writing group; the Department of Political Science and International Affairs; GRSL (Global Racial and Social Inequality Lab); the College of Liberal Arts; the Center for the Humanities; Louise Buckley and the Dimond Library staff; and the students in my classes in which I taught from this book over time.

The Hadassah-Brandeis Institute (HBI) afforded me two grants at key stages of this project: in 2010 for my earlier work (and to Sue Levi Elwell for support with that proposal) and in 2021 as a Scholar in Residence (though not many of us were physically in residence due to a high COVID-19 count in Massachusetts that semester).

The UNH GRSL and Departments of Political Science and Women's and Gender Studies and the Hadassah-Brandeis Institute student research assistants, including Patrick Baga, Richard Barney, Alyssa Brady, Michael Branley, Marina Cardoso-Vianna-Vaz, Samantha Costa, Katie Clark, Caroline Cundy, Angelina, Joelle Galatan, Caroline Hall, Jing Huang, Bethany

Kaminsky, Elisabeth Loehmuller, Nick Pasquale, Jessica Rosenthal, Sofia Siegel, and Leah Trachtenberg.

B'not Esh, very specially, which has challenged and embraced me for more than thirty years and helped me work out so much of my life and of this book.

The members of the HBI feminism, Zionism, and antisemitism working group, who quickly also became good friends and a calm in the numerous storms in this period; the Jewish Multiracial Network for living and thinking in practice; Chani Getter and the Women's Nehirim for being an extraordinary home for a while and where, one year, Sabrina Sojourner took us on a journey that was central to the development of this book; the community of the National Havurah Institute; and the fabulous women of political science in our expedition to Mexico City and back to La Casa Azul and Leon Trotsky's next home there before his assassination.

Lanie Resnick, Alexandra Adler, Ana Gomes, and Mariana Chemaly for their unique modes of support, on their own and together.

For their reading, friendship, and/or support throughout and at crucial moments: Dawn Rose; Carol Conaway; Ruthie Berman and Connie Kurtz; Evelyn ("Evi") Beck, Patricia Moynagh (thank you for getting to the Arendt chapter!), and Lori Marso; Beth Martin and Penina Weinberg; Sarra Lev and Dianne Cohler Esses; Nina Davidson; Sara and Michael Pasche-Orlow; Jane Litman and Sonya Pilz; Robin Hackett (particularly for her support on the Stein chapter) and Siobhan Senier; Jeannie Sowers and Mary Malone; Sandy Sussman and Rebecca Lesses; Barbara Johnson and Judith Plaskow; Kathy Ferguson and her fantastic (including her much appreciated critique of my own) work on Goldman; Eve Sicular and also Tamara Cohen for Meir contacts in Jerusalem; and Nina Judith Katz also for her work beyond editing. I thank Gannit Ankori and Evi Beck for pulling me out of a pit at the last minute before I hit "send" on the manuscript.

Bonita Nathan Sussman and Gerald Sussman, for their friendship, for our work together, and for their Miami Beach apartment as a retreat for the final rewrite.

As always, to Beth and Nina, Paris and Toni. Thanks to my parents, who taught me to ask questions, and for the love and support of my grandparents and family.

Early and/or brief versions of the Kincaid and Goldman chapters were published as follows: the Kincaid chapter as an entry in the Jewish Women's Archive's *Shalvi/Hyman Encyclopedia of Jewish Women*; in *African Zion: Studies in Black Judaism*, edited by Edith Bruder and Tudor Parfitt

(Cambridge Scholars, 2012); and in *Fifty-One Key Feminist Thinkers*, edited by Lori Marso (Routledge, 2016); and the Goldman chapter as an entry in the *Oxford Bibliographies in Jewish Studies*, Naomi Seidman, editor in chief (2021).

V.
Miami Beach, Florida
Portsmouth, New Hampshire
2024

Chapter 1

Introduction

This book is a Jewish study of diaspora and colonialism, of genocidal settler colonialism. This work in Jewish feminist political thinking focuses on six twentieth-century Western women. Each is a transnational figure, and this project undertakes a Jewish analysis in a transnational context.

I have been working on this project since the early 2000s.

I have been working on this project all my life.

Here, I explore how these six brilliant and talented mischief-makers can help us as we create our Jewish lives and multiple communities vibrantly. I ask, How can thinking with these simultaneously broken and whole troublemakers helps us get on with the projects of making our lives more generally: individually, collectively, and as Jews, feminists, antiracists, queers, anticolonialists, and justice seekers? I have long been working out how we can best attend to anti-Jewish issues at both the interpersonal and structural levels in our diversity as Jews and in deep solidarity with others. Thinking with these six helps me to do that. In our worlds where vessels shatter, shards are gathered, again and again.

The six women you will find in these pages are a distinctive set of unusual public figures. I have been researching each figure individually, sometimes in various combinations, as well as all together as a group. Here, readers will find chapters on Jamaica Kincaid, Golda Meir, Hannah Arendt, Frida Kahlo, Gertrude Stein, and Emma Goldman. I have chosen to let my engagements with each of these extraordinary people stand mainly on their own, making one woman the focus in each chapter. At the same time, my work with all of them led to fruitful cross-fertilization that made the whole of this book possible.

As in the subtitle of this book, what does it mean that I am thinking with each and all? To call the figures I explore here thinkers is to make them, and our relationship, more static than they were. Yes, I was doing research "on" them, but that came to take the form of thinking "with" them. I asked questions, and so did they. I challenged them, and they challenged me. They turned the kaleidoscopes of their lives and saw new vistas; they asked me to come take a look with them. They held out on me, afraid, confused, or even ecstatic; I asked gently to walk beside them; I also pouted, got angry and frustrated, demanded. There is no one answer to the questions, What is a theoretical analysis? a Jewish, or feminist, or political one? This project demonstrates that we need to build new modes of inquiry.

In this book, I use what I call a political-as-personal methodology.[1] What feminists often mean by the vision "the personal is political" is that we need to see that much of what we have called private or personal actually operates through public discourse on a political stage. Readers will find that method brought into this study. I also look at the public aspects of my subjects' legacies (i.e., their art, politics, work) to consider how these might have mattered to their making of what some might take as the private aspects of their lives (their sexualities, gender orientations, choices of where to live and how to present themselves, what they liked to read, what to make of their family ties, etc.).

I take the figures' work, politics, art, life, and activism *together* as I explore each one. Who are these women? Who are we? I have been working to explore how new approaches, ones that activate our hearts together with our spirits and heads, might tell us more about these figures and their milieus. I ask, How can new multivalent looks at these historical figures help us experiment with creative ways to be Jewish in our time? I wonder, How can insights gleaned in a Jewish feminist study of this unexpected gathering of those who came before us transform the thinking and collective projects of both Jews and non-Jews?

Honestly, I really want to know how to be Jewish in the world with our neighbors. I mean that. How can we be Jewish, Jewish women, and people? Every so often over the past couple thousand years, some people seemed to think they had this figured out. Still, this challenge has been far from smoothed out by 2025.

Martha Ackelsberg once shared that she thought of this book as a salon. That comment helped me to understand some of what I was doing. I am delighted for you to join me, for you to bring yourself into this conversation.

As for me, I use my capacities as a political theorist to tackle this expansive inquiry. While each figure has been the subject of extensive commentary, sometimes academic and sometimes popular, each troubles or poses challenges to standard ways of defining one or more of my focal categories: Jewish, feminist, political, thinker. My tousle with these troublemakers stems from a deliberate choice: an aim of this feminist work is to critically reexamine these categories, together and separately, and particularly in a Jewish context. Some readers will have issues wrapping their heads around my feminist thinking with these women. Some will not get, at first, that sometimes I'm exploring whether (and when, how, why) Jewish crumbs might make sense in new ways if we see them as part of a trail, a trail of Jewish crumbs. Challenging these categories is a generative undertaking and a signal contribution that feminist work done in a Jewish frame can provide. Central to my feminist Jewish political theorizing is that my approach here works simultaneously and explicitly with numerous mutually constitutive (some might say intersectional) analytic tools, primarily queer, critical race, class-based, and de-colonial theories. Their troubling of the four categories of this book was a good starting point. That was just the beginning. What happens when we assume from the start that these women are troublemakers, ask questions about the Jewish context of that troublemaking, and then ask how they went on with the project of living their lives? How did they go about being Jewish, Jewish women, and people all at once?

While the subjects of these chapters overlapped in their historical contexts to varying degrees, and most of them also overlapped geographically, at least intermittently, they did not necessarily seek each other out as comrades. They did not even engage much with each other as nemeses. They required neither friendship nor critique from each other. But each of us leaves a legacy beyond the conscious entanglements we take on during our lives. Hanging out with each and with all of them together has been valuable for me. In presenting this book, I hope that this work will also be beneficial for you, as well as for Jewish feminism and social justice movements in general. And I look forward to folks picking up my approach and thinking with other interesting people.

Okay, So Who Are These Women? In Brief

I do not present these chapters in chronological order of my subjects' births but rather in a way that gets us started analytically and increasingly cultivates our skills toward the work we need to do with Emma Goldman, as the last chapter. I realize that many readers will not know much about the women of this book. At the risk of repetition, I thus present brief biographies here before I say more. Here are my six:

Jamaica Kincaid (1949 to present) was born Elaine Cynthia Potter Richardson in Antigua, a Caribbean island colonized by the British. Kincaid is a prolific writer and political thinker. Although she had been a good student, in 1966, before she could graduate from high school, her parents sent her to the US to work as an au pair. In 1973, she began publishing her writing, both fiction and nonfiction. She began writing regularly for the *New Yorker*, published in an array of popular and literary intellectual journals, and eventually authored many books. Generally, her work focuses on diasporic and postcolonial Caribbean feminist themes. These are also significant Jewish themes.

Golda Meir (1898 to 1978) was born in Kyiv and came to the US with her family in 1906 to flee anti-Jewish violence. Her family was active in overlapping socialist, labor, and Zionist movements. The main strains of the Zionist movement at this time were understood by many globally as a Jewishly particular aspect of a comprehensive international liberation movement made possible by an infinite variety of oppressions and ways of life experienced within local contexts. Thus, historically and as a political theory, fraught as is any big theoretical paradigm, Zionism has included a broad range of transformational strategies as part of human collective engagements in the long historical arc toward justice. Meir joined the Labor Zionist movement, and then she made aliyah (moved to Palestine) in 1921 as the region was undergoing a significant shift in its colonial occupiers: from Ottoman to British. While she prioritized kibbutz living, Meir lived mainly in cities, and as her political career developed she came to live in urban centers exclusively. Meir emerged among a small group of pre-state Jewish leaders who transitioned to ministerial positions in the new Israeli government. Meir became foreign minister, minister of labor, and, eventually, the fourth prime minister of the country (from 1969 to 1974). She is still the only woman to have served as Israeli prime minister. A tough politician, she built and held her power base in part through her ongoing ties with Jewish women's groups internationally. Her rise in the political ranks of the pre-state Yishuv in Palestine was further supported by her history of grassroots community organizing in the US, where her fiery oratory continued to impress English-speaking audiences.

Hannah Arendt (1907 to 1975) was born and raised in a middle-class Jewish family in Germany. Arendt studied philosophy at the University of Marburg, an avenue then quite unusual for both Jews and women, and especially for Jewish women. In 1933, the Gestapo arrested and jailed her for investigating Nazi antisemitic propaganda. They released her after one week; she fled and ended up settling in Paris for a significant period. Over her lifetime, Arendt was active in various Zionist initiatives: intellectual, political, and direct service. Among her concrete Zionist actions was her work in Paris for Youth Aliyah, a project that was able to bring many stateless Jewish children and young people to Palestine in 1935. In 1940, with the Nazi takeover of France, Arendt was arrested again and detained with thousands of Jewish women and children. She and many of the others were sent to an internment camp in the south of France. Arendt managed to escape the camp. She fled to New York in 1941 on a rare emergency visa organized for some of Europe's most threatened intellectual and cultural elites. Once in the US, Arendt lived mainly in New York City and held a number of positions in academia, publishing, and Jewish communal institutions. Hannah Arendt published extensively and emerged as one of the major political and philosophical thinkers of the twentieth century.

Frida Kahlo (1907 to 1954) was a Mexican painter, a leading figure in the *Mexicanidad* arts and revolutionary movement, a bisexual, and a communist. Kahlo represented herself as hailing from a mixed family, with a Hungarian German immigrant father and a mixed Spanish Catholic and Indigenous mother. After a short time in Mexico City's prestigious German elementary school, Kahlo contracted polio, which forced her to leave school. In 1925 Kahlo was badly injured in a bus accident. The injuries she sustained in the accident affected her for the rest of her life. While in bed recovering, Kahlo began to focus seriously on painting. Her intense health struggles would also eventually make her an important inspiration to the disabilities movement. While she remained based in Mexico City, throughout her peripatetic life she situated herself in the center of art, politics, and intellectual circles across Europe and North America, making art, creating community, and fighting antisemitism and all aspects of fascism of her time.

A genre-defying writer and a major figure in the art world, Gertrude Stein (1874 to 1946) was also out as the life partner of the Jewish Alice B. Toklas. Stein wrote novels, plays, operas, essays, and numerous portraits in prose. Born in the US to a wealthy German Jewish family, she spent most of her adult years in Paris, where she hosted a salon that brought together intellectuals and artists from around Europe as well as expatriate and visiting luminaries from the US. Stein survived World War II in France. Though a US citizen, as a Jew, intellectual, and out lesbian, she was a target for fascists, and her work was on the list of banned works in France during the Nazi occupation. She and Toklas left Paris with the German invasion and sought refuge in the "free zone," the Vichy-controlled south of France (until Germany took over that region as well). While not always able to find publishers for her work, she wrote prolifically and gained significant renown during her lifetime, and even more posthumously.

Emma Goldman (1869 to 1940) was born into an Orthodox Jewish family in the heavily Jewish Lithuanian city of Kaunas/Kovno, then part of the Russian Empire. After a few moves with her family, in 1885, at fifteen, Goldman and one of her sisters fled the anti-Jewish violence of their native Europe and joined their older sister in Rochester, New York. Over the course of her lifetime, Goldman worked many jobs for pay, and she became notorious for her anarchist feminist thinking, activism, speaking, and writing. Her anarchism brought together critiques of church, state, militarism, and capitalism with challenges to patriarchy and heteronormativity. At the same time, her work theorizing and interrupting these oppressive institutions inspired her revolutionary visions of beauty, the arts, and sexual freedom. After spending most of her life in the US and Russia, and after years in multiple exiles, she spent the last years of her life in Toronto.

Jewish Feminist Political Thinking through Diversity

While the main subjects of the following chapters have enjoyed a good deal of celebrity, they have not been the focus of extensive scholarly inquiry in a Jewish feminist frame. This was very much the case when I began this study. I am glad to have encountered more material over time.[2] Some of them have been the subjects of writing from a feminist or a Jewish studies perspective. For example, Seyla Benhabib engages Hannah Arendt in a Jewish feminist political theory framework. Jennifer Ring (1997) does a mighty job exploring Arendt through both a gendered and a Jewish lens. Feminist or not, still too few studies have touched on the questions of how their Jewish context and Jewishness might have mattered to them and their lives, work, and politics, or how their lives, work, and politics might matter Jewishly. In this work I prioritize a multilayered Jewish feminist frame in my approach to learning about and thinking with each and all of these women.

In working on this project, I draw on my status as an insider/outsider. What does it mean to say that I am an insider/outsider in this context, with these mutually constitutive categories? Like many—particularly Jews; feminists; queer theorists; those who do critical race, class-based, or de-colonial work; and certainly Jewish feminists (people, scholars, artists, activists) who do all of these—I am alternately dismissed or embraced for being too this or too that. I am too Jewish, or not Jewish enough. I can be rendered suspect among feminists, queers, antiracists, class critics, de-colonialists, and an array of activists and critical theorists for being so Jewish and for a host of other particularities. In academia, my work is too multi- and interdisciplinary for some. As a theorist, my work is at times cast as either too engaged with the mundane or too much a product of the ivory tower. Each of these aspects of my work is also a strength that helps me to make a contribution. Grounding my work in the multiple and inherently connected analytical tools and political commitments of feminist, Jewish, critical race, queer, class-based, and de-colonial theories and politics renders me unintelligible to some and a reliable resource and ally to others. In these pages, I offer some of the process and product of such insider/outsider training, experience, and commitments. I bring all of my insider/outsider self to the work on this project.

Time and again, this work has reaffirmed for me that a dedication to doing new work in new ways can yield new insights. So obvious? It turns out, this is neither as obvious nor easy as it sounds. This commitment has been a basic premise of diversity studies founded on highlighting that which has been degraded and dehumanized in a wrangle of (in)justice politics—including those long excluded from the activities and practices in which we make meaning—and bringing us into the worlds that we create from what we value and deem worthy of attention. This approach does far more than merely add the new into previously existing realities. I entered this work with the hunch that including those previously excluded could change our paradigms themselves. Further, even when facing difficulties, I trusted my long-held practice of drawing on alternative methods that can help us shift our actions in and beyond academic scholarship. A Jewish feminist work that is foundationally queer, race-critical, class-based, and de-colonial (at the very least in aspiration, as these are ongoing and never complete projects) will find aspects of wonder, interest, and connections previously unidentified, unnamed, unexplored, and underexamined. In the course of this project, I have found this to be the case over and over again.

I ask a lot of questions. With many others over time, I have worked to heighten curiosity and hone my skills of inquiry. In this project I ask,

How can Kincaid's complex grappling with diaspora demonstrate for us the importance of centering colonialism in diaspora studies undertaken in Jewish contexts? How can a Jewish feminist analysis of her work contribute Jewish insights to larger diaspora and de-colonial theory and politics? In what ways can a Jewish feminist analysis show us Golda Meir not merely as a head of state or ideologue but as one who smashed multiple boundaries in ways that have become crucial to critical theory and political activism today? How does this examination of Meir's fraught legacy come into relief in ways that are politically productive for us in our time? How does using a Jewish feminist lens to look at Hannah Arendt reposition her work on the Jewish salonnière Rahel Varnhagen as central to the intellectual direction of Arendt's life? How does Arendt's work on another historical Jewish woman demonstrate that challenging the genocidal contours of assimilation politics for the despised is central to Arendt's theorizing justice? What can Kahlo's transnational web of Jewish relations in the first half of the twentieth century help us learn about the robust ways we are, and can be, Jewish today? What can a Jewish feminist analysis offer to the throngs of Kahlo acolytes, scholars, artists, and a range of ordinary folk? What of import for us today can a Jewish feminist approach to Gertrude Stein's life, art, politics, and work show us about Stein and a legacy of Jewish women creating transnational community? And into the final chapter: In what ways can a Jewish feminist analysis of Emma Goldman generate fresh understandings of anarchism and also offer a profoundly new frame for Jewish studies? These are some of the main questions that animate this examination, bringing in new subjects of study in new ways that support us as we innovate for ourselves and our communities in societies that are still based in power hierarchies.

Women? And Why These Women?

Over the course of this study, others have asked me many questions as well. While I have endeavored to speak to many of these questions in the coming chapters, a few of them deserve attention here at the start. For example, some have asked me why I am focusing on women as such when I agree that a binary gender system is a social construction and has been a violent one at that. For decades, I have been lucky enough to create communities with women and with people using a range of pronouns and in which I am often given space to dynamically note, express, and change my gendering. For me, trans, conceptually and as lived experiences, means many things. In particular, I experience and seek to develop trans as a process of becoming, in connection and in transgression, on my own and in communities. In all of this, women in my historical time and place are truly important. There are many aspects to my commitments to women. This book is one of them. It has been vital, personally and as a politics, to explore this question with others.

With nudging, more or less gently, another question that I have pondered is about Ashkenormativity and thinking more deeply with Sephardis, Mizrahis, and Jewish women beyond these ethnocentric Jewish groupings. I have been doing what I call Jewish critical race theory for a number of decades now. I'd say that my selection of the six in this book is far from normatively Ashkenazi. That doesn't make this book a Sephardi study source, but it does help with Ashkenormativity. I hope that others with more training than I have take up new studies on people such as Doña Gracia Nasi (ca. 1510 to 1569), Esther Handali (d. 1590), Esperanza Malchi (d. 1600), and Glückel of Hameln (ca. 1646 to 1724), among others.

Many have asked me, Why these women and not others? I love hearing the array of people my project brings to mind for others. This is one book. That necessarily limits its scope. I look forward to many more adventures with many more women and all people, with those who use the methods you will find here and with new ones as well. I can't speak to all the great potential subjects folks have asked me about. Here are some more on my own list:

While chronology is not an organizing principle for this project, there is an era that I focus on here. The time frame for this book spans from Jamaica Kincaid, who is with us today, to Emma Goldman, born in the late 1800s. In a historical sense, Jewish studies folks are still in the process of constructing "the contemporary" as a field set off from the modern. In political and feminist theory, the contemporary is sometimes thought of as following a modernism invented by scholars of the time period and since.

While I am not a historian, clustering figures chronologically to look at this question (Whom else from history might it be fun to think with?) lends clarity about some among our extensive choices. I would love to see inquiries on other eras and ones that could stretch this era without necessarily breaking it, looking for instance at Rose Emma Salaman (1815 to 1898) and Adah Isaacs Menken (1835 to 1868). There are good questions: If I have focused here on Emma Goldman (1869 to 1940) and Gertrude Stein (1874 to 1946), why not Emma Lazarus (1849 to 1887), Rosa Luxemburg (1871 to 1919), Esther Moyal (1874 to 1948), and Luisa Capetillo (1879 to 1922)? I look at Golda Meir (1898 to 1978), Hannah Arendt (1906 to 1975), and Frida Kahlo (1907 to 1954), as they emerged for me as a cluster more or less at the center of the era I am constructing. Given that time span, I look forward to future projects on some of their contemporaries, such as Sulochana, born Ruby Myers (1907 to 1983); Pramila, born Esther Victoria Abraham (1916 to 2006); Jacqueline Shohet Kahanoff (1917 to 1979); Betty Freidan (1921 to 2006); and Beki Luiza Bahar (1926 to 2011). More immediate contemporaries of Jamaica Kincaid (1949 to present) with whom it would be wonderful to work are Hélène Cixous (1937 to present); Carolivia Herron (1947 to present); Ada Fischer (1947 to 2022); Paula Jacques, born Paula Abadi (1949 to present); Lani Guinier (1950 to 2022); Brigitte Peskine (1951 to 2020); and Chochana Boukhobza (1959 to present). What? These women are Jews? Yup. What is my response to these queries about why not other women? Please do these studies. Show me what I am missing. Show us all new ways of living rich Jewish lives.[3]

Each of these six figures enabled me to think through specific subjects and do certain kinds of thinking. Perhaps prompting Ackelsberg's comparison of this book to a salon, I have been engaging and thinking with these women for years, in talks and conversations, and others have joined me. Now I invite readers to come in. In a salon, a host might start out announcing that the evening will focus on discussing transnational communities seeking justice. Then, the participants in the salon take the topic wherever they do (at least in the unruly spaces I have been in). Letting these women speak to and guide me has been an amazing process. I did not only, or fully, impose my issues on them. Though, I do keep asking—with and of them—my central questions regarding how to be a Jew and how to be a person altogether.

When I was starting the book some decades ago, I was fairly preoccupied with diaspora, and especially with alienation and diaspora. You will find my explorations of this theme central to each chapter. We start with Kincaid because with her we work out some things we need to for the work of the book as a whole. We then complicate matters and explore further as the book progresses so that we will have the tools that we will need to use in our thinking with Emma Goldman. The book begins with Jamaica Kincaid because we needed to start out deeply politicizing diaspora in the way that she does. Bringing a critical assessment of colonialism into work in diaspora studies at the start opened my understanding of diaspora for multivalent and co-constructed Jewish studies. Building on that as I learned with Kahlo and the others, I have come to realize that this diasporic inquiry is also about examining genocidal settler colonialism. But I get ahead of myself.

Does the variety of figures I focus on here make conceptual coherence, or Jewish coherence, categorically impossible? At times, over the many years in which I have been working on this project, I have thought about whether the answer to this question might be simply that this group of thinkers only seems so disparate because no one has previously thought of them together. Or did my interlocutors determine that these historical figures are so different because we have not previously appreciated them in a more multivalent, Jewish feminist (feminist, Jewish, queer, critical race, class-based, de-colonial) frame that takes in a fuller complex of their life, work, politics, and art? Once I began asking these questions, I encountered a font of overlapping innovation and imbricating pressures. Once I let these figures speak on their own and together, dynamic and mutually enriching modes of investigation emerged. The question of what it means to normalize marginalization is worth exploring. Must cogent examination itself require sameness? Can exploring different examples of how we might sustain vibrant Jewish living help us with one of the most necessary matters before us: creating life-affirming Jewish worlds?

Good folks have asked, How can I presume to explore Jewishness by studying these figures, in all their diversity, in a Jewish context? If I center difference, does our very diversity not lead us to defy collective conceptualization? No, quite simply, it does not. Coherence does not require sameness. As Wittgenstein discusses his (Jewish queer) idea of family resemblance, and as I have explored in my work with mutually constitutive theory since the 1980s with *Cornerstones of Peace*, we can have clusters of context that overlap and might relate to each other inherently (Brettschneider 1996). We may echo Gertrude Stein, who famously declared "there is no there there," in saying that any "there," Jewish or other, is constituted through diversity. This has been a pillar of diversity theorizing for decades. It still works for me. I hope it is helpful for many of us. In doing work through diversity as a base, we also find that we need to rethink and re-vision central categories within which we make meaning, community, and politics.

Challenging Constitutive Categories

All of the subjects of this book trouble at least one of the framing categories of the project: what it means to be Jewish, feminist, political, and a thinker. They are not the only potential subjects who could do so. But their troubling effects are a significant part of why I chose these six, and part of what has made engaging with them such a treat. There always seems to be someone policing our boundaries. Who among us is truly beyond being ruled out of some important category by normalizing policing? How can thinking with historical boundary breakers using contemporary critical theoretical tools open new routes for us today? Shift our visions to seeing new roots?

Over the years, foes, friends, colleagues, and comrades have asked whether these women are even *feminists*. When I first studied Hannah Arendt while in graduate school for political theory, my professors presented her as horribly antifeminist. This was in the 1980s. Feminist analyses of Arendt have blossomed since.[4] Frequently, I have heard the refrain that Golda Meir was no feminist. People have regaled me with tales of Gertrude Stein's antifeminist conservatism. They have repeated that Emma Goldman liked to hang around with the "big boys" and that she whined endlessly about failed heterosexual romances. Some say that Jamaica Kincaid harms women by portraying them so "negatively." They note that Frida Kahlo let Diego Rivera walk all over her and so she should not be hailed as a feminist role model. Do we need to remind ourselves that to be of interest for feminists, one does not have to be a feminist role model? Or to ask, What is a feminist role model, anyway?

As readers will note, I do not bother making an argument about whether these women are feminists. Instead, I can be a feminist who engages with these women in feminist ways for feminist aims. And they have rewarded me handsomely for this. I hope you will be inspired to search for your own feminist treasures by honoring the thorny life quests of these women and others who have come before many of us. Might this help us more compassionately take up the knotty legacies of our own lifetimes?

How can I call these women *political?* Kahlo was a painter, Kincaid and Stein were writers, and Arendt was a philosopher, if also a political theorist. But they all have their detractors. I have heard some people seek to degrade Goldman's political street cred by claiming that her thinking is derivative and that she never really organized grassroots movements. Okay, Meir was a head of state, but critics will say that her vision of justice as a Zionist was too compromised to be of any use for us today. But these criticisms are based in limited and limiting concepts of what is "political." I argue that these women were all political, as we are. We live, alone and together, within constantly refracting power dynamics in which we are always both agents and objects in a lot of ways. A geologist once told me that everything is geology. I'm a political theorist, and I enjoy addressing politics everywhere. I encourage you to take up the practice; it is liberating.

What is Brettschneider up to, including (choose your foremother) in a study of Jewish *thinkers*? Over the years I have heard people reiterate that Goldman never produced a "great work" of anarchist theory; Meir was, at best, a tedious strategist; Kahlo wasn't a communist leader or theoretician; whoever claims to understand Stein's writing is lying; and what does it say about Kincaid's thinking when we look at her writing style? "Okay, maybe we'll let Arendt stand as a theorist," some will say, but then still reduce her work to presenting a series of Aristotelian dualisms. In working on this book, it was not always clear to me who are the thinkers: sometimes it seemed that they are, and sometimes it seemed that I am. In retrospect, I know that the answer is both. They were thinkers. So am I. Whose thinking have I been examining and developing, theirs or mine? Each and all of ours. I consider that a strength. You can try your own version of this.

Jewish feminist political theory is an act of love. Love has many manifestations. In this case, it consists of taking troublemakers and rabble-rousers seriously and critically analyzing them and their work. The benefits are endless. This is particularly so for the ways these women trouble the boundaries of Jewishness.

I understand that, for some, inclusion of each of the people in these pages in the category of *Jewish* is open to question. I hear you. For some, a question about this currently in vogue regards Frida Kahlo. The narrative of Kahlo's having been raised by a Jewish father was challenged only years after her death. Jewish feminists had just recently come to claim her as "one of us" by around the turn of the Christian millennium. In 2005, a book arguing that Kahlo's father was not Jewish was published in German and initiated a burst of conversation (a good deal of it is way more nasty than "conversation"). Many challenged me lovingly about this. You have made the project so much better. Also, honestly, some challenges weren't so loving. Some who challenge me about Kahlo's identity read German (thank you, Evi Beck), but most of those troubled by this acknowledged to me that they have not actually read this work. There wasn't a ton of published deep thinking with Kahlo on a Jewish feminist sensibility even when people often casually referred to her father as Jewish. Kahlo was in Europe on the verge of World War II, well into the murderous Nazi rage against Jews, the Left, intellectuals, and artists. Kahlo was in Paris with numerous key figures of the time who became direct Nazi targets. She lived in Mexico during the Nazi Holocaust in a city increasingly impacted by German Nazi influence. Nevertheless, we rarely find serious inquiry into whether or how the new biographical note about her father's paternal lineage might have made a difference for Kahlo or for anyone who interacted with her or her work. The main exception is the work of Gannit Ankori. You will notice that in the Kahlo chapter I do not say whether Kahlo is Jewish, nor do I examine that as a question. I'm looking at the way she created transnational webs with Jewish connections at their center. That seems to me like a pretty good way to create a Jewish life.[5] Perhaps asking each other more questions will allow expansive conceptualizations of Jewishness? "Does it matter that I have never/only ever had a Jewish lover?" A rabbi friend often counsels "yes" to those who ask her this when thinking about themselves on a Jewish journey. We can only see.

This question of who is sufficiently Jewish came up with all the others, beyond just Kahlo. Engaging with these figures requires us to get curious about Jewishness as a potentially meaningful category. In some ways, my least controversial subject from the point of view of the Jewish category might appear to be Hannah Arendt. Arendt spent a lifetime at the center of transnational Jewish progressive intellectual life only to have her status as a legitimate daughter of Zion rescinded when she was charged by former allies and close friends with lacking *ahavat Israel* (love for the Jewish people). A Zionist and German Jewish survivor of the Holocaust, Hannah Arendt is generally accepted as one of the leading intellectual figures of the twentieth century. Arendt was long a respected darling of the Jewish intelligentsia, from the US to Israel, but she experienced a dramatic fall from grace upon the publication of her account and analysis of the trial of the accused Nazi war criminal Adolf Eichmann (originally published serially, as had been contracted, in the *New Yorker*). She also understood that engaging the Zionist project required co-creation with Palestinians. When an array of strands of Zionism collapsed under the historical weight of the British partition plan on the heels of the havoc wrought by the Holocaust, Arendt continued to argue against a statist version of Jewish self-determination. Despite her apparently obvious status as a Jew, including her Holocaust "credentials," stellar mind, and work for Jewish and Zionist organizations, her political and intellectual work caused many to call her a traitor to her people and to position her outside the boundaries of Jewishness. Even some longtime allies of Arendt participated in this rejection. Many Jewish feminists know that our acceptance and position as community members is never simply a given. For many of us, it is always conditional; our politics, ideas, and actions often override other seemingly basic facts of our Jewishness. In the year following October 7, 2023, leftists frequently valorized Arendt, including many energetic anti-Zionists and those who refused to interact with anyone near a Zionist, somehow forgetting that Zionism was central to her lifelong thinking, politics, and activism.

Is so-and-so Jewish? The answer can always be provisional, usually in ways that call into question the strengths and the very dignity of the person. This challenge to our positionality frequently serves as a form of Jewish—and other—cultural or political policing that confers power and prestige on some while removing others from the ranks of those acknowledged as worthy of care or study, or even acknowledged as important. For example, biographers of Gertrude Stein reliably note that she came from a German Jewish family and then go on to ignore the many ways in which that might matter. At times, there is an intermediary moment between the claim of her Jewishness and its dismissal. Stein will often be introduced in the following manner: "Born to German Jewish parents, Stein was not raised religiously . . ." or with some other term to connote that Jewishness was not important to her life trajectory. Such a dismissal also means that one can then ignore Stein's significance in a Jewish context. However, a pinnacle of this sort of dynamic didn't occur until decades after Stein died, when she was subjected to a new, Jew-on-Jew witch hunt decrying her as a turncoat to her people. By around 2000, after years on the sidelines of Jewish communal inclusion in staking out our cultural history, like Kahlo, Stein finally began to be the subject of honored examination (with much feminist attention to get her to this place). In a flurry, numerous Jewish museums curated exhibits on her. In response, a coterie of right-wing, male, Jewish political figures chose to challenge her Jewish identity as part of a campaign to vilify her bequests to Jewish life. It was only upon a distinctly Jewish and often feminist celebration of Stein around the year 2000 that these gatekeepers sprung into action with this perceived threat to their concept of "who is a Jew" and what sorts of laundry it is okay to hang out in public. We can find similar disdain of any particular Jews from non-Jews, sporadically rising to public outcry.

Gatekeepers can target anyone. This targeting seems endemic to the politics of policing identities and group membership. No one is ever safe. Various empowered and marginalized communities face the pitfalls of what is often referred to as "respectability" politics.[6] We need specifically feminist analysis to unpack this gatekeeping. It is not surprising that the Jewishly troubling subjects of this book are all women. All are boundary pushers in their own ways.

I am asked, "Does it matter that so many of the close associations of this or that communist were Jewish?" Or I am told, "I'm pretty sure that anarchist wouldn't have hung out with all those Jews if they weren't anarchists." And, "She only surrounded herself with all those Jews because they shared the same values." Likely, yes. I'm pretty Jewish. You don't know me all that well yet. You may already realize, however, that you don't expect me to seek out rabid fascist Jews for my new "revolutionary rest" book group. Of course not. Are you gonna tell me that things Jewish don't matter to me since I gravitate toward Jewish versions of the many aspects of life I consider worth living? Or that I can't prove that I seek dynamic Jewish communities because additional facts of my life include that "some of my best friends" aren't Jewish?

Emma Goldman was a political person whose Jewishness was rooted in revolutionary thinking and action in the streets. She experienced extreme anti-Jewish hatred firsthand. She reached for beauty and justice like a prophet. In contrast, for example, to Abraham Joshua Heschel or even Isaac Deutscher, Goldman did not pair these facets of herself with traditional Jewish religious or scholarly credentials. She has been nearly cast into oblivion as a Jewish thinker. Goldman is rarely treated as worthy of inclusion in Jewish studies outside of rare feminist and radical political circles. Spoiler alert: I did NOT unearth a trove of letters Goldman exchanged with Alexander Berkman on their Jewish souls. How can I center Jewishness in my thinking with her? Not the same, but certainly related: in a political environment post–October 7, 2023, in which so many Jews are being told they are not welcome in too many spaces (even spaces with many Jews who have somehow, at least temporarily, passed some test), I imagine Goldman being "canceled" like so many. (Wait for it: Goldman considered immigrating to Palestine in her later exile.)

None of those with whom I think in this book was religiously observant. People often state that Goldman was not religiously observant as a way to mark that she had a break from her family of origin and that Jewishness was not important to her. Goldman's family may have operated within Orthodox cultural norms while still in Europe, but "religion" was not central to the family's functioning during her life in the US. People tend to forget that Goldman remained in close contact with her family throughout her life, and numerous members of her family remained cherished allies and supporters even during her most difficult times. Golda Meir's close family of origin consisted of socialist Jews, labor activists, and socialist Zionists. Arendt was an intellectual and was active in an array of Jewish and Zionist communal organizations, some of them comprising intellectual elites and others engaged in refugee rescue work. The Jewish aspects of Kahlo's life were not religious but rather centered on her extensive Jewish ties and Jewish cultural upbringing.

In this book, I examine the Christian, and particularly Protestant and Liberal, cultural imperialism of recasting Jewishness as, and reducing it to, a religion. This anti-imperialist investigation is vital to how we can do this sort of feminist Jewish work. Think of it a little like a Jewish consciousness-raising group: "Oh, I never thought before about how Jewish that is. Hey, I do tend to hook up with Jews, and there is kind of something special about those relationships. Jewish, that's the word for it. I sort of always knew that, but I didn't realize there was a word for it. That's a thing? How come nobody told me that it's a thing?"

By thinking with Kincaid, Meir, and Arendt, we will be ready to address this aspect of our inquiry directly by mid-book, in the Kahlo chapter. The topic of what one can call a Jewish life and who gets to define that has particular implications for feminism. Jewish women have always been necessary to the functioning of Jewish life. Historically, they were also generally barred from the creation of, and even participation in, what might be called formal and hegemonic Jewish religious knowledge networks; this can, for sure, still be the case. We find a mutually reinforcing dynamic of Protestant inability to recognize life forms outside of its discursive range and internal Jewish patriarchal processes of valuation that both separately and together render Jewish women largely incomprehensible or invisible. In this work, I think with a series of extraordinary women in ways that enable us to reclaim and re-vision both ordinary and radical Jewishness without necessarily referencing religious frameworks.

Ordinary Jewishness. Yeah. Oh, and "radical Jewishness" is my term, not that of these women. In the 1990s, a student gave me a bumper sticker with the following message: "Feminism is the radical notion that women are people." Okay, decades of activism and scholarship have reimagined this. It is also true. In 2025 pregnant women in Texas are forced to carry fetuses to term that were created from a rape; reminding people that we are human isn't such a simplistic message. When trans rabbis are feeling that they must resign their posts at beloved congregations due to increasingly explicit anti-trans legislation in their states, insisting that we are all people is worth struggling for. I would have liked to remain in my dreamland that there were no longer people actively teaching that enslaved persons, brought forcibly to the lands that became the US, were happy and better off than they had been before their harrowing journeys through the Middle Passage; alas, such teachings are more prevalent now in the media and public schools than perhaps at any other period in my lifetime. Who had to prove rapes were acts of war in southern Israel in 2023, even as those who gave the orders to point an unimaginable amount of bombs at Gaza would JUST NOT

STOP? In that vein, radical Jewishness operates and shifts with affirmation (all too often needed as a demand) that Jews are worthy as people and as a people, that we can be oppressors and oppressed, that we (can) actively and freely participate in world making, and that we might face horrors and still—somehow—celebrate.

For sure, frameworks of quotidian Jewish communal life are not our only feminist frameworks. Many women and feminists have, indeed, participated in religious, spiritual, liturgical, and ritual life. In this book I highlight multiple modes of Jewishness. One must do so in order to bring out Jewish women and feminists as visible and recognizable (even as we remake processes of recognition). One must also do so in order to actually engage Jewishness generally. This is a charge to Jews, non-Jews, and people on the margins of Jewishness. If we stay within Christian and Liberal imperialist paradigms or internal Jewish patriarchal ones, we will miss women and most things feminist. We will miss much of what is, and can be, Jewish.

Let's look at the example, here, of Jamaica Kincaid. Kincaid was raised in a non-Jewish family. My scholarship on Kincaid concentrates on her life, her work, and her political commitments in a Jewish context. I am frequently questioned about how and when she became a Jew. No one has asked me this question of the other five women in this study. Editors, reviewers, and commentators consistently ask me to state upon a first mention of Kincaid that she converted; they ask me to note when, and often why. Many who ask me about this are sincere. Others may be haters. There is likely to be interesting political theory to make of Kincaid's story related to conversion, but that is not the political theory I am doing with her for now. Importantly, while Kincaid has published more than a dozen books and many interviews related to her own story, I have not seen her address this question.

Jews celebrate conversions if the convert invites that. Generally, however, Jews go with the ancient wisdom to not make a big deal about conversions. Still, over the past decade or so, I have thought about these questions and attempted to answer them in various ways. In response, at times I have attempted to summarize the arguments I have made about Kincaid's contributions to Jewish feminist political thinking. These seem to be powerful rejoinders available to a scholar regarding the question of the import of Jewishness for Kincaid and of Kincaid for Jewishness. Often, however, the only reply that has quieted certain interrogators is when I report a tidbit I once read that she had served as president of her synagogue. As the years passed, I would also sometimes add that she has been interviewed many times in the Israeli press (this had not been the case in the early years of my research on Kincaid and her work in a Jewish feminist context). Connection to a religious institution or to Israel seems to put those challengers at ease. I find this problematic. Additionally, I am usually stunned that there is never a follow-up query about the nature of the relationship to her synagogue or the content of the interviews. The question for us for now is why these potentially incidental bits of news seem to provide safe passage through the gatekeeping that challenges her Jewishness. Why don't people ask me why these statements matter?

In this book, my focus emerges along with my grappling with the double standards for Jews who get to be Jews (if presumed to be "biologically" Jewish—more commonly complicated these days by the many among us who are born with a variety of sperm and egg donors, the wombs that provide homes to fetuses, and mixed sperm of known fathers, etc.) and those whose Jewishness must be explained. This restrictive standard is damaging in so many ways, including basic feminist challenges to assumptions that parentage defines one's biology and that people called and even experienced as mothers and fathers must necessarily have anything to do with gametes, gestation, labor. Halacha (Jewish law), interpreted differently over time and in different places, makes key contributions. A basic feminist challenge also questions why we would assume such biological determinism, even if it is to claim another "member of the tribe" in a world history full of the erasure and destruction of Jews, often by forced separation of Jews from Jewishness. Instead, this book is an exercise in exploring what might matter and why, in some of the ways that I can for now. My work in this book is to make meaning of some of our experiences, contributions, and relationships. To that end, in this work I think with these six flawed and outstanding women within their and our larger networks of politics, knowledge, people, and experience.

Chapter Briefs

Chapter 2: Jamaica Kincaid: Diasporic and De-colonial Interstices

I begin with Kincaid. My study of Jamaica Kincaid emerged within my larger, decades-long project exploring African-heritage Jews in their diversity. Using a Jewish feminist lens, I immersed myself in Kincaid's writing, in the interviews she gives, and in the biographical and scholarly work about her. When I began this project some decades ago, I wasn't really finding studies of Kincaid in a Jewish context, so I aimed to see what this process might teach me about Kincaid that others might not yet have explored. What might Kincaid have to offer Jewish studies, and what lines of questioning might a Jewish examination open up for her fans and scholars? Out of that process, I have since published other work on Kincaid, and I am still learning from her. In this chapter I offer a close reading of her profound essay "On Seeing England for the First Time" in the context of her oeuvre as a whole.

Diaspora is a common theme in Jewish life and thinking. Bringing Kincaid into our diaspora theorizing opens the field in exciting ways. For Kincaid, critiques of colonialism are usually linked to discussions of diaspora, and this linkage is common outside of Jewish studies. Despite the Jewish historic base of the concept of diaspora in its current usage and the inherent connection between diaspora, empire building, and colonial takeover, colonialism is rarely interrogated in understanding contemporary Jewish experiences with diaspora. Thinking with Kincaid, we can see the specific relevance of including colonialism and de-colonial theorizing in Jewish diasporic studies.

In addition to grappling with the diasporic in our lives, particularly after the 1791 French Emancipation of the Jews, each of the women in this book wrangled with genocidal ideologies and practices of settler colonialism in ways both similar to and different from Kincaid's experiences. Bringing colonialism into the Jewish conversation at the beginning of this book provides a lens through which we can learn more about the politics of Jewish diasporic circumstances and activate a more critical analysis. At the same time, this Jewish inquiry can contribute to diaspora and de-colonial studies in which Jewish work has been noticeably absent. Kincaid gets us started.

CHAPTER 3: GOLDA MEIR: SMASHING BINARIES OF GENDER, DIASPORA, AND ANTICOLONIALISM

We next move on to Golda Meir's kitchen (where she did a good deal of her politics before and while she was Israeli prime minister). Neither a scholar nor a writer, Golda Meir did not leave a coherent written body of work for our twenty-first-century investigation. As an international political actor, however, she left us a notable legacy. Many have heard of Meir as one of the first, and still rather few, women to serve as heads of state. Serving as prime minister of Israel made her well known, but it seems to have also curtailed what we might learn from her. In a patriarchal frame, Meir is often the subject of study because she was prime minister, and often her time as prime minister is the primary focus, or impetus, for study. Feminist work on Meir has looked at her a bit more broadly. Unfortunately, even feminist scholars can limit themselves to an empirical biographical accounting. Critical investigations rarely go beyond a dualistic framing as to whether Meir was a feminist or not.

My study of Meir utilizes the political-as-personal methodology that I am developing in this book to take her seriously in the full context of her politics and life experience. This method enables me to reframe what might be of interest about Meir for feminists in our time. We can use multiple registers to understand how she was both a target of and participant in potentially genocidal settler colonialisms. No longer prioritizing Meir as a prime minister in my analysis leads me to view her in new ways in comparison with Emma Goldman, known for her grassroots organizing and anti-state anarchism. The personal-as-political approach allows us to see just how similar these two flamboyant leaders were. They both spoke extensively to huge adoring audiences across the globe and were enlivened by these encounters. Both expanded their power bases through community organizing and engaging face-to-face with the masses.

Along with what we learned from Kincaid, seeing Meir not exclusively as a head of state and as like Goldman in some significant ways allows us to get to the deep ways in which she pushed boundaries of primary concern for many feminists today. Using feminist queer theory to look specifically at the dogma of binary theoretical paradigms in diaspora thinking, de-colonial work, and gender studies, we can see Meir in new and exciting ways, as one who smashed binaries and contributed to radical feminist vistas. After our thinking with Kincaid, in chapter three we get to trouble the diasporic in new ways with Meir as we recall the anticolonialism of her activism and its common cause with transnational anticolonial struggles, particularly across Africa.

CHAPTER 4: HANNAH ARENDT: *RAHEL VARNHAGEN* AND DIASPORIC DE-COLONIAL JUSTICE THEORIZING: ON PARIAHS AND PARVENU?E.S

Okay. Hannah Arendt. Arendt, too, needs to be understood in terms of the diasporic. She, too, navigated genocidal settler colonialism. Political theorists are likely familiar with Hannah Arendt's theories of plurality, freedom, revolution, and totalitarianism. Many Jews will know of Arendt for her analysis of the court proceedings of Nazi war criminal Adolf Eichmann. As were many other Zionists, she was critical of Zionist leaders both for not responding to Nazism in a concerted and forceful enough way and for not working enough with Palestinians in the context of their national aspirations for self-determination shaping also Palestinians' right to a homeland. Progressive Jews frequently revisit a 1944 Arendt essay in which she categorized and assessed those she determined to be pariahs or parvenu?e.s.[7] While scholars know of Arendt's work on the eighteenth-to-nineteenth-century German Jewish *salonnière* Rahel Varnhagen, rarely is an examination of Varnhagen brought into focus with Arendt's work on parvenu?e.s and pariahs.

This chapter centers the Varnhagen work as a life project for Arendt in order to provide a new view into Arendt's work, life commitments, and thinking on justice. The Varnhagen book was the first work Arendt undertook following her PhD dissertation, and it was nearly completed in 1933 before she fled Nazi persecution in Germany. Arendt managed to keep the manuscript together through harrowing and violent dislocations, including imprisonment in a jail in Nazi Germany, displacement to other European countries, asylum in Paris, her time in an internment camp in the south of France, and, eventually, exile in the US. Arendt only published the Varnhagen book decades later, in 1958, after reaching the relative safety of New York and publishing other significant works. In this book, Arendt struggles in a gendered frame through the tangle of how to be a Jew in the world.

There have been political theorists who have cast Arendt as creating a dichotomous system of universals and particulars, and explicitly eschewing particulars. Feminist critiques have already enabled us to "un-think" such accepted assessments. We can also find Arendt's de-colonial theorizing of justice through this complex Jewish feminist critical race analysis. Taking up a variety of cues as we center Arendt's work on a Jewish woman who navigated diasporic and imperial particulars and universals, we see in different ways how to live well as a Jewish woman in the world. Arendt's insights regarding justice in this case are deeply grounded in the material world and politically radical. We can see that Arendt had already been doing the thinking that would enable her later analysis of pariahs and parvenu?e.s in the earlier *Varnhagen* project, which she carried with her, quite literally, throughout her life. Arendt's grappling with the alienation inherent in a diasporic and colonial condition becomes core to her call for collective action, in solidarity across groups, to challenge the assimilationist and genocidal presumptions foundational to Western notions of freedom and equality.

Chapter 5: Frida Kahlo: On Creating Vibrant, Transnational Jewish Networks

And here we arrive at Kahlo. Long before I ever imagined this project, some people in my circles told me that supposedly Frida Kahlo's dad was Jewish. By late in the twentieth century, the prickly and hallowed community of Jewish feminists, lesbians, and fellow travelers began to welcome Kahlo among its legendary members. This inclusive move is now largely on hold. In her lifetime, Kahlo offered a narrative of growing up in a mixed family with a European immigrant Jewish father and a Spanish, Catholic, Indigenous mother. Talk about embodying and coping politically with genocidal settler colonialism. Recently, the Jewish aspect of this narrative has been challenged, and ensuing doubts have derailed serious Jewish scholarship on Kahlo. Still, we can do new Jewish feminist work on Kahlo now with insights gleaned in the early chapters of this book.

This de-colonial and multilayered Jewish feminist analysis looks at the life, work, art, and politics of Frida Kahlo to puzzle through how we might create meaningful Jewish lives steeped in connection. Kahlo wove dense webs of Jewish relations across countries and continents. Committed to and an architect of *Mexicanidad*, Kahlo immersed herself in transnational intellectual, artistic, and political networks of friends and lovers, colleagues and comrades. She also worked actively against Nazi fascism, and she did so as a person claiming Jewish ancestry. Thinking with Kahlo in a Jewish feminist modality allows us to see these intense ties and risk taking in new ways. The analysis that this leads to brings into relief Jewish themes in her work, which most Kahlo scholars and art critics have ignored or failed to notice.

Our thinking with Kahlo in the context of Mexican history here also invites us to explore a centuries-long Sephardi legacy of Jews in the Americas in addition to a modern Ashkenazi history. This Sephardi Jewish history in the Americas moves from the fifteenth-century Catholic Spanish Inquisition to the early-twentieth-century breakup of the Muslim Ottoman Empire. Allying with Kahlo in this way also offers us a dynamic vision of Jewish feminist possibilities beyond Protestant imperialist inventions of Jewishness as a religion, orthodoxies, and gatekeeping.

Chapter 6: Gertrude Stein: A Queer Feminist Jew-ing: Constraints and Possibilities for Post-Emancipation Jewish Lives

Gertrude Stein. Go ahead, try to read some of her work. Perhaps this chapter, alongside those on the other subjects thus far, will help you make sense of it. Most accounts of Stein's life and work emphasize her relationships with men and downplay her Jewishness. Existing Jewish and feminist scholarship on Stein rarely situates her among combinations of Jews, women, and Jewish feminist freethinkers. The multilayered Jewish feminist approach to Stein's life, work, and art in this chapter analyzes the ways in which she was steeped in Jewish history and then-contemporary Jewish trends. Stein surrounded herself with women, often associated most closely with Jewish women, and grounded her life in significant, then-current trends that impacted her Jewish ethnic identity. These dynamics constrained her as a woman, gender bender, lesbian, and Jew living among antisemites, including both intimates and strangers. The same dynamics also enabled her unique life path and work.

Thinking with Stein provides us with additional possibilities of how to live as a Jew / Jewish woman and as a person. Along with her Jewish life partner, Alice B. Toklas, Stein survived the Holocaust in Vichy France. Yet another Jewish woman working to survive and thrive through an intense period of anti-Jewish genocidal settler colonialism. A political-as-personal analysis that focuses on these issues allows us to identify Stein's distinctive role as she carried forward the still-underappreciated and notably Jewish women's tradition of the salon. Additionally, through this analysis we note the similarities between posthumous, extreme critiques of Stein by Jews (albeit largely right-wing ones) and those faced earlier by Arendt, including those from the Left. In linking this situation between Arendt and Stein, we can note how such critiques mark a misogynist, anti-queer orientation against prominent Jewish women who do not play the role of the "nice Jewish girl."

CHAPTER 7: EMMA GOLDMAN: ANARCHIST FEMINISM, A NEW FRAME FOR DIASPORIC LONGINGS AND JEWISH STUDIES?

We are now ready to learn from and with Emma Goldman. Do not be surprised that, like the subjects of the earlier chapters, Goldman spent a good portion of her life fleeing anti-Jewish genocidal settler colonialism. Given the background from our investigations thus far, I focus on how Goldman navigated various exiles and diasporas across several authoritarian regimes and always remained on the move. Emma Goldman was notorious already in her own lifetime as an anarchist, a feminist, and a Jew. Unfortunately, outside of anarchist circles, too little attention has been paid to anarchism as a political theory generally, and still less to anarchism as specifically pertaining to or emerging from diasporic Jewish life. Similarly, there is too little work prioritizing Jewish feminist perspectives in examining Emma Goldman: her life, activism, politics, and thinking. She is among those in this book whose biographers frequently note that she was born to a Jewish family but then broach no further inquiry into whether and how that might make a difference in our understanding of her or her contributions. Adding to these lacunae has been a patriarchal bias against looking seriously at her contributions to political theory, anarchist or otherwise, as her legacy cannot be distilled into a single theoretical text or a series of explicitly theoretical articles.

As Kathy Ferguson and Lori Marso show us, a feminist approach to Goldman that examines the political-as-personal can highlight the contours of her thinking in her life, activism, and constellation of allies, as well as in her oratory and written work. A multilayered Jewish feminist approach can disclose myriad ways in which Jewishness enabled her life's work. We can also ask questions about situations such as the temporal alignment between when Goldman was most depleted and when she also "just happened" to be cut off from Jewish comrades and communities.

In appreciating this intersectional Jewish feminist base for understanding Goldman and her transnational life, work, and politics, we come to find a radical resituating of a theoretical framework for understanding Jewish life historically and for pursuing Jewish studies in the twenty-first century. Through this new study of Goldman, we find that anarchist political theory is best equipped to explain and chart options for Jewish life. Jewish existence, in its diversity, situated transnationally in diaspora for millennia, also functions through an ontological alterity, at least to the Protestantism that has become hegemonic in modernity. These aspects of diasporic Jewish civilization provide deep and abundant case studies for anarchist inquiry, as anarchist theory can be seen as a versatile and elegant theory of Jewish life.

Carefully exploring each of these women, chapter by chapter, individually and together, helps us to build a coterie of new historical and political insight and apparatuses for our current and future life and study. In each chapter we visit one of these six imperfect and still remarkable figures on new terms. Mutually constitutive Jewish, feminist, queer, critical race, class-based, and de-colonial theories open new pathways for scholarship, insight, compassion, relationships, and problem solving. We learn new modes for understanding the ways they fashioned lives in a broken world full of violence and disruption, beauty and love, yearning for dignity and seeking justice. We find complex patterns of ways in which Jewishness may matter to so many of us, even if we cannot always articulate them for ourselves.

With this work, I endeavor to help us articulate this and overcome obstacles for such articulation and interrogation. We can locate Jewishness, in its diversity, at the nexus of the intricate and shifting strategies that this constellation of historical figures employed to survive and to thrive. Each navigates alienation and the fertility of the diasporic; each gets on with the project of their lives in the context of genocidal settler colonialism. We can appreciate in new ways how Jewishness made a difference for these six cultural icons. They provide us with an array of options for how to live as Jews, as Jewish women, and as people. We need them because this seemingly simple idea, to live as a Jew and as a person, remains a challenge today. We need them because this simple idea of living as a person and as one with any abject particularities remains beyond reach for too many of us today. It is time to stop erasing Jewishness as itself a foundational category of experience and of impact in the world. In these chapters, we find the Jewish import of those whose celebrity is already established. How might others continue and hone this spirit of inquiry, and bring out the contributions of many others, especially those who are not yet famous?

Equipped with these new tools, how might we develop our capacities to appreciate feminist modes of life building? Multivalent Jewish feminism can contribute to this project for all feminists. Each chapter in this book enhances our specific and overall sets of tools for reimagining and transforming specifically Jewish possibilities. This nuanced study, with close readings of each agent of change building the work as a whole, from Kincaid to Goldman, enables us all to re-vision prospects for lives of justice, kindness, and peace, and potentially to create infinite new ones.

Chapter 2

Jamaica Kincaid

Diasporic and De-colonial Interstices

. . . who are these people . . . who forced me to think that the world I knew was incomplete, or without substance, or did not measure up because it was not England; that I was incomplete, or without substance, and did not measure up because I was not English.

. . . there they were, the white cliffs, but they were not that pearly majestic thing I used to sing about . . . that created such a feeling in these people that when they died in the place where I lived they had themselves buried facing a direction that would allow them to see the white cliffs of Dover when they were resurrected.

—Jamaica Kincaid, "On Seeing England for the First Time"

I have been doing scholarly work on Jamaica Kincaid for some time.[1] In 2010, the newly formed International Society for the Study of African Jewry launched its inaugural conference, at which I was to deliver a paper on Kincaid's work. The ISSAJ Jews and Judaism in Black Africa and Its Diasporas conference—please hold your delight and condemnation—was convened at London's School of Oriental and African Studies. While England's resources made it possible for us to gather for this Jewish studies conference, I also thus felt it incumbent upon us to critique English colonialism, its role in the Atlantic slave trade, and its central place in the creation of an African diaspora in a Jewish context. While Jamaica Kincaid is mostly known for her fiction, she is also an insightful essayist. Upon the occasion of the conference, I found myself particularly drawn to an extraordinary early essay of Kincaid's telling of her first visit to England as a survivor of British colonialism in the Caribbean. Emerging from that paper and work I have done in these intervening years, in this chapter I analyze Kincaid's essay "On Seeing England for the First Time" utilizing a comparison between Kincaid's castigation of colonialism and the otherness of colonial subjects scattered about the empire with notions of diasporic conditions.

Colonial and diasporic living are far from singular or easily compared in a binary frame. They are also rarely lived as self-contained and separative modalities. An aim of this chapter is to have a layered Jewish feminist analysis of Kincaid assist us in understanding ways that they are often simultaneously constructed. To do so, at times, I slow down the thinking to enable us to highlight each thread. Such a choice, I realize, risks essentializing and segregating the phenomena. My intention with taking such risks is that we will be able to build bold insights into the de-colonial diasporic and the diasporic de-colonial, Jewishly and more broadly. That work must operate on multiple co-constitutive levels. The analysis here begins our thinking with Kincaid and also sets us up to complicate this thinking as we move through this book.

Jewish engagement with the growing field of diaspora studies is a rich site for multilayered examinations of politics, the movement of peoples in history, and core matters of justice. My work in the field and in this chapter is based in a study of African-heritage Jews in the Americas and takes a theoretical approach to how we might more fluidly make sense of somewhat balkanized emergent fields of diaspora studies in order to place Jewish experiences globally in new ways. Thinking how the political is also personal and grounded in a study of Kincaid's full body of work, this chapter focuses on her essay "On Seeing England for the First Time" as a primary example of the dexterity of Kincaid's relentless critique of colonialism, even as she published this essay so many years ago. While postcolonial studies is a crucial aspect of diaspora studies and is required in examinations in African and Latin American diaspora studies, Jewish work is not adequately integrated into these overlapping fields. Kincaid's work can help us do so and has enabled me to engage de-colonial theories also in the coming chapters.

Jamaica Kincaid was born Elaine Cynthia Potter Richardson in 1949 in Antigua—a Caribbean island colonized by the British. Kincaid is a prolific writer, often said to "represent a quintessential Caribbean woman's voice." Her work stands out in any study of Africana, Caribbean and African

American, and African diaspora literature. Among the central themes in her work, we find explorations of the ravages of colonialism and imperialism, migration and diaspora, exile and loss. Kincaid is also Jewish, and these are likewise perennial Jewish themes.[2] However, among the extensive literature on Kincaid there is a marked absence of attention to the fact that she is Jewish and to Jewish matters of interest in her work.[3]

Bringing a Jewish feminist lens to the study of Kincaid's work and including Kincaid among those of significant import to study in a Jewish context will enrich and expand the scope of both fields. Including new peoples and aspects of the community in Jewish studies will require transforming the frameworks and central categories of inquest in the field. For example, analysis of Kincaid's work necessitates taking colonialism seriously, an endeavor not undertaken in most Jewish studies paradigms.[4]

How does the Jewish lens deepen our analysis of Kincaid's contributions? Kincaid's work tends to name a focus on colonialism, not directly on a diasporic condition. In fact, in 1987 Kincaid reflected, "I don't have the luxury of longing to be a displaced person" (Cudjoe 1989, 402),[5] suggesting a difference in her thinking between the experiences of colonial and diasporic living. However, elsewhere, Kincaid presents being displaced, in a clear and embodied exile of the diasporic, as an experience that might give clarity to the tumultuous feelings, the confusions involved in the difficulty of making sense of her life as a colonial subject in such a way that can enable proper subjecthood.[6] We can bring these two modes, diaspora and de-colonial theories, together. According to Kincaid, the cultural imperialism involved in the genocidal colonial project robbed her of her capacity for independent sense making, a faculty she considers necessary to the development of agency that might facilitate productive resistance strategies.[7] But how can she launch such resistance strategies for which she has become famous? Kincaid relates that it is her diasporic condition that makes this possible.

While the focus on the colonial experience serves as the "text" in this text, there is thus also a "subtext" of the diasporic, more explicit at some times than at others. Kincaid's critique of colonialism often hints at parallel facets of diasporic phenomena, particularly Jewish ones. For example, in the second opening quotation above, Kincaid notes acerbically the "religiosity," the well of feeling that the White Cliffs of Dover aroused in her British colonizers and their ritualistic turning to face that direction.[8] For millennia, it has been a common Jewish practice, particularly of the diaspora, to say prayers in the direction of Jerusalem, a mytho-cultural-religious Jewish center. Kincaid does not offer an explicit Jewish parallel in this particular text. It is my argument here, though, that bringing a Jewish feminist orientation to a study of Kincaid's political thinking exposes interesting aspects of her work, here and more broadly, undetected when that combined lens is absent.[9] Further, studying Kincaid in a Jewish feminist context creates opportunities to broaden and deepen Jewish political thinking, linking discourses of the diasporic commonly found in Jewish studies with a critique from postcolonial studies often not found in this field.[10]

While Jewish political thinking has long focused on the realities and concept of diaspora, rarely has such thinking brought into the frame insights from a critique of colonialism. The lack of a critical awareness of colonialism is a gap in Jewish discourse contributing to a less-than-full ability to recognize broader contexts of power in Jewish diasporic trajectories. Jewish feminists seek to make explicit critical analyses of power. And, with this in mind, we find that diasporas are almost always created out of circumstances similar to, and often the same as, those that are more commonly understood as colonial. Introducing a critique of colonialism can contribute to Jewish, and particularly Jewish diasporic, theorizing.

The term *diaspora* is connected inherently to both Jewish and colonial phenomena. The word *diaspora* was originally used to reflect the experience of colonizers in an imperial victory. Only after the creation of the Jewish diasporas of antiquity did the term become used to reflect the experience of the subjects of inquisition. A study of Jamaica Kincaid's work proves a fertile beginning for efforts to bring together anticolonial critique and diaspora studies in a Jewish frame, given her situation at the nexus of multiple layers of colonial and diasporic dynamics as well as the intense and complex nature of her capacity for insight into and analysis of these dynamics.

Biographical Note: Kincaid

First, a biographical note. Jamaica Kincaid was born Elaine Cynthia Potter Richardson on May 25, 1949, in St. John's, Antigua, a Caribbean island colonized by the British. Kincaid was raised Christian and in relative poverty by her mother and stepfather. An excellent student who loved literature, she had the ambiguous experience of having the best of an island British colonial education. The birth of her three younger brothers created a rift for her with her mother, given a shift of her mother's focus to the boys' needs. As a gendered manifestation of her situation as a poor and female colonial subject, in 1966, at the age of seventeen, prior to earning her high school diploma, Kincaid was sent to New York to work as an au pair, separating her from her family back home for many years.

Having earned her high school general equivalency degree during her time in New York City, Kincaid was awarded a full scholarship to the then recently opened and short-lived Franconia College in New Hampshire. She attended school there for about a year in the late 1960s and never earned a college degree. She later earned honorary degrees from numerous universities.

In 1973, when she began to publish her writing, she changed her name to Jamaica Kincaid, primarily because of her family back home's disapproval of her writing. She wrote for the *Village Voice* and *Ingénue*, and her short fiction was published in the *Paris Review* and the *New Yorker*. Kincaid became a staff writer at the *New Yorker* in 1976 and stayed for twenty years; she was a featured columnist for the *New Yorker*'s Talk of the Town for nine years and continues to contribute essays in the *New Yorker* and other outlets. An award-winning writer, Kincaid has published numerous books, including fiction, nonfiction, works on gardening, and a children's book. She has also published many article-length works of fiction and nonfiction. Her first book, the collection of stories *At the Bottom of the River*, won the Morton Dauwen Zabel Award from the American Academy of Arts and Letters and was nominated for the PEN/Faulkner Award for Fiction. Her anticapitalist nonfiction work on neocolonialism in *A Small Place* (Kincaid 1988), written from the lens of an Indigenous islander to the masses of tourists from the Global North who come to the islands to "get away," was woven into the narrative of Stephanie Black's 2001 documentary, *Life and Debt*. Kincaid has been both a finalist for and the winner of a stream of prestigious national and international awards for her writings bringing forth Caribbean tableaus and sensibilities. In 2021, Kincaid won the prestigious Langston Hughes Medal from the City College of New York.[11]

In 1979, Kincaid married composer and Bennington College professor Allen Shawn, son of *New Yorker* editor William Shawn, with whom she had had a productive professional relationship. After living mainly in New York City, she lived for many years with Shawn in Bennington, Vermont, where the couple raised their two children, Harold and Annie. Kincaid and Shawn divorced in 2002, and since her years living and writing from Vermont, Kincaid has held a position as professor of African and African American studies in residence at Harvard University. Active in her Jewish communities, she served for a time as president of her synagogue in Vermont and more recently has been featured prominently in Jewish and Israeli news publications.

Methodological Notes

> In Bath, I drank tea in a room I had read about in a novel written in the eighteenth century. In this very same room, young women wearing those dresses that rustled and so on danced and flirted and sometimes disgraced themselves with young men, soldiers, sailors, who were on their way to Bristol or someplace like that, so many places like that where so many adventures, the outcome of which was not good for me, began in Bristol, England.
>
> —Kincaid, "On Seeing England for the First Time"

Let us next take note of how Kincaid's method resonates with modes of resistance central to Jewish historical consciousness (that I would like to bring forward in this work). Like the midwives of Exodus who defy the Egyptian pharaoh's decree to kill Jewish newborn males, Kincaid's mode is to stand up to the mightiest power source of her experience. As she notes in an interview, "I hate tyrants. I hate tyranny. . . . It's better to be dead than to have people forcing you to do things that are a violation" (Garner 1996). Kincaid's method inspires and instructs us in how to speak truth to power. In doing so, Kincaid's methodology as a writer is, and enacts, a politics.

Key to Kincaid's method is to start with power dynamics.[12] Her method then calls into question the position of the dominant and attends to the view of the less powerful. In creating the very frame from the view of the dominated and speaking from this position, she makes those at the margins, their experiences and knowledges, primordial—of the first order.[13]

Kincaid's method teaches us to turn history on its head for a new view, one better equipped to answer to questions of justice, even if with (her characteristically complex) engagement with hope and despair.[14] For example, in her essay "On Seeing England," Kincaid writes that the stories of glory taught in her colonial education "never end well" for her, the colonial subject. The histories of empire come at the expense of her and her history.[15]

Demonstrating how her method derives from and enacts a politics, Kincaid tells the stories of the people who make the canonical tales and realities possible: the laborers.[16] Kincaid turns the unseen not only into the seen but into the subjects of the story. In doing so, she reorients the reader's focus from the *victors* to the *spoils* of history so that we might be able to undertake a reckoning. This is part of the process of holding those responsible for the "spoiling" accountable for their position in historic events of subjugation.[17] For example, in the article centered here, Kincaid tells of a ride in the English countryside with a white friend, a sympathetic friend with whom she has traveled to England. They notice the endless hedges Kincaid has long read about in the fiction taught in her British colonial education. The friend comments on how the owner of one set of such plantings has been complaining about the upkeep of the hedges as if the owner is the subject of a look at the hedges.

For Kincaid, however, it is the laborers—who have toiled to plant and keep up the hedges over so many years—who are the proper subject for rumination. She writes, "And the countryside did have all those hedges and hedges, fields hedged in. I was marveling at all the toil of it, the planting of the hedges to begin with and then the care of it, all that clipping, year after year of clipping, and I wondered at the lives of the people who would have to do this, because wherever I see and feel the hands that hold up the world, I see and feel myself and all the people who look like me" (Kincaid 1991, 373).

As Jews, many times "the conquered," and as a people so long of the diaspora, we also have had to develop our own histories.[18] We could not accept the versions of the story told by the conquerors.[19] We are called to, choose to, revitalize a plenitude of texts and lore that destabilizes the frame that the powerful intend to bequeath to history.[20] We have similar opportunities, as Jews, to employ Kincaid's method, building together a future also in terms of the power dynamics *within* our own communities. We can learn from Kincaid that as those of the African diaspora, as women, queers, *am ha'aretz*, we have a claim to this legacy and also a keen awareness that the claim in our case has been unfulfilled. For example, we are taught that we all stood together at Sinai, we all have some power, and yet so many within Jewish communities, globally and locally, are marginalized.[21] Utilizing Kincaid's methods, we can see that, unlike the disenfranchisement of the colonized, which always ends in a dead end for the subject in Kincaid's rendering, Kincaid in diaspora, as with some of the marginalized within Jewish communities, can reference this supposed inheritance as a basis for a claim.[22] It is crucial to employ this method in our use of Kincaid's work on colonial textual power to highlight aspects of diasporic difference and guide a Jewish feminist vision of politics.

Text in Colonial and Diasporic Cultures

> The naming of the kings, their deeds, their disappointments—was the vivid view, the forceful view. There were other views, subtler ones,

> softer, almost not there—but these were the ones that made the most lasting impression on me, these were the ones that made me really feel like nothing. "When morning touched the sky" was one phrase, for no morning touched the sky where I lived. . . . The world was theirs, not mine; everything told me so.
>
> —Kincaid, "On Seeing England for the First Time"

Of course, there are many instantiations of imperial and colonial processes, as there are in the diasporic. There cannot be only one way, therefore, to compare the colonial and diasporic. Let us take a moment to appreciate aspects of each regarding "texts," as we are nurturing vigorous and nuanced analysis.

Broadly, texts serve a number of similar functions in the postcolonial critique developed in Kincaid's body of work and for many in diasporas, Jewish and otherwise. While different texts are primary to different Jewish communities, there are central texts for many Jews in diaspora. While there might be no text quite as central to colonial life as something like the Jewish bible or Talmud,[23] in Kincaid's rendering, there are often central texts of colonial education, both "vivid" and "subtle."

The texts of Kincaid's colonial education forced into her view specific knowledges, vividly portrayed, of the lives of British kings, "their deeds, their disappointments" (1991, 34). Even more destructive than the hard facts in the texts, Kincaid writes, were the subtleties of imagery in the texts, resounding with experiences of those in diaspora as well as her colonial past.[24] Texts functioned here as key parts of the political context of colonial circumstance.[25] Central to the strategies of her subjugation was that in the truth texts of her British colonial education the facts of imagery and metaphor did not correspond to her lived reality.[26] This practice negated her lived imaginary and its meanings.[27] They undid her personhood.

In the case of diaspora, the relations can sometimes operate differently. I might not know firsthand the beauty and import of imagery of the morning dew in the Jewish bible, for example, but many Jews in the diaspora keep these images alive culturally.[28] They also are not our lived experience in exile, the place of living that is not the "home place." Many in diaspora can revel in the beauty of the place of living. The world is a big place with much beauty. Still, we can also delight in coming to understand what the images in the diasporic texts mean, sometimes precisely because they are not obvious to us in diaspora.[29] Simultaneously, while Jewish texts have been used for oppressive circumstances within the Jewish community, and to hold up unjust hierarchies among Jews, and between Jews and non-Jews, we—including those persecuted within Jewish contexts—can also engage with these texts, and increasingly so during Kincaid's lifetime. And then perhaps we contest them, and I make new metaphors with these images, a process of making our lives meaningful, of making connections for us in our time across time and across wherever our peoples have been scattered.[30]

To varying degrees, we in diaspora are taught the original language of "our" texts, familiarity with them generally, their images and stories, our history (see figure 2.1). With millennia of fecund cultural production and also frequent oppression, these varying degrees likely exist by now in some geographic locales as much due to personal preference as due to internal Jewish and larger social inequalities. Still, it is in large part through our relationship (however fraught, mobile, and reconstructed) to the people, language, imagery, and history of these texts that we remain and grow as a people, richly diverse.[31] Often it is in relation to our texts, in our (differentially situated) grappling with them,[32] that we find spaces of agency as communities in diaspora. Often it is in these differential ways of relating to texts that we can mark both our presentness and our exiles and struggle to create individual and collective lives of dignity in diaspora.[33]

Figure 2.1. Text in colonial and diasporic cultures. *Source*: Created by the author.

Text in Colonial and Diasporic Cultures

Colonial Cultures	Diasporic Cultures (Jewish)
• British Literature • British Histories • Texts of Colonial Education	•Bible •Other Jewish Authoritative Texts
"THEIRS"	**"OURS"**

Seen through Kincaid's vision, the ways in which the colonial texts, perhaps intended to be beautiful, are out of step with the actual lives of the subjects in a colonial context serve to create and perpetuate exploitative power dynamics. Kincaid describes this power dynamic worked with and through text in the colonial context in this way: "the world was theirs, not mine" (1991, 35).[34] Kincaid's writing on the colonial experience helps bring into relief some of the functions of text for at least Jewish diasporic life via comparing and contrasting the power relationships inherent within each.[35] Thus, let us use this particular text of Kincaid's to further engage a comparison of multilayered colonial and diasporic experience.

The Home Place as Truth

> When my teacher had pinned this map up on the blackboard, she said, "This is England"—and she said it with authority, seriousness, and adoration, and we all sat up. It was as if she had said, "This is Jerusalem, the place you will go to when you die but only if you have been good." We understood then . . . that England was to be our source of myth and the source from which we got our sense of reality, our sense of what was meaningful.
>
> —Kincaid, "On Seeing England for the First Time"

Of course, many of us have experienced many diasporas and many colonial takeovers, in our own lifetimes and in those of our communities over time. We make our lives with many "homes" and many "aways," many "heres" and many "over theres." For those in the Jewish diaspora, and likely similar for many diasporic circumstances, the diaspora is not always experienced in a lived way as an alienation from a specific geographically other location. Diaspora, in its multiplicitous manifestations, is somehow often both geographically inflected and not only a spatial situation. The anticolonial critique we find in Kincaid's work helps us parse this complexity, even as it helps to clarify some geographical aspects of diasporic conditions.

In Kincaid's experience, through the project of colonial education, England becomes the source of all sanctioned reality and myth. It is interesting for this Jewishly inflected study that in order to disprove the "truth" of England, Kincaid juxtaposes England with Jerusalem. The Jerusalem reference gives her access to a critique and an authority to note that the truths of England are false.[36] Here Kincaid's work veers into a central lane of Jewish diasporic history, referencing Jerusalem as a home place, as a grounding for the creation of Jewish meaning making over millennia. Jews frequently do this even if they have never stepped foot in Jerusalem or find themselves relatively satisfied with their lives at a particular time and place in diaspora.

With her acute attention to power and the dynamics of domination, this aspect of Kincaid's work also highlights some general distinctions between colonial and diasporic phenomena. While there are similarities, there are also fundamental differences between the distance and alienation of those colonized in their homelands and those sent into diaspora (see figure 2.2).[37] Those still at home but subjects of colonial rule develop a sensibility of "over there," as do those in diaspora.[38] But for the colonized the place "over there" is not theirs; it is the colonizers'.[39] It is a place from which the colonized will be permanently alienated but whose truths they are taught nonetheless.[40] The very creation of the place "over there" comes at the expense of those with whom Kincaid is primarily concerned: the colonized. The "over there" is itself made possible by the colonization, and its truths are developed in part through the negation of the varied truths

Figure 2.2. The home place as truth. *Source*: Created by the author.

The Home Place as Truth

Colonial Subjects
Home = "Here"
(Place of Living)

"Over There"
Truth
Good
Beauty
History

"Here"
Oppression
Unworthy

Diaspora Subjects
Home = "Over There"

"Here"
(Place of Living)
Exile
Oppression
False Truths

"Over There"
Redemption
Meaning

among the colonized.⁴¹ Despite the historical experience, knowledges, and values of the colonized in their diversity, the colonizers' view of what is true, meaningful, and important is presented as real—inculcated as the myths, dreams, and aspirations worthy of being considered authentic.⁴²

This aspect of the relationship of home place/over there to falsehoods/truth stands in contrast to some common traditions of those in diaspora. For many in diaspora, the home place may be "over there." Thus, similar to in the colonial experience, "truths," stories and myths, can be generated from (or re-created over time in relationship to) a life elsewhere. Diasporic existence is one where there is a dominant truth in the place of living but it may be overridden by, or is at least explicitly in tension with, truths of the "over there." However, the power dynamics within the colonial and diasporic are often somewhat inverted.

To whatever extent communities might be settled in any given historical moment, in diasporic mythology, the place of living is not exclusively the home place. The "over there" functions as (also) a home.⁴³ Among African and African-heritage peoples as well as all sorts of Jewish cultures, even after millennia in diaspora and significant attempts to ground new Jewish cultures in diasporic spaces, there remains for many Jews a connection to an "over there" as home—stronger for some than for others, but central still to Jewish thinking in its broadest sense. In a Jewish context, one does not need to espouse a specifically Zionist agenda to acknowledge the significance of a historically situated home place "over there."

For many in diaspora, in contrast to the relationships in the colonial dynamic, the knowledges of the place of living are challenged as exploitative.⁴⁴ For example, many Jews in the US celebrate the diasporic as enabling dynamic modes of Jewish living, in community and with our neighbors. It is clear, at the same time, that to live best in this particular diasporic circumstance we must also work to clarify and resist the role of discrimination in this place of living as we do with its role in domination across the globe. As an ethic in itself, as a survival strategy, as a mundane feature of living among the peoples of the world, many in diaspora form deep allegiances and alliances over time with others in their place of living.⁴⁵ This is the case particularly with those also marginalized, even if the relationships are often fraught.⁴⁶ At the same time, one of the goals of peoplehood in diaspora is to keep intact and grow many facets of "truths" from (and created in exchange with those from) afar. The work of firming up and building on the knowledges from "over there," working creatively to apply them in innovative ways "here," is the work of justice, or can be central to working against injustices of exile. In direct contrast to this aspect of Kincaid's focus on the colonial experience, working in these truths from afar often sets one against the truths that oppressors attempt to teach in the diasporic place of living. Finding ways to resist the universalization of the truths of here and to learn and adapt the truths from the home place is liberation work.

Awe and the Home Place:

> I did not know then that the statement "Draw a map of England" was something far worse than a declaration of war . . . there was no need for war—I had long ago been conquered. I did not know then that this statement was part of a process that would result in my erasure . . . I did not know then that this statement was meant to make me feel in awe and small . . . : awe at its existence, small because I was not from it.
>
> —Kincaid, "On Seeing England for the First Time"

Hearing the story, sometimes loud and sometimes a whisper, of a diasporic trope in examining the role of colonialism, we find that awe and the home place are important to understanding the multivocality of Kincaid's work. Kincaid's accessing of the concept of awe is spoken in the colonial frame amid diasporic murmurings—like the sounds of the many voices during the standing "silent" prayer in a Jewish service. Awe has the potential to manifest in varied ways, with significant political differentials. Knowledge of the home place of diaspora is intended to create a certain kind of relationship: to ennoble, to enlarge the spirit of those still connected. In the colonial frame, the home place serves a different function; it is meant to make Kincaid invisible, "erase" her very being through feeling small and in awe.[47]

After the first generation, those in diaspora may be said to no longer be formally "from" the home place. This shift in making meaning about where one is "from" can occur in such a way that breaks the people, which succumbs to the violences of the diasporic circumstance. Within diasporic cultures, many insist on naming ourselves, a kind of being from the other place, in this case the home place, as an aspect of seeking life, a life together to determine our cultures and futures. This can be the case even when the "other place" does not really function as an other place on a map but another place discursively, culturally. The activity of maintaining that we are "from" over there can be an aspect of our freedom work.[48] As freedom work, it is often fraught and dangerous work.

In her life in diaspora in the US, Kincaid undoubtedly is often asked, Where are you from? In a diasporic context, Kincaid likely answers this question with reference to Antigua, the Caribbean. In the colonial context, in Antigua, this question is a nonissue. She is the one from "here"—the conquered. But Kincaid's multilayered experience demonstrates that contexts and political demands shift, in this case from the complex colonial to the multifaceted diasporic. In the shifting locales of home place, from the place of living to "over there," one's people's situation as a small and a large group also often shift. In this, power relationships shift as well.[49]

In response to my (Ashkenazi) "foreignness" in the US, especially during my life in New England, I am often also asked where I am from. "From New York," I say, repeatedly to the repetition of the query when my response does not seem to satisfy. The answer the "American" is looking for from me with the question "But where are you from?" can only be answered with the phrase "I am Jewish." Differences among Jews are significant. Unlike for Kincaid, it does not answer the "American's" questioning of my "foreignness" to say that I am from eastern Europe, the actual place from which my grandparents sought refuge on these shores. I cannot say "from Jerusalem" as a concrete location on the globe to answer the question. I intone "Jewish" and connote an ancestral homeland that makes my minority ethnicity and questionable personhood in the United States stand out as geographically—and otherwise—foreign. Kincaid lives at the crossroads of numerous "other places" in a similar way and, significantly, also differently than I do.

When the diasporic and neocolonial context has race reconfigure diverse peoplehood in other ways, the "American" does not imagine that Kincaid could answer "Jewish" as well. Kincaid knows the unspoken intent of the inquisition. While we both might be called to account for our accents and other markers of foreignness and minority, she is being called first to account for the specific color of her skin and her beautiful accent in relation to matters of pigment.

A justification for oppression of colonial subjects is oft explained to be that they are inferior for not being from "there"—the colonial home country. On the contrary, those in diaspora are often the target of discrimination in the place they live precisely because they are considered not from "here."[50] Within diasporic cultures, active work of "not being from" the places in which we are living is part of the project of resisting the genocidal, assimilative tendencies of diaspora. The question of whether we can remain a people in diaspora, whether life in the diaspora will not require us to participate in genocidal processes, is key in both colonial and diaspora studies, as it is in Jewish life and thought.[51]

A significant link to Jewish experience with text and diasporic life is embedded in this aspect of Kincaid's critique of colonialism. Out of her colonial experience, Kincaid links the perception of "smallness" to "awe" in the context of power. These are not unrelated in Jewish, particularly diasporic, thinking either. The concept of awe, for example, is central to Jewish communal and often spiritual experience. Kincaid's experience of feeling small in this context is clearly an aspect of oppression, meant to suppress the spirit.[52] In the colonial situation, Kincaid is of the majority numerically but of the disenfranchised in terms of power. In the diaspora, she may be, equally if differently, disenfranchised but part of a numerical minority. Diasporic sensibility demonstrates that one may be among the "small" numerically but that power can come from attachment to one's people, a larger group, which works differently for disempowered majorities under colonial rule.[53]

Similarly to Kincaid's use of the concept of awe, in the context of Jewish reference to what is "true" or sacred, feeling small is often noted and is frequently positively valenced. In the different power context, this same "feeling small" is feeling appropriately humble or affirmingly part of something larger than oneself.[54] This version of awe and feeling small *opens* opportunities for hope and connection.[55] In this Jewish diasporic example, in potential contrast to Kincaid's colonial example, awe can have a liberatory function. In the colonial context, a liberatory option may be achieved through a global anticolonial movement and multicountry solidarity. Jews can embrace and reframe the anti-Jewish rendering of our communities as rootless cosmopolitans. I rather like being a so-called rootless cosmopolitan. But I do know that many Jews do not experience themselves as rootless, and some do not even associate with being cosmopolitans. Globalism in this context can serve aspirations for justice in both diasporic and colonial contexts.

Forgetting and Not Learning the Lesson

I did not know much of anything then, certainly what a blessing it was that I was unable to draw a map of England correctly.

. . .

The reality of my life was conquests, subjugation, humiliation, enforced amnesia. I was forced to forget.

—Kincaid, "On Seeing England for the First Time"

Under the colonial view, not learning the ruler's version of the truth makes one less worthy and becomes part of the justification for oppression.[56] In a resistive move, Kincaid inverts the colonial view, noting that it was a blessing that she never learned to draw the map of England properly. Despite Audre Lorde's extraordinary critique, historically, some have been able to learn the masters' tools to bring down the masters' house.[57] The double-edged sword of using the masters' tools is crucial to acknowledge in the many ways that learning the masters' lessons often requires unlearning one's own people's ways. The colonized also often must work to "forget" the lessons they have learned from the colonizers as part of the work in expunging colonial rulers, to take back or create anew their capacities for self-determination in the home place.[58]

In addition to the central work of Fanon (2004) helpful here, thinkers such as Du Bois (1961) discuss the need for conquered subjects to develop a double consciousness—one in which they learn the ways of the masters in order to survive in the masters' world yet also ways of their own people to protect and build spaces of freedom as a conquered population.[59] Here, Kincaid notes the nearly holy good fortune—the blessing—of never having learned the colonial texts, the truths, accurately. Resisting learning the colonizers' truths, from over there, imposed upon us over "here" provides opportunities to see through the modalities in which colonizers conquer.[60] Never really learning the lessons of one's history and culture from within the location of the colonized place of "here" is a loss—especially if due to violence, both physical and that of cultural imperialism.[61] *Not* learning the colonial cultural touchstones can also enable access to our not-colonized texts, meaning the varied truths of the here, the home place under colonial rule, in order to resist modalities of our conquest.

Often those in diaspora face similar challenges. Being forced to forget one's own knowledges and take up those of the colonial powers is often an assimilative and ultimately genocidal aspect of the diasporic and of both colonial and settler colonial living. Developing cultural fluency in one's histories, texts, languages can also be fraught with tensions under the pressure to learn and function in the cultural frame of the dominant in the place of living. Syncretism, the influence of new cultures into one's own, can often enliven one's culture—even if one's own is the subject culture. How much and in what ways is it best to learn the modes of the place of living? What to learn and in what ways in order to function, to survive, to learn the rules of the hegemonic game in order to lessen oppression, to inspire new depths in a diaspora community's culture? As in Kincaid's relief when she realized that she had not learned certain lessons, how do we determine what is best not to learn, what and how to unlearn aspects of hegemonic culture in the place of living for those in diaspora?

For those in diaspora, the politics of forgetting can be equally complex. There may well be many aspects of one's home culture worthy of letting go to history. How can we let go with agency when the oppressive context of our lives in diaspora requires forgetting?[62] Sometimes dominant forces' pressures to lose a subject's history can be holistic and also problematically selective. It is a matter of distillation. How do we come to clarity about what might be best to forget among the truths learned/forced upon us in diaspora, especially when we have been schooled by our diasporic communities to think that adherence to such truths is crucial to our very survival among the hosts of our exile? When done in empowering ways, the process itself is indeed a blessing. Kincaid reminds those of us in diaspora, as well as those colonized, often one and the same, that the fruits of the labor, then, can be blessings as well.

History

> I knew the names of all the kings of England. . . . Their disappointments, their triumphs. . . . It wasn't as bad as I make it sound now; it was worse. I did like so much hearing again and again [about] Alfred the Great . . . I loved King Alfred. My grandfather was named after him; his son, my uncle, was named after King Alfred; my brother is named after King Alfred. And so there are three people in my family named after a man they have never met, a man who died over ten centuries ago.
>
> —Kincaid, "On Seeing England for the First Time"

In this text Kincaid recalls that she loved King Alfred, the man she learned of in history. This love was inculcated also through her family's acceptance of the valuations of British history, to such an extent that three men in her family are named after this Alfred. However, this love and this naming are also cast clearly as factors of oppression and othering.[63] Kincaid brings this aspect of her upbringing under scrutiny in order to demonstrate a colonial process of distorting and warping history.[64] The colonizers' historical project includes the erasure of the subjects' history.[65]

Shifting a prism to the diasporic, if Kincaid had a tie to early Carib figures, African stories, biblical characters, they too would be people she "didn't know" in a technical manner. However, in contrast to the stories of the colonizers, she could "know" them in a different sense. In knowing these iconic personages, instead of intentionally severed from them, as a diaspora subject she can be connected and brought into connection.[66] In naming generations in exile and the names alive in our cultural stories, we bring ourselves and each other into history.

In the colonized frame of Kincaid's essay, the grandiosity of history serves to estrange and disempower. In her critical capacity, acknowledging how long ago the kings she was forced to learn about lived represents their irrelevance to her life.[67] Yet legends of African, Jewish, and African Jewish history teach of figures who died even longer ago. For Jews and many in diaspora, the historical timeline of so many centuries told in our tales can be a grounding factor, not only an explicitly alienating one. In the African, Jewish, and African Jewish contexts, to count oneself among peoples with millennia of lineage conveys a dignity, a gift, and exaltation for individuals otherwise facing a potentially daily crushing of the human spirit in the commonplace violence too often an endemic feature of exilic living.[68]

In the colonial instance, for Kincaid, the rulers' projects of teaching history pervert subject peoples' capacities to live and love in right relation.[69] Kincaid points out the dynamic of oppressive hierarchical relations between colonized and colonizers.[70] Set in history this way, the relationship can be nothing but abusive.[71] She is also clear that living in this violent historical context contorts the potential for relationships of equality horizontally, among the colonized as well.[72] People in diaspora often know this dynamic too.[73] It is hard to learn to love, honor, and treat each other with dignity when the context of our circumstances situates diasporic subjects as foundationally and only detestable.[74] Many in abject communities work at this, whether their circumstances are diasporic and/or colonial, at least in a certain sense. Women and all of us learning to love women, instead of devaluing women, is revolutionary work in white supremacist patriarchy. Loving oneself and queers is radical in cis/heteropatriarchy. We can take up Kincaid's insights and critique of diaspora and colonialism "domestically" within countries as well.

Conclusion—Text and Imagery of Place: Connection and Subjugation in Colonial and Diasporic Contexts

> I went to Bath. . . . The landscape was almost as familiar as my own hand, but I had never been in this place before, so how could that be again? . . . It was all those years of reading, starting with Roman Britain. Why did I have to know about Roman Britain? It was of no real use to me, a person living on a hot, drought-ridden island, and it is of no use to me now.
>
> —Kincaid, "On Seeing England for the First Time"

The descriptive aspects of English literature that Kincaid would never know as her own reality functioned as components of her oppression. The architecture of imagery of place in the colonial texts of her experience is the scaffolding of her "othering," of her distance from the colonial real, meaning England and the English. In the colonial sense, Kincaid can never make a claim. The colonizers' imagery will always and only mark her status as never measuring up, as conquered.

In discussing imagery and connection in the diasporic context, a contrast with the colonial experience can at times be stark. For diaspora communities, we often intend to maintain the textual imagery as ours despite its differences from the place of living. Or we may lament our distance from the textual imagery and then develop methods of survival so that the differences between text and diasporic living not only effect disaffection but inspire the longing to connect. While some societies have allowed individual "others" to integrate into their normative cultures, this is rarely the case for communities. As we will see with Arendt and others in upcoming chapters, those retaining group ties in diaspora are generally relegated to the margins of cultural production and meaning in the place of living. This is particularly so when those in diaspora insist on publicly being their othered selves and do not actively participate in genociding their difference. In this case, in diaspora our feelings of alienation can also be from what we claim as our own, not only from what relates to the conquerors. But having our own texts in exile enables possibilities of collective autonomous self-making for minorities even while within a dominant culture. This can be especially so when that dominant culture remains largely "other" to one's own.

Kincaid's conjuring the familiar that is out of place—that everything is familiar in Bath, but she has never been there—is a mark of her position as a colonial subject. While truth-making strategies can often be confused—usually for specific political ends—with truths themselves, a difference from Kincaid's rendering can be signified in stories told by Jews who go to modern Israel, for example; see things they have only known in stories; and comment on feeling connection. Of course, many contemporary Jews feel mainly alienation in visiting modern Israel. Both are clearly possible. In the diasporic context, still, familiarity with the place "over there"—that from which we have been exiled—can allow for a claim, a groundedness, connection. This familiarity with a place that is different from the place of living is one mode of truth making. This can be so even in negation of our centralizing the place of our historic centers. Certainly, methods of truth making can also serve imperial designs. At the same time, often in diasporic cases the capacity for truth making via grappling with history and text (and the ways that some histories and our texts may appear "foreign" to our circumstances in diaspora) is also a core method of establishing agency through recourse to not-completely-conquered versions of reality.

Kincaid's scathing text placing the sources of colonial oppression in (as the title names) "On Seeing England for the First Time" highlights interesting and sometimes distinct facets of power and resistance strategies for the colonized and those in diaspora. Many of us, such as Kincaid, are multiply situated: in diaspora and colonized, and perhaps also colonizer or one who has returned "home" (see Abbasi 2017). From Kincaid's position in the nexus of colonized subject and member of the African, Caribbean, and Jewish diasporas, we can see that her incompleteness as a British subject is an oppressive aspect of colonial rule and also see that such incompleteness is simultaneously an invitation to connection and revolution. In this analysis of Kincaid's case, we can see that she brings together these many knowledges in identifying alienation as a call to justice and social transformation.

Kincaid's critique offered in her text "On Seeing England for the First Time" is itself a political act. The methods employed in her writing serve as a politics themselves. In these processes, Kincaid brings together many of the differences as well as much of the overlay of colonial and diasporic conditions. Kincaid's critique of the roles of text in the form of subjugation, that is colonialism, unexpectedly also highlights aspects of note for the political roles of text for those in exile.

Chapter 3

Golda Meir

Smashing Binaries of Gender, Diaspora, and Anticolonialism

[Golda Meir] was my big childhood icon.

—Natasha Lyonne, born in 1979

Golda Meir was a smart and strong woman. Our multilayered method of the political-as-personal will let us see new facets of Meir's life, struggles, and legacy. Meir was a boundary smasher. Here, I highlight two aspects of my investigation: one at the level of gender and one at the level of diaspora. These two are not separate. However, since I tend not to be understood when I say multiple things at once, I will explore them in turn below.

Meir served as prime minister of Israel from 1969 to 1974, during a time that included the September 1972 massacre of eleven Israeli athletes at the Munich Olympics as well as the 1973 Yom Kippur / Ramadan War between Israel and its neighbors, primarily Syria, Iraq, Egypt, and Jordan. She also had a long and active career in politics and as a community organizer in the US, where she arrived as a young woman, a refugee from anti-Jewish violence in the Russian Empire. After she moved to Palestine in 1921, her life in politics and her move into leadership in the Yishuv, the Israeli pre-state government, put her at the center of some of the main events of Israel's history. The fact that she became prime minister is likely the main reason so many people know of her, when we tend to know about so few women political activists in history. Prime Minister Meir and her Zionism have also been excoriated in public discourse over the years.

Perceptions of Zionism and Meir's role as head of state have likely prevented numerous potentially interesting conversations about her and interfered with our learning from her.

I want to look at Golda Meir using various tools and starting from the perspectives of the creative wisdoms of contemporary feminists and queers, within de-colonial, class-based, and race-critical frames offered by both activists and those in the academy. Using this approach, I find a more radical legacy left to us by this extraordinary and controversial woman. After I spent some time in different Israeli archives and doing other research about Meir, it became clear that I needed to follow my own heart and the approach of this book more generally to use the political-as-personal method linking her work with her life, passions, activism, and struggles.

Meir is often compared to former British prime minister Margaret Thatcher.[1] Given the paucity of women heads of state, this comparison makes sense from a patriarchal political view. Both are considered to have been hawks. And while Thatcher headed the party in opposition to the British Labour Party and Meir was a leader of Israel's socialist Labor Party, by reputation both have been considered conservative and typecast as "impenetrable" (an interesting adjective for women in patriarchal systems). In this chapter, I make no apologies for the many aspects of Golda's legacy that are fraught. The following is neither a defense of Meir's hawkishness nor of her leadership during the 1973 war, which resulted in tremendous casualties for Israelis, Palestinians, and those in the Arab and Muslim states involved. I offer no attempts at excuses for Meir's misunderstanding, lack of empathy, and problematic record with respect to Palestinians and to Mizrahi Jews in Israel. I utilize my de-colonial critiques of Meir's Zionism, but perhaps in some ways that will be new to readers. What I argue in this chapter is that when we look at Meir from a multilayered, transnational, feminist perspective, bringing to bear the critical insights of queer theory, we find a Golda Meir surprisingly similar to the fantastic whirlwind that was Emma Goldman, another political Jewish woman from whom we have a great deal to learn.

I will be honest: when some leftists and anti-Zionists hear that I have been working on Meir, they caution me not to sully my reputation with including a chapter on her in this book. (I actually have been warned similarly about other chapters of the book.) I have had similar responses from some mainstream and progressive pro-Zionist feminists. Whether they listen to what I'm saying about what I seek to do in this chapter or not, some are clear that Meir is not worthy of inquiry. She is not deserving of our attention as feminist scholars and activists. I want to continue engaging with people I have long sought out who challenge me on many issues, in many ways. As in other difficult conversations, I assume it will be okay for us to talk and, if so, to ultimately disagree. In the case of Meir, too often they tell me not to bother.

When Israelis of most political persuasions hear me speak of Goldman and Meir together, they tend to get furious. How could I "downgrade" a founder of Israel to the likes of a radical political activist? I reply as a feminist: the extensive transnational and grassroots organizing, community building, and network nurturing of these two women link them and are worthy of study. Meir's methods of doing politics were quite similar to Goldman's. Yes, even though one was formally an anarchist (meaning against the state, among other things) and one a builder of what turned out to be a new state on the global map. Emma Goldman engaged in some violent acts when she was younger before shifting her vision of anarchism, and she was often thrown in jail for her activities. She was deported from the US. Yet, in another time and place, Meir's actions supporting the Haganah (pre-state Israeli defense forces—not an army sanctioned among the official nations of the world) and secret incursions into Nazi-occupied Europe might not be considered so far from Goldman's at-times-illegal and desperate attempts to make tangible her political imperatives. These actions often brought each into conflict with the law of their time and place. Meir's long legacy of activism, job history, and concrete planning for the settlement and needs of new refugees and immigrants to Israel would, I assert, have made the likes of Emma Goldman proud. Both women never ceased to be busy with meetings, organizing with ordinary folk as well as with the leaders of their movements, working for some very specific plan of material benefit for activists and communities, and promoting their radical visions of justice.

And what does Meir have to offer us as contemporary feminists opening up to the revolutionary legacy of our Jewish foremothers beyond comparisons to Emma Goldman? Rather than accept the staid PR version of Golda Meir as an "iron lady,"[2] a Margaret Thatcher type, a "tough guy in women's clothes," we will take the political context of this drag performance seriously.[3] As we bring out the Meir beyond the stoic stereotype, the woman behind the "neuter" who played with the big boys in the creation of the Israeli state, infamous for not recognizing the Palestinians as a people and for saying that Mizrahi activists in Israel were not acting like "nice boys," we find a complicated feminist legacy very different from standard descriptions of her. Even with my dovish, race-critical, de-colonial, and queer views, and not in spite of them, Meir has now endeared herself to me deeply. That doesn't mean I have to agree with her or ignore what I consider inexcusable. I hope that I can share this Meir who now increasingly travels with me, just as Goldman has for so much longer.

Thus, this chapter looks at the ways that Meir smashed overlapping binaries central to contemporary Jewish life and thought. Specifically, I explore them using diaspora and queer gender theories, aided by de-colonial work, each which is important for feminists and for all of us. This work has compelled me to look at my own life experiences and to explore, together with others,[4] the many ways in which we are still constricted by binary gender expectations. It has led me to look more constructively at strategies for both challenging and accepting these expectations within ourselves and each other as we work to transform them. Golda Meir lived and engaged in politics, created meaning, and did her part to change the world for Jews, women, and all. She did this as a Jewish, secular, anticolonial socialist caught in a constellation of impossible and contradictory expectations of her as a woman. She did this as part of a global anticapitalist movement applying numerous Western racist frameworks in the context of the Middle East and North Africa. She is iconic in how much she stands for these cis-gendered, heteropatriarchal conundrums. In examining her rather extreme situation, I hope that we can take stock of our own current circumstances and perhaps find new ways forward as we continue the exceptional—and yet everyday—work of *tikkun olam*, healing and transforming the world.

This chapter will also argue that Meir's binary-smashing impact does not stop with gender issues, as important as they are. Her incredible life and work also slash through the either/or framework of diaspora theorizing, co-constructed as it often is with colonialism, so central to Jewish thought for millennia and crucial to so many on this planet, rife as it is with displacement (not only in the modern period). Building from the exploration of diaspora studies in Jamaica Kincaid's work, I argue that we could see Meir's life and situation as a paradigm of the binary presumptions in much Jewish diaspora thinking, which divides locations into "home" and "away." A standard assumption is that home is good, away means oppression, and we all ought to seek to return home. While the particulars are significantly different, like Kincaid, Meir lived and also forged a complex diasporic politics in her time and place. Born into oppressive circumstances in the diaspora of the Russian colonial Empire, then a refugee in the US, Meir became a Zionist. As a young woman she made aliyah, that is, moved to what would become Israel. Moreover, changing direction post-Holocaust, she became a central player in making a strand of Zionism that was a prominent version of the Zionist dream into a reality—creating a Jewish state. Who could embody this home/away diasporic dichotomy more? But, like most narratives regarding Meir, this story turns out to be far less simple than it first appears. In the second part of this chapter, I nudge open the discussion from Kincaid yet a tad more. I retell Meir's diaspora/Zion story in a new way in the context of more contemporary critical and queered feminist diaspora thinking. As we learn with Kincaid, diaspora tales are all the richer when placed within gendered, classed, raced, and de-colonial analyses. In doing so I demonstrate that even Meir, usually upheld as a quintessential example in a Zionist paradigm, shows us a nuanced and multifaceted complex of diaspora/home. This complex cannot be contained by the more commonly traditional declassed, degendered, desexed, deracinated, and binary models inattentive to colonial foundations.

This chapter proceeds as follows: First, I share some background on my research process for diving into this study of Meir. The process itself taught me a lot more about Meir than I had originally expected. Then, before we can go any further, we take a break. It seems that we need a breath and some history in order to journey together in this chapter. Once we gain some shared footing from this history review, we can then reenter Meir's life in terms of her basic biography. We will need the material of these first sections when we unravel some of her biography in the next section on Meir smashing gender binaries. And, finally, we will look together at another great feminist, queer, class-based, de-colonial example of Meir smashing binaries as we develop our diasporic theorizing in this book and its relationship to genocidal settler colonialism in a Jewish context.

The Research Process and Golda Meir

I became seriously involved in both feminist and Jewish politics at around the same time, in the early 1980s, when I was somewhere between sixteen and eighteen years old. This was only a few years after "the age of Golda Meir," in which so many girls, especially many Jewish girls such as Natasha Lyonne, dreamed of becoming Meir (Conte 2020). In 1980, Andy Warhol included a portrait of Golda in his series *Ten Portraits of Jews of the Twentieth Century*.[5] Meir's early years as prime minister were marked by enormously high approval ratings, and she was considered iconic around the globe.[6] Yet after the Yom Kippur / Ramadan War and moving toward the mid-1980s I no longer heard much about Golda Meir.[7] In my feminist, peace-activist circles, the only thing positive said about Golda Meir was the occasional reference to her reply to an Israeli cabinet member suggesting a curfew for women at a time when rapes in Israel were on the rise. Meir answered, "Men are committing the rapes. Let *them* be put under curfew" (Cottin Pogrebin 1997, 909). People in my circles at the time spoke disparagingly, as if the remark were the only thing she ever did for women.

This project led me to begin to study Meir's life and contributions more seriously. Over two research trips to Israel, I was able to work in a few of the archives holding materials on Meir.[8] In particular, on a research trip in Israel in 2010, I was able to visit the kibbutz where she lived briefly but which remained a beacon in the inner landscape of her life's meaning. I had the opportunity to meet with the curator of the museum there and to spend some time in the Kibbutz Merhavia archives. By chance, one evening that summer at dinner with dear friends on a nearby kibbutz, someone mentioned to their ninety-year-old father that I was heading to Kibbutz Merhavia to look into Meir's life. Vitzo was a Slovakian Holocaust survivor and a founder of his kibbutz, affiliated with the socialist Zionist movement Hashomer Hatzair and its political party Mapam (which opposed Meir's Labor Party and its affiliates, including its affiliated kibbutzim). Vitzo began to tell me what he thought of "Golda." I was not prepared for the experience. Until that point in my research I had been exposed only to polished analyses in books and scholarly articles. Vitzo was raw, animated, and intense as he fervently recounted his memories of Meir. After that, I began to ask more everyday folk about her, and in 2013 I undertook another research trip to Israel during which I purposely made time to have conversations and ask questions of people of all ages, in addition to doing additional archival work and other formal research.

The conversations proved important to the analysis I offer in these pages. It may, therefore, be surprising to hear that many people did not have too much to say that was interesting. I don't say this to be mean. Of course, most people I spoke to were interesting people, and we had lively and challenging conversations. Many people hadn't thought about Golda in a while and it was fascinating to watch their memories and emotions build over the course of a conversation, often in dialogue with others. Most significantly, I learned a great deal from what turned out to be the banality of so many of these conversations. What do I mean by banality? Over and over, most of the people with whom I spoke, regardless of age or other demographics, (a) told me that there was nothing interesting to say regarding Golda Meir, then (b) proceeded excitedly to tell me the exact same handful of stories about her. At first, I found this quite odd, but eventually I started to make sense of the phenomenon.

The people who were gracious enough to share their time and thinking with me came from all walks of life. Initially, I specifically spoke with people in at least their eighties so that I could hear people's own adult memories of their personal experiences of Meir's active years. I spoke with teachers, men who were soldiers during the 1973 war, neighbors who ran into her in the *makolet* (small neighborhood grocer) where she bought her own milk and eggs, political activists (whether inside formal political party structures or not), scholars, journalists, and ordinary people who voraciously followed the news, as many Israelis do. Then, realizing that it would be interesting also to hear how people experienced her legacy as taught in Israeli schools over the decades, I shifted the age range of my interlocutors. I talked to educators, mothers with grown children, and young mothers of school-age children to hear about their Golda Meir school projects.

In the many informal exchanges I had, my experiences tended to repeat, despite the variety of people with whom I spoke. Frequently, my interlocutors acted as if they were giving me inside information or a sweet morsel of select news. Most people focused directly and only on Meir's time as prime minister.[9] Generally, the people with whom I spoke seemed to know nothing about or were explicitly not interested in discussing her life or her activist accomplishments prior to being prime minister. They mentioned the ever-infamous "Golda shoes," remembered as dark, clunky shoes that were the butt of many a joke. Ashkenazis almost always wanted to talk only about her responsibility in the Yom Kippur / Ramadan War.[10] Mizrahis and Ashkenazi leftists said she had been racist when she said that the Black Panthers (an Israeli movement of Mizrahis standing up to Ashkenazi oppression) weren't being nice in their protests against Ashkenazi hegemony in Israel. Arab and Palestinian Israelis and various activists on the left were furious with Meir's refusal to acknowledge Palestinian peoplehood. Truly, a total of approximately five stories circulated . . . and that was it. As for the special inside information people thought they were giving me, it was the same few stories. Meir's reaction to the Black Panthers was extremely problematic and continues to deserve new critical interrogation. The people with whom I spoke, however, did not offer their own analyses of the situation. They just mentioned the headline. It was the same with her rejection of the fact of Palestinian peoplehood.

What could it mean that the legacy of a controversial national and international leader had become so staid? Where does it leave us today in our capacity for undertaking complex justice work and seeking fulfilling lives when Meir's negotiation of multiple modes of settler colonialism (by others, with others, and with portions of her own Jewish community) while leading an international revolutionary anticolonial movement at a point of extreme crisis for the Jewish people gets so simplified? Moreover, what is lost when analysis of imbricating inherent contradictions, required to take seriously a woman functioning in male arenas of power, has been boiled down to a few hegemonic snapshot stories?

In the US, I tried asking friends from my younger activist days, a crew then hovering around fifty years of age (yeah, I've been working on this project for way over a decade), whether they ever think about Meir. "Nope." What do they think of when they think of her? "She was a hawk and not good for Israel/Palestine peace." "She was racist against non-Ashkenazi Jews." What else do they know about her? "Not much more than that." These are people I thought of as so "in the know." As I continued my academic research, I branched out with my casual inquiries. I asked anyone I could: women in their seventies who were Christian ministers, family members, and so on. We all had the same story: the Margaret Thatcher comparison, hawk, stubborn. These definitely were not offered as compliments.

Along the way through these conversations in both the US and Israel, I found some distinctly gendered and generational patterns. Jewish women, particularly those over sixty at the time of our conversations, were more likely to eventually begin talking to me in increasingly personal and emotional ways about what Meir meant to them. In particular, they spoke about how important it had been to them that she was a woman. Older mothers eventually got around to talking to me about how they tried to make certain that their daughters paid attention and learned about "Golda." If we were talking one-on-one or with a small group of women, this subject came up sooner. If the woman was with her husband or with men in the conversation, it seemed to take a lot more time and courage for the women to shift the thread to their admiration for Meir "as a woman." Over time, this pattern suggested to me that the official PR version of Golda Meir was largely constructed within the pressures of militaristic and heteropatriarchal contexts. Ordinary women had more to tell if they were able to hang onto the space of conversation long enough. What interventions can contemporary queer feminist scholars and activists make into this reified, sedimented portrait?

Interlude

Wait a minute.
    Time out.
    I think that we are getting mired in some confused history and jumbled storytelling.
    Maybe you get the sense from current history that all Jews and Jewish organizations are Zionist, or that they would ever agree on what that term could mean. Maybe you have absorbed a prideful or an antisemitic fantasy that Jews know what they want and work in step together for shared goals? I realize that most of us today likely do not know that Zionism was a minority Jewish movement among so many that sought to end anti-Jewish oppression; this was one aspect of Meir's challenges in her international Jewish work. Since Zionism is often castigated as a European solution to a European problem, probably most of us do not realize that, even if a minority among Jewish movements generally, Zionism has a long and respected history in Sephardi and Mizrahi, Ottoman Empire, Middle Eastern and North African, and other locales of Jewish life. Meir's work, for better and worse, was not only with Ashkenazi Jews in Palestine and Israel but with masses of Mizrahi and Sephardi Jews. Today, Moroccan Israelis form the largest Jewish ethnic group in the country.
    Exploitation is real and it is deadly, but also, so much for a simple rendering of white supremacy. Sometimes these Jewish ethnic groups worked together and sometimes they did not. For example, Jewish life does not have a central authority structure, but there is a long tradition supporting a position of chief rabbi in Jerusalem, Gaza, and other places around the globe. So much for anyone envisioning halacha, Jewish law, as "the" law. In the land of Israel today, there must be two chief rabbis, one Sephardi and one Ashkenazi. Intra-Jewish matters of contention have run deep when it comes to Israel. Western Jewish elites often worked to limit publicity of Zionist activities. When support for the creation of some sort of Jewish homeland (the aim of statehood was for most of pre-state politics a minority interest among Zionists) began to grow, western Jews frequently characterized east-

ern European Jews (who mainly became the founding leaders in the European Zionist movement) in European colonial terms such as ragged radicals.

It can be tricky to learn to think in different ways about Meir and others from the vantage point of current international events. For example, it may be news to many of us that, outside of the Jewish community, the term *Zionism* was really only used in the way it is today, in 2025, in the context of the history of the Russian and Soviet machinery of antisemitism. What many of us take to be basic alliances among Jewish groups and across communities have rarely been stable. Those presented as Israel's foes or friends have not always lined up the way they do today. Most of us are surprised to learn, for example, that Israel had open borders with Iran long after its independence and longer than with most of its regional neighbors. They had an unspoken alliance as the two non-Arab states in the area. Formal diplomatic ties were cut after the 1979 Islamicist Iranian Revolution. Back channels between the countries remained open particularly during the decade or so of the Iran-Iraq War from 1980 into the early 1990s.

Here's another bit about shifting alliances that I learned only as an adult: in 1948, the Soviet Union was actually the first country to recognize Israel as an independent country. This act by the USSR was followed by recognition from various other countries. The US only came on board later in 1949. Then Israel got kicked to the US side of the Cold War in what soon seemed like an unbreakable tie. That was the global lineup for my entire life, leading to the amnesia about early Soviet support for Israel. Then, on October 7, 2023, following years of violence between Israel and Palestine, came the brutal Hamas attacks in southern Israel and an ensuing humanitarian crisis in Gaza resulting from Israel's "merely using its right, under international law, to defend itself." For a while, those alliances regarding Israel since the Cold War remained intact. March 22, 2024, marked a major shift. The Jewish and larger Left demanding a ceasefire from the start of Israel's retaliation had been excoriated. The US had been, somewhat predictably, vetoing United Nations resolutions for a ceasefire. At the end of March 2024, the US led the way for a ceasefire demand that was even less in line with Israel's position in the previous UN calls (for example, not requiring Hamas to free any of the 130 hostages that remained in captivity), and it was Russia and China who vetoed the resolution in the UN Security Council. Geopolitical shifts happen.

It is dangerous that any of us can forget how small a percentage of Jews worldwide, across countries and continents, survived the genocidal settler colonialism of Nazi-led anti-Jewish movements from Europe to the Middle East and Africa. Most of those whom we designate as "survivors" barely survived at all. Decimated communities were not only Ashkenazi but also Sephardi and Mizrahi. It was not only Yiddish Jewish culture that was nearly wiped out but Ladino-speaking Jewish culture as well. Some of us learn about certain Arab leaders collaborating with the Nazis and that local and other Arabs and leaders pushed the Ottomans and the English to slow and stop legal immigration of Jewish refugees to Palestine. I'd like to know more about that.

Were you also taught that many Arab communities in Palestine and countries in the region worked to *support* the passage of Jews into the relative safety of Palestine? They did this for Jewish refugees from the Russian Empire during the intense period of pogroms, from various countries and continents during the Holocaust, and from other places and times where and when Jewish lives were in danger. During the Holocaust, for example, it was often only unexpected countries who opened their doors to Jewish immigration (such as Albania, China, and the Dominican Republic), exacerbating the massive refugee crisis. I had to learn that on my own as an adult.

Here's another example: even with Zionism's many problems, with country after country shutting its doors to Jewish refugees fleeing the genocides and displacements of pogroms and the Holocaust, globally it was not uncommon for liberals and even anarchists, socialists, and communists from various countries and nationalities to support the right of Jews to settle in Israel. This support for settling refugee Jews in Palestine, however comparatively small it was on a global scale, included many anti-Zionists as well as Palestinian and Arab groups.

This probably means that, like me, you had forgotten that founding Israel was, in the post–World War II age, part of a broader anticolonial movement, in alliance with those of many Arab, Asian, African, Indigenous, and Latin American peoples and others. Yes, you likely have heard of animosity between Jews, Muslims, and Christians in the lands of biblical Israel over the past couple of thousand years and in the past century. This has had devastating consequences. Have you ever heard of the histories of many "Jewish/Arab" collaborative projects in pre- and post-state Israel? Of the heritage of many local joint "Jewish/Arab" initiatives, from long before Israel declared independence and today's efforts at a shared society? Historically, these initiatives frequently focused on shared issues of agriculture, commerce, education, sanitation, irrigation, and throwing off the yoke of Ottoman and then British rule.

Did you know that Israel was created as a secular socialist country? As we will see, this was at times awkward for Meir when doing her work raising support for Israel from international Jewish communities. Wealthy donors in the US, for example, by the 1940s were often no longer socialists. (We will explore more on that in the Goldman chapter.) Moreover, US Jewish elites—particularly in the Reform movement—were busy re-creating Jewishness as a religion (we'll get to that more when we think with Kahlo), so it was not always easy to understand efforts to create a secular, socialist Jewish country. It still is not for many.

I find this similar to some people seeming perplexed that there could be a Jewish state that is also a democratic state. Most of us educated in the West suddenly get a mind block when it comes to Jewish politics. A huge swath of countries across the globe has national "religions" or state-supported ones, including what are called the democracies in western Europe. The world remains home to many countries with still-functioning monarchies, again including Western(-style) democracies. Call me Eurocentric, if you like, for reminding us that many of the countries that those of us in the West were taught in public school are "democracies" are in Europe or were created out of European settler colonialism. In my Eurocentric New York public school education, I was never given proper tools to take on many of the conundrums I would find in my adult life, such as the argument of some that Israel cannot be a Jewish state and a democratic state. But why, then, as a politics major at US universities, was I forced to study England, that democratic beacon, for so long? England has both a state religion and a monarchy. What? Right. Well, we are told that we have to look at on-the-ground civil liberties there. Life in England and its occupied states can be super racist, homophobic, anti-Jewish, Islamophobic, colonial, and patriarchal, but supposedly that does not have anything to do with England being a nation-state with a monarchy and national religion. Hmmm? Is there a relevant application of this idea to Israel?

So many years of violent conflict for the peoples of Mexico and most of those in Latin America, in the US and Canada, in Australia and New Zealand result from the fact that their countries were created out of lengthy settler-colonial policies of a handful of other countries. Many across this planet call for national self-determination. This hasn't yet helped too many of the earth's inhabitants, such as the Kurdish, the Armenian, and the Palestinian people. Efforts for national self-determination continue to wreak havoc in eastern Europe and Asia, impacting international grain supply chains (diminished) and arms sales (increased). Many countries of Europe were established with the post–World War I work of a small group of world leaders in the 1919 Versailles Treaty. It is plain to see that Israel was founded within geopolitical borders in which numerous other peoples had also made their homes, likely for centuries. After World War II, areas that had struggled under colonial rule saw the British create new states supposedly partitioned according to nationality in places such as India and Israel and then flee the scene, leaving the inhabitants in those lands with bloody legacies and border disputes still actively tearing people's lives apart today. One with a public middle or high school US education might recall that dozens of the countries in Asia and Africa were basically created after World War I by a small group of Western diplomats. For most, the world is a mess. We all have a role to play in this and personal choices to make. Most of it occurs well beyond the level of individuals and individual countries, empowered and constrained in a global setting. A lot of people work hard to get their segments set right. It is not easy work. Check this out.

Admittedly, too few US citizens have even (or recently) read the US Declaration of Independence. At least, that is the sense I get from teaching US politics to undergraduate students in US universities. It might not be surprising that most of us have also never seen the Zionist Israeli Declaration of Independence, which states,

> The state of Israel will be open for Jewish immigration and for the Ingathering of the Exiles; it will foster the development of the country for the benefit of all its inhabitants; it will be based on freedom, justice and peace as envisaged by the prophets of Israel; it will ensure complete equality of social and political rights to all its inhabitants irrespective of religion, race or sex; it will guarantee freedom of religion, conscience, language, education and culture; it will safeguard the Holy Places of all religions; and it will be faithful to the principles of the Charter of the United Nations. (*Declaration* 1948)

I know that it is "just" a document. Still, nice going.

Arguably, it can be tough to parse that the constant references in US media to Israel as a democracy stand on shaky ground. But does that not mean we also need to revisit our curriculum on democracy more broadly? Shouldn't we also ask what it means to say that the US was the first modern democracy when it was founded on slavery and the dispossession of Indigenous peoples on this land? In World War II, the US fought the Nazis with a racially segregated military. And what have we been taught of the roles that most of the rest of today's Western "great democracies," such as Germany, France, the Netherlands, Belgium, Italy, and Spain, played in the Atlantic slave trade, colonialism, Christian missionizing? Admittedly, the concept of democracy can be a tough nut to crack. And yet, many of us never learned that, in addition to receiving condemnation, Zionism was also lauded by the international Left as a revolutionary movement. This was due partly to the way it challenged the nature of democracy found "even" in the West, where we are taught to take for granted an assertion that countries are democratic, and also to Israel calling upon itself to be more of a democracy than many of these great powers.

Loss of this history is a problem. Pre- and post-October 7, 2023, we have seen that thousands of people around the world have lost the knowledge of so much of our radical democratic history. We never knew, or we forgot, that Israel was celebrated among many anticolonial movements and other recently de-colonized countries across what were then called the second and third worlds. Most of us never knew that Golda Meir, as Israeli Foreign Minister, visited many African countries that were fighting their own socialist and anticolonial battles—because activists and newly independent governments invited her. She was brought to these neighboring lands so that they and the new Israel, which had many challenges but did just throw off the yoke of British colonial rule, could share their experiences fighting similar causes. When she stepped off airplanes in these countries, she was met by huge audiences and resounding rounds of applause. I'm thinking that means that you, like me, may never have known that Israel worked closely with many Global South and newly postcolonial countries. Israel and these countries shared scientific advancements about how to better feed their people through agricultural development in desert regions, social studies regarding new public transport systems, and institution development as they all struggled to meet the demands of newly free peoples.

It is important to affirmatively attend to the Palestinian refugee crisis, particularly since 1948. There should be no question about this. We must meet history on the terms of real people rather than on the basis of some of the very skewed narratives we hear coming from different communities. We must work to overturn anti-Jewish ideas and systems. Jews and many allies are well positioned to work in this area. Certainly, Jews know of many of the horrors of being displaced, sent into exile, and rendered stateless. No two cases are alike. Sure, Jews can point to the expulsions and exiles resulting from colonial takeovers in the ancient Jewish kingdoms. We can look back to the Visigoths and the Crusades in our history with similar calamities, the wreckage of the Spanish Inquisition, the destruction of the Nazi-based Holocaust. We can plainly see that Jews have a direct interest in working in cross-community and intercountry coalitions to address all such cases.

Still, it often also seems that too many (i.e., Jews in the West and others worldwide) did not get the memo about the approximately 800,000 Jews exiled and forced in various ways from their ancestral homes in the Middle East and North Africa in relation to the creation of Israel. Jewish communities in most of this region were ancient, predating the Christian, Muslim, and Arab takeovers of these lands. Over only a brief period in the twentieth century, they were reduced to remnants. It may be news for some of us to learn that Lebanon briefly experienced a growth in its Jewish population at this time. Many of the dispossessed Jews say they still keep the keys to their homes in Baghdad in their pants pockets. We know that across countries, with different permutations in each country, some new government rules allowed the Jews to take only one suitcase each with their belongings and forced them to forgo their businesses, land titles, and other holdings. Jews know the lethal imprecision between what get labeled "pull factors" and "push factors." When Jews sought out new homelands in their efforts to end brutal discrimination and grinding poverty, the factors leading them to leave are called pull factors. When governmental decree, murderous antisemitism, and expulsion (under various names) forced them into exile, these reasons for leaving are called push factors. Important distinctions. It can be hard to see a clear demarcation line.

Hmmm . . .

Okay,

take a breath.

Let us get back to this Golda Meir story. Perhaps our thinking with Meir can help us sort through some of these gaps in our education and some of the confusion in our thinking. Perhaps this will help us become ready to note and change the mortal impact of too much of our policy.

Meir's Biography

Golda Meir was born Goldie Mabovitch to Blume and Moshe in Kyiv, in the Pale of Settlement, on May 3, 1898. When her father immigrated to New York City in 1903, Blume and the three of her daughters who survived early childhood (five children older than Golda did not survive) moved to Pinsk, Belarus. They lived there with Blume's family from 1903 to 1906.

Meir's father, Moshe, moved to Milwaukee in 1905. In 1906, when Golda was eight years old, the rest of the family joined him there. All the members of the family were socialists or socialist leaning. Meir's father was active in the labor movement, her sister was active in the Labor Zionist movement, and their mother also helped to make their family home a center for Jewish political actors, refugees, and new immigrants from across the spectrum of the Left—labor, socialist, anarchist, and communist, both Zionist and not.

People always characterized Meir as clever and quick. After graduating from the Fourth Street School (later renamed the Golda Meir School) as class valedictorian, she aspired to become a teacher, one of the greatest futures most girls could imagine at the time. Despite their support of her early studies, Golda's parents considered a middle school education sufficient for a girl who would likely become a worker. After bitter and dramatic family struggles, at age fourteen, Golda ran away to Denver to live with her older sister, Sheyna, and her brother-in-law, Shamai Korngold, so that she could attend high school. Sheyna's home was also a center for leftist argument of all types, so Meir continued her political as well as her formal education in Denver.[11] While living there, she met Morris Meyerson in 1913. They would marry on December 24, 1917.[12] Before that, she returned to Milwaukee and her parents, finished high school, and attended the Wisconsin State Normal School, where she served as the vice president of her class.

We will look more closely at the contributions of Emma Goldman later in this work. For now, it is interesting to note that there are strong parallels to Goldman's early years here, and in their later years we find both similarities and differences. As refugees from eastern Europe, both Meir and Goldman were from communities Westerners (including Jewish Westerners) considered backward and "oriental." There is important critique of Western Jews and early Zionists internalizing and employing European colonial views such as modern/backward, patriarchal/free, healthy/disease-carrying, and so on. It is also true that more Western Jews and Zionists of the time (including early Zionist Sephardi community leaders, both men and women) associated the likes of the Meirs and Goldmans, together with others from the poor and autocratic lands of the Russian Empire, with the degraded aspects of these binary pairings.

From their youngest years while still in the Russian Empire, both Goldman and Meir were inspired by older, politically active sisters. Both fled anti-Jewish persecution and violence in eastern Europe for refuge in the US. As adults, they each traveled frequently and lived across national borders (both chosen and not). Meir was able to continue living with her family for longer than was Goldman. Quite unusual at the time, Meir's sister and parents also made aliyah. Biographers of Goldman tend to emphasize her awful relationship with her authoritarian father, while Meir is noted to have often enjoyed support from her family. However, Goldman received support and respect from many of her family members of at least three generations. Unfortunately, Goldman's early excitement for her husband quickly waned, and her marriage dissolved. While Meir's marriage to Meyerson eventually came to exist in name only, they started off as quite a pair. Both women kept a series of lovers over their lifetimes. The two had somewhat unusual profiles regarding parenting. Goldman did not have children and would have needed a serious operation had she wanted to try. Meir had an abortion in her first year of marriage and later raised two children.[13]

In 1921, Golda, Morris, Sheyna, and Sheyna's two children immigrated to the British Mandate of Palestine. The details of their voyage are harrowing. With almost no resources left, they finally arrived at the Tel Aviv train station, which was basically covered in sand. Meir applied with her husband to live on Kibbutz Merhavia, but their first application was rejected because they were a married couple. The Merhavia members also judged that as an "American" woman, Meir would never be able to handle the rough conditions. Their second application was nonetheless approved. Meir often joked that the only reason they were accepted was that Morris had a phonograph. While living on the kibbutz from 1921 to 1924, Meir was chosen as representative to the Histadrut (General Federation of Labor). Due to Morris's poor health and the pressures on Meir to live a more "normal" (gendered) life, they left the kibbutz for Tel Aviv and then moved to Jerusalem in 1924. In these years they struggled with poverty.

Golda and Morris had two children. Menachem was born in 1924 and Sarah in 1926. In 1928 Golda left Morris and moved to Tel Aviv with her young children. There, she took a job as secretary of the Histadrut's Council for Women Workers.[14] This job led her to relocate with her children, for a time, to New York City, where she worked from 1932 until 1934. Meir became incredibly successful in her work for the women's council, and she moved from there into mixed-gendered posts that were increasingly politically well-positioned. Her separation from Morris was finalized in 1938, although they never legally divorced. He died in 1951. Sarah quit high school in 1943 to move south to the newly forming Kibbutz Revivim in the Negev. (Yes, for close readers of the news, Kibbutz Revivim is close to those directly attacked on October 7, 2023.) Meir took enormous pride in her daughter's kibbutz involvement (Blashfield 2010, 62). Menachem was also quite gifted, went into music, and later published a rather sentimental memoir about his mother (M. Meir 1983).

Approaches in 2024 to the drastic escalation in the war between Israel and Hamas echoed some of the strategies that Meir and other leaders in the Yishuv devised. Some work; many don't help matters much. Examples of some of these approaches, used in the early years of the Jewish state as well as across the globe, include looking toward military solutions, intercountry back-channel negotiations in a world too divided to conduct more of them in the open, years of inadequate modes of citizen involvement in policy development, and exploiting fear and insecurity among the populace.

In 1934, Meir became a member of the Executive Committee of the Histadrut, rising to head its political department in 1936. During World War II, she held several important positions in the World Zionist Organization and in the Jewish Agency. Meir served as acting head of the Jewish Agency and was its spokesperson in dealings with the British from 1946 until the end of the mandate in 1948. During this period, Meir was active in the decision taken by the pre-state Jewish leadership to reject the British policy to bar new Jewish refugees and immigrants. She was part of the illegal effort to smuggle Jews into Palestine and was also involved in finding ways for Jews in Israel to support Jews in Europe and the war effort there by clandestinely infiltrating behind enemy lines. As Jennifer Ring (1997) insightfully discusses in relation to the Israeli response to Hannah Arendt's later work, the gender politics of Israeli responses to the Holocaust was intense, as Zionists (with a largely male leadership) clamored to claim agency and to protect the emerging ideology of "the new Jewish manhood" in the face of horrific oppression and genocide in the diaspora. Meir was a central player in these strategy sessions against genocidal settler colonialism.

Meir volunteered in January 1948 to solicit twenty-five million dollars from the US Jewish community for the newly created state of Israel. This was considered an amazing sum. No Jewish or Zionist fundraising venture had ever come near to this target goal. Meir's proposal was accepted: she spoke English and had a good bit of earlier success on extensive US speaking and fundraising tours while a representative of the Histadrut's Council for Women Workers. Meir activated her grassroots networks through Jewish women's groups across the US, and these networks proved foundational to skyrocketing her political career back in Israel. On this particular trip, Meir succeeded in raising fifty million dollars due to her network building, organizing strategies, persuasive rhetoric, and the urgency of the Israeli War of Independence (upon being attacked by numerous neighboring countries).

Meir was in the first Israeli government, and she served as Israel's first ambassador to the USSR, from September 2, 1948, to March 1949. In

1949, she was elected to the first Knesset, in which she served until June 4, 1974 (the eighth Knesset). After declining founding prime minister David Ben-Gurion's invitation for her to be deputy prime minister, Meir served as minister of labor from 1949 to 1956 and was then appointed foreign minister, a post at which she served from 1956 until 1966, when she retired from office at age sixty-eight.

Meir's retirement was short-lived. A few months later, she returned to political life as secretary general of her party, Mapai. In 1967 she became secretary of the united Labor Party. When sitting prime minister Levi Eshkol died of a heart attack, her colleagues convinced her to take on the role of prime minister. They deemed that she would be the best person to help the party avoid a feared split from the increasing internal power struggle between Yigal Allon and Moshe Dayan. Meir was elected as prime minister in the next national election, and she served in that post from March 17, 1969, until 1974.[15] Incredibly popular, Meir was then reelected, but she chose to resign as prime minister on June 4, 1974. She died in Jerusalem of lymphoma on December 8, 1978, at age eighty.

Those Gender Binaries

Golda Meir and her legacy get caught in a binary system of gendered thinking. It is common for people to refer to her as "manly."[16] One of the most famous lines quoted about Golda Meir comes from Ben-Gurion, who said that she was "the only man in the Cabinet" (Butt 1998).[17] This characterization is a double-edged sword. It was meant to be a compliment suggesting that all the less worthy ministers in the cabinet were acting like women. To push the metaphor, it is a double-edged blade with rich potential for slashing at gender binaries. At the same time, its cutting edges are so worn down from use that neither side can slice even a tomato. We need a new analysis, one more dialectically systematic and less superficially contradictory. Meaning, instead of accepting the meanings of gender within a traditional binary frame, it will be fruitful to work with the mutual constitution of multiple identity factors, systemic oppressions, and movements for justice. The deeper contradictions in Golda Meir's gendered legacy have much to teach us about her and about our situation today.

Meir was considered a powerful political player. As most people had no way to make sense of a woman in this role, they often transformed her into a man in their imaginations. They described her in a laudatory way as tough, stubborn, shrewd, and a tireless worker who was able to withstand pressure and normal human physical and mental stress at superhuman levels, like a soldier. There are many stories of political leaders gathering at her home and calling at all hours of the day or night for analysis and strategy sessions with her. People needed her to make the tough calls. During her years in the public sphere, Meir faced some serious health issues, and yet she kept them secret and continued to carry on her duties. For example, she undertook an intensive series of radiation treatments for cancer in the middle of the night while she served as prime minister.

It is likely that there is truth to these characterizations of her, and they have also helped people muddle through a gender contradiction that they had no tools to understand. How could a woman be a paragon of these many "manly" qualities? In the popular imagination she becomes a man in drag—and not the fabulous queer kind, but a somewhat grotesque caricature of cisgendered thinking and heteropatriarchy. In this frame, there are two separate and solidly formed genders that are mutually exclusive: male and female. These genders emerge from socially constructed systems of beliefs, and each corresponds to a discrete set of characteristics and practices considered fitting to only one of the categories. While the dichotomies have shifted over time and place, class and culture, the system in which Meir functioned will still be resonant for many today.

Jewish men tended not to fit in the male side of the dichotomy in European categorizations. In the West, for example, *Jewish* gender norms often cast Jewish women as strong and independent relative to the broader society within the raced, classed, and sexed hierarchies in which Jews navigate Christian hegemonic norms. Internally to Jewish communities, however, girls and women also occupy a second-class status related to these characteristics. Within the Jewish community, these expectations are not revered, just required. Revered characteristics were associated with learnedness (in ancient Jewish texts and reasoning). Such prized characteristics could only be developed among boys and men, as girls and women were barred from Jewish houses of study. Meir was known to be a woman, and in normative modern and Western Christian cultures she would be expected to be demure, more passive in the presence of men, and more associated with the private sphere than the public, despite any paid work that she did. Women are expected to be beautiful according to the standards of their cultures and to take primary responsibility for childbearing, childrearing, and many additional tasks of caretaking.

In Western Christian schemata, the strong man Meir accordingly becomes an ugly and problematic woman. Meir is desexualized and almost always presented as matronly or grandmotherly—at whatever age. Her clothes are presented as old and unstylish. Her sturdy shoes were famous, providing comic relief. Meir was often questioned and criticized for "neglecting" her children. A powerful woman who must be a man must also be a bad mother. For men and the masculinized public, she was a trans and queer sort of successful man and therefore a failure as a woman.

Later in her life, in many Jewish feminist and (pro-)Zionist women's organizations, this successful man, Meir, was also considered a failed feminist. Women's political organizing changed from her early days, when endless Jewish and Zionist women's organizations invited her to speak on the situation of women in the Yishuv, on kibbutzim, and so on. By the 1970s, she was known by some in feminist circles as a successful woman who had succeeded by turning her back on women generally, "women's issues," and the "woman that she was." Viewed as suspect, as a man in drag (in an anti-queer trope), in the 1980s she was considered a bad role model for feminist leadership. In Israeli feminist circles, the view circulated that Meir might have gotten her start in women's organizations but that she later abandoned them for opportunities to play in the very male political professional league. She was portrayed as physically unattractive and dowdy. Who could use her as a poster figure for the new Israeli woman, strong and beautiful, accomplished but still so sexy? She had a husband and children, but feminists and the press complained that she never saw them.[18] Did this mean that women had to make an either/or choice? Public success or family and womanhood? The world of men and "power" or the world of women and care (Margalit Stern 2009)? Women, and many in marginalized groups, continue to face these either/or choices daily. We still need to find ways beyond this dead end. We can learn from historical examples: Golda Meir would not give in to these closed options.

Contemporary feminists often talk about Meir as if she could relate only to men and left individual women and the politics of feminist aspirations behind. This is likely to have been true in many instances. Insightful US Jewish feminist Letty Cottin Pogrebin published a book on Meir in 1991 and then wrote the entries on her for important feminist encyclopedia projects, including the biographical article on Meir for the Jewish Women's Archives. Cottin Pogrebin (1997, 908) quotes Colette Avital ("who began her career in Israel's foreign ministry under Meir's tenure" and became "one of her nation's top-ranking foreign service officers") as saying that Meir "disliked women, never really helped women." I have no reason to challenge Avital's characterization as what she experienced. At the same time, in my view, this is likely an unfortunate misreading of Meir's life and legacy as a whole.[19] I want to bring to the fore a variety of additional aspects of Meir's orientations and legacies. We will look at a range of examples of Meir "helping" women. In rewriting this story, we can start with her close relationships with women whom she clearly liked and also loved.

From childhood until her days as an elder and a stateswoman, Meir not only surrounded herself with strong women and maintained intimate relationships with women but also publicly acknowledged the importance of these relationships and networks to her. In opening her autobiography, Meir makes a point of noting the important woman in her own family genealogy. She tells of her great-grandmother Golda, after whom she was named. That Golda was "known for her will of iron and for her bossiness" (G. Meir 1975, 18). It was that Golda who helped Meir's grandparents approve the love marriage of her mother with the man who became Meir's father, whom her mother wanted so badly to wed at a time when the more common practice was to use a matchmaker. As gender-bending, strong women can sometimes pass their legacies across generations, perhaps it will not be surprising that people also often complimented the great-grandmother Golda by saying that she had "a man's mind" (Klagsbrun 2017, 10).

Appreciating the strength of women in her life, Meir describes the mother she knew as similarly feisty and then introduces her sister Sheyna, Golda's senior by nine years. Sheyna had a profound influence on her younger sister. Becoming a revolutionary with the socialist Zionist group in Pinsk by age fourteen, at risk of arrest and brutality by Russian authorities, Sheyna intrigued Meir and pulled her into her world of courageous political organizing from her childhood years. Meir recalls that on Saturdays while her mother was at synagogue, Sheyna would have meetings in their home, an action as dangerous as her weekday evenings out at "mysterious meetings." When her mother returned home, Golda would walk outside, almost patrolling in her own ritual, as would a sentry, so that she might warn Sheyna's group if a policeman came close. Golda's father, Moshe, had moved to the US by this point with the goal of earning money and then returning to the Russian Empire. It was largely Sheyna's illegal revolutionary activities as a socialist Zionist and their danger that led Golda's mother to insist that the family join Moshe in the US in 1906. While no accounting is seamless, we can see that Golda grew up in a family context in which women were courageous grassroots political activists who took responsibility for each other's actions and set the course of the family's histories.

While Israelis often commented in my conversations that Meir was not a great orator in Hebrew, many Israeli English speakers noted that she was an extremely effective public speaker in English. It seems that she began this career quite young.[20] Meir had a small circle of very close girlfriends in her youth with whom she shared her politics, tales of love, and aspirations. A child fellow traveler of Sheyna and her politics, Meir began her own grassroots political organizing career in 1908, when she was in the fourth grade. Meir and her close friend Regina Hamburger (who later joined her on aliyah) formed the American Young Sisters Society to raise money to buy textbooks for students in their area who could not afford them. Their activities included a fundraising effort in a large rented hall, where Golda spoke publicly. After graduating from high school, Golda taught for a while at a Yiddish school in Milwaukee, organized protest marches, was a favorite street-corner political speaker, and formally joined the Poalei Zion (Labor Zionist) organization.

Most biographies of Arendt, Stein, Kahlo, and Goldman point out the influential men in their lives. Kathy Ferguson has done extraordinary feminist scholarship addressing the gap in knowledge that this leaves and recovering "Emma's women."[21] Similarly, most biographies of Golda Meir point out the many important men with whom she was close and who influenced her political thinking. They do not, however, prioritize, or often even mention, the networks of women with whom she regularly worked and organized from a young age in Milwaukee until the end of her life. As with Stein, Kahlo, and Goldman, many of the women in these inner circles became close personal friends. In Meir's case, these intense women's networks also enabled her meteoric rise in politics, including in grassroots politics in the US and, eventually, state politics in Israel. Yet the political impact of these relationships receives insufficient analysis.

While Meir loved and admired her father and his labor activism in Milwaukee, it was her mother who made their home the vibrant political and intellectual space where she thrived. Meir continued to be inspired by and close to Sheyna for the rest of her life. Her close friend Regina Hamburger Medzini helped her plan her escapade of escape to Denver for refuge with Sheyna, a brave act for all three. In Wisconsin at the time, teachers could not marry, and Meir's parents worried about her future marriage prospects if she were to become a teacher. At this young age, Meir began to experience more directly the constraints of the societal either/or construction between so-called womanhood and personal happiness, on the one hand, and public or career aspirations, on the other. Meir's flight from Milwaukee deeply affected her parents, especially her father, but they eventually reconciled and rejuvenated their parent-child relationship, and their mutual respect for each other as comrades continued to grow. Another aspect of the power of the daughters' role in the family appears in their parents' eventual decision to follow them to Israel. Multigenerational aliyah was quite unusual for Jews in the US, and it was also unusual for the younger women in the family to pave the way in such a relocation.

The gender politics of Meir's familial ties are complex. She lived in the US at a time when women did not have a clear status as citizens in their own right. This had implications for Meir, as it did for Emma Goldman.[22] In 1917, Meir achieved derivative US citizenship because she was under twenty-one years old when her father attained his US citizenship. But women citizens of the US at that time lost their citizenship if they married men who were not US citizens.[23] When Golda married Morris, who had not become a US citizen, her own recently acquired US citizenship was called into question. This problem also curtailed her freedom of movement and agency as an activist at a time when she was beginning to travel extensively for political work for Poalei Zion, and it was particularly problematic when she was trying to cross the border into Canada. We can note this same lack of rights for women when we consider that they gained the right to vote in the US only in 1920, shortly before Meir left to make aliyah to Israel. This situation for politically active women, such as Emma and Golda, hits home for me and many feminists. I often think about how my grandmother and great-grandmother risked and lost so much in fleeing from the Russian Empire to the US at a time (just around when Meir left for Israel and Goldman was deported from the US) when women did not even have the right to vote here.[24]

It remains unclear why Meir's start in women's organizations makes her later success in broader political spheres so painful for many feminists, as if her career trajectory embodied only loss for women. It is a common situation that we still face today. When a colleague gains administrative experience in a women's organization or as director of a feminist studies department and then goes on to positions that are not exclusively in women's and feminist arenas, she is often considered suspect or held to higher scrutiny. If we believe that the place of feminists is everywhere, or nearly everywhere, then we ought to continue our relationships with and support for women and feminists who shift bases in their careers. While I cannot speak for individuals who may have felt personally abandoned by Meir's rare career trajectory, the historical record is clear that Meir maintained her close ties to the women she met and worked with as a grassroots activist in the US and in the Israeli women's council. As a young woman, she also forged strong, lifelong bonds with the women in the US branch of the Council of Women Workers and in Pioneer Women.

Meir began engaging in political campaigns under a female-gendered banner in the fourth grade. She continued to distinguish herself in mixed-gender political groups from a young age. For example, she attended the first convention of the American Jewish Congress in Philadelphia as the youngest of the delegates. She returned to "women's" organizations with her first Histadrut appointment and then moved back out to more general posts. But what about the quality of the work she did? Did she abandon traditionally female, and feminist, commitments to real people and their needs—to the "politics of care," as Joan Tronto (1993) calls it?[25]

When we look at Meir's long life in politics (and not only at her success at the apex of the Israeli political structure as prime minister), we find many examples of concrete commitments that Meir made to doing work for "the people." She routinely took into account women's lived realities, and she continued doing "care work" even as a political official. This is rare for any politician, as most often seem to forget real people's day-to-day needs once in office. Noting this also contradicts the feminist criticism that Meir "did nothing" for women and for feminism. Here is an interesting illustration: around 1946, British officials rounded up many male political leaders of the Yishuv. The British had no idea what they were in for when they left Meir as the acting head, and then the head, of the Jewish Agency's political department. For example, at this time, a group of Jewish refugees headed to Palestine began a hunger strike when they were detained aboard two ships in Italy. As head of the Yishuv, Meir led the effort for leaders of the community in Palestine to join them in a solidarity fast. Although she had recently been in the hospital for a gallbladder attack, she insisted on conducting the public fast herself. I consider this part of a feminist legacy of care that I want to teach to my students and my daughters. Similarly, in 1947 Meir traveled to Cyprus as a Yishuv representative with the unenviable task of helping detained Jewish refugees decide who would enter Palestine first under the pitiably small quota of Jewish immigrants allowed in. She chose to argue for giving first priority to families with children, despite arguments in many socialist circles that adult male workers had more value. Standing her ground on her commitments to the needs of children, Meir largely succeeded in her persuasive efforts.

Women and feminists from numerous communities fought many battles during the years when Meir was active politically in Israel. I make no pretense that she was always publicly on the side of official women's organizations. I have not conducted a feminist analysis of the specific demands of these organizations from a contemporary intersectional standpoint. Likewise, I cannot presuppose that even largely excellent work by "women's" organizations served all women constituents in their diversity. I do not mean to sweep over this lengthy, and likely fraught, history. Further study is warranted to integrate Mizrahi Jewish and Palestinian critiques of Jewish women's organizations in this time frame with the existing feminist critiques of Meir's relationship to these same women's organizations. This will likely transform those critiques when operating in separate lanes. Similarly, scholars have not yet adequately analyzed Meir's commitments as a socialist. These warrant consideration in the context of a more complicated re-gendered story of Meir's role in a solidifying Ashekenazi hegemony among Jews in Palestine. Meir's socialism is also worth examining in the context of her successful international solidarity work with other (eventually fledgling) nations in their struggles against colonialism. As a parallel, we can note that Emma Goldman was also often castigated by feminists of her day, for example, for her refusal to join the women's suffrage effort. Most of us today understand that this did not make Goldman an antifeminist. Neither case is as straightforward as many presentations suggest. Important questions remain: What is the actual work that we expect of feminists in their diversity, and how can we get beyond the litmus tests and double standards for women who become successful in mixed and also largely male spheres of power? This problem continues to challenge women politicians today in the US, in Israel, and likely around the world.[26] We can see this conundrum in standard receptions for all the subjects of this book.

In her many years as labor minister, for example, Meir did extraordinary work that ought to be valued, particularly by feminists. Meir refused Ben-Gurion's invitation to serve as deputy prime minister in order to work as labor minister, a position in which she was able to create large infrastructure projects to secure both housing and work for a vast number of new immigrants to Israel. Israeli leadership was steeped in Eurocentric presumptions, and policymaking often had severely differential impacts on Ashkenazi and Mizrahi immigrants. We need to learn Meir's role in this setting more specifically. We know, however, that when planning the layout for the new housing projects, Meir prioritized women's traditional work in the home across communities. In this, she saw her role as helping to assist masses of new immigrants in creating homes and communities rather than just state housing and alienating living spaces that might serve to isolate women across class situations.

There is much more that we might study in this case. Meir was also involved in initiating social legislation such as the National Insurance Act, which had a direct impact on the well-being of women, children, and all those settled in the new state. Even on the level of symbolic politics, in her speeches and writings, Meir constantly referred to "men and women" instead of the more usual, supposedly universal term, "men." We can see that in these many ways, over the course of her life's work, Meir did not leave women behind but instead included women centrally in her vision of a bold and revolutionary project of Zionism, as well as in her understanding of the heart and toil of the Jewish people. Some also point to this legacy as a concrete political contrast to Meir's racist public statements about Mizrahi refugees: in her mundane work in labor and housing, Meir did much to attend to the daily and familial needs of many of Israel's poorest and most marginalized. Meir's commitment to ending poverty was not only political and socialist. Meir herself was raised poor and spent years as an adult trying to raise a family in poverty while living in Jerusalem. In multiple places and stages in her life, she had personal experience with poverty that she later recounted as beyond dreadful. This mattered in her political work. It is time for new feminist and queer studies of the architects of early Israeli public policy to work with class-based, critical-race, and de-colonial tools. It is my hope that this more nuanced queer and feminist critique of Meir can support such future research.

In the meantime, when women in the US enter politics today, they still face similar scrutiny for their feminist qualifications. I don't mind holding women public figures to high standards. At the same time, it is clear to me that feminism means that we ought to hold *all* public figures to these standards. During Hillary Clinton's run for US president, we heard over and over the question, What does she do for women? In various ways, when women run for office, from Kamala Harris and onward in US elections, we hear the questions, What does this woman candidate do in terms of the real care work (à la Tronto 1993)? What is her stance on welfare, abortion, violence, education, single mothers, health care, housing? Meir's record on such specific issues demonstrates a long history of doing this care work and attending to women and to feminist concerns, including to the daily conditions of women as workers. She maintained her attention to these issues long after her years working with explicitly women's organizations.

As a woman, Meir was constantly in a position where the world around her demanded adherence to changing and conflicting gendered norms. There are many examples in her career where people paying tribute to her named her specifically as a woman. For example, Meir's famous 1948 talk in Chicago is often referred to as the speech that made possible a Jewish state.[27] But hear the gendered language of this tribute in a new way: David Ben-Gurion, Israel's first leader, commented that when the history of Israel is written, it will say, "There was a Jewish woman who got the money to make the state possible" (qtd. in Meir 1975, 214).[28] Similarly, she is also repeatedly castigated politically for being a woman, as when the religious bloc opposed her appointment as labor minister in 1949 specifically because of her gender. At other times, her comrades made interesting strategic use of her status as a woman in patriarchal settings. For example, Meir was sent to meet secretly with Jordan's King Abdullah. For the dangerous journey, strategists had her dress in the women's Arab dress considered traditional at the time, including a veil, so that she would not be recognized.[29] Meir's gender was utilized, praised, exploited, and critiqued in numerous ways, suggesting that even in the highly charged world of international politics, gender, as queer theorists today argue, is far more malleable than is usually presumed.

There is also no safe or simple space for her as a sexual being or in relation to domestic duties. She had a passionate love affair with and then marriage to Morris. She was hardly asexual, and she was reported to have had other love affairs later in life. But there are multiple contradictory standards for women; if they are to be sexually active, they must be married. If married, they must suppress themselves in service to their husbands. Men, of course, could be active in their careers and still have families. There are many men in apparently monogamous relationships who are reported to have affairs. Meir met no one's standards at the time. She never divorced Morris, and they maintained good relations with each other, as each did with the children when Meir took the kids and moved back to Tel Aviv without Morris. There was no social category for her relational life with Morris. The story as usually told omits that Meir sacrificed her ideals to leave Kibbutz Merhavia due, at least in part, to pressure from Morris. This is a different story from that told of the spoiled "American" woman, too feminized and soft to function on a kibbutz. Was she to stay with Morris forever and deny her aspirations? On the one hand, she was expected to be asexual, for sexual women are seen only as women, inherently in contradiction to politically successful persons. On the other hand, to have had affairs would also mean that, somehow, she was not working hard enough or was a stain on her family name. There was no way to step outside these discourses of gender with the scathing critiques Meir faced: to be seen as a sexual being would have feminized her and meant that she could not be taken seriously as a person; being perceived as asexual somehow still dehumanized her, because men are expected to be sexually active to demonstrate their prowess.

A woman, a man, a man in drag. Meir could not win under any set of gender expectations. Few of us can.

Similarly, being a "good mother" can be seen as categorically impossible because of the incongruous and unattainable expectations of motherhood. I cannot say whether Meir was a "good mother." Meir worried that critiques of her as a bad or neglectful mother might be true. She schlepped her children to political meetings in Tel Aviv, since she had no one to watch them.[30] Does that make her a bad mother? It can also be seen as affording her children an extraordinary education. I schlepped my kids to plenty of meetings; I generally considered it a good thing. In 1932, when Meir arranged to go to the US for Pioneer Women, she did so in large part to enable her daughter, Sarah, to get expert medical treatment for a life-threatening kidney disease. Meir then also had to work very hard while in the US. Bad mother or ingenious parenting?

Meir was often portrayed as frumpy and unable to meet feminine standards of beauty. Yet she was supposedly meticulous about ironing her clothing and always wore pressed clothes. This contrasting fact ironically contributed to people criticizing her for being a "privileged American," feminized, bourgeois, and therefore weak. Additionally, it is interesting that in the many young adult biographies of Meir, she is often portrayed as "pretty." Is this characterization there merely because someone presumed it was required so that girl readers would see her as a role model? She seems to me to have been quite "pretty." I wonder whether Natasha Lyonne cared about that? I don't know that it was part of the calculation of teachers introducing Meir in such a position of esteem to Jewish kids like me, born in the 1960s. Was it Platonic demands for the truth, editors, authors, or marketing departments that decided to put those descriptions into the books?

Ultimately, the questions are not whether Golda Meir was a good or bad mother, good or bad wife, fastidious in appearance or sloppy, pretty or "manly." We are all in drag, performing ourselves within various vectors of constraints and capacities (Sontag 2018; Butler 1990). Drag is a politics, an art form, and a creation, expression, or camouflage of identity. At times, Golda went in drag as a woman to do the men's work of international peacemaking. Some of us are more conscious of our drag performances. Many of us comport ourselves according to expectations within systems of power over which we have little control. Ultimately, instead of continuing to criticize Meir for versions of her strategies for coping with often-sexist demands or trying to find "the facts" about her, aren't we, feminists, better off honestly acknowledging the multiple sets of contradictory and impossible expectations that she faced and considering how we may be facing similar circumstances in our own era?

In what ways do we pressure ourselves and each other to manage these unmanageable demands? Can feminists wear stilettos? What about flannel shirts or double-breasted suits? What "feminine" touches need to be on a woman's work clothes for her to avoid heterosexist or transphobic gender speculation and critique? Women still have to be careful when being assertive; women will be policed for being "aggressive," while male colleagues win praise for being "strong." Tiresome to many of us, but still the case. How often does anti-Jewishness operate for many of us in gendered ways? For example, have you heard articulate, outspoken Jewish women identified as masculine or too pushy as Jews? Too feminine? Not feminine enough? For straight women, dykes, bisexuals, trans folk, and all sorts of queers from both and variously marginalized and dominant communities, these issues take on additional, explicitly queer meaning. Most of us end up queerly gendered, whether by choice or because of the unreachable and clashing requirements of our particular societal milieus . . . like Golda Meir, the only man in the Israeli cabinet.

Diaspora: The Russian Empire and the US

This section explores an example of how we might use queer, feminist, and de-colonial theories together in a Jewish context to complicate the notion of diaspora. Our work with Kincaid on the relations between colonialism and diaspora brings us, in part, to this section. Also required for our work here is further learning about and bringing queer critiques of binary thinking into our examination of Meir in new ways. To do more binary smashing, we will first take a new look at aspects of Meir's assignment as the first Israeli ambassador to Russia. Meir held this post at a crucial moment in the development of Cold War alliances. We can witness a historic shift in

Cold War alliances during Golda Meir's career. Thus, we will next assess the complexities of her ties to her second diasporic home, the United States, including to Jewish women's groups in the US. Looking through the frame of Meir's life and politics, we will note in many concrete as well as abstract ways how this diaspora became foundational to a nation's re-creation of a long-lost home.

On the first page of her autobiography, *My Life*, Meir (1975, 13) recalls "poverty, cold, hunger, and fear" as she remembers the dread and frustration of her early life in the Russian Empire; similar deprivation would recur many times in her life. She writes of "the consciousness of being different and the profound instinctive belief that if one wanted to survive, one had to take effective action about it personally." Living under an oppressive regime, facing additional hardships, particularly as a Jew, during her time in the Russian Empire, Meir recalls, "And I myself have never felt—not even for a minute any nostalgia for the past into which I was born" (19). These experiences followed her when she became a refugee to the US, where she lived among other Jewish immigrants. They seem to have contributed to her decision to maintain Sheyna's fervent socialist Zionism—and later return to it as a young woman setting out to rebuild a Jewish homeland. After an extremely difficult start in Palestine, where, like most of the Jewish community there at that time, she faced terrible poverty and other uncertainties, Meir found meaningful employment, began to make ends meet, and rose to the top circle of leaders who directed the course of the many thousands working to create modern Israel. This telling of Meir's diaspora and return story presents the Zionist dream realized. It even seems that she never looked back to the fleshpots of Egypt on her way to the promised land. But this is only one version of Golda Meir's diaspora/Zion story.

A number of contemporary Jewish political thinkers have endeavored to rework the home/away binary of particularly Jewish diaspora theory. Their work has much to offer, although Meir would have likely hated it. Golda Meir was an unapologetic Zionist. Zionism was her chosen Jewish path for being part of a worldwide revolutionary and de-colonial workers' and justice movement. Many of the Jewish diaspora thinkers whom I find interesting are also expressly pushing back against the dominance of Zionism for Jews of modernity and the supremacy of Zion in the age-old Zion/diaspora dichotomy that has existed for Jews since the fall of the ancient temples in Jerusalem. These thinkers challenge us to consider the binary in traditional understandings of diasporic conceptualizations in new ways. It is mainly the Jewish feminist Melanie Kaye/Kantrowitz who articulates a vision of diaspora with the complexity I seek in the critical retelling of Meir's story that I present here.

Kaye/Kantrowitz's work is the least academic of the cluster of these diaspora scholars, and this may be part of what helps her to articulate a feminist vision so useful for us today. Kaye/Kantrowitz's life's work was situated within multilayered, diverse coalitions of grassroots activists. Meir might not see herself in Kaye/Kantrowitz's work, and Kaye/Kantrowitz might have found it surprising that I place a Zionist prime minister in the context of her vision of radical diasporism. Nevertheless, I hope to demonstrate in the remainder of this chapter why I consider them a generative pairing both for new diaspora theorizing and for making sense of Meir's legacy in new ways.[31]

I have taken note of Jamaica Kincaid's multiple home/away locales as an avenue to exploring how she complicates a traditional diasporic binary. Still, that Meir's diaspora had two primary locations does not necessarily disturb the general binary model of most diaspora thinking. The Jews in diaspora wandered, so Meir's people wind up in the Russian Empire and then, in her lifetime, her family of birth migrates to the US. This is the story of millions of Jews of Meir's time. My grandmother's family did the same. Curiously, though, when my grandmother's family left the Russian Empire, they originally set off to make aliyah to Israel. Tragedy befell them; a notorious leader of the White Army murdered my great-grandfather. Without the man of the family, the women continued on their own but needed a change in destination because those bringing them to Israel did not want them without the man who was expected to be the family wage earner. After this change, it took them two years to make their way to a ship bound for the US, and that is how my family arrived on these shores. Despite Sheyna's active Zionism, the Mabovitch family likewise came to the US, and only later, as young adults, did the two sisters, Sheyna and Golda, undertake an independent decision to make aliyah.

Meir says that she never looked back or had any nostalgia for Russia. I wonder about such statements, as I was raised on a steady contradictory diet of stories of virulent antisemitism and oppression against my family and Jews generally in the Russian Empire of Meir's time interwoven with endless memories of luscious smells, tastes, songs, relations, and shtetl life. Once in the US, my family, like Meir's, mixed mostly with other Jews without formal schooling and who had fled pogroms in eastern Europe. I cannot say that nostalgia was not operative in these stories; otherwise, why would we have eaten so much kasha in New York City? Despite Meir's assertions, there are elements in her story that suggest that her heartstrings were not completely severed from her birthplace. Lessons from her seemingly emotional reminiscences can inform our politics and Jewish feminist political theorizing.

After noting that she had no nostalgia for the Russian Empire, Meir (1975) continues in her autobiography to note, "It [the Russian Empire] deeply colored and affected my life and my convictions, about the way in which all women, men and children, everywhere and whoever they are, are entitled to spend their lives—productively and free of humiliation—and, even more, about the way in which Jews, in particular, should live" (19). Noting parallels to lessons learned in our study of Kincaid on diaspora theorizing, we see here, yet again, that we learn not only from the home place but also from diaspora.

Meir had an unusual life trajectory that demonstrates some complications with the home/away diaspora binary. She served in the first Israeli government and was appointed Israel's first ambassador to the USSR from September 2, 1948, to March 1949. For this post, Meir was also issued the first Israeli passport. The story goes that when she received her new Israeli passport, Meir relinquished her US passport.[32] I am not certain whether this was a requirement within the new Israeli government, but it was a strong Zionist statement, one not many ordinary Zionists have made when given the choice. Comparatively, while the percentage of US Jews making aliyah to Israel is smaller than those from other countries, most who do so keep their US passports. A history of anti-Jewish oppression makes many mistrustful, and most feel the more passports, the better. We cannot know what might have been different for Hannah Arendt if she had had passports from countries other than Germany in her escape from Berlin and then again from a Nazi internment camp in France. But Meir chose to move forward into history with her new Israeli passport only.

Meir's post as the first Israeli ambassador to the Soviet Union gives us much to consider for new nonbinary diaspora theorizing. For example, Meir was concerned about what language she should speak with other Jews in Russia. She felt that she could not converse in Russian at a diplomatic level, and she was not sure whether she should try her Yiddish with other Jews or just speak in English. Her fluent English from her diaspora upbringing in Milwaukee assisted her tremendously on this official Israeli state business in Russia, and, here again, the binary line of away versus home turned out to be a tad more complex in reality.[33]

Being sent as the first Israeli ambassador to the USSR was no honorific, throwaway assignment. Stalin was a world leader, and Soviet support was essential to Israel's founding. From late 1944, banking on the projection that the new country would follow some version of socialism and speed the decline of British influence in the Middle East, Joseph Stalin had adopted a somewhat pro-Zionist foreign policy. The Soviet Union saw relations with the unusual kibbutz-based socialism in Israel as a potential means to further the Soviet position in the Middle East, an important arena in the burgeoning Cold War. (Remember: cold wars depend on hot wars occurring outside the primary metropoles with additional levels of imperialism and defense. Israel's case is exemplary here, striving for autonomy as also a tool in Cold War imperial politics, and Meir navigated much of this over decades.) In November 1947, the Soviet Union, together with the other Soviet bloc countries, voted in favor of the United Nations Partition Plan for Palestine, which paved the way for the creation of the State of Israel. On May 17, 1948, three days after Israel declared its independence, the Soviet Union was the first nation to officially grant de jure recognition to Israel and only the second country to recognize the Jewish state altogether.[34] In addition to Soviet diplomatic support, arms from Czechoslovakia, part of the same Soviet bloc, were key to Israel's strength in the ensuing 1948 Israeli war with regional powers (although it is customary in leftist circles to state that Western, as in primarily US, support gave Israel military supremacy at this time and during this way). Thus, in the growing Cold War (manifest in these multiple hot wars), the Soviet Union was a crucial ally of the nascent Jewish state, and Israel's ability to secure the weapons it needed was contingent on good relations with the communist superpower. A case study of Meir will also be an interesting option to challenge binaries of Cold War discourse. Despite the initial Soviet support of an independent country, anti-Jewish sentiment and policy was intense in the Soviet Union at this moment. Soviet ideology by then considered Zionism a "socially retrogressive," reactionary, "bourgeois nationalism," and the relations between the two states were extremely precarious. Meir had her work cut out for her as the first Israeli ambassador there.[35]

Was she cautious? How did she approach her mission? Meir was not at all an observant Jew. However, she arrived in Moscow in October of 1948, on the cusp of the Jewish High Holy Days. She decided to go to synagogue.[36] Meir was now the official representative of the new State of Israel. As a woman, however, she would be expected to sit upstairs in the women's gallery and not be seen or heard by the men in the service. Talk about an apparently impossible gender bind. On October 13, 1948, Golda Meir paid an unauthorized visit to the Moscow Choral Synagogue to attend

High Holy Day services. Word spread, and, at significant risk to their own and their families' lives, throngs of Russian Jews came into the streets of Moscow chanting for her and for Israel. This was a momentous time for Jews in the Soviet Union. It was a mere five months since the establishment of the State of Israel. World War II and formal genocidal anti-Jewish policies had ended only a few years prior. Disturbing antisemitic attitudes and policies continued.

In other years, approximately two thousand Jews might have attended High Holy Day services at the Moscow synagogue. But not in 1948. Meir (1975) recalled in her autobiography, "'The street in front of the synagogue had changed. Now it was filled with people, packed together like sardines, hundreds and hundreds of them, of all ages, including Red Army officers, soldiers, teenagers, and babies carried in their parents' arms" (183). She writes, "For a minute I couldn't grasp what had happened—or even who they were." Meir continued, "And then it dawned on me. They had come—those good, brave Jews—in order to be with us, to demonstrate their sense of kinship and to celebrate the establishment of the State of Israel. Within seconds they had surrounded me, almost lifting me bodily, almost crushing me, saying my name over and over again."

Approximately fifty thousand Jews converged on the synagogue; nothing like this had been seen in Moscow for more than twenty years. It was the city's largest public gathering since the 1920s and an almost unprecedented display of communal action by Russian Jews. Golda Meir, born of circumstances similar to these fifty thousand demonstrators, had returned as the head of a free and independent Jewish people's internationally recognized country. One can argue that swarms might have gathered for whoever was the first Israeli ambassador. Meir was careful always to tell the story as not so much about her personally as about Jewish solidarity. And still, it is uncanny that this small Russian-born Jewish woman was the focus of this outpouring of Jewish solidarity, even in a community under anti-Jewish duress. That she had begun her life's journey in the Russian Empire was important to the way she was adored by Moscow's Jews. Even if Meir reported no nostalgia for the Russian Empire, it was extremely meaningful for these Russian Jews that Golda was Russian.

The Moscow synagogue story is tremendously moving and also had tragic consequences. The assertion of Jewish identity enraged the Soviet government, whose authorities saw it as an outburst of particularist nationalism subverting Soviet authority. The joy of Meir's visit in 1948 was soon crushed by persecution and arrests in the following years, when Jews faced harsh repercussions during the bleak years at the end of Stalin's reign.[37] Meir kept her ambassador post for under a year. But she remained vigilant, watching the situation for Jews in the USSR for the rest of her life. Her historic ties to the Russian Empire made her active in the moves of Israel and worldwide Jewry to monitor the treatment of Jews there and to push for granting refuseniks permission to exit the Soviet Union. In her role as a tough negotiator and national leader, Meir maintained a lifelong soft spot for the fate of Soviet Jewry. She may never have wanted to return to Russia, but her diaspora ties remained significant for her and her policymaking.

And what of Meir's unusual relationship with the US, her second diaspora home? Israel's and Meir's roles are central to understanding strategic global shifts of power. The Cold War, and too many hot wars to follow, made a significant shift in direction at this historical moment. Not long after Meir's time as Israeli ambassador to the Soviet Union, Stalin shifted alliances, ended relations with Israel, and linked with the Arab bloc in international affairs. The United States, however, not as clearly pro-Israel as the USSR to start, now became Israel's principal ally among the major world powers.

US support for Israel was due directly to the US elite's imagined strategic interests in the oil industry and the Middle East in general during the Cold War. It was fueled by Christian millenarian ideology and the out-size role of Christian evangelicals in US politics. This Christian theological engine of US "pro-Israel" attitudes and policy is even more publicly evident today. In an unexpected way, Stalin's crackdown on Jews after Meir's visit to the Moscow synagogue was among the influences that set in motion the Soviet investment in Iran and numerous Arab countries in the Middle East, and thus also prompted the US to react by allying with Israel. This shift in US foreign policy further strengthened the power of the Christian evangelical Right over time. We are still living out the consequences of Meir's work and its role in this history of shifting geopolitical alignments.

It is common to debate the "power" of the "Jewish lobby" and to infuse such discussions with long-held anti-Jewish tropes of some invisible but cabal-like Jewish mastery over global politics. (In just about any day of news, one will find evidence of this coming from both the Right and the Left.) The so-called special relationship between the US and Israel that remained in place for decades was largely an outgrowth of Christian evangelical pressure in US politics. Many Christians believe that Jews must return to the ancient land of Israel to ignite Armageddon and usher in the new age of Jesus's return. However, Jews, those who do not accept Christ as their personal savior, and a variety of other no-goodniks will not gain access to the kingdom of heaven. They will be destroyed in the fires and catastrophes of Armageddon. Christians engaged in this sort of Armageddon initiative take a special interest in Israel and the doings of Jews. There was nothing natural or inevitable about the controversial US role in supporting Israel since the 1950s in some of the ways that it has. To demonstrate this point further, notably, when Israel has not complied with elite US interests or has presented interests of its own that might not meld with elite assessments of US preferences, the special relationship has not looked all that special.[38] More of us need to know about this. Christian evangelical "Zionism," the flood of Christian money into Israel and certain Jewish groups, lobby initiatives, and getting Jews back to Israel, is extremely well funded and well organized. I am astonished when leftists and politically astute comrades don't realize the role of these movements in the US, in Israel, and worldwide. Some activities occur in secretive modes, but plenty of it is quite accessible to the public. How has the public story of Israel's favored role in US foreign policy been cast?

Meir was at the center of these developments. The so-called unique relationship that developed between Israel and the US was also due, at least in part, to a relatively large concentration of Jews in the US (historical accident or predictable?). While a tiny minority of the US population, at that time, the largest portion of post-Holocaust world Jewry lived in the US. Meir played a key role in organizing relations among US Jewish communities and among ordinary Jews, not just with heavy-hitting US political power brokers.[39]

The relationships a young Meir had developed within a dense web of grassroots organizing in the US Jewish community was unparalleled among the Israeli political leaders of her day. She began building these relationships as a girl. Then, as a young woman, she moved into extensive political organizing for Poalei Zion, gave speeches, arranged meetings, and raised both awareness of the Zionist cause and the funds to support it. In her early, pre-state position touring the US for Pioneer Women, which she sought in part to enable her daughter, Sarah, to get the medical treatment that she needed, she continued her grassroots organizing and expanded her networks in the US Jewish world. Women's groups around the US jockeyed for her visits and clamored for information about her.

When Meir returned to the US in 1947 for her major fundraising tour, which surpassed any projections of success, she needed to interact with US Jews of a somewhat different sort than those with whom she had been accustomed to doing political work. This time, she needed donations that wealthy communal players could provide. That need meant engaging more with German-heritage and more-Americanized Jews than the eastern European immigrants whom Meir knew better. While all European Jews, these different Jewish ethnic groups were not automatically fast friends, as we will note more in the Arendt chapter. Meir was in a new arena. Imagine that still, in my day, I have had close Midwestern friends of German Jewish descent need to find a way to tell me, "No, our parents probably won't get together when they end up retiring at the same time in that town in Florida." Despite how close my friend and I are, she knows that her kin wouldn't give mine the time of day. Can you imagine what Meir had to do to successfully lobby these US Jewish political leaders in the 1940s?

We see here an important example of binary thinking just not holding up in actuality. Meir's situation in her first diaspora of Russia was complicated on many levels, as was her emerging role as an Israeli icon in the US. Meir was an active socialist who detested Stalin, the authoritarianism of Soviet rule, and the direction these took the potential of the Russian Revolution. In this, she was similar to Emma Goldman. Deported from the US for her anarchist influence, Goldman also returned to Russia for a time, where she hoped to learn the truth about the revolution and to help in its efforts. Both Meir and Goldman returned to Russia as politically accomplished adults with semi-independent statuses, although Russia was now firmly under the thumb of Soviet rule (Goldman was there when Lenin was in power). Devastated by the path of the revolution in Russia and by Soviet treatment of anarchists, Goldman finally escaped. While back there as adult political leaders, both Goldman and Meir met with many Jews (even though Goldman was not there in an official Jewish role). Both Goldman and Meir were publicly critical of the antisemitism they found in eastern Europe.[40] But when the adult Meir, a committed socialist, returned to the US midcareer to secure support and US Jewish funding for the Israeli War of Independence, she was required to act in a field of elite Jews and US capitalists. This experience was not completely foreign for Emma Goldman either. Goldman had long walked a fine line as a radical creating alliances with nonanarchist groups and wealthy progressives, often along the lines of support for free speech, for particular purposes. Meir, from 1947 onward, had to engage in diplomacy with top US political officials, as well as with wealthy, assimilated, "Americanized" Jews in a capitalist context with which she had no real prior experience.[41] Also, recall that most of the US Jewish establishment was not aligned with Zionism at this point in history and had long been explicitly hostile to Zionism.

Both Goldman and Meir were fed by their experiences speaking to large, adoring US audiences. Each gave these talks in both English and Yiddish. Goldman was able to speak to more audiences in English, widening her transnational base as her language skills improved, but she also continued to operate in Yiddish her entire life. As Meir's sphere of influence widened and the stakes of her rallying support for Israel intensified, her talks were also increasingly delivered in English. I have no information on whether the young Meir ever heard Goldman speak. Regardless, she was likely fired up by Goldman and the influence that Goldman's Midwest speaking tours held over her political comrades.[42] Meir returned to the US many times for speaking tours, in addition to the many formal speeches she delivered at the UN as Israel's foreign minister.[43]

Meir was considered a hero in the US Jewish community. Additionally, she never lost her ties with old friends from her early organizing days. Even as an Israeli statesperson, Meir spoke positively about what she learned in the US regarding the possibilities of democracy and freedom. Once an Israeli citizen and political leader, in addition to surrendering her US passport, Meir eventually caved to pressure from Ben-Gurion to adapt her married diaspora name Meyerson to the Hebrew Meir. Overall, however, as an international Zionist leader, Meir was never required to completely disconnect from her US diaspora experience. The US remained a type of home for her on multiple levels. It was a place where she could do her political work in English, easier for her than public work in Hebrew, and where she understood the political context. In those years, even among those who had previously lived in the US, few Israelis traveled from Israel to the US as frequently as Meir did. On a more internal level, then, the US remained a beloved place, full of dear friends and comrades from the movement, to which she had retained unusual access as an Israeli political leader often sent on diplomatic ventures.

Far from being only an either/or dynamic, we see that Meir's time in diaspora in both the Russian Empire and the US mattered to her life, politics, and experience of success. Meir's time in Moscow as Israel's first ambassador there fed her lifelong soft spot for Russian Jewry, beginning with her reception by throngs of Jews who risked much to come out to cheer her in public. Meir's relation to the USSR became more complicated over time as Israel's place as a pawn in the Cold War gained importance and as she became a state leader responsible for Israel's safety in the complex, developing set of satellite imperialist hot wars in the region. Additionally, formal USSR policy increasingly reviled this committed socialist for her Zionism.

Meir needed to learn new skills to undertake diplomacy and fundraising with wealthy US Jews who differed from her in both class and ethnicity. Meir also wanted her Zionist life path to serve as an example to excite other Jews in the US to make aliyah. Yet Israel came to depend on an active US Jewish diaspora in ways unimaginable in Meir's early days as a political organizer. Meir's capacity to leverage her diaspora ties and political prowess in the US foundationally enabled the building of the Jewish homeland in Israel. It simultaneously emboldened the public political activities of the US Jewish community, a tiny diasporic minority.

Conclusion

In terms of diaspora theory, Golda Meir may look like a classic example of the binary model of a diaspora of oppression contrasting with a home of triumphant return. With a slight shift in the kaleidoscope, and as a challenge to simplistic assumptions of some diaspora models, Meir got to have her proverbial cake and eat it too. She lived the Zionist dream of a return at a most intense level, often surviving on coffee and cigarettes as she worked eighteen-hour days for the Jewish homeland. At the same time, not only was she able to maintain her diaspora ties, but deep engagement with them fueled her in her personal and public work. As do most of us, Meir lived in a world in which binary thinking appears hegemonic. With the insights of feminist queer and de-colonial theory, however, we can see a far more dynamic, multilayered, and dialectical field of actualities reliant on and shifting co-created Jewed, gendered, classed, raced, and imperialist dynamics.

The realities of Meir's life, work, and passions provide us with a similar interruption in the repetition of a dominant version of binary gender thinking. A woman who rose to leadership in male spheres of power, Meir was often characterized as a man in a dress, a cross-dresser. These have not been favorable, pro-queer portrayals. In both patriarchal and feminist circles, people usually cannot get beyond the numerous incompatible and unattainable dichotomous expectations of Meir. Seeing her fail to live up to these irreconcilable expectations, they stereotype her as asexual, a bad wife and mother, a career woman who sacrificed her family and the concerns of women for personal success, a woman who rose to the top without doing anything for other women, or a woman needing to prove her testosterone levels by being more hawkish, more intransigent, and more stoic than most men. These portrayals judge but do not analyze or theorize Meir's circumstances.

Was Golda Meir a flawed woman, person, and politician? Of course. And yet Meir was also a woman, and a smart, talented, caring soul who fought for what she believed in for Jews both because Jews deserve to be treated humanely and as part of a transnational socialist and anticolonial movement. A multilayered theoretical analysis demonstrates that she was smashing binaries in many directions. I supposed that Meir lived her life as best as she could within significant constraints and committed herself to a Jewish version of an international social justice revolution.

Meir was a courageous woman. I do not have to like her, support her choices, or agree with her political vision to acknowledge that she was a unique historical figure who left us an important legacy as contemporary feminists. Legacies do not have to be simplistic and glossy. Her legacy is revolutionary, at least in the terms argued here. Meir defied one of the most basic oppressive power dynamics of modernity, binary thinking, in at least two significant arenas: diaspora theorizing and gender norms. That is quite a legacy.

Additional Resources on Golda Meir

Norman Provizer and Claire Wright, "Chronology of Golda Meir," Golda Meir Center for Political Leadership at Metropolitan State University of Denver, https://www.msudenver.edu/golda-meir-center/golda-meir/chronology/.

Archives with Material on Meir

1. University of Wisconsin—Milwaukee Libraries
2. The National Library of Israel
3. American Jewish Committee Archives
4. American Jewish Committee Oral History Collection
5. Schusterman Center for Israel Studies, Brandeis University
6. Archives of Kibbutz Merhavia
7. The Ben-Gurion Archive, Sde Boker (materials on Meir in the diaries)
8. Central Zionist Archives, Jerusalem
9. Histadrut Archives, Tel Aviv

Documentary Films on Meir

Golda, directed by Sagi Bornstein, Udi Nir, and Shani Rozanes (Israel / Germany: Gebrueder Beetz Filmproduktion / Go2Films / UdiVsagi Production, 2019).
Intimate Portrait: Golda Meir, directed by Kathleen Murtha (New York: Lifetime, 1999).
Line of Life with Golda Meir, directed by Herbert Krosney (Israel: NMC United Entertainment, 1977).
A Woman Called Golda, directed by Alan Gibson (United States: Paramount Domestic Television, 1982).

Articles on Additional Documentary Film Work

Nathan Burstein, "From Rhoda to Golda," *Jerusalem Post*, May 15, 2007.
Terri Ginsberg, "Film Review of *1948: Creation and Catastrophe*," *Arab Studies Quarterly* 40, no. 1 (Winter 2018): 73–79, https://doi.org/10.13169/arabstudquar.40.1.0073.
Shelley Glantz, "Golda Meir: A Profile," *School Library Journal* 44, no. 7 (1998): 53.
Ali Jaafar, "Smoke & Mirrors: 'Snakes' on a Middle East Blacklist?" *Variety* 402, no. 11 (2006): 6.

Plays

Golda: A Partial Portrait, written by William Gibson, directed by Arthur Penn, Theater Guild, New York, 1977.
Golda Meir: A Play, written by Darlene E. Resling (Baltimore: Learning Well, 1997).
Golda's Balcony, written by William Gibson, produced by David Fishelson, Manhattan Ensemble Theatre, New York, 2003. Revival, 2023–24.

Chapter 4

Hannah Arendt

Rahel Varnhagen and Diasporic De-colonial
Justice Theorizing: On Pariahs and Parvenu?e.s

In this chapter I explore Hannah Arendt's excavation of Rahel Varnhagen and analysis of the pariah and parvenu?e as foundational to her thinking about justice and political engagement. Arendt keenly articulates an existent human condition of alienation due in large part to dehumanization and a lack of meaningful freedom. Arendt offers a critical and coherent assessment, grounded in an analysis of the situation of Jews in the European diaspora, of what she argues is the *only* defensible role for those on the boundaries of their societies, given inequalities and social hierarchies. She makes a commitment to difference. I argue here that Arendt's work has implications beyond her stated subjects—Jews and other self-consciously marginalized political actors. Arendt's analysis of outsiders exposes flaws in the system for all inhabitants of Liberal democracies. This makes her arguments about the situation of outsiders directly relevant to everyone, regardless of their location on a map of power. Arendt's radical anti-assimilationism speaks clearly to our time, whether one considers oneself an activist, marginal, or not.

In activist circles where Arendt's ideas are constantly tested, it can still be trendy for progressives, and particularly progressive Jews, to use the language of pariah and parvenu?e. Cyclically, we find well intentioned and often smart folks within activist groups returning to Arendt's text and mining it for insights usable for their own historical moment. This work is often important, as it is inspiring for street activists and intellectuals alike.

Rarely is it ever discussed that Arendt's insights and analysis offered in her 1944 essay "The Jew as Pariah: A Hidden Tradition" were developed years prior in Arendt's work on the life and conundrums of another German Jewish woman who lived a century prior: Rahel Varnhagen. Arendt's efforts to think lived Jewish circumstance, enabling her work to make sense of the human condition, as she sought to do over time, were made possible by examination of the detailed particularities through which the historical figure Varnhagen succeeded and failed and did so again and again to live as fully as she could imagine as a woman, a Jew, a human.[1] Arendt's commitment to the full Jewish and universal personhood of Jewish women tends to get lost in these occasional blasts unearthing the essay with her articulation of pariahs and parvenu?e.s directly and what we together can rethink as her theorizing justice.

I have also heard colleagues say that people work on Arendt's Varnhagen text as an obvious choice for feminist inquiry. While Arendt's book on Varnhagen is on a particular Jewish women, I do not find it more or less feminist than many of her other works. I choose to prioritize this text for this book for a somewhat different reason. I focus on Hannah Arendt's work on Rahel Varnhagen because it is here that a young Arendt developed her theories on the pariah and parvenu?e that are central, for example, to justice work such as critical race theory today. Arendt's attempts to make sense of herself and her own prospects as a Jewish woman are found in her early study of Varnhagen. That is one of the most interesting aspects of the text. In it, however, as I will develop below, Arendt also makes significant contributions to a critique of Liberalism and to discussions of options for radical democratic change.

In this chapter thinking with Hannah Arendt, we move on from the work on Jamaica Kincaid in the first chapter, linking de-colonial work with diaspora studies, and on Golda Meir in the second chapter, rethinking binaries of gender and diaspora. Here, we are thus able to place the interpersonal thinking that Arendt did with Varnhagen as an aspect of Arendt's political thinking in the context of diaspora theorizing. It is also significant that Arendt, as an individual, somehow kept track of the unpublished manuscript in times of displacement amid a severe anti-Jewish genocidal settler colonialism. Arendt took time, decades, to let her early experiences thinking with Varnhagen percolate and mature.[2] She did not publish the work until 1958. The diasporic frame highlights the ways that discourses constituting the nation are both exclusive and assimilationist. This work is a signal contribution of Arendt's work addressing the pressure to assimilate in Liberal democratic theory's understanding of equality and freedom. The primary model of freedom and equality developed in Liberalism, which emerged at least in part out of the experiment of the 1791 Emancipation of the Jews of France (and later Germany and other parts of Europe), is rooted in a sameness paradigm.

In situating Arendt's work on this eighteenth- and nineteenth-century Jewish woman and European Jews more broadly in the context of diasporic theorizing, I ask, What opportunities of agency for diasporic communities exist in such circumstances? What does justice have to do with options for coping with the alienation often inherent in the diasporic? In exploring these questions, the chapter appreciates Arendt's move toward a broader theoretical frame for democratic social transformation. Arendt exposes the fallacy of Liberal egalitarian aspirations and selective success for individuals in marginal communities. She offers a vision of an actual democratic political role for pariahs and those who refuse to leave their abject communities behind. She carries her analysis of the pariah category further in "The Man of Goodwill," her assessment of Kafka's *The Castle*, which emerged from her semiautobiographical book on Rahel Varnhagen. It is in making clear the diasporic nature of Arendt's thinking that we can more fully appreciate her conclusion that the vision from Varnhagen and then Kafka can and must be extended from an individual framework to that of a community—even more, that communities must act in concert with other communities. As long as the systems of which we are a part operate hierarchically, there are no individual solutions, whether for parvenu?e.s or pariahs. Arendt demonstrates that assimilation, even as elites pursue this imperialist (and sometimes genocidal) model, is itself impossible. Given existing inequality, whether for individuals or communities, there is no actual option to live a "normal" and decent life, as there is no normal or decent existing life that we can strive to fashion our lives like.

The core problematic of Western Liberal concepts of equality is that they rely on a sameness, assimilationist model rooted in and mobilized with the Emancipation of the Jews of France in the early 1800s. It is important to note that women were not even conceptualized in this Liberal model. Those French Jews who were newly granted access to the rights and duties of citizens were certain Jewish male heads of households. Studying Varnhagen, a Jewish woman, pushes Arendt's analysis of the problems of the Liberal model. It helps her work beyond gender difference as configured in patriarchy, which does not even acknowledge women as part of the Jewish package. It enables her to see not only how a French (and later other) mention of

Jews erases Jewish women but that this historic mention of Jews erases all Jews, including Jewish men, by requiring Jewish assimilation for any Jew to be able to access citizenship. The Emancipation was based on a very partial experience, the prospects of "parvenu?e.s," who achieved individual success largely by ridding themselves of their Jewish markers. This is where contemporary critical race theory must look in order to dissect the problematic and reimagine options that have the potential to be more liberatory. Similarly, while much of critical race theory in the United States operates within a domestic paradigm, a focus on Arendt can enable scholars and activists to explore the relevance of the diasporic to such domestic theorizing. In the process, this Arendtian and Jewish grounding also performs the significant task of internationalizing US feminist critical race theory and bringing into clearer view the situations of immigrants, migrants, refugees, asylum seekers, and other outsiders within US borders still today.

Ultimately, stemming from Arendt's work on Varnhagen, we see the relationship between domestic and international inequalities in the context of the Emancipation's equality problematic. There is a long international history of critical race theory, including from US-based writers. Reinvigorating domestically focused critical race theory's more radical vision of equality requires an understanding of the justice issues inherent in the diasporic. Arendt helps us to identify that the "problem" of alienation for diasporic peoples is as much a problem of *injustice* inherent within host/dominant societies as it is so often a part of the diasporic condition. Based on Arendt's analysis of the particularities of a Jewish woman, I argue, thus, that "correcting" the problem of alienation at the core of much diaspora theorizing ought best be understood as part of a larger justice project.

To go about this, the chapter proceeds as follows: we first take a look at Arendt's basic biography. In this case, Arendt's life commitment to the German Jewish woman Rahel Varnhagen and the Varnhagen project become clear. After brief note on Arendt's major works, we take up our study of Varnhagen. Here, readers will also find a brief biographical sketch of Varnhagen and then explore some of Arendt's thinking with her. From there, we can move on to working out how Arendt rethought central categories of Western political thought. We will do so by accompanying Arendt on her considered tour through an option of a parvenu?e and various kinds of pariahs. We will clarify with Arendt key confusions regarding Liberalism through looking at the eighteenth-century Emancipation of the Jews of France. Arendt shows us that this movement, usually associated with equality and freedom, was made possible by one of the most significant acts of disassociation in the

West. The so-called freedom of the Jews in Western modernity is the creation of its own diaspora. The way out, or back in contact, is with a political formulation of contact itself through collective action.

Biographical Note: Arendt

Hannah Arendt is one of the major political thinkers of the twentieth century. She was born in 1906 in Hanover, Germany, as the only child into a middle-class, largely secular, Jewish family. Her father died when she was young. Biographers comment on the antisemitism Arendt experienced as a child and as a university student in Germany. Arendt pointed out that other Jewish children in her school were more directly targeted with antisemitism than she was—particularly those less assimilated, such as eastern European Jews more recently arrived in Germany than she was. She told interviewers that her mother taught her to have faith in and always stand up for herself. She took this attitude with her through her youth and into her university days, allying with other Jewish students and standing up to professors as the Nazi threat grew.

Arendt's identification with Germany and thus seeing eastern European Jews in a somewhat different category of person is not uncommon among Western Jews. (Readers may recall from the Meir chapter that awkward situation with my dear friend from the Midwest.) Such is a dynamic also often found in other communities around the world. Her own family hailed from Russia, despite her imagined distance from Ostjuden, Jews of the East. The very term *Ostjuden* was a twentieth-century concept created out of the experiences of a certain class of Jews in the lands of the German Empire, in what we now might call central Europe. We can find its larger historical development mobilized through and reflected in the particularities of the trajectories of families such as Arendt's. It was a conceptual framework devised by those assimilationist-trending Jews whose imagination of the east and of Jews went no further than the boundaries of the European continent. Its purpose was to create and sediment the then-imagined Western Jews' distinction from Jews of the Russian Empire. Despite her commitment to democracy and the eastern origins of many Jewish people in Germany in this period, we can find what is often thought of as Arendt's antipathy to the masses. We can include in the general bias, sometimes said of Arendt and of many German Jews still, a more specific distaste for the masses of Russian and eastern European Jews. Many of these Jews were seeking an escape from extreme antisemitism and flocked to Germany for better life chances as Jews. Soon thereafter, with the rise of Nazism, these Ostjuden kept their westward move, and, like Arendt, landed in France. There, however, even German Jews such as Arendt, rendered stateless by the Nazi Party, faced a mortal threat on par with these same Ostjuden.

In the Germany of the early 1900s, it was unusual for Jews of any class or ethnicity to attend university (though somewhat more common for an occasional member of the group of middle-class, assimilated Jews of Arendt's social milieu), and more so for Jewish women to do so. Arendt demonstrated her unusual intellectual capabilities from a young age and, in 1924, began her studies in philosophy at the University of Marburg. There, she met and studied existentialism with the world-class thinker Martin Heidegger.[3]

As is always mentioned at this point in her biography, the young Arendt had an affair with the married professor. Arendt ended the youthful affair when she went to study with Karl Jaspers in Heidelberg in 1926. After receiving her PhD in 1929, Arendt married a Jewish man named Günther Stern in Heidelberg. Heidegger became a controversial figure, as he joined the Nazi Party in 1933. While Arendt and Heidegger broke off ties for many years, many have criticized Arendt for not more publicly denouncing Heidegger for his relationship with the Nazis.

Until the early 1930s (when leftist politics, open intellectual exchange, and simply being Jewish in Germany were no longer possible), Arendt mixed in elite intellectual circles filled with thinkers and activists. She was also continuing to prove the expansive and incisive capacities of her distinguished mind. Her circles were mixed, comprising German and international figures, with Jews among them. In a way that was reflected later in her thinking and writing, she never disconnected from Jewish affairs and remained engaged with both the worst-off among Jews and the leading Jewish activists, thinkers, and issues of her day.

Arendt was among a too-small number of Jews who assessed the power, direction, and danger of increasing Nazi influence in Germany relatively early. In 1920, the Nazi Party in Germany gained prominence (with three thousand followers), and Hitler became the leader of the party. By 1930, the Nazi Party won roughly 20 percent of the parliamentary vote. Hitler came to power in Germany in 1933, first as chancellor, then as a dictator. By the early 1930s, Arendt pressed her colleagues and comrades to pay attention to the reality of the threat the Nazis posed. Most did not take Arendt's advice. As we know, so many suffered dearly for not being able to read antisemitism and the Nazi form of totalitarianism for what they were in Germany and beyond in the 1930s. During the rise of the Nazi Party in both formal politics and everyday life, Arendt acted with the German Zionist Organization; she was arrested and jailed in 1933 by the Gestapo for investigating antisemitic Nazi propaganda. She was released after one week.

Following that imprisonment, Arendt fled Germany. She spent brief periods in Czechoslovakia and Switzerland, eventually being able to settle for a time in France. In Paris from 1933 to 1940, she regrouped among local and expatriate intellectual circles and activists. While there, Arendt continued her research and writing and, importantly, stepped up her active engagement in political organizations. Given the dire circumstances for Jews in Europe at the time, it is important to note that Arendt was working with a number of Zionist and Jewish refugee organizations, including Youth Aliyah (an organization that helped thousands of Jewish children to escape Nazi-occupied Europe, mostly to Palestine).

While in France, Arendt met another German radical in flight from Nazi power, Heinrich Blücher. In 1936 Blücher became her primary partner, and he remained so for the rest of their lives. Blücher was a communist and was not Jewish. Due to their refugee situation, it took Arendt some time to formally divorce her husband, Stern; she and Blücher were legally married in 1940.

Meanwhile, upon the Nazi invasion of France, Blücher and Arendt were both arrested and placed in separate internment camps in the southern part of the country. We will address this situation more broadly when we look at both Kahlo and Stein. Arendt was sent to a camp in Gurs and escaped shortly thereafter.[4] Arendt then fled to New York in 1941. Both she and Blücher obtained emergency visas with help from Arendt's former husband, Günther Stern, who was already in the United States. These visas were made possible through the networks developed by the now-noted Varian Fry and comrades. In addition to ordinary people, these visas were meant particularly to assist numerous figures of Europe's intellectual elite in escaping Nazi reach. Once in New York, Arendt's mother assisted in Arendt's reunification with Blücher.

In the United States, Arendt held a number of positions both in academia and in activist Jewish communal institutions. It is amazing that this woman who is acknowledged as a world-class political philosopher was not just an ivory-tower thinker. In the US, Arendt held numerous prestigious academic positions: she was the first female professor at Princeton University (she hated to be noted as the first woman x or y) and went on to hold posts at other elite institutions such as the University of Chicago,

Wesleyan, and finally the New School for Social Research. Arendt was also directly engaged in political and social service work. From 1944 to 1946, for example, she worked as a research director at the Conference on Jewish Relations. From 1946 to 1948 she served as the chief editor at Schocken Books, and from 1949 to 1952 she was the executive director of Jewish Cultural Reconstruction. Arendt died on December 4, 1975, at her home in New York City.

Overview of Major Works

Arendt was a prolific writer, publishing regularly in a number of leading intellectual magazines and journals, including *Aufbau* (a German-language monthly journal for Jews around the world), the *Journal of Jewish Social Studies*, and *Jewish Frontier*. She was also author of numerous books. While her first book, published in German, was based on her PhD dissertation on the subject of love in the works of Saint Augustine (Arendt [1929] 1996), she is best known for later books such as *The Origins of Totalitarianism* (1951; see Arendt [1951] 1973), *The Human Condition* (1958), and *Between Past and Future* (1961). Arendt also became notorious for her journalistic and analytic accounting of the trial of Adolf Eichmann in *Eichmann in Jerusalem: A Report on the Banality of Evil* (Arendt 1965), originally published in 1963. During her lifetime after *Eichmann*, in addition to the many articles, Arendt wrote *On Revolution* (1963), *Men in Dark Times* (1968), and *Crises of the Republic* (1972).

There sometimes appears to be a split between those who know Arendt as a Jewish thinker and those who know her as a political thinker more generally. While the communities of intellectual Jewish thinkers and academic political theorists are not often in direct conversation, the split is not necessarily generated from Arendt's own work and commitments. The view emerges from marking this Jewish/non-Jewish split as corresponding to her earlier works, more focused on politics and political action, and her later works, often deemed more philosophical. Jewish scholars tend to disagree with the conceptualization of a split.[5] Most notably, Jennifer Ring (1997) articulates the multiple ways that Arendt's work is foundationally both gendered and Jewed.

As I have noted, this chapter focuses on a work of Arendt's that is less well known than the books named above, *Rahel Varnhagen: The Life of a Jewish Woman* (see Arendt [1974] 1997). The Varnhagen book is an odd and also truly fascinating work. It is the work that the young Arendt began after completing her PhD dissertation. It is also important for its position in Arendt's own life and intellectual development and how the concerns she explored there remained primary for her for the remainder of her life.[6]

Rahel Varnhagen: The Life of a Jewish Woman, or Two

Many leading thinkers and activists keep personal journals, some published during their lifetimes or posthumously. Others write memoirs for publication. Arendt did neither. What she did do is study the life of a Jewish woman, Rahel, who lived in Germany more than a century before her. The Varnhagen project is as close as Arendt got to a personal exposé or memoir of herself as a Jew, a woman, a lover, and a political thinker and actor. The Varnhagen text is important for its content and also in order to see more clearly how Arendt might want us to think about our own situation. I argue here that the book shows us the development of Arendt's belief that the only way to approach one's personal circumstances is to take responsibility in a political manner. What this means in this context for Arendt is that the way to deal with criticisms, dissatisfactions, alienation, myriad large or small indignities we might have in our lives is to take a stand for justice in the context of collective political action.

In *Feminist Thinkers and the Demands of Femininity: The Lives and Work of Intellectual Women*, Lori Marso (2006) insightfully examines the ways that we might look to the relation of the political and personal in the lives and thought of our feminist foremothers in order to open new ways of understanding these thinkers and their contributions for us today. Marso also does excellent readings of how women political thinkers and actors have utilized their relationships with other women—personally, politically, and intellectually—to explore, make sense of, and articulate their own concerns when speaking in their own voices might not have been possible. I understand Arendt's project on Varnhagen in a similar vein. Instead of writing her own autobiography, Arendt offered a study of Rahel, a middle-class German Jewish woman born in 1771.

Biographical Note: Varnhagen

Rahel Varnhagen was born Rahel Levin on June 19, 1771, in Berlin. Her father was already established in the community as an affluent jeweler. She was raised in a Jewish home with little religious practice. In 1795,

Levin became engaged to a Christian German aristocrat, Count Karl von Finckenstein. She broke off the engagement, however, after four years. In the years that followed, her home became a meeting place for intellectual and political thinkers of the day. In 1801, she became engaged to the secretary of the Spanish Legation, Don Raphael d'Urquijo. Soon, that engagement also ended (in 1804). After her father's death in 1789, Levin lived in Paris, Frankfurt am Main, Hamburg, Prague, and Dresden. In September 1814, she converted to Christianity, becoming a Protestant before her marriage to Karl August Varnhagen von Ense the same month.[7] Due to the demands of Varnhagen's diplomatic career, the couple moved to Vienna in 1815 and then to Karlsruhe in 1816 before settling back in Berlin in 1819.

We will explore more about Jewish women's traditions as *salonnières* in the coming chapter on Gertrude Stein. Of import for us in this chapter is that, throughout her time in Berlin and elsewhere in Europe, Rahel hosted salons and informal gatherings for political, social, and intellectual thinkers. Particularly for the first salon in her Berlin garret (1799 to 1806), Rahel took advantage of the social upheaval of the time to bring Jews and non-Jewish intellectuals and cultural figures together in ways that were impossible before and would be again for many years afterward.[8] Rahel passed away on March 7, 1833, in Berlin.

Arendt on Varnhagen

Arendt was first introduced to the writings of Rahel by a Jewish woman friend, Anne Mendelssohn.[9] When Arendt began to take up the biography project after her PhD dissertation (and what turned out to be toward the end of her time in Germany), Arendt called Rahel "my closest friend, though she has been dead for some one hundred years" ([1974] 1997, 56). While Arendt felt very "at home" in many ways in Germany as a successful member of the German Jewish middle class, she was in part attracted to Rahel for their similarity in being "homeless" (Young-Breuhl 1982, 57). Being a "homeless one" here is not meant to suggest they did not have a place to live.[10] Nor is it a direct geographical reference, such that Arendt would later know as a formally stateless person, but a statement of despair and alienation that Arendt first understood as the survivor of a failed romance.[11] Building on the understandings of diaspora in Kincaid and Meir, we can note that Arendt came to personally appreciate the political significance of this alienation later, with the Nazi project to annihilate the seemingly safe and well-positioned German Jewish community. Arendt herself became, effectively, a visitor in a host country, a diaspora subject within Germany, in a way she had not understood previously, and then in other countries as a refugee. This concept of being in diaspora while still in one of one's homes adds to our understanding of the diasporic developed in the first two chapters.

There are some important differences between the two women's situations, though Arendt generally reduced these to instances of historical timing. Rahel's situation was precarious as a Jewish woman without independent means. Like Arendt, Rahel was young when her father died. Rahel had to rely on her brothers to support her and, later, on the search for a husband who would grant her the financial and social status she desired and felt entitled to (and that became increasingly closed to her as a Jewish woman).

As unusual as it was, Arendt was able to attend university and provide for herself. She did not have to rely on any one man or romantic partner for her income. Of course, Arendt regularly relied on intimates and strangers, particularly to secure her safety during the Nazi Holocaust. However, it is important to note that Arendt did not have to rely on a male romantic partner in order to be a part of history in the ways that she was—to be a full member of the most elite and active intellectual and political circles of her time. Rahel had neither such access nor such opportunity. When the historical moment allowed, she hosted her first salon.[12] But as times and the political situation of Jews and women changed, Rahel needed her Christian husband in order to be able to form and host her second salon.[13]

Arendt began the Varnhagen book when she was still quite young and living in Germany. Interestingly, she did not publish it then. Even though she wrote most of it (supposedly all but the last two chapters) at that time, she could not bring it to a close. She schlepped it (imagine schlepping manuscripts and notes before computers and photocopy machines), held onto it, worked at it for decades. It cannot be overstated that these decades included her flight from Germany after Nazis imprisoned her to destinations around Europe. She made her way to Paris, where she worked on the project again. Arendt further experienced the forced dislocation of her time in and escape from the Gurs internment camp as well as her harrowing journey to relative safety in the US. With this unique history, Arendt returned to the project later in life while living in New York. After so long with this project, working it out over time, Arendt finally published the work as a book in English in 1958.

The story of the book itself reveals interesting and important insights into the meaning of the work for Arendt. What more did she need from the project that she didn't bring it to a close in Germany? or publish it while in exile in Paris, where she is said to have completed it, or a version of it, at one point? Why did she hold onto the manuscript, through so much turmoil, and finish it only more than two decades later when, in that time, she had published widely and worked on numerous other projects? It seems that she needed to come more fully to terms with the basic thesis of that work: that being a Jewish woman was central to her life. She needed other Jews, and a Jewish perspective in the context of a diasporic striving to live among non-Jews as an equal, in order to be able to live a meaningful personal, intellectual, and political life. Arendt wrote in the preface (dated 1974, written in 1956), "The German-speaking Jews and their history are an altogether unique phenomenon; nothing comparable to it is to be found even in the other areas of Jewish assimilation. To investigate this phenomenon, which among other things found expression in a literally astonishing wealth of talent and of scientific and intellectual productivity, constitutes a historical task of the first rank" ([1974] 1997, xvii). Arendt notes that her Rahel investigation "can be attacked only now, after the history of the German Jews has come to an end." She clarifies, "The present biography was written with an awareness of the doom of German Judaism (although, naturally, without any premonition of how far the physical annihilation of the Jewish people in Europe would be carried)." On the perspective afforded by the delay of finishing the manuscript, Arendt writes, "At that time, shortly before Hitler's coming to power, I did not have the perspective from which to view the phenomenon as a whole." The intervening years walking a path set out in the privacy of her mind and heart alongside another Jewish woman struggling for dignity, love, and affirmation afforded Arendt the opportunity to develop this more comprehensive view, which could more centrally pair the Jewish struggle for recognition of personhood with the false promise of the Emancipation.

In drafting those last chapters in Paris and returning to the project decades later in the US, it appears that Arendt had finally begun to figure out what was most important to her about Rahel. In the way that the book is a kind of memoir by proxy, in the intervening decades, Arendt made sense of what was at stake to her and clarified the most challenging tensions in her own life: how to be a Jewish woman and a human. It may thus not be surprising that, in order to do this, she needed to be older than the young woman she was in the 1930s when she began the study. She needed time and experience to work out how she might take her rightful place in the world. With the perspective of those years, Arendt was more able to imagine how she could "weave [her] strands of . . . Jewish genius into the general texture of European life" without writing in an explicitly Jewish language such as Yiddish or Hebrew and without suffering the fate of others like her who she claimed "have been given short shrift and perfunctory recognition" due to their status as Jews (Arendt 1944, 99).

We can see that Arendt, most crucially, is exploring what options there are for Jews to engage in the world and what roles Jews and all humans must embrace for themselves. Yet while Arendt is talking about Jews and is specifically concerned with Jews, her work is relevant to all those at the margins and ultimately to anyone living in a Liberal democracy (or those aspiring to do so). In the process, while still a product of numerous biases of her class and time, Arendt offers an incisive critique of power relations and injustice. She ends with her most valued insight about the fundamental responsibility of humans to engage in the activity of thinking—but not as an end in itself. She was no ivory-tower philosopher or armchair Liberal. For Arendt, thinking is a path to collective political action in an unjust world.

Arendt took the insights she came to by the end of the work on Rahel and wrote up this theory more directly in articles. We can also find it reflected in other aspects of her life's work along the way and after that point. I will now focus on one main work to demonstrate how her insights gleaned over time through her engagement with Varnhagen can be found in subsequent, more accessible works. Given the centrality of how we may think differently about Arendt's exploration of justice by centering her work on this courageous and of course constrained Jewish woman, Rahel Vanhagen, I now examine Arendt's views on the problem of Liberal equality and assimilationism via an article she wrote for the journal *Jewish Social Studies* in 1944 and which has become intermittently popular within the Jewish Left, "The Jew as Pariah: A Hidden Tradition."

Diaspora, the Emancipation of the Jews, and Liberal Equality

Jews functioned as a quintessential "other" in Christian Europe for centuries. Understood as foreigners, a people in exile from their own homeland, Jews were at best barely tolerated in various European host countries, hated, exiled often, and generally persecuted. This relationship of Europe to Jews in diaspora survived the transition from the Middle Ages through to modernity, when the basis of anti-Jewish views was largely transformed from a religious one to a national and racial one. This is the world into which Rahel was born in the eighteenth century. During the rise of Liberalism and nationalism, Jews were considered outside the nations that were being reimagined in the creation of modern Europe's nation-states. A rights paradigm entered this stage of history along with the Liberal revolutions of modernity, one in which people are no longer to be understood as inseparable parts of their social caste or community (peasant, noble, etc.) but given rights as individuals.

The wretched situation of nearly all of the Jews in Europe had long been referred to as "the Jewish question" or "the Jewish problem." It is often said that we must correctly understand this as Europe's problem with Jews. Arendt clarifies that, actually, the Jewish question is the problem of the wealthy Jews. The problem is their Jewishness, their association with Jews in general, the destitute masses of despised Jews.

Below I will discuss the parvenu?e, an option select Jews were able to access to better their individual status.[14] For Jews, an answer to the Jewish question seemed to come with Napoleon's set of codes, begun in 1806, resulting in a bumpy process often referred to as the Emancipation of the Jews in France. Like other ideas of the 1789 French Revolution, the tenets of Jewish Emancipation spread unevenly through western European countries over time. As many have noted, basic rights were extended to certain Jews in a framework understood as being "a Jew at home and a man in the street." While not all those who have discussed this paradigm have taken the gendered phrasing seriously, it is appropriate, as the promise of Emancipation was extended only to male heads of households (see Levitt 1997). Rahel Varnhagen lived in a turbulent time when such Liberal ideas made their way to Germany and were rolled back and reinstated, impacting her life and prospects directly.

Between Arendt and Varnhagen, we can see workings of the diasporic on a number of planes in a European context. One level reflects a traditional understanding of the Jewish diaspora generally: exile with the Babylonian and later Roman conquests of Jerusalem. Chronologically, a second can be said to be a result of the Emancipation of the Jews of western Europe (while not uniform in method, timing, duration, or consequence). For Arendt, a third level is the destruction of German civilization as she knew it, through the rise of Nazism and her exile from Germany. While the first and third instances are somewhat well known, I will clarify the signal matter of the second: the Emancipation as a diaspora.

What was it that the "emancipated" Jews of Europe would be liberated from, specifically? The Jewish case turns a number of European Liberal presumptions on their heads. The extension of Liberalism is often discussed as a "spread" of principles universally sought such as freedom and equality. This is so, as if the principles are actually universal and many cultures over time and place might not have had their own particular understandings of freedom and equality. Additionally, Liberalism tends to presume that all peoples aspire to its version of freedom and equality.[15]

As Arendt came to note in her study of this Jewish woman, however, the paradigm of Liberal equality relies on a concept of sameness, so that those who are different from the ruling elite must remain "less than" as long as they continue to be associated with their difference. Emancipation is usually understood with the dominant group in the subject position and abject groups seeking to end whatever obstacles are barring them from participation in the dominant modes. There is also a view of "the Emancipation" that it offered select "liberation" from the narrowness of requiring Jewish compliance to Jewish communal rules, regulations, and dynamics. The promise of equality (to those in the dominant group; this is not necessarily a concern for life within the abject group) could be accessed, given various levels of actual and ideological antisemitism, if (mostly male, wealthy) Jews fled their ghettoes and communal institutions. Thus, ideologically, Emancipation functioned like other imperial takeovers (even while "domestic"), "allowing" the dominant culture to enter into the ghetto and the inner life of Jews in new ways, with norms of the dominant culture valenced positively and those of the ghetto still despised. As in other settler-colonial paradigms, the goal of this takeover was to rid the land of the history of the conquered population. In cultural context, this means that the goal of this conquest, often referred to as freedom in the West, is to rid the place of Jewish history.

The Emancipation's requirements for Jews to "enjoy" the rights of citizens to freedom and equality are an ideological form of settler colonialism within a given territory. It is, ultimately, genocidal.

Elite members among the marginalized were invited to enter the dominant culture, but only on the latter's terms. As practiced in Arendt's time in Nazi form, Arendt ([1974] 1997, 250) notes of Varnhagen, "The central desire of her life had been escape from Jewishness, and this desire proved unfulfillable because of the anti-Semitism of her milieu, because of the ban, imposed from the outside, against a Jew's becoming a normal human being."

Freedom of choice in this case becomes the creation of a new diaspora. If any individual Jews had a "choice"—meaning, had the means and aspiration to move from the ghetto, family, home, and communal support networks like any good capitalist entrepreneurs—they were those who were already self-selected from among those sufficiently similar in ideological individualism and entrepreneurial spirit to elites in the host culture.[16] In her examination of Rahel, Arendt notes that the Emancipation, in actuality, created another layer of diaspora—elite Jews in flight from Jewish association and community. Through her study of the life of Rahel, Arendt learned about the failure of this assimilationist paradigm, required with the fanfare of the great promises of freedom and equality of Liberalism. Arendt came to realize that not only was this "universal promise" not very universal, it also came at an enormous cost. To the degree that the Emancipation succeeded, it meant the disappearance of the Jewish people as a *people*.

Further, there was a more universal question Arendt articulated from her work on Rahel: assimilation into what in an altogether unjust social order?

Many Jewish thinkers have celebrated the Emancipation as an opportunity for Jews to be treated as and have the opportunities of "humans." As equals of all "mankind," Jews would now be able to participate in the creation of history. Jerome Kohn (2007) writes, however, that "it is clear to Arendt that the Emancipation Edict of 1812 did not, and was never intended to, preserve the Jewish identity of the Jews as a people" (xv).[17] For Arendt, the central question regarding this vision was, How would Jews participate in this creation and with what goals? The premise of that question exposes a gap in the vision of Liberalism itself: Liberalism's foundations have never been too troubled by the existence of social inequalities. Would emancipated Jews expect to participate as equals with those on the upper end of social hierarchies, as citizens but among those without concern for decency and democracy?

Arendt relies on Rahel's predicament as a proxy for her own, as she ends up living through more than a cultural aspect of genocide against Jews. Arendt survives through the Nazis' and their affiliates' total genocidal, settler-colonial war against Jews and too many others. I was taught that Marx saw two trajectories for Liberalism: democracy (as most of us in the West are taught is Liberalism's future) and totalitarianism (with civil society eventually crushed under the awesome sovereign of Hobbes's imagination). Together, we can see that Arendt's analysis brought her to the critical awareness that the paradigm of the Emancipation of the Jews was nothing more than Liberalism's somewhat more corporate extension of the Jewish individualist option of a parvenüe. Let us explore what exactly the parvenüe option is and what options are left if one rejects (or could never properly access) the false promise of Emancipation.

The Jew as Pariah, the Allure of the Parvenüe

In her 1944 essay, "The Jew as Pariah: A Hidden Tradition," Arendt takes the insights she developed through her long examination of the life—loves and intellectual activity—of Rahel Varnhagen and focuses them politically. Here, Arendt discussed the limited options available to Jews as political actors, given their circumstance as diasporic subjects. Emerging directly from her engagement with Rahel's life story, Arendt notes that we can see two major trajectories in the European case, and possibly beyond: parvenüe.s and pariahs. It is in this dual trajectory that we understand the parvenüe option as an instance of what becomes the false promise of the Emancipation and of Liberal equality more broadly. Arendt's challenge is then to come to terms with the harsh realities of the limited alternatives if one refuses to participate in cultural genocide masked as freedom in Liberalism and also if one cares about social justice.

The Parvenüe

Parvenüe.s are those who utilize their individual wits and capacities to become what are sometimes called "court Jews." These Jews (who can be read in the US context as those from marginalized communities) act individually, ingratiating themselves in personal ways to particular nobles or elites. They are ready to shed any signs of their marginal communal origins, willing to assimilate as much as is allowed in order to be given provisional access to dominant modes. This setup serves elites when it is determined that the marginalized also have something much needed by the nobles: connections, money, information, and so on. Elites often also figure out that they can position parvenüe.s in between themselves and the masses to deflect accountability, making the "middlemen" what Arendt calls their lackeys and henchmen (1944, 109). Parvenüe.s are usually isolated, individual Jews in arenas of mainly non-Jewish power.[18] They tend to connect back to their communities only to the extent that such connections afford them the resources that will hold and advance their individual places among the elite.

While many in the parvenu?e circumstance might use their individual money, power, or influence to help Jews or Jewish communities (for example, through internal philanthropy), they are often also complicit in systemic antisemitism. Their individual situation, their place at the table, so to speak, is based on the whims of the host. Given the precariousness of their circumstance, they fear rocking the boat or trying to use their position for systemic change. As individual actors, proud to have risen above their communities of origin, they are invested in their own advancement. They do not want to risk whatever provisional status they have succeeded in attaining by bringing up their communities as well.[19] One can certainly argue that, in real life, we have seen variations of the parvenu?e, or scales of acquiescence to systemic demands. For Arendt, parvenu?e.s participate in the extinction of their culture by opting out of it individually and assisting the dominant culture to hobble along with the status quo, continuing to oppress the marginalized.

Pariahs

Pariahs, on the other hand, are just that—outcasts, marginal. Like Jews as a people often, historically, pariahs are abject persons and/or communities. Arendt finds in the Jewish example of esteemed pariahs a more universally human example. But there are different kinds of pariahs or ways to mobilize potential power within a pariah position. Arendt explores four kinds of pariahs as outsider options for political agency. In this essay, Arendt names each category, attaches it to a historical figure, and tells us about that figure and their historical moment. She then also tells us the potential and limitations of each option.

Despite the origins of her thinking on the matter in her study of Varnhagen, in this oft-quoted 1944 essay, Arendt discusses only men. In her study, Arendt looks to Heinrich Heine, Bernard Lazare, Charlie Chaplin, and Franz Kafka's protagonist, K., from *The Castle*. Each figure lived in a different historical, political, and cultural milieu. While each was a pariah, they had different life circumstances and made different political and artistic choices. Common to all pariahs is their affiliation with the common people. Thus, Arendt's theory of the variations of the pariah can tell us not only about Jews as abject people but also about abject people(s) more generally, those she calls "oppressed and despised" (1944, 104). While she has compassion for all the pariahs she explores, she clearly builds a valuation of them into her analysis.

Heinrich Heine—The Schlemihl

Arendt first discusses Heinrich Heine (1797 to 1856). A journalist, essayist, and literary critic, Heine was one of Germany's most famous poets and became known as the people's poet. Heine was born Jewish. His radical politics brought him notoriety, and many of his works were banned. Like Arendt and Varnhagen, Heine spent time as a radical German expatriate in Paris (he lived in Paris as an expat for his last twenty-five years).

Arendt (1944, 101) calls Heine's sort of pariah the "schlemihl" and "lord of dreams" (*Traumweltherrscher*). *Schlemihl* is a Yiddish word meaning an awkward person, one who trips over "him"self. The schlemihl is not to be confused with a schlimazel, who is also awkward but also just has really bad luck. In a classic Jewish vaudeville skit, it is a schlemihl who spills his soup into a schlimazel's lap. Arendt does not use the word as a slight. She uses the term to convey social ostracism and a political manner of innocence.

Throughout her examination of pariahs, Arendt is also examining the role of art and beauty. In this section on the schlemihl, she notes a natural equality among us but argues that such is also the weakness of the schlemihl. He is a lord of dreams; the beauty and equality of nature he loves do not translate into the world of human society and politics. Here, one has one's head in the clouds, in a way ultimately dangerous for one's people. The problem of attending only to the beauty of art and nature is that one is too easily indifferent to political structures and to seizing the mechanisms of power. Even though Arendt says of Heine individually that he "takes his place today among the shrewdest political observers of his time" (1944, 107),[20] the schlemihl pariah is "always remote . . . stand[ing] outside the real world and attack[ing] it from without" (105).

Bernard Lazare—The Conscious Pariah

The second type of pariah is exemplified by Bernard Lazare (1865 to 1903), a French Jewish literary critic, journalist, and an anarchist in his politics. Lazare moved to Paris to pursue his interest in literature in 1886, the year that Édouard Drumont published his notorious antisemitic pamphlet *Jewish France* (*La France Juive*). By the early 1890s, Lazare had connected with Ahad Ha'am (born Asher Zvi Hirsch Ginsberg), the writer and political activist who was among the founders of the early Zionist Hovevei Tsiyon (Lovers of Zion) movement.

Due to Lazare's reputation as an outspoken activist and his work on Jewish affairs, when Captain Alfred Dreyfus, a Jewish officer in the French army, was accused of treason, which most Jews and the French Left saw it as an antisemitic move, Dreyfus's brother asked Lazare to defend Dreyfus. He ended one of his important attacks on the prosecution with the phrase "J'accuse," which was later made famous in a letter on the incident by Émile Zola in 1898 (see Zola 1992). Lazare was a radical and over time became more involved in Zionist and Jewish affairs generally. He was eventually ousted from the Dreyfusards for his radicalism. This fact becomes important to Arendt's analysis.

In her study of Lazare, Arendt calls this category the "conscious pariah" (1944, 101). Arendt frames a new subcategory because her example of this type of pariah lets go of the innocence of the schlemihl and comes to understand themselves as a political actor, denouncing oppression and the pariah's abject position. Like Lazare, conscious pariahs must not accept the debased position of their people in part because in doing so they become partially responsible for it. Instead, the oppressed must become conscious of their opposition and force themselves into the political arena. Arendt writes that "Lazare's idea was, therefore, that the Jew should come out openly as the representative of the pariah, 'since it is the duty of every human being to resist oppression'" (109).

While she clearly had a lot of admiration for Lazare, still, Arendt noted the limitation of a "pariah who [simply] refused to be a rebel" (110). Ultimately, Lazare was not able to bring the Jewish masses along with him on his radical path. He lost the following of his own people. Thus, crucial to her critique of the conscious pariah is that Lazare preferred to "play the revolutionary in the society of others, but not in his own." He was not able to mobilize his own community to act in concert with him.

Charlie Chaplin—The Suspect

Next, Arendt presents an analysis of Charlie Chaplin. This is an especially interesting study in part because Chaplin was not Jewish. Nevertheless, there had been much speculation that he was Jewish, and, during his life, Chaplin was called Jewish—as a slur—by others due to the radical content of his work. Arendt holds him up as a quintessential example of a Jewish mode of being political, mainly due to what she analyzes in his work and impact but also in part because he was often taken to be a Jew.[21]

In the figure of Chaplin, Arendt identifies a kind of pariah who is the perpetual "suspect" (1944, 110). She explains the suspect pariah with the insight that "the law is his perennial enemy and society treats him with mistrust." She notes the particularly grotesque portrayal of his suspect character, as is common in antisemitic imaginings. In Chaplin's case, she says, "Often he is punished for crimes he does not commit, yet he is also ingenious enough to get away with many crimes that he is responsible for."

We might see in this study of Chaplin that the suspect pariah is a more modern schlemihl, though not in the visionary, transcendental sense Arendt portrays with Heine. Perhaps in focusing on Chaplin, a more urban persona, Arendt sees that he is consistently confronted by the real world and can find no retreat in nature. With Chaplin, we see a sometimes hapless creature—likened to the dreamer—but it is clear that *his* oppression is political. She notes, "Chaplin's heroes are not paragons of virtue, but little men with a thousand and one little failings, forever clashing with the law" (1944, 112). Pure love of beauty, art, nature, and lofty ideals are not sufficient to get him through the trials of politics and injustice.

For Arendt, the primary limitation of the suspect pariah is that they do not yet have a *systematic* analysis of power, or more importantly do not convey a *systematic* strategy for the masses to overturn oppressive power relations. They use their wits and acquaintances to survive the oppressive power of the state and class inequality. But, unlike the parvenu?e, it is clear that they do not translate this into thinking they are therefore individually worthy. The luck involved in his near escapes remains haphazard and individualized; it does not allow him—or us—to view his as an earned success or his little gains a systemic option for liberation. Again, unlike the parvenu?e, Chaplain is working to mobilize political insight on a broader scale than that of one person. But therein lies the limitation of the suspect pariah.

Arendt writes of Chaplin's career trajectory, "But then came unemployment, and the thing was not funny anymore. He knew he had been caught by a fate which no amount of cunning and smartness could evade. Then came the change. Chaplin's popularity began rapidly to wane, not because of any mounting antisemitism against him, but because his underlying humanity had lost its meaning. Men had stopped seeking release in laughter; the little man had decided to be a big one" (1944, 113).

K. in Kafka's "The Castle"—The Man of Goodwill

As the fourth model and the one most elaborated upon, Arendt takes up Kafka's character K. Kafka (1883 to 1924) was born to a middle-class Jewish family in Prague. He attended a gymnasium and university in which the language of instruction was German. While he trained as a lawyer and worked for an insurance company, he considered his fiction writing his real work. Most of his stories and books were published posthumously by his longtime Jewish friend Max Brod (even though Kafka had made Brod promise to destroy his manuscripts). Kafka was one of six children; the other three still living at the time of World War II were probably killed in the Holocaust. As a young man, Kafka identified with anarchists and antimilitarists, and later as a socialist and atheist. He studied Hebrew in anticipation of his Zionist move to Palestine (which did not come to pass given his early death from tuberculosis). His surreal portrayals of alienation, the dehumanizing realities of bureaucracy, and the irrational operations of power have created the term from his name, Kafkaesque.

Arendt's section on Kafka is the most complex, with numerous twists and turns. This is the case in part because Arendt is most drawn to this pariah option and thus it appears to her most perplexing. In particular, she looks at primary characters in two of Kafka's works, K. in "Description of a Struggle" and K. in *The Castle* (Kafka 1958, 1992), focusing mainly on the difficulties of making political sense of K.'s journey in *The Castle*.

In *The Castle*, the protagonist is a village resident and attempts a parvenu?e solution to his alienation in reaching for entry to and acceptance by those in the nearby castle. Ultimately, he abandons this strategy and resolves to define himself and achieve some sort of affirmation of his human dignity through his own efforts in the village. Eventually, because society has no place for such a man of goodwill, he becomes exhausted and dies. But it seems that the death of this character is not the main tragic note Arendt hopes to convey. We can see this from her interest in K.'s efforts to expose the flaws that had previously seemed simply natural to others and to prompt the villagers to develop a political consciousness. Moreover, in her analysis, Arendt is telling us that the pariah (and, indeed, all of us) must "confront the real world through thinking"—not an idealized one[22]—through, as Arendt later frames it, thinking what we are doing. This is no mere sloganeering. [23]

We have seen the societal pressures of an assimilationist model in the case of the parvenu?e. For the parvenu?e, the only escape from discrimination is to stop being different, to deny one's community and connections (as pariahs are discriminated against for their difference). The parvenu?e takes on the ~~herculean~~ (Pat Moynagh corrects me: Sisyphean. That is different. Pat is correct.) Sisyphean task of attempting to shed difference, to abandon any markers of Jewishness or other pariah status, and to join the ruling elite by becoming like them. But this leaves parvenu?e.s in a perpetual state of anxiety and likely to be forced to act as stooges of the ruling class in oppressing their own people, or pariahs in general.

In Arendt's analysis of *The Castle*, we see how the assimilationist option plays out for ordinary people, or those who reject the parvenu?e option. To attempt to assimilate without trying to be in the ruling class (trying just to "be human" and afforded human dignity by living a simple life and fitting in among the masses) is to confront the central problem of politics. There is no option to merely meld into the masses, shedding one's markers of difference in order to live well. This is so because "the masses" do not get to live with basic human dignity either. Rejecting the elitist version of assimilation of the parvenu?e leaves no viable option of assimilation for those who don't want to oppress others, those who just want to live their lives.[24] There is much propagandistic hoopla in US mythology regarding the so-called common man, the upright middle class of every politician's speech. However, because the systems of which we are a part operate hierarchically, there is no option for a pariah individual or community to live a "normal" and decent life as there is no normal or decent life one can strive to fashion one's life after.

Arendt's vision arising from Kafka's protagonist must be extended from an individual framework to that of a community. It is not merely in K.'s individual situation that Arendt finds this point but in its implications for all the people of the village. Her conclusion moves further to note that communities must act in concert with other communities. Jews and other abject groups will not be able to mobilize the more radical potential of the conscious pariah acting alone. Arendt's argument does not remain parochial even when shifted from an individual to a communal context. She does not stop with an answer to ending Jewish oppression, for example, with an argument for ending oppression of Jews only. This is not even possible. In fact, this formed the basis for the kind of Zionist thinker she became. Arendt was clear that to whatever degree it would be possible for Zionists (historically, pariah Jews) to achieve collective self-determination (considering this a primary goal of Jewish Emancipation, to become "simply" like the other nations of the world) would merely make a pariah Jewish people into a pariah Jewish country.[25] In a version of what we might now consider an example of Eve Kosofsky Sedgwick's 1990 majoritizing view in her *Epistemology of the Closet*, Arendt's Zionist theory was in line with those that sought a Jewish homeland along the way of a more widespread global movement for justice.

Conclusion

Arendt spends much of the project on Rahel focused on despair and alienation on a personal level.[26] By the end of the work, made possible in the harrowing intervening years and by Arendt's growth during that time, Arendt recasts the personal problem of estrangement as a political problem for Jews as a whole. But the Jewish problem is not only a problem for Jews, it is one that exposes flaws for everyone in Liberal democracy and in other systems. The "problem" of alienation for the diasporic, for other abject peoples, and for any others who don't "fit in" in a variety of ways is a problem of *injustice* inherent within host or dominant societies as much as it is a problem within the diasporic condition itself. Thus, thinking with Arendt, we can say that the problem of alienation at the core of much of diaspora theorizing and experience is best understood also as part of a larger justice project.

This view reaches us all, whether one considers oneself alienated, marginal, or neither. In Arendt's work on the pariah and parvenu?e, we come to see that complacency is deceptive and dangerous. Those in an abject position can barely afford it. Complacency also serves as a deceptive desire for those of us who think we are doing okay, with the circumstances to live well, and so we can ignore the problems of "others" and the "larger world." One may achieve a modicum of success and try to insulate oneself from big-city and larger political problems. Doing so does not, however, make one actually safe or one's situation just. We must demand more.

To establish options of liberation beyond bourgeois notions of Liberal freedom and self-aggrandizement, one must engage in the political world and do so in concert with others. It is a dead end to really getting to one's personal happiness to imagine oneself risen above one's humble origins—as in the US quintessential bootstraps ideology. It is a fallacy to consider oneself fitting in and not really part of the communities one might be consciously or unconsciously distancing oneself from. It is an illusory state: you are where you are only as a guest and as long as you please the dominant characters.[27] Moreover, along the way, while you think you are hurting no one by just doing your own individual thing, you are actually participating in the very oppression of the communities from which you distance yourself. It is not enough to say, I did wrong to nobody today. Arendt is clear: "Society, we are told, is composed of 'nobodies'—'I did wrong to nobody, nobody did wrong to me; but nobody will help me, nothing but nobodies'" (1944, 113). In this seemingly innocuous way, we each divest ourselves of any responsibility, and monumental injustices continue with no one to hold accountable.

Arendt wrote, "That the status of the Jews in Europe has been not only that of an oppressed people but also of what Max Weber has called a 'pariah people' is a fact most clearly appreciated by those who have had practical experience of just how ambiguous is the freedom which emancipation has ensured, and how treacherous the promise of equality which assimilation has held out" (100). She utilizes the situation of the Jews of Europe to debunk the myths of modern Liberal democracy, which are also our myths in the contemporary United States. Arendt's work demonstrates that the particular situation for Jews and demands for assimilation expose the fantasies of freedom and equality for all of us in the US today.[28]

Many among the populace are perhaps like K., well-meaning people. But Arendt demonstrates that to act here and there, follow the news, stay informed and care some, vote, write a letter, and so on just helps keep the deception of US democracy—that we are a free and equal people—intact. We are not a free and equal people. Most of us are far from free and do not enjoy the dignities of equality. Political action only has efficacy if part of a collective action. Arendt is opening a way for abject Jews and others to remain connected and committed to their peoples in the context of a revolutionary project. She is also warning those of us who might think we are doing okay to be careful: we might find ourselves wooed into the position of the parvenu?e, thinking we are worthy and powerful and beneficent (writing our checks to our charities or political campaigns) but really being part of the problem. In contrast, by exploring the life of this eighteenth- and nineteenth-century Jewish woman, Rahel Varnhagen, and the Jewish problem more generally, Arendt concludes that, given the basic fact of social hierarchies, the only way to live a decent life with human dignity is to take on injustice directly and in concert with others.

Chapter 5

Frida Kahlo

On Creating Vibrant, Transnational Jewish Networks

What happens if we place Frida Kahlo's Jewish story as core to her art, politics, and life? Beyond her relationship with her father, Kahlo kept Jewish friends, comrades, fellow artists, and lovers close. Kahlo's work to counter antisemitism and Nazi fascism was key to her politics and art, just as work against right-wing antisemitism, and against the Right generally, remains critical for many contemporary Jewish feminists and others. But this is not the Frida Kahlo best known to history. Kahlo's deeply embedded Jewish relations and concerns remain occluded, as so many stories of the Left omit Jews, Jewish movements, and Jewish issues. It's time to explore Frida Kahlo and the Jewishness of her life within our Jewish feminist story.

This chapter looks at the art, politics, and life of Frida Kahlo. I seek to reintroduce readers to the feminist Kahlo in a Jewish context. While many scholars and biographers have noted that Kahlo presented her father as Jewish, they do not look at Kahlo through a Jewish lens.[1] Feminists, Jews among them, helped give Frida her proper place on the map of art and art history.[2] Most, however, do not examine her work for its Jewish import, for what Jewishness might have meant to her and how it inspired themes in her activism, love, and work. The most impressive counterexample is the work of Gannit Ankori, which will be discussed at length below. It was Ankori's curated work on Kahlo for a pivotal 2003 Jewish Museum exhibit that sparked my interest in exploring Kahlo for this project.

I intend to stage this reencounter with Frida Kahlo in a Jewish feminist context by looking at the opportunities of and limitations on how Kahlo and others may have understood her (and our) Jewish situatedness. I shall explore those prospects and constraints historically in ways that I hope will be of assistance to Jewish feminists and others today. As central as Jewish ties and history seem to have been to Kahlo, I wonder how she might have come into connection with other Jews with whom she could make love, art, and politics with a different understanding of themselves and their relations to each other as Jews and/or in a more explicitly Jewish context.

The challenge of understanding a Jewish context for Frida Kahlo continues to be difficult for many today. Here, I examine this challenge to make meaning of Kahlo's Jewish ties in the context of multiple dominant paradigms of orthodoxy, empire, colonialism, diaspora, capitalism, and Protestant cultural imperialism. Differently from the other women of this study, though similar in the broad strokes, Kahlo's very existence in Mexico during her lifetime is made possible through numerous cross-cutting eras of genocidal settler colonialism. When you think about it, most Jews are where they are as a result of luck and murderous imperialist warring. Perhaps this is true of most people? These paradigms are still with us, even as many continue to forge vibrant Jewish communities and diversity more broadly in the face of hegemonies that exploit and homogenize difference. Following a brief biography of Frida Kahlo, I look at a history of Jewish immigration to Mexico, each wave of which is significant for Kahlo's life. We can then specifically address some barriers to seeing Kahlo in a Jewish context. With this groundwork laid, we will look anew at the intricate web of Kahlo's Jewish ties in her art, politics, and life over time.

Brief Kahlo Biography

A typical contemporary biography of Frida Kahlo will say something like this: Frida Kahlo is a widely celebrated Mexican artist best known for her self-portraits.[3] Often considered a feminist icon, she is credited for her prominence and activism in the *Mexicanidad* movement. Kahlo was born on July 6, 1907, in Coyoacán, Mexico, and died in the same neighborhood on July 13, 1954, at the age of forty-seven. Kahlo grew up and died in "La Casa Azul," her family house that her father, Wilhelm/Guillermo Kahlo, built. Kahlo presented her father as a Hungarian German Jew from Baden, Germany. He immigrated to Mexico from Germany in 1891. Kahlo's mother, Matilde Calderón, was a devout Catholic of mixed Spanish and Indigenous Mexican descent.

Kahlo's mother originally sent the young Frida to Catholic school. Frida's father then enrolled her in Mexico City's German elementary school, Colegio Alemán. When Kahlo was seven years old, she contracted polio, which eventually forced her to leave school. Among the lasting effects of the illness were stunted growth in her right leg and contortion of her right foot. Kahlo's battle with polio kept her from school for some years before she returned to her studies at the prestigious National Preparatory School in 1922. It is likely that it was at this point that Kahlo falsified her age and claimed to have been born in 1910. Some argue she did this to make herself younger so that she could still attend school. Others claim that Kahlo changed her birth year to align herself more closely with the Mexican Revolution, which began in 1910. At the National Preparatory School, Frida Kahlo met the renowned Mexican artist Diego Rivera.

In 1925 Kahlo was on a bus heading home from school when the bus collided with a trolley car. In the collision, a piece of iron went through Kahlo's pelvis and back. The injuries she sustained in this accident affected Kahlo for the rest of her life. She endured at least thirty operations over the course of her lifetime due to the accident and the polio. Her intense health struggles would eventually make her an important inspiration in the disabilities movement.[4] While in bed recovering from the bus accident, Kahlo began to focus seriously on painting. Her father encouraged her, and the painting intensified their bond. Kahlo never returned to school.[5]

In 1928 Kahlo joined the Mexican Communist Party. She worked closely with the photographer Tina Modetti and the muralist Diego Rivera. Kahlo and Rivera quickly entered into a romantic relationship, and in 1929 they married. The couple separated and got back together multiple times, divorcing and remarrying. Both Kahlo and Rivera had multiple affairs; Frida's partners included both women and men.

While it is often said that she did not attain fame while alive, Kahlo achieved considerable recognition in her lifetime. Her paintings were shown not only in Mexico but around the world, including in galleries in New York, San Francisco, and Paris. MoMA (the Museum of Modern Art) in New York City and the Louvre in Paris requested Frida's paintings. Still, while Kahlo's paintings sell for millions today, she never was able to support herself financially from her own artwork. Despite constant struggles with her health, Frida frequently traveled internationally, socializing with some of the best-known artists, thinkers, and activists of her time. In particular, she maintained connections with an international network of communist, antifascist, surrealist, and *Mexicanidad* political artists.

Most Frida Kahlo biographies would say more about Diego Rivera than does the above. While even the briefest biographies generally say that she presented her father as Jewish, Kahlo's own Jewish context and its import for her do not receive lengthy attention. Scholarly works have not tended to explore the meaning of Jewishness for her life, art, and politics.[6] In my view, this is a significant omission. Kahlo noted the primacy of her father's influence on her and on her becoming an artist. Her connection to Rivera contains a Jewish inflection. Kahlo continued to surround herself with Jews—Jewish artists, comrades, friends, and lovers—throughout her life. She took a keen interest in Jewish history and ideas, which are also key to her communist politics. Gannit Ankori opened up a new avenue of research into the rich meanings that Jewishness had for Kahlo's art. It is time to further examine the Jewish angles and to broaden them to include the possible roles aspects of Jewishness played in her politics and life. Let us begin by exploring the Jewish Mexican context of Kahlo's circumstances.

Jewish Mexican Immigration

Today, the Jewish community in Mexico numbers about forty thousand, comprising slightly under 0.04 percent of the population. This community has historically been centered in and near to Mexico City. The Jewish history that forms Frida Kahlo's story is rich and interesting. It is said that approximately 95 percent of the community is currently affiliated with formal Jewish organizations associated with both Sephardi and Ashkenazi communities (Frydberg 2014). The Mexico City Jewish community of today shares with that of Guillermo and Frida Kahlo's era the combination of a relative high quality of life for Jews in the city when they stay within Jewish circles and ongoing social marginalization and antisemitism in Mexican society more generally.[7]

The Jewish presence in Mexico is often discussed in terms of three primary waves. Each of these waves is significant for understanding Jewish matters of importance to Kahlo. The first major migration of Jews to Mexico was Sephardi (Frydberg 2014). *Sepharad* means "Spain" in Hebrew. Sephardis are Jews who trace their roots to the flourishing Jewish community of Spain during Muslim rule (CE 711 to 1492). Maristella Botticini and Zvi Eckstein (2012) estimate that in the year 1500, half of the world's Jewish population (which they estimate at one million) were practicing Sephardi Jewish traditions.[8] The Spanish Inquisition, which sought to purge Jews and Muslims from Christian Europe, began with the fourteenth-century Catholic reconquest of Spain.⁹ In 1492, the new Spanish Catholic monarchs, Queen Isabella and King Ferdinand II, established the Alhambra Decree, an edict of expulsion directed at the Jews and Muslims of Spain. During a catastrophic period for both Muslims and Jews, masses fled the country, opting for exile over persecution, death, or staying as forced converts. In the first dozen years of the Spanish Inquisition, more than thirteen thousand Jews were put on trial. The Spanish Inquisition did not officially end until 1808. It is estimated that over the course of the Inquisition, 31,912 people were burned at the stake as heretics and approximately 291,450 survived.

Important also for us in this chapter, Diego Rivera's twentieth-century family came to Mexico as part of this wave fleeing the Inquisition. The Catholic reconquest of Spain grew over time along with other new European imperialist moves globally, including colonization in what came to be called the Americas, the Atlantic slave trade, and Christian missionizing. Many Jews who fled the Inquisition settled in Mexico for a time. Many of the Spanish Jewish exiles migrated as converso/as, Jews who either converted to Christianity or publicly claimed that they had converted in order to avoid torture and death. Often, descendants of this great migration are known now also as *anusim/anusot* (Hebrew for "forced ones") or crypto-Jews (those who held onto and passed down Jewish traditions secretly while actively and publicly practicing other faiths).¹⁰ They often got to the Americas by hiding on ships of conquest. Power dynamics in history rarely proceed along neat oppressor/oppressed lines.

During the Inquisition, approximately one quarter of Spain's 125,000 to 200,000 Jews were baptized, joining 225,000 of the descendants of the forced converts of previous generations. The Inquisition was only formally stopped in Mexico in 1820. Yeah, I'm serious. By then, approximately one hundred crypto-Jews had been put to death, and many still were in prison (Ferry and Nathan 2000; Gitlitz 1996). Of interest for Kahlo, the Nazis of Kahlo's day, in both their thinking and their practice, revived many aspects of the Inquisition. Some of the more obvious similarities between Nazi and Inquisition anti-Jewish interests included obsessions with the fiction of blood purity as well as requiring yellow and other clothing markers for Jews.

Many Spanish Jews fled first to nearby countries, such as Portugal or Italy. However, the Inquisition grew in scope over time. For example, in 1496, the Inquisition expanded to Portugal, where 40,000 Jews were put on trial, 1,800 of whom were burned (Botticini and Eckstein 2012). The Portuguese Inquisition extended to colonies in Goa and Brazil. Jews fleeing the Portuguese Inquisition migrated to Italy, the Netherlands, Belgium, the Muslim-controlled Middle East, and the Ottoman Empire.

In 1535 Spain established colonies in the Americas, referred to as New Spain, with Mexico City as the capital. Over the course of time, the Spanish Inquisition extended to many areas that Spain had conquered as well, such as Mexico, the Philippines, Guatemala, Peru, New Granada, and the Canary Islands. Throughout the 1500s, Spain directed and pulled back from a variety of initiatives to purify (in Christian terms) the newer Spanish territories. These included occasionally barring converso/as from moving to the territories, allowing them to live in the territories only with specific policing, or requiring them to return to Spain. For example, in 1523 a decree against Jews was issued in Mexico City requiring all Jews to leave New Spain within six months. Still, despite the magnitude of oppression, Jewish converso/as continued to emigrate to and live in Mexico, often with falsified documents (Wiznitzer 1962).

By the second half of the nineteenth century, the public Jewish community of Mexico comprised approximately thirty families. At this time, the second wave of Jewish immigration began. This second wave consisted of two internal waves: Sephardi and Ashkenazi. (Ashkenazi Jews trace their roots from the Jewish communities of northern, central, and eastern Europe.) Mexico had entered into a period in which leaders encouraged European immigration in order to "whiten" the country. This made it easier for some Jews to come to Mexico, despite not being considered among those of the race of their host countries and also significant levels of antisemitism still operating in Mexico. For example, in 1865, in another effort to increase the country's European population, the French-imposed Mexican emperor Maximilian I issued a decree of religious tolerance. As a result of this edict, a new wave of mostly Ashkenazi Jews came to Mexico from Germany, Belgium, France, and Austria. Following Maximilian's assassination in 1867, Mexican president Benito Juárez established Mexico as a secular state, welcoming more Jewish immigration (Alt Miller 2015). In 1884, Mexican president Porfirio Díaz also sought increased European immigration, and his policies permitted more Jews of various Jewish ethnicities to immigrate.

The instability at this time, in regions where Ashkenazi life had often flourished, coincided with a period of tremendous upheaval in Sephardi life. This period of transition marked a significant shift in Jewish life in what was then Palestine as well as in the Americas. Given our history tour with Meir and all of our subjects, we'll take a moment to note that Jews had lived in Palestine and then were there under Ottoman rule for centuries.

Ottoman control over a changing and vast region lasted for approximately six hundred years, into the twentieth century. The empire spanned regions we would name today as in North Africa, western Asia, southeastern and some of central Europe. At different times, different areas enjoyed peace and prosperity. Ottoman rule, as with most empires, was also pocked with brutality; many populations were massacred time and again. Upon the breakup of this very diverse empire, there was a major nationalist, pro-Islamic push to re-create Turkey. These are some of the contexts for the more well known (though not well known enough) Armenian and Kurdish massacres, and these communities still seek recognition today. As the Ottoman Empire began to crumble on the verge of World War I, discrimination against Sephardi Jews remaining in Palestine and areas across the empire increased. At this time there were also massacres of Jewish communities, for example, in Istanbul. For our context, it is helpful to recall that Golda Meir moved to Israel in 1921, at the heart of the fall of the empire and the rise of modern Turkey. This major geopolitical shift had a tremendous impact on Jewish life in Palestine and the development of the Zionist movement. In particular we must also note an anti-Jewish massacre in 1934 in Thrace, which sent thousands of Jews on the run. Many joined existing Jewish communities in Palestine and other parts of what had been Ottoman territory. As a result, many Sephardi Jews also fled to Mexico and South America. Given the Spanish language base, Mexico and other Latin American regions were primary destinations for Sephardi Jews fleeing the terrors of the breakup of the Ottoman Empire and the transition to the new nation-state of Turkey.

During this period, Kahlo's father emigrated from northern Europe to Mexico. Guillermo Kahlo came to Mexico City at a time when very few Jews lived in the city. He married a local woman, Maria Cardeña, and later married again to Frida's mother. According to Ankori, Frida and Guillermo actively participated in German, and specifically German Jewish, cultural life in Mexico City. Before we explore that, let us briefly note the next significant historical moment (for Mexico, Jews in general, and the world), which also had a direct impact on Mexico City's Jewish context during and for Frida Kahlo's life.

The third wave of Jewish immigration to Mexico followed the end of World War I, amid the growing racist nationalism that also led to the rise of Nazism. (As we see, the "waves" history scholars point to are also not so neat and separate. That's okay.) While estimates vary, by 1912, the Jewish population in Mexico counted approximately five hundred people (Bureau of Jewish Social Research 1921). In 1921 and 1924, the United

States passed new racially based laws restricting the immigration of Jews along with a number of southern and eastern European groups. One consequence of these laws was a new rise in both Sephardi and more northern European Jewish immigration to Mexico (Frydberg 2014).

The Jewish community in Mexico City grew again at this time, and both Ashkenazi and Sephardi Jews contributed to the soaring numbers. Moving toward World War II, after the US, countries such as Mexico were appealing destinations for many Jews fleeing Nazi oppression, especially for Ladino (a Jewish language mixing Spanish and Hebrew)-speaking Sephardi Jews. Most people seem to know less about the targeting and murder of Sephardi Jews during the Holocaust. Nazi influence and rule, with its genocidal anti-Jewish policies, spread not only to southeastern Europe (home to large and old communities of Sephardi Jews) but also to the Middle East and to North Africa. International failure to more forcefully resist Nazism and to open immigration resulted in the murder of approximately ninety percent of the Ladino-speaking Jewish world, along with the mass murder of Ashkenazi Jews. While Jews streamed into Mexico, antisemitism was also rising in Mexico City at the same time. German cultural influences and community had been significant for Kahlo because of her father and many of their associates as well as her time at the German school in Mexico City. During Kahlo's adult years, the German cultural influence in Mexico City became increasingly pro-Nazi and anti-Jewish.[11] This development appears to have had a key impact on Kahlo and her life, work, and politics.[12]

Even if Kahlo's father associated with Jewish establishments, it is likely that formal Jewish religious institutions in Mexico City, Ashkenazi or Sephardi, would not have counted Frida as officially Jewish during her lifetime. Historically, most interpretations of rabbinic law reckon Jewish descent by the mother's line. Kahlo claimed no maternal Jewish ancestry. Then, as now, this religious obstacle to Jewish affiliation slows down but does not stop many individuals from making meaning and associating Jewishly.[13] Beyond the religious sphere, below I discuss Kahlo's cultural Jewish connections.

Barriers to Seeing Kahlo in a Jewish Context

In this section I critically examine a phenomenon of creating Jewishness as a religion and its likely role in (mis)understanding Kahlo's vibrant attachments. We will find that this reconfiguration of Jewishness as a religion occurs within significant geopolitical shifts moving into modernity and remaining very much with us in the contemporary period.

Other than protecting Frida from antisemitism, what else might go into confusions regarding Kahlo's Jewish bonds? Yes, in the Orthodox religious milieu of her day in Mexico City, someone such as Frida Kahlo might have had to undergo formal conversion to have been counted as Jewish within religious Jewish organizations. There is no record of Kahlo undertaking religious conversion. Still, we can query how Kahlo's many Jewish associations might have been valuable to her. Additionally, Kahlo might have been designated as Jewish under Nazi laws. But there are important reasons why many non-Jews (and some Jews as well) might have disassociated Kahlo Jewishly despite her many significant connections that were Jewish. The most obvious might be an effort to spare her an increasingly pernicious anti-Jewishness. On this note, some cognitive separation of Kahlo from Jewishness might have been intended to make it easier for others to value her in a period of prevailing antisemitism, even within the Left. Clearly, we must note her lack of religious Jewish affiliation as a factor.

To make sense of why this lack of religious relationship would matter, particularly to non-Jews, we need to examine Kahlo's life in the context of the rise of capitalism, empire, and Protestant imperialism, all of which align with historic European antisemitism even in predominantly Catholic Mexico. Like many Jews I know today, Kahlo forged numerous ties in Jewish contexts despite having no religious communal status. In my own experience, it is not always easy for non-Jewish friends and colleagues to understand that being Jewish is not simply a religious matter. In my US context, it is through assimilationist pressure within domestic Christian imperialism that Jewishness has been refashioned as a religion. Jewishness as a religion is a Christian concept. Lacking a paradigm for things outside its experience and refusing to allow for significant difference, it is a Christian imperialist move to try to fit the round fullness of Jewishness into the delineated square peg of the Christian category of religion.

Some have argued that this orientation is predominantly a Protestant form of internal (domestic) cultural colonization and global empire building. We will look at this further back in time soon enough; for now, one can note its origins also clearly in the German Protestant tradition in the context of the political upheavals and relations to Jews in the era of the development of modern nation-states (a move impacting the life chances of Rahel Varnhagen and continuing for others in this study). These historical

European developments, like the Spanish Inquisition before them and Nazi antisemitism subsequently, also made possible the development of modern capitalist Catholic Mexico, which allowed the Kahlos refuge. The dominance of this Christian paradigm in the West makes it difficult to see the Jewishness of Kahlo's webs of relations.

If not a religion, a race? Attempts to categorize Jews post-Holocaust, for those not seeking to reinforce traditions of murderous anti-Jewishness, has not been easy for many. For most Jews that I have known, being Jewish has more to do with something akin to peoplehood. It includes cultural and communal senses of identity, even with significant diversity across time and geographic locale. In modernity, the West has also considered Jewishness a racial designation, a modern western Christian concept close to the "ethnicity, "peoplehood," or "civilization" paradigms that Jews experience.[14] The very word *race* emerges from the medieval Spanish *raza*, used to denote breeds of dogs, horses, Jews, and Afro-Muslims (Gordon 2016). One can note this link in the Mexican context into the twentieth century: around 1939, the Mexican Ministry of the Interior developed the specific term "racial refugees" to refer to Jews fleeing Nazi anti-Jewish persecution in Europe (Gleizer 2013).

If not a race, then a religion? Generally, being Jewish has a religious component, Judaism, practiced and understood in quite different ways over time and place. Judaism, as what we might name today as a religious aspect of Jewishness, has been important. Still, neither knowledge nor practice of Jewish religious tradition is a requirement of Jewishness, nor is it central to many modern Western Jews' understandings of themselves and their relationships to each other. This is partly the basis of how the white supremacist Christian Right has trained the right wing of the Republican Party to complain that most Jews in the US are not really Jews (and why many hate-based Christian evangelicals will claim that they, as believers and devout religious practitioners, are more Jewish than most US Jews). While Judaism is usually described as a monotheistic religion, there is no required profession of faith or belief that makes one a Jew. Jews may follow clusters of common practices that relate to Judaism, but there is no set of practices that must be performed for one to qualify as Jewish. One does not have to believe in God; atheist, secular, and humanist Jews have long and honored histories, including among rabbis and Jewish communal leaders. (This is, apparently, increasingly upsetting to the Christian Right and its fellow travelers.)

Responding to this reality, Isaac Deutscher (1968) coined the phrase "the non-Jewish Jew" to refer to those Jews who stand in the Jewish social justice tradition but sometimes find themselves at odds with prevailing understandings of Jewishness. Deutscher's paradigm can be of help to us in clarifying the Jewishly inflected contexts that Kahlo formed for herself. A Deutscher reminder here may also be helpful for many Jews today who have trouble articulating their self-understanding as cultural Jews in the context of dominant Christian paradigms of Jews as a religious (or, today, some use the equally colonizing Christian euphemism "faith") group. We all, including western Jews, have been subject to imperialist overt and covert acts of re-creating Jews as a religious grouping. As we saw in our thinking with Arendt, if some Jews do not have much of a formal Jewish education that clearly names the roles of such hegemonic antidifference praxis for Jewish contexts, it is likely that even many Jews will draw on these dominant Protestant notions about Jews. For those who have been trained Jewishly in the social justice tradition, which in some estimates can be seen as the majority of US Jews, it can be difficult to articulate their cultural and political situation as Jewish (not, necessarily, as "Jew-ish," as many might joke today).

I was introduced to Deutscher's legacy by Melanie Kaye/Kantrowitz, first executive director of Jews for Racial and Economic Justice (jfrej.org), an organization I imagine Kahlo would have loved and one which would have loved to have had the likes of Kahlo among its ranks. Actually, JFREJ likely counts many Kahlo-like Jews among its members and allies. Kaye/Kantrowitz (1992) has helped generations of cultural Jewish leftists connect and make meaning and politics Jewishly. Back to Deutscher: born in Poland in 1907, Deutscher moved to the United Kingdom at the start of World War II. Deutscher hailed from a religiously observant home and community, where he was considered a prodigy of Talmud and Torah. As a young man, he left the religious fold to become a Marxist,[15] scholar in the secular world, and leader in Poland's underground communist movement. Like Hannah Arendt, he later began to see commonalities between Nazism and Stalinism. The Communist Party eventually expelled him for daring to publish his critical and independent views.[16]

Most relevant for our discussion of Frida Kahlo, Deutscher's attempt to articulate his adult Jewish identity is best summed up in his now-famous formulation of Jewishness based in history, culture, and leftist political values committed to vibrant forms of Jewish life in diaspora. Deutscher (1968, 51) states, "Religion? I am an atheist. Jewish nationalism? I am an internationalist. In neither sense am I therefore a Jew. I am, however, a Jew by force of my unconditional solidarity with the persecuted and exterminated. I am a Jew because I feel the pulse of Jewish history; because I should like to do all I can to assure the real, not spurious, security and self-respect of the Jews." I can't say that Deutscher had the Kahlos and the array of my comrades and intimates on the Jewish Left in mind when he came up with this. Perhaps Frida Kahlo could have said the same, but she did not have Deutscher's pedigree.[17] As we will see, Rivera sounds a lot like Deutscher. Like Kahlo and most Jews, Deutscher was not a Zionist prior to World War II. Like Meir and Arendt, after the Holocaust he supported the creation of a Jewish state. And particularly like Arendt, Deutscher was critical of the emerging Israeli response to the situation with Indigenous Muslim and Chrisitan Palestinians.

My scholarly capacities to work with this historical power analysis of Jewishness as a religion have been helped along the way by lots of Jewish folks of all stripes—feminists, lesbians, and queers whose writings appeared on the stage of history just as I was becoming old and smart enough to read them. Evi Beck's (1982) *Nice Jewish Girls*, on and by Jewish lesbians, was paradigm shifting in many ways. The work and its reputation recast outsider Jewish lesbians as insiders. Projects such as Kaye/Kantrowitz and Irena Klepfisz's (1986) special double issue of the lesbian journal *Sinister Wisdom*, titled *The Tribe of Dina*, further empowered waves of Jewish cultural and political (however spiritual and ritual-oriented) activists to place themselves Jewishly. Decades on, this conceptual shift enabled me to understand the critique of Arendt and Gertrude Stein, which I will discuss later in this volume, in new ways. For a more detailed exploration of this concept, I turn now to Leora Batnitzky.

Batnitzky (2011) has done excellent work carefully tracing the origins of how Judaism became a religion.[18] Batnitzky analyzes the idea that Judaism as a "religion was invented in the modern period, and the many conceptual tensions that followed from it" (1). She writes that "Like the notion of Jewish religion, the modern concept of religion more generally is not a neutral or timeless category, but instead a modern, European creation, and a Protestant one at that." Batnitzky's contribution to naming these tensions can also assist us in identifying some barriers to including the Kahlos among us within a Jewish feminist history. Let us take a closer look.

The Protestant Reformation was not an isolated religious revolution. We need to see this momentous religious shift also, at least, in economic and political terms. The corresponding European Christian transition from feudalism to capitalism took place through a series of economic and social revolutions that resulted from and brought about a series of political and cultural changes. These interweaving changes included also a Liberal political introduction of the individual rights of citizens in new nation-states in Europe (and, eventually, in much of the rest of the world). The understanding of religion as a discrete facet of life was a direct result of these changes, particularly among Protestant communities in western Europe, and soon in the Protestant-dominant US.

What about matters Jewish in Catholic Mexico? In contrast, Jews have historically lived and understood themselves as a collective body inhabiting the nexus of what we in the Protestant West today might call religion, culture, and nationality. Thus, while individual Jewish communities could be quite different from one another in many ways, they also knew themselves as part of a larger collective of the peoples of Israel and transnational, intergenerational exchange. It is helpful to understand the situation of the Jewish communities in Mexico during Guillermo's and later Frida's life in the context of even these Protestant developments. Readers may recall from the Arendt chapter our discussion of the lethally assimilationist political aspects of this in the eighteenth-century French Revolution. Note that France at the time was a Catholic country as well. While Catholic, Mexico was struggling to become an international, modern country modeled on the Protestant West. Mexico then declared itself a secular country under law. Its leaders proclaimed religious tolerance and sought to attract non-Catholics, including, at certain historical turns, Jews. As with France's revolutionary extension of the franchise to Jewish male heads of household, Mexico was acting within the still-developing Protestant norms of an ascendant political Liberalism. In the case of Latin America, these norms maintained that immigrants of minority religions, such as non-Catholics in Mexico, could integrate into the Liberal nation-state and promote its position within the demands of international "free" enterprise and colonial conquest.

With the rise of the European political construction of the individual as a politically viable entity, having an internal landscape that is due rights, Protestantism developed what we tend to term religion as a private sphere separable from politics, economics, and the social, at least in formal terms. It would not have made sense to consider Jewishness merely a religion prior to this Protestant formulation, nor did it make sense during the same period in other culturally distinct parts of the world, such as feudal Catholic Europe or a largely Muslim Ottoman Empire. It was this Liberal Protestant conceptualization, central to both imperialist capitalism and to the rise of the nation-state,[19] that made possible the second wave of Jewish immigration to Mexico, which brought those like Guillermo Kahlo to the increasingly cosmopolitan metropolis of Mexico City.

In the final chapter we will come back to the role of reconnecting to Jewishly defined selfhood in our study of Emma Goldman. Zionism has been one way for Jews to claim a right to collective self-determination. It was, and remains, far from the only version of such a claim. With a bit more history, our look at Frida Kahlo's life, politics, and art can assist us in defining Jewish self-determination in our own ways today. There are various stories of Frida and Rivera publicly claiming Jewish roots, especially when they determined that it really mattered. Possibly apocryphal, likely suggestive, it is the case that Guillermo, Frida, and Diego Rivera could all respond to the question "Are you Jewish?" with the reply "I am an atheist." Many of my non-Jewish close ones still have some trouble wrapping their heads around that one. Both realities make sense outside of Protestant colonizing norms. Culturally identified and secular Jews today, including many on the Jewish Left, are seeking to reclaim Jewish cultural space from Christian cultural imperialist conceptualizations. We will see that this orientation certainly impacted the ways that many considered Gertrude Stein not Jewish in any meaningful way.

England began experimenting with these Protestant political ideas in the sixteenth and seventeenth centuries. It was, however, the anticlerical and anti-Catholic French Revolution of 1789 that most explicitly embedded the new ideas of rights and citizenship into the new European political context of nation-states. It took more than a simple linear path to adapt these views to the nineteenth-century German context for Guillermo's family. Directly impacting Rahel Varnhagen's life chances, Germany and France entered into a prolonged period of political and military struggle in which each country claimed control over patches of borderlands. With each change of political rule, the Jews of these areas were alternately emancipated or stripped of their new rights (as also impacted Marx's family lines). Still, Germany considered itself the center of civilization and advanced philosophy and viewed German culture as the most developed. During this period, a German Jewish middle class developed that sought to end its second-class status and gain full access to German education, culture, and the world of ideas. Gertrude Stein's parents came from this milieu, as did other members of their immigration wave from Germany to the US. Later, this would be the German Jewish world into which Hannah Arendt was born. Being eastern European immigrants in the nineteenth century, Emma Goldman and Golda Meir did not function as much within this Germanic Protestant context.

A central paradox emerges in the Protestant German context. German Jews faced the question of how best to argue for civil rights so as to end obvious forms of anti-Jewish discrimination and (most directly impacting the middle class and those aspiring to it) denial of access to universities and public life. In nineteenth-century Germany, as Batnitzky (2011) states, there was a significant "gap between the ideal of full Jewish integration into the German state, and a far more incomplete and vexed political and cultural reality" (5). The emerging Christian German reality was framed by Kant's "rational religion ground in the autonomous self" (Batnitzky 2011, 7). German Jewish thinkers sought to construct a description of Jewishness intelligible in the new German Protestant, increasingly Liberal and capitalist, context. They hoped to win recognition that would enable German opinion makers to stop perceiving them as a threat to the new state, so that "worthy" Jews—those who fit the mold of German Liberal Christian ideals of civilized individuals rather than those of a Jewish collective—could integrate into the German nation-state and public life. Batnitzky demonstrates that in the context of a tense exchange with Christian elites, the man whom many Western Jews consider the founder of modern Jewish thought, Moses Mendelssohn, "invent[ed] the modern idea that Judaism is a religion" (14).

At a time when it was rare for Jews and Christians to interact, Mendelssohn was close to the Christian figures considered the greats of German philosophy of his day, such as Gotthold Ephraim Lessing and Immanuel Kant. Their work and period became central to the context for Rahel Levin Varnhagen's life and to Arendt's thinking. Lessing, Mendelssohn, and others participated in Varnhagen's salons, which then became an important Jewish women's cultural legacy for Stein. That Mendelssohn could engage with Christian philosophers and still remain Jewish was incomprehensible to even "progressive" German (Christian) thinkers. Thus, in 1769 Swiss theologian Johann Caspar Lavater challenged Mendelssohn to "either refute Christianity or convert" (Batnitzky 2011, 15). While not quite as physically violent as the "option" presented to the Jews of Catholic Spain ("convert or die," which led many to flee), Lavater's words followed a similar underlying structure. (Jews within reach of the Nazis were not given an "option" to convert, mostly only to die.)

Mendelssohn (2013) responded to this challenge by writing *Jerusalem; or, On Religious Power and Judaism*, in which he defended Judaism as rational (thus recognizable and acceptable to Protestantism) and made a case for Judaism's compatibility with the ideals of the new German nation-state and philosophy without "offending" Christians. It is here that he offers the most comprehensive Jewish articulation of the Protestant Enlightenment ideas of separation between church and state (brought into Mexican politics in its nineteenth-century period of racialized empire building). He argued that Judaism is a religion and that Jews can thus coexist with the political reality of the new German nation-state, able to offer it their full civil allegiance. This framework then became a paradigm utilized in other European contexts, including the emerging international (i.e., culturally largely European), capitalist Mexico, which invited Jewish immigration from Germany and thus attracted Guillermo Kahlo. These developments did not greatly impact self-conceptualization within the formal Jewish community in Mexico City, as those affiliated with religious institutions were largely Orthodox, whether Ashkenazi or Sephardi. Similarly, it had little influence on Jews from the first and second immigration waves, who, for the most part, had emigrated from non-Protestant countries. Many Jews continued to see themselves one way; modern European Christians defined Jews another way.

Batnitzky argues that this cultural and political pressure to reduce Jewishness to a religion was not found in the Orthodox or Catholic countries of eastern Europe, which remained feudal longer than did the northwest. Under Muslim Ottoman rule, much of southeastern Europe did not initially participate in this Protestant cultural and political context. The eastern Europeans (such as were Emma Goldman's and Golda Meir's contexts) and Sephardi Jews who made up most of Mexico City's early Jewish community rejected this translation of Jewishness into the Protestant model of a religion. On the contrary, they continued to practice a vibrant Jewish cultural life. This cultural Jewish life was available to Jews and others of Frida Kahlo's generation, including those who, like her, could not, in the dominant religious ideology, be named as Jewish. Thus, Kahlo met many Jews in her Western international political and artistic circles who would not have named Jewishness as a primary public religious identity. Still, for many, as I argue here for Kahlo, their Jewish ties could be meaningful for them, individually and in relation.

Making Jewish Meaning in Frida Kahlo's Art

Recall that I began to imagine this chapter and this book after I viewed the Kahlo exhibit at the Jewish Museum in New York City in 2003 entitled *Frida Kahlo's Intimate Family Portrait* (Ankori 2003).[20] This exhibit was primarily a study of Kahlo's 1936 painting *My Grandparents, My Parents, and I*. An Israeli scholar, Gannit Ankori, curated the exhibit, demonstrating the many Jewish meanings of the work. In doing so, Ankori opened up new opportunities to explore deep meanings of Jewishness for Kahlo. Ankori focused mainly on Kahlo's art. Over years of research, I have been able to expand the boundaries of Ankori's look at the possible centrality of Jewishness to Kahlo's politics and life. Much of the import of Ankori's work and its impact on me has survived the storm of the publication of the 2005 Franger and Huhle book genealogically demonstrating that Kahlo's father's paternal line was Lutheran.

Ankori has done groundbreaking work placing Frida Kahlo in a decidedly Jewish framework. While Kahlo's life, art, and politics cannot be separated, in this section I will discuss Ankori's critique of two central Jewish sources in Kahlo's art: the horrors of anti-Jewishness in German Nazism and in the Spanish Inquisition. Ankori's work on Jewishness in Kahlo's art via these two primary themes has been so groundbreaking that it deserves considered attention before we move on to other areas of Kahlo's life and politics. Most scholars characterized *My Grandparents, My Parents, and I* (sometimes referred to as "Family Tree") as merely "whimsical" and "amusing." Ankori takes the painting seriously. In doing so, Ankori has not only transformed what might be Kahlo's artistic legacy but also opened up space for larger Jewish feminist reclamations.

Jewishly contextualizing Kahlo can be understood by way of her affinity for her father (however fraught) and the life she made for herself with strong Jewish ties. Pop cultural references tell us that she often spoke of herself as "half-Jewish." Although there is no such category within Jewish law, many apply such an appellation anyway. This designation could have made sense for someone like Kahlo.[21] Also, if her maternal grandmother did come from a Jewish line, with the Nazi ideology becoming increasingly dominant during the course of her adulthood, she could have suffered a Jewish fate if she had been in Europe. Additionally, Ankori (2003) notes, "After Hitler's rise to power, Kahlo is reported to have been deeply concerned not only about Nazism in general, but specifically about her Jewish relatives who apparently still resided in the vicinity of Baden-Baden."

Modernizing the Spanish Inquisition's mania regarding pure bloodlines, a key aspect of the Nazi government's Nuremberg Laws of 1935 aimed at establishing Aryan racial purity. Nazis promulgated the use of genealogical charts, based on the Western "family tree" model, to prove (or disprove) one's Aryan lineage. Such charts became popular in Mexico City as well, with the increasing Nazi presence there. Important for Kahlo, "by 1936, Nazi oriented manuals on how to conduct 'genealogical research' were introduced and distributed in Kahlo's alma mater, the German School of Mexico

City. Most of the school's teachers had by then joined the Nazi party and encouraged their students to sketch their 'pure' origins and to chart their 'family trees'" (Ankori 2003). In her artistic work on her family tree, Kahlo used this tool to resist the growing Nazi influence in Mexico City explicitly by demonstrating her mixed heritage.[22] Ankori takes a new look at what could be Jewish identifications in Kahlo's art in this framework. Ankori also demonstrates a relationship between Kahlo's work in this painting and Isaac Berliner's poems as a Jewish European immigrant to Mexico. The images and story in Berliner's Yiddish poems are reminiscent of Guillermo's journey and also represent the mixing of cultures, Mexican and German, at a time of Nazi emphasis on cultural purity (Berliner and Rivera 1996).

Ankori notes that *My Grandparents, My Parents, and I* introduced several symbolic elements that became central to Kahlo's overall body of work. For example, Ankori (2003) observes that renditions of land and sea, insemination with sperm and eggs, and "a womb-like cactus flower in the act of pollination" initially appear in this 1936 painting. We also see Kahlo use a clock with an eye, which Ankori suggests may be related to Jewish modernist artist Marc Chagall's explorations of multiple cultural inheritances.[23] Thus, it is interesting to pay attention to images that Kahlo worked on both in preparation for and as part of this work when they resurface in her subsequent paintings. Ankori argues that each time Kahlo uses symbols such as sperm and eggs, as she often did in later works, they indicate Kahlo's engagement with her Jewish heritage.

Ankori also provides a fascinating discussion of the influence of Alfonso Toro's (1944) two-volume *La familia Carvajal* on Kahlo's writing, politics, and artwork. This work examines the history of Jews and the Inquisition in sixteenth-century New Spain, specifically the oppression of Jews in Mexico.[24] Ankori catalogues the impact of Kahlo's examination of these volumes during 1944 to 1945 and later. In the diary writings, sketches, drawings, and eventually paintings that follow this reading, Kahlo returns to the use of land and sea that she first developed in *My Grandparents, My Parents, and I* and also begins to incorporate images of torture, particularly of women. Ankori argues that Kahlo's renditions of torture emerge from her engagement with the humiliation and torture depicted in Toro's work and are not only artistic renderings of Kahlo's own horrendous health and medical care (as they are usually interpreted to be in the absence of any Jewish context).

Numerous images from Kahlo's diary sketches appear in a full oil painting in 1945, *Without Hope*. Scholars, including Herrera, have analyzed this painting without noting the relation to Toro's work or Kahlo's interest in Jewish history. The painting contains many elements of interest to Kahlo that critics have long remarked upon, including sperm inseminating eggs (Ankori notes that Kahlo had not, at this stage, used this image in any of her paintings since her 1936 *My Grandparents, My Parents, and I*), science, disease, and war. But in *Without Hope*, Kahlo turned many of these into a "depiction of cells adversely affected by poison gas" at the historical moment when news of the Nazi gas chambers and other torture techniques used on Jews was becoming known to the world. Ankori notes that Kahlo's personal library included a copy of the 1943 *Black Book of Nazi Terror* (in which artists and writers from sixteen countries tell their stories of Nazi atrocities).[25] The Inquisition and Nazi obsessions with purity and torturing Jews come together in Kahlo's *Without Hope*. Ankori's analysis (quite different from Herrera's) can help us ask new Jewish questions about Kahlo's *Moses*; her engagement with Freud's *Moses and Monotheism*, which she was reading and painted in the same year as *Without Hope*; and other aspects of Kahlo's life.

Reclaiming the Jewish in Kahlo's Politics: The Jewish Anecdotes and Beyond

There are a couple of often-told stories of Jewish interest that I heard numerous times as I began my own Jewish feminist study of Kahlo.[26] When shared, these anecdotes are emphasized as if they express all that there might be to say about Frida Kahlo and Jewishness (similar to the sedimentation of the few stories people often told of Golda Meir's legacy). Further, the stories are often told in isolation, without the solid grounding of what my post-Ankori study revealed was a rich Jewish infusion in Kahlo's politics, life, and work. When placed in a Jewish context, we can inquire in what ways Kahlo's known political association as a communist was likely (as for many leftist Jews of her day) not only deeply related to her antifascism but a primary component of her resistance to the antisemitism of Nazism.

One anecdote frequently retold occurs at a dinner party at the home of Henry Ford, a well-known antisemite. During the dinner, Kahlo is reported to have asked, "Mr. Ford, are you Jewish?" Her feisty resistance to the accepted silences lives on.

A second tale is told about a time when Kahlo and Rivera were staying at the Wardell Hotel in Detroit. Upon learning that Jews were not allowed to stay at the hotel, both said publicly that they had "Jewish blood" and threatened to leave. The legend maintains that the management changed the antisemitic policy in response.

Ankori helps us to look at Kahlo's art through a Jewish lens. Further, Kahlo's art is never divorced from her life and politics. Kahlo's participation in the Communist Party is often subsumed under Rivera's political commitments. When biographers and scholars note Kahlo's own communist affiliation, they present it outside a Jewish context. Like many particularly Jewish communist activists, Kahlo explicitly mobilized her communism in directly anti-Nazi, antifascist ways. Many Jews of her time developed their tools in this way for resisting the deathly antisemitism of the period.[27]

Kahlo was well aware that, according to her understanding, Nazi law would have classified her as Jewish.[28] She understood that this meant that if she had been living in a formally German-occupied or German-allied land, she, too, would have been targeted in what came to be known as an explicitly anti-Jewish genocidal settler colonialism. Even during the early portion of the war, Kahlo knew, at the very least, that antisemitism was a scourge and that Jews in Europe were in grave danger. She is said to also have been specifically concerned for the fate of her Jewish relatives in Europe.

The anecdotes with Henry Ford and at the Wardell Hotel suggest small but public ways in which Kahlo resisted. There are other bits from Kahlo's biography that are best contextualized in this communist, antifascist, anti-Nazi, antisemitism-resisting context. For example, Ankori also tells of Kahlo's public support for a Lionel Reiss art exhibit in New York in 1933. The Reiss portraits of Jews aimed to take on the antisemitism of Nazi and other popular ideologies. By showing Jews in their diversity and humanity, Reiss sought specifically to counter Nazi anti-Jewish propaganda. This was important to Kahlo. Often considered the start of the Holocaust, 1933 marks (among other significant atrocities) the rise of the Nazi Party into power, anti-Jewish book burnings, the start of anti-Jewish legislation, and the formation of the first concentration camps. From the start of the Holocaust, then, the communist activist Kahlo associated publicly with Jewish solidarity and resistance to Nazi antisemitism.

Interestingly, Ankori further discusses the Jewish and political presence in Kahlo's personal library, linking Kahlo's communism with her concern for the antisemitism of Nazism and the growing fascism of her day. Filled with histories and literature of Mexico and beyond, Kahlo's library also included many works on the Soviet Union and communism. In her diary, Kahlo noted that she reread her many volumes by Marx, Lenin, and Stalin. As noted above, Ankori also remarks on the presence of a two-volume history of Jews in the Spanish Inquisition and the *Black Book of Nazi Terror* among her collection of books, along with other works on Jewish subjects.

Clarifying direct connections of Kahlo's political commitments to resisting fascism and particularly Nazi antisemitism with her communism does not detract from understanding Kahlo's politics as a communist. On the contrary, exploring the deep roots of Kahlo's commitments provides us with a vigorous appreciation of her leftist values and her engagement with communism. Ignoring the Jewish aspects of Kahlo's life and primary touchstones leads to more anemic understandings. Instead, using a Jewish lens helps us to conceptualize the fullness of her communist politics, as using a Jewish lens does for so many Jews on the left in her time and today.

Jewish Ties in Kahlo's Life

We can see lively Jewish connections in Kahlo's personal relationships, family ties, various of her communities in Mexico City and abroad, and what she read as well as the artists, intellectuals, and activists with whom she lived a vibrant life. Honestly, however, to say that Kahlo liked some of the products of Jewish giants in the make-up industry is not to say much of Kahlo's Jewish ties. (How much does it say about your Jewish identity if you prefer Revlon products over those of Helena Rubinstein?) Similarly, to say that numerous famous Jews collected Kahlo's art does not really help our study with the proper depth. It is well known that a number of wealthy Jews were collectors of Kahlo's work. This is some of the content of the post-2005 reframed hoopla regarding "Kahlo's Jewish ties." Perhaps folks will show us things in these references that I am not seeing. For now, there are a number of important Jewish relations in Kahlo's life that do warrant further investigation.

For example, there is a noteworthy Jewish communal dimension to the Jewish works in Kahlo's personal library. Ankori discusses the numerous books in Kahlo's library that were printed by a German Jewish publishing house organized in Mexico in 1942. In addition to various volumes printed by this publisher, Kahlo also had several books by German Jewish intellectuals on Jewish themes published by yet another German Jewish publishing venture in Mexico City. Moreover, she also kept Spanish-language writings on Jewish themes, work by the Sephardi Jewish poet Yehuda Halevi, and other volumes that would have been circulated among the Jewish community in Mexico City of her day. Even with a quick perusal of the books still kept in Kahlo's personal library at La Casa Azul (now a museum), one also finds Yiddish titles along with others attesting to her extensive interests.

In addition to her ties to German Jewish publishing efforts, Kahlo was close to Alberto Misrachi and the crowd he gathered at his bookstore. Situated in Mexico City's Centro Histórico, where Jews of Guillermo's generation often settled, Misrachi's bookstore was a center for politicians, intellectuals, and artists. A Greek Sephardi Jew, Misrachi later opened an art gallery. Misrachi's gallery exhibited Kahlo's works, among others by Mexican luminaries, and he became a primary broker and supporter of Kahlo's paintings.

As Ankori deftly demonstrates, with these many Jewish connections, it becomes of new interest to view the primacy of Frida's relationship with her father in this Jewish context. Kahlo was quite specific that her father was her main familial tie and that her life as an artist was bound to the person whom she presented as her immigrant European Jewish father.[29] Because she made herself into a representative of *Mexicanidad*, many people look for Spanish, Indigenous, and Catholic sources of inspiration in Kahlo's art. These sources are evident. Acknowledging the foundation and importance of Jewishness to Kahlo does not imply any lack of interest on her part in exploring these cultures. Kahlo was enriched by her mixed heritage (as noted in her 1936 anti-Nazi work on her family tree).

Ankori's work is critical: Understanding Kahlo's "deep emotional bond to and profound empathy for her father," juxtaposed with her negative emotions toward her mother, illuminates the artist's complex and conflicting systems of identification, and "the more deeply we probe this issue, the clearer it becomes that beneath the overt layers of *mexicanidad*, Kahlo, at some level, always maintained a view of herself as 'other' " (2002, 49). Deutscher claims a marginalized standpoint experience as Jewish, but others have not always acknowledged it as such. Ankori writes, "This self-image was, to a large extent, shaped by the artist's strong identification with her father, who remained forever an outsider. For although Wilhelm officially became Guillermo, he never completely integrated into Mexican society" (49). Guillermo's perpetual status as outsider resonates with themes Arendt problematized in the work on pariahs and parvenu?e.s that she developed in her early study of Rahel Varnhagen. As with Arendt and despite German antisemitism, Guillermo continued to revel in the cultural greats of German literature, music, philosophy, and art. Frida came to share these loves. The world has largely forgotten their import for Kahlo's life, work, and politics. The scholarship on Kahlo does not fully attest to the impact of her tie to this central relative, whom Kahlo often publicly associated with a Jewish context.[30]

Was there really a Jewish tie with Rivera? Scholars of Kahlo usually overfocus on Rivera. While Rivera looms large in Kahlo's life and the scholarship on her, the Jewish tie in their relationship is generally overlooked. For example, in writing about Rivera and Jewish themes, often noted is that he illustrated Isaac Berliner's Yiddish book of poetry, *City of Palaces* (1996). Rivera was working on this Berliner project in 1936 when Kahlo was producing *My Grandparents, My Parents, and I*. Less frequently investigated is that Diego Rivera's mother was a conversa. Despite a dearth of scholarly exploration of Jewish meaning in Rivera's politics and work, Rivera himself stated the importance of his Jewish heritage explicitly in 1935: "My Jewishness is the dominant element in my life. From this has come my sympathy with the downtrodden masses which motivates all my work."[31] I warned you that Rivera could sound a lot like Deutscher. Without a Talmudic (a high-level textual and usually religious) education, almost no one notices this about Rivera. I suggest that leftists and all those interested need to read Deutscher's essay "The Non-Jewish Jew" and re-situate both Kahlo and Rivera in Jewish terms. In my experience, like Kahlo and Rivera, many people on the margins of the Jewish community continue to connect with each other over various layers of marginalized status.[32]

Beyond family narrowly defined, throughout her adult life, many of Kahlo's closest ties were to Jews and other members of her artistic and political circles with significant Jewish forebearers. These included Kahlo's close friends Lucienne Bloch, whose grandparents were Jewish, and Sergei Eisenstein, the Russian filmmaker and theorist, who grew up hearing Yiddish from his father, a German Jew who converted to Christianity (we keep seeing the modern Rahel Varnhagen paradigm of Jews converting to Christianity, particularly in German-related cultures, in their aspirations to live decently).

There is also a Jewish story to tell of Kahlo's many lovers. One of Kahlo's best-known affairs was with Leon Trotsky. In 1937, when Trotsky was exiled from the Soviet Union, he and his wife Natalia Sedova came to stay with Kahlo and Rivera in Mexico. Kahlo put them up in her family's house, La Casa Azul. While Trotsky was staying with them, he and Kahlo had an affair. Kahlo's affair with Trotsky is often noted in "Fridamania," but it is not usually mentioned that Trotsky was Jewish and that antisemitism played a distinct role in his vilification and exile. Kahlo's affair with Trotsky on its own might not tell us much of Kahlo's attraction to Jews. Before and after this well-known affair, Kahlo had numerous other Jewish lovers and associated closely with many other Jewish artists and comrades.

In 1931, for example, Kahlo began a decade-long affair with Nickolas Muray, a Jewish Hungarian photographer living in the US (Kaminer 2015). During this period, Kahlo and Rivera were traveling back and forth between Mexico and several US cities, and Kahlo was quite busy with her health and her work. In July 1935, Kahlo journeyed to New York with two Jewish women who were close friends of hers, Anita Brenner and Mary Schapiro Sklar. This was Kahlo's first trip abroad without Rivera. Brenner, a well-known author of children's books on the art and history of Mexico, was the daughter of Latvian Jewish immigrants to Mexico. Toward the end of that same year, Frida met the Japanese American sculptor Isamu Noguchi, with whom she had an affair (Noguchi's mother, Léonie Gilmour, was educated in New York humanist and heavily Jewish ethical culture schools; Marx 2013; Matsui 2010).

In April 1938, the artists André Breton and Jacqueline Lamba traveled to Mexico on Breton's cultural commission by the French government. Breton was a writer who is generally considered the father of surrealism. Lamba was a painter, performer, and surrealist. Breton and Lamba sought to meet Trotsky and so met Kahlo. At that time, Kahlo and Lamba began an affair. By this time, Germany had succeeded in annexing Austria in its genocidal settler-colonial aims to take Europe all the way east and would soon take other parts of eastern Europe. Mexico was already involved in numerous international forums to discuss the European refugee crisis resulting from German aggression (Gleizer 2013).

At the time of Lamba and Breton's visit to Mexico, Frida was working on her painting *What the Water Gave Me*. This painting intrigued Breton, and he encouraged Julien Levy, a New York–based Jewish art dealer, to showcase Kahlo's works (Mahon 2011). Thus, in October of 1938, as Germany began to deport Jews to Poland, Kahlo travelled to New York for her first solo art exhibition at the Julien Levy Gallery. The exhibit ran from November 1 to 15. Levy's gallery was a widely known stepping stone for Latin American and European surrealist artists seeking to make a name for themselves in the United States. Among Kahlo's works on exhibit was her *My Grandparents, My Parents, and I*. Half of Kahlo's twenty-five paintings were sold at this show, where she also received commissions for new portraits by prominent art personalities.[33] During her time in New York, Frida resumed her affair with Nickolas Muray (Kaminer 2015).

While Kahlo's work was on exhibit at the Julien Levy Gallery in New York in November 1938, the Nazis undertook what came to be called Kristallnacht, the Night of Broken Glass. From November 9 to 10, countless civilians joined the Nazi SA paramilitary forces (Sturmabteilung, referred to in English as storm troopers) and the Hitler Youth in a wave of pogroms throughout Germany and German-occupied territories. In these anti-Jewish massacres, Nazis killed Jews and rounded up Jewish males. In addition, Nazi officers and ordinary civilians collaborated in ransacking and destroying thousands of Jewish homes, stores, schools, hospitals, and other visible Jewish spaces and burning down approximately one thousand synagogues. This wave of massacres and destruction, marked by broken glass from smashed windows, garnered broad notice in the international press and is often regarded as the start of the Holocaust.

As Herrera (1983) discusses, Kahlo traveled to Europe despite Hitler's rise to power and the already-well-known anti-Jewish hysteria of Nazi enterprises. Soon after the New York gallery exhibit, at Breton's invitation, Kahlo went to Paris for the first time, in January of 1939. This came a mere few months before Germany invaded Poland and World War II formally began for the West. Within days of Germany's invasion, in September, France and Britain declared war on Germany. Germans swiftly responded by occupying France. During this tense period, Kahlo was in Paris to participate in the exhibit *Mexique* at the Colle Gallery. During her time in Paris, Kahlo stayed with the Bretons and then with Kurt and Arlette Seligmann (Mahon 2011).[34] At the *Mexique* exhibit, Frida's works were showcased together with Breton's collection of Mexican art and Manuel Àlvarez Bravo's photography. Àlvarez Bravo was an acclaimed Jewish Mexican photographer renowned for his Mexican themes. During this visit, the Louvre purchased Kahlo's painting *The Frame*. With this purchase, Kahlo became the first twentieth-century Mexican artist whose art was purchased by the Louvre. During Kahlo's stay in Paris, Lamba and Breton introduced her to more Jews and others in artistic and political intellectual circles, overlapping with the circles of German exile Hannah Arendt and US expatriate Gertrude Stein.[35]

As will be discussed in more detail in the next chapter on Gertrude Stein, in the south of France, the French set up a collaborationist government known as the Vichy regime. In 1939 the Vichy regime constructed the Gurs refugee camp with the intention of interning leftists fleeing fascist Spain. By 1940, Germany had occupied Paris and much of northern and eastern France. The Vichy regime then also began using the camp at Gurs to detain thousands of German Jews as well as leftist and other dissident political leaders. It was during this time that Hannah Arendt was captured in Paris and sent to Gurs.

Those of Kahlo's female relatives in Europe she seems to have identified as Jewish would have faced a horrific development. Jewish women who had remained in Baden (Jewish men from Baden had already either been sent to concentration camps or fled) would have been evacuated by the Nazis and imprisoned in Gurs. Almost all of the 7,500 remaining Jewish girls and women of Baden were sent to Gurs, where they suffered imprisonment and terrible living conditions. Arendt managed to escape Gurs. Members of the same circles that Breton and Lamba had introduced to Kahlo managed to smuggle Arendt out of Europe to safe haven in New York; these circles also assisted Breton and Lamba in their flight from Nazi-occupied France. By 1942, the approximately five thousand Jews (including the remaining Jewish women and girls from Baden) still interned at Gurs were sent to the Drancy concentration camp in Paris. By this time, Gertrude Stein and Alice Toklas had left Paris for the south of France. Most of the Jewish former inmates of Gurs were eventually sent from Drancy to Auschwitz and some other Nazi death camps, where they were murdered. Arendt and others such as Breton survived by fleeing, Stein and Toklas survived in the south of France, and Kahlo left Paris on the verge of the nightmare that, by the end of 1939, was growing exponentially. Understanding the fate of any of Kahlo's relatives as well as many comrades, fellow leftist artists, and friends can help us understand the central place that the German-initiated genocide of Jews held for Kahlo, both politically and personally.

Kahlo's Declining Health, Postwar Recognition, and Additional Close Jewish Ties

In the ensuing period, Kahlo had her art on display in numerous venues and lived as fully and as passionately as possible while she also faced increasing complications from her health. In January 1940, Kahlo's *The Two Fridas* and the now-lost *The Wounded Table* were exhibited in the *International Exhibition of Surrealism*, organized by Breton and Wolfgang Paalen at the Gallery of Mexican Art.[36] Kahlo also exhibited her work with the *Contemporary Mexican Painting and Graphic Art* exhibit at the Palace of Fine Art in San Francisco's Golden Gate International Exhibition. Later in the year, *The Two Fridas* was shown in New York at MoMA's exhibition *Twenty Centuries of*

Mexican Art. In 1940, Kahlo had an affair with Jewish art collector Heinz Berggruen while in New York City (Stechler 2005).

At this time, Kahlo was suffering greatly from health issues. She was also briefly detained in prison in Mexico for political reasons. On May 24, 1940, a Stalinist group made an unsuccessful attempt on Trotsky's life. Trotsky and his wife moved out of La Casa Azul to a more secure location. Rivera, who was wanted for questioning, went into hiding and later fled to San Francisco. On August 20, Trotsky was assassinated. The Mexican police took Kahlo in for questioning and held and interrogated her for two days before finally releasing her.

From the early 1940s into the early 1950s, as Kahlo was receiving even more recognition for her art, her health crises were increasing. Nevertheless, she continued her work and also her political involvement. For example, in 1941 Frida was one of twenty-five artist and intellectuals chosen by the ministry of education as founding members of the Seminar of Mexican Culture.[37] More and more of her works were exhibited in major cities in Mexico and across the US. At the same time, Kahlo's health continued to decline severely. She experienced great pain and underwent numerous additional surgeries.

Kahlo established personal connections with her many caregivers. This is understandable, given the centrality of pain and extensive health-care needs for most of her life. But the fullness of the relationships, as well as their Jewish dimensions and their relation to Kahlo's art and politics, are unusual. For example, Kahlo and Rivera met the US Jewish doctor Leo Eloesser in San Francisco when Kahlo was twenty-three. She originally consulted him regarding her foot and ended up maintaining a deep, multileveled relationship with him until her death. A young Kahlo painted a portrait of Eloesser and gifted it to him in thanks; she also gave him a self-portrait that she had painted. Eloesser spoke Spanish, loved the arts, and shared Kahlo's passion for left-wing politics. His boldness and radical spirit attracted Kahlo. In addition to being known for medical developments, Eloesser had helped to open the first Jewish orphans' home in San Francisco in the 1870s and stayed on as an officer (Kahn 2002, 228–29). Later, Eloesser went to Spain many times during the civil war to serve as a doctor with the Abraham Lincoln Brigade. After World War II, he traveled to China to assist with the people's medicine. Over their many years of close friendship, Kahlo and Eloesser shared their love of art and politics. Eloesser supported Kahlo when she was deciding to have an abortion and appreciated the artwork she did in relation to this event. He also helped facilitate her reunion with Rivera.

It is well known that Kahlo had many friends, but the fact that quite a lot of those closest to her were Jewish has not received adequate scholarly attention. Over the years, Kahlo's many friends and supporters played a crucial role in her survival, her art, and her politics. Kahlo surrounded herself with Jewish friends, forging and fostering many intense and intimate connections over her lifetime. In addition to those noted above as examples, among these were Galka Scheyer, founder of the artists' group the Blue Four, and Arcady Boytler, the Russian-born filmmaker to whom Kahlo gave her 1945 painting *The Little Deer*, and his wife, Lina.[38] Among her long-term, close Jewish friends were also Elise Haas of San Francisco, heir to her great-uncle Levi Strauss (who had no children of his own and whose family remains among the largest Jewish philanthropic donors to Bay Area artistic and progressive causes); the historian Meyer Schapiro; and the painter Olga Costa, another German Jewish immigrant to Mexico. In this extraordinary group we also find Ella and Bertram Wolfe, Raquel Tibol, and the painter Marc Chagall. While I do not pretend to provide an exhaustive list here, this accounting of Kahlo's close Jewish friends further includes the Mexican film producer and art collector Jacques Gelman, the artist Alfred Stieglitz (husband of Georgia O'Keefe), the art patron Albert Bender (often referred to as the best-known Jew in San Francisco in the 1930s), the painter Walter Pach, and the Romanian-born Edward G. Robinson (née Emanuel Goldenberg), who emigrated to the US, where he became a well-established actor and was blacklisted by McCarthy.

It was in 1944 and 1945 that Kahlo first began her serious study of Toro's two-volume work on Jews in Mexico during the Spanish Inquisition. Additionally, after reading Freud's *Moses and Monotheism*, in 1945 Frida painted *Moses*, an interpretation of Freud's work. In 1946, the Mexican Secretariat of Public Education awarded Kahlo the National Prize of Arts and Sciences for her *Moses*. In 1948, Frida reapplied for and was accepted back into the Mexican Communist Party (from which Rivera had been expelled in 1929, leading Frida to leave in solidarity; Rivera was not accepted back until 1954).[39] In the early 1950s, the incredible artist Gisèle Freund, a German Holocaust survivor, had traveled to Mexico to speak about her art. She connected with Kahlo at that time and ended up staying in town for a couple of years. Joining Kahlo's community seemed to have that sort of impact on people. In 1953, photographer and Kahlo's close friend Lola Àlvarez Bravo organized the first solo exhibition of Kahlo's works in Mexico. The exhibition ran from April 13 through 27 at the Galería de Arte Contemporáneo. Kahlo's doctor had told her she was not well enough to attend the opening. Kahlo had her bed loaded onto the back of a truck and driven to the exhibition. She attended the opening lying in her own bed.

On July 2, 1954, counter to the advice of her doctors, Kahlo took part in a demonstration against North American intervention in Guatemala. This turned out to be Kahlo's final public appearance. On July 13 Kahlo died in the Blue House. That afternoon, her coffin was placed in the entrance hall of the Palacio de Bellas Artes, attended by an honor guard. The next day, hundreds of people came to pay their respects. Kahlo's body was cremated later that day, and her ashes were placed in a pre-Columbian urn, which remains on display in La Casa Azul.

Conclusion

Despite the context that Kahlo created for herself, rich in ties with many Jews and entwined deeply with her life, politics, and work, I rarely encounter a scholar or pop enthusiast who has much idea that Kahlo had any such connection to the Jewish world. Kahlo's fame continued to build posthumously. Interest in her grew with a later burst of feminist energy. As a result of this new interest, biographers and scholars have plumbed virtually every aspect of Frida Kahlo's life for insight into her work. Even the performance artists and political graffiti group the Guerrilla Girls have a Frida Kahlo persona.[40] We know such an extraordinary amount about Frida Kahlo that the lack of awareness of her understanding of Jewishness and what it meant to her and for her art, life, and politics is quite striking.

In 2003, Gannit Ankori put a Jewish analysis of Frida Kahlo's art onto the map. Kahlo did not make it into *Jewish Women: A Comprehensive Historical Encyclopedia* (Hyman and Ofer 2006). However, she was then listed among the many feminists celebrated by the Jewish Women's Archive in their online exhibits ("This Week," n.d.).[41] As of today, her entry remains on the website. A Jewish feminist exploration of Kahlo that purposely brings together her life, politics, and art offers us many new opportunities to understand Kahlo, what was important to her, and her legacy.

A multivalent Jewish feminist examination of Kahlo also enables us to better understand additional important historical developments oft understudied. While any talk of Guillermo Kahlo usually operates within an Ashkenazi frame, we cannot really understand Kahlo's Mexican Jewish world without recentering Sephardi history. Further, A multilayered Jewish analysis of Kahlo allows us to spotlight the role of Protestant imperialism in defining Jewishness in narrowly religious (Christian) terms that fits the needs of expansionist global capitalism. We can see the ways that such colonial occupation contributes to a cultural genocide that erases Jewish lives, cultures, communities, and contributions. A lack of appreciation for Jewish ethnic diversity and Jewishness beyond a European frame contributes to anti-Jewish tropes found in critiques of Jews as elite puppet masters. Such a dearth of knowledge about Jewish multipositionality also functions by limiting the various and textured ways in which Jews understand that they can live, connect, make art, and engage in radical political transformation. Jewish feminist studies of the life and work of Frida Kahlo continue her resistance to antisemitism and call to us to create new forms of relation courageously and Jewishly.

Chapter 6

Gertrude Stein

A Queer Feminist Jew-ing:
Constraints and Possibilities for
Post-Emancipation Jewish Lives

The Jewish lesbian author who coined the infamous "a rose is a rose is a rose" and "there is no there there," Gertrude Stein was likely the first person to use the word "gay" in writing to refer to homosexual people, and she used it in a short story about two women ("Miss Furr and Miss Skeene"). It is also Stein who coined the now-famous term "the Lost Generation" after World War I. Some critics say that she brought down and rebuilt patriarchal language.

In this chapter I approach a study of Stein in a novel way, grounded in the multivalent Jewish feminist political thinking and methods used in the earlier chapters. This reorientation of Stein is intended to disorient a long line of interest in Gertrude Stein that does not take her Jewishness seriously. From this, I come to see Stein in a new manner, helpful for Jewish scholars and ordinary folk interested in Stein and to demonstrate how a Jewish focus can greatly expand ways that Stein-literature and other scholars can understand her, her work, and her legacy. Here we find (1) a Gertrude Stein steeped in the cultural women's Jewish traditions of her class, time, and family as core to her life's work, and (2) that understanding hostility toward Stein is best approached in feminist terms of her queerness and Jewishness.

Gertrude Stein (1874 to 1946) was a writer, a major figure in the art world, and the life partner of Alice B. Toklas. She wrote novels, plays, operas, essays, and numerous portraits in prose. Born in the US, she spent most of her adult years in Paris, where she hosted a salon that brought together intellectuals and artists from around Europe as well as expatriate and visiting luminaries from the US. While not always able to find publishers for her work, she wrote prolifically and gained significant celebrity during her lifetime. Stein is now considered an important literary figure, and, as F. W. Dupee (1962) noted, Stein had already gained prominence among modern literary giants by the early 1930s.[1]

In the mid-1930s, Stein returned to the US for the first time since 1903, for a highly successful lecture tour. Dupee (1962) states, "Just before her death her sayings and doings over there were much in the news in America, and her later writings, cast in a much-modified Steinese, were sought by the popular magazines . . . delivered from her hospital bed [is] the last specimen, and one of the most searching and comical specimens, of Steinese. 'What is the answer?' she inquired, and getting no answer said, laughing, 'In that case, what is the question?'"

I was first drawn to study Stein by seeing the feminist scholarship on Monique Truong's (2003) *The Book of Salt*. Truong is a Vietnamese-born US lawyer with a degree from Colombia University. *The Book of Salt* centers on her character Bính, a Vietnamese gay man living in Paris and working as a cook for Stein and Toklas. The story grew out of a reference made in Toklas's now-infamous memoir and cookbook to two Indochinese men working for Stein and Toklas as cooks (Toklas [1954] 2010).[2] Truong's novel portrays Stein's creative and radical use of language as inspired by Bính's struggles to learn a new language.[3] The character Bính also finds a journal Stein has been keeping on him; he recognizes his name in the journal but cannot read the rest of the English text.[4] *The Book of Salt* is a fabulous piece of fiction as well as political critique. Truong uses the novel medium both as art and as a significant critical engagement with colonialism. Stein's alternative brilliance, and indeed all art by radical Westerners, is implicated directly as colonialist: stealing from the colonized for what becomes their own benefit, in part through subjecting the colonized both to the imperial gaze and to the concretely exploitative economic relationship between the Global North employer and the Global South employee. Written from the perspective of Bính, this critique becomes all the richer by presenting Bính as a whole person, with a past and complex present, rather than a secondary figure (Stein's cook) referenced through a Global North figure (Stein). I loved that reversal, turning a colonial subject into a full human. At once intrigued and disturbed to find a Jewish, lesbian, gender-bending woman representing the colonizer, I needed to know more. More than a decade after I first read Truong, that "more" became this chapter.

After the previous chapters, readers will not be surprised to learn that most accounts of Stein's life and work emphasize her relationship to men and downplay her Jewishness. In biographies of Stein, the men who became some of the greats of modernism, such as Pablo Picasso, Henri Matisse, Ernest Hemingway, F. Scott Fitzgerald, Sinclair Lewis, and Ezra Pound, always appear central. Biographies of these men, on the contrary, rarely mention Stein and do not position her as an introductory figure to prove the eminence of the others. Feminist literary scholars and lesbian and queer activists and scholars have heralded Stein, although they rarely situate her among Jews, women, and feminist freethinkers, except for references to her long-term relationship with Alice Toklas. While there is Jewish-studies scholarship on Stein, even these studies rarely mention or analyze the ways that her life and work are steeped in Jewish history and contemporary Jewish trends. This chapter rectifies these gaps and brings into relief Jewish and Jewish feminist aspects and influences in Stein's life, work, and art.

Critics usually assume that Stein had little Jewish sensibility, and Jewishness is rarely the subject of serious academic analysis in Stein studies.[5] Interestingly, at the same time, some prominent contemporary Jews have vilified Stein in much the same way that many Jewish thinkers and organizations vilified Hannah Arendt after her work on Eichmann was published in 1963. Jennifer Ring's (1997) critique of the sexism and gendered aspects inherent in the vitriolic response to Arendt's work on Eichmann helps us understand the anti-queer and gendered sexism at work to marginalize Stein. Arendt became suspect as a woman intellectual who, while still a student, had had an affair with her professor, Martin Heidegger, later a member of the National Socialist Party. Extreme Jewish critiques of both Arendt and Stein mark an anti-queer orientation against prominent Jewish women who will not play the role of the "nice Jewish girl."

As we will see, Stein surrounded herself with women and often associated most closely with Jews. Jewish women figured prominently in both of these groups of Stein's closest associates. Moreover, Stein's life was grounded in the main trends impacting her Jewish ethnic identity at the time. This Jewish grounding played an important role in the numerous limiting and creative dynamics for her also as a female. These dynamics constrained her as a woman, a gender bender, a lesbian, and a Jew among many antisemites, both intimates and strangers; they also both constricted and enabled her unique life path and work. Stein's Jewish, feminist, lesbian, genderqueer, and simultaneously economically privileged ways of life and work formed mutually constitutive identities that, together with their attendant oppressions and access afforded, created the base for the independent intellectual and artist that she became.

It is time to do a feminist "Jew-ing" of Stein. In doing so, we will find unique lessons from Stein's legacy. As we saw in the chapters on Hannah Arendt and Frida Kahlo, a central post-Emancipation challenge is how Jews can be Jews and *also* people in the world. In some ways, Gertrude Stein provides a good case study of one who managed this multiplicity, her multiple positionalities, to a large degree. She had some of the most privileged and best experiences living an expansive life enabling her own unique expression while also nestled within generative collectives. But the example of her life and thinking also demonstrates to us that no one ought to expect that even a relatively successful Jewish life path as both particular and universal is going to be easy. Even with her family's wealth, Stein also faced tremendous challenges, as a woman, a lesbian, a gender nonconforming person, and a Jew. Additionally, in particular with a Jewish lens, Stein faced some of the worst examples of limitations on and genocide against Jews. While Arendt was a German citizen (until her citizenship was revoked under Nazi rule) who sought refuge in the US during the Holocaust, it is interesting to examine the example that Stein presents: a US citizen who seeks a personal and cultural refuge in France and then ends up living under the specter of Nazi occupation throughout the duration of the Holocaust. Stein lived through the Holocaust in Vichy France as an out Jewish lesbian who was older at the time. Her writing was on the Nazi lists of banned works by Jews. In this chapter, I will demonstrate that a significant lesson we can learn from a multilayered Jewish feminist study of Stein is that Jews who manage to live independent lives as both Jews and as people (and as women, and lesbians, and gender nonconformists, inhabiting multiple power positions such as in relation to colonialism) ought not expect that they will not face backlash. We live within intensely unjust systems. Even if one is doing relatively okay, backlash should be expected. For Stein, this backlash extends out seventy years postmortem to efforts to vilify her and her strategies for survival through one of the toughest situations for Jews in modernity, the Nazi Holocaust.

To do this feminist Jew-ing of Stein, I will first (re)present her basic biography. While I examine Stein through the prism of politics, the chapter then follows a mostly chronological structure. In part two, I explore

German Jewish migration to the US and the Stein family's US Civil War context, and then move on to the Vienna years and the Oakland base. In the next sections, I take a new look at Stein's early adult years at Radcliffe College in Cambridge and also at Johns Hopkins University in Baltimore. I address issues of the political context for women in the Jewish Reform movement before placing Stein's Parisian salon in the tradition of Jewish women *salonnières*, such as Rahel Varnhagen (explored in the chapter on Arendt). In the last section, I take up some aspects of Stein's situation as a US Jew (and an intellectual and out lesbian) in World War II France and a postmortem attack on Stein at a moment when her work and legacy were receiving a great deal of public recognition.

Feminist Jew-ing of Gertrude Stein

While even cursory biographies of Stein will note that she was born Jewish, not many scholars explore the centrality of Stein's Jewish context to her life and work. On the contrary, it is not uncommon for researchers to explicitly note that Stein created a life apart from Jewish influence and community and even accuse her of crimes of Nazi collaboration. Similarly, while scholars will note the close ties Stein had to clusters of creative men, they usually do not note the reality and import of Stein's relationships with women beyond her primary relationship to Toklas.[6]

The following is a version of the usual brief biography of Gertrude Stein: Gertrude Stein was a German Jew born on February 3, 1874, in Allegheny, Pennsylvania, to Daniel and Amelia Stein. Her childhood was rather nomadic, as in 1875, Daniel moved the family to Vienna, Austria, and three years later to Paris, France. It was not until 1879 that the family returned to the United States, settling in Oakland, California. Gertrude Stein's parents died when she was relatively young, her mother in 1888 and her father in 1891. After the death of her father, Stein moved to Baltimore to live with her aunt.

In 1893, Stein applied and was admitted to the Harvard Annex, a women's educational program preceding Radcliffe College. Gertrude Stein matriculated, having completed only one year of high school, primarily in order to join her brother Leo in Cambridge, Massachusetts. When Radcliffe was founded the following year, Stein enrolled there and proceeded to study psychology under the tutelage of William James. Following her graduation from Radcliffe, Stein enrolled in medical school at Johns Hopkins with a view to becoming a psychologist. After two years of medical school, she left the university.

Following some travel, in 1903, Stein moved to Paris to live with her brother, Leo. Their apartment at 27 Rue de Fleurs became the site for their famed salons, which hosted a number of well-known musicians, artists, and writers. Her home gallery walls featured works by Renoir, Cézanne, Matisse, and Picasso, and it is in large part through the Steins' support that these men became the renowned painters they are considered to be today. In 1907, Stein met Alice B. Toklas, who would become her life partner. Born into an upper-middle-class Jewish family in San Francisco, Toklas studied music at the University of Washington briefly before moving into Stein's Paris apartment in 1909. Due to a confrontation, Leo moved out of the apartment in 1913.

During her time in Paris, Stein wrote a number of what became her famous works, including *Three Lives* (1909), *The Making of Americans* (written 1903 to 1911), *Tender Buttons* (1915), *The Autobiography of Alice B. Toklas* (1933), *Wars I Have Seen* (1945), *Brewsie and Willie* (1946), and *The Mother of Us All* (1947). Only once, in 1934, did Stein travel back to the United States. The occasion of her return was for the opening of her opera, *Four Saints in Three Acts*. Following the opening, she went on a successful university tour across the US.

As World War II began to sweep across Europe, Stein and Toklas moved from Paris to Belignin, in southern France, and ultimately to Culoz, France, where they struggled through the Nazi occupation. Allegedly, Stein and Toklas used Stein's friendship with Bernard Faÿ, a prewar colleague who worked for the Vichy government, to avoid arrest during the war, and some controversy remains regarding Stein's purported involvement with the Vichy government. Undoubtedly, Stein and Toklas mobilized any number of strategies to survive. Stein and Toklas returned to Paris in 1944. In 1946, Stein died of cancer in Paris.

In this chapter, I will push this standard biography of Gertrude Stein in layered feminist ways and using a Jewish critical lens. Stein is known for innovations in writing that mirrored (and were mirrored by) the new movement among the painters whom she gathered and promoted. Stein undid our familiarity with language in her literary version of cubism to enable a "presentness." Her work cannot be reduced to the categories with which it is sometimes associated, such as surrealism (with which Kahlo is often associated in painting) or automatic writing. Innovative with language and style, she sometimes employed a playfulness that is politically quite serious. Stein's work is politically radical, calling into question core fictions of modernity with its investment in narrative and a presumption of a unified and coherent subject. By displacing the naturalness and centrality of narrative and subjectivity in modernity, Stein challenges not only artistic orthodoxies but political fallacies that bolster vacuity in supposedly democratic politics. Fascism exploited this vacuity, which enabled devastating systems and individuals to operate while refusing to recognize the fullness of a person's humanity.

Biographers usually make brief mention of the fact that Stein's parents were German Jewish immigrants to the US. However, Stein's relative lack of Orthodox religious upbringing apparently suggests to such biographers that her parents' heritage marks the end of Stein's Jewish context. Biographers will also point out the notoriously antisemitic and Nazi men with whom she kept company, such as Ezra Pound and Bernard Feÿ, but they ignore the ways that she built her life always grounded in deep primary relationships with other Jews. When we explore a bit more carefully, we find a very different story than the common biography of Stein. Although biographers most closely associate Stein, like Kahlo, with famous non-Jewish men, Stein re-created affective ties with Jews, particularly Jewish women, in most places where she lived during her unusual peripatetic youth. This web of Jewish relationships extends to the adult Gertrude Stein of Paris.

The adult Stein made her first home in Paris and launched her Parisian salon life with her Jewish brother, Leo. Her other brother and his Jewish wife also joined them in Paris. Additionally, as is well known, Stein made her adult life with Alice Toklas, a Jew from San Francisco, near Oakland, who was connected to that local community where Stein had passed part of her youth. Here, I will situate the mature Stein of the Parisian salons within a context of a long and vibrant tradition of European-heritage Jewish women *salonnières* who brought traditional Jewish intellectual and discursive traditions into the secular worlds of arts, culture, and politics. Following the Enlightenment, both hosting and attending salons, such as Stein's, became a contribution often distinct to Jewish women within cultures that significantly circumscribed the agency and participation in public life of most women, and especially of Jewish women. I argue that hosting a salon was among the ways in which Stein brought a Jewish association into her life and work as an adult in Paris. This assessment of a Jewish and women-centered Stein allows us to take a new look at posthumous anti-queer and gender-based sexist attempts to vilify Stein as a traitor to Jews and as a Nazi sympathizer. In this analysis we will find a range of possibilities for post-Emancipation Jewish life, both fraught and innovative.

The German Jewish Migration to the US and the Civil War Context

In this chapter, I use a Jewish, feminist lens to resituate Stein Jewishly and to recognize the primary relationships she had with women, Jews, and especially Jewish women. It is time to "Jew" Gertrude Stein. To do so, let us further unpack the brief biographical sketch provided above. This project will require a reorientation for Stein that may be somewhat disorienting to many readers. This move is necessary because of the nature and significance of Stein's literary and political contributions. Among her contributions, here I note in particular her contributions to modernism, which intended to decenter certainty and expose the disunity of the subject in the face of Liberalism's creation of a unified subject founded on the exclusion of all outliers. This decentering task itself is characteristically Jewish. This disorientation to reorient is crucial. Here we will Jew Stein and Stein's Jewishness, find a Jewish Stein, and explore new meanings that this work enables.

A nineteenth-century wave of German Jewish immigration to the US marked a significant new moment in US Jewish history. The first two waves of Jews to what became the US were those fleeing the Spanish Inquisition (called, from the Hebrew for those from Spain, Sephardis; Gorsky 2015) and those stolen from Africa during the Atlantic slave trade (Brettschneider 2015). The third significant Jewish migration to the US occurred with masses of Germans coming here. In the mid-1800s, the German states were experiencing an economic shift from small-scale family farming to industrialization. Seeking prosperity, many Germans relocated from rural areas to nearby cities only to discover high unemployment and little opportunity ("German Immigration" 2004). This rampant economic strife sparked a wave of mass migration across the region. From 1850 to 1880, over one million Germans immigrated to the United States, the majority of them Protestants, and roughly one-third Catholics ("German Immigration" 2004).

Of direct relevance for our study of Stein, during this same period, thousands of Jews from central Europe were also fleeing the region for the United States (Wineapple 1996, 10). In addition to economic strife, these immigrants were also seeking freedom from increasingly restrictive laws targeting Jews (Zollman, n.d.). For example, the *Matrikel* laws in Bavaria, enacted between 1813 and 1861 (Lowenstein 1981, 94), prohibited Jews from settling in their birthplace, starting a family, or often establishing businesses (Barkai 1985, 312, 313). As a result, approximately 150,000 German Jews made the journey to the United States during the mid-1800s (Diner 2009). Many of these newcomers initially became peddlers or traveling salespeople, particularly in the rural Midwest (Diner 2009). However, some soon shifted to opening industrial and commercial businesses in regions such as the Northwest and the East Coast. Several established their status in a burgeoning, although relatively segregated, Jewish high society in the US (Barkai 1985, 315).

Stein's grandparents were part of this German Jewish immigration, and it is within this Jewish context that Stein's family emerged in the transitioning Jewish racial and social order of the US. Originally from Bavaria, Stein's paternal grandparents arrived in Baltimore in 1841 (Wineapple 1996, 10). Their sons founded a clothing-manufacturing firm. This company became prosperous and, over time, propelled the family into the emerging higher echelon of Baltimore Jewish society (11). While less affluent than Stein's paternal grandparents, Stein's mother's parents were also successful German Jewish immigrants who settled in Baltimore. Her maternal grandfather opened a dry goods store, and her grandmother belonged to one of Baltimore's foremost Jewish families (11). Before marrying, Gertrude's parents had attended the same synagogue, the Orthodox Baltimore Hebrew Congregation (12). Thus, their marriage joined two well-respected German Jewish immigrant families. Gertrude's brother, Leo, later classified the Stein family as belonging to the "old bourgeois Jews of Baltimore," a societal ranking at the time above the then newly arriving eastern European Jewish immigrants but below the Sephardis, who were viewed as Jewish "aristocrats" (12).

It is important to note that, fleeing persecution and seeking economic opportunities, Stein's grandparents immigrated to the US and to Baltimore just prior to the US Civil War (1861 to 1865). At that time, Maryland was officially a slave state. The lived reality in this border state was complex. For example, free African Americans made up one-quarter of Baltimore's population, and the economy benefited from its mix of southern plantation slavery with northern mercantilism. There was no one "Jewish" experience of the US Civil War, as Jews lived in both the North and the South (and fought in their small numbers for both armies during the war). Stein's family is a good example of this. They were merchants, invested in the US clothing industry that required both southern cotton and northern manufacturing. In

1862, mid-war, Stein's father moved to Pittsburg, part of the Union, while much of her family remained in Baltimore, part of the Confederacy. Some members of Stein's family supported the Confederacy; others supported the Union (Roth Pierpont 2000, 35; Wineapple 1996, 12).

While neither serving as slaves nor considered Black, European-heritage Jews in the US (even those who emigrated from Germany) were not considered white and faced significant discrimination in both the Union and Confederacy. As Jews, they were seen as potential traitors, and the community's ties across the North and South aggravated these suspicions (Korn 1951; Rosen 2000; Rosengarten and Rosengarten 2002). In late 1862, the year Stein's family moved to Pittsburg (Hobhouse 1975), Ulysses Grant issued General Orders 9 and 10 banning Jews from traveling to the South and then General Order no. 11 expelling Jews "as a class" from territories controlled by the Confederacy and giving them twenty-four hours to get out. (Order no. 11 served to strengthen the previous General Order no. 2, regarding "cotton-speculators, Jews and other Vagrants.") While Stein's family was able to prosper economically (the new armies needed uniforms for their soldiers), these were also terrible times for Jews in the US generally, and especially for Jews in the areas impacted by these orders. As merchants and with family across the Union and Confederacy, Stein's relatives would have been at significant risk. Many Jews were forced out of their homes, stripped of their possessions, imprisoned, and generally terrorized. Lincoln rescinded the order in early 1863.

The Vienna Years

Motivated by both business prospects and his commitment to providing an urbane, cosmopolitan education for his five children, Stein's father relocated the family to Vienna in 1875, when Gertrude was three. After the Jewish Emancipation of Austria-Hungary in 1867,[7] Jewish immigrants from other areas in Europe moved to the city in droves, seeking the economic, cultural, and social opportunities that Vienna afforded (Rozenblit 1984, 22). By 1880, 726,105 individuals resided in Vienna, and 73,222 of them, more than 10 percent, were Jews (17).[8] Unlike the new gentile immigrants in Vienna, Jewish immigrants ascended the Viennese socioeconomic ladder in deliberately formed clusters. This route was in part dictated by the restrictions of operative antisemitism. These Jewish immigrants created their own Jewish middle-class communities and "provided themselves with an efficient brake against total assimilation" (88, 147). The connections among Jewish immigrants extended beyond religious affiliation, as Viennese Jews established charitable and literary societies as well as political organizations (147). Such networks obviated the need for Jews to enter into Christian intellectual society, from which they were often barred due to rampant antisemitism.

Below, we will see the ways that Stein carries through her lifetime the vibrancy of this relatively secular, and profoundly Jewish, context from her childhood world in post-Enlightenment Vienna. For the Stein family, Viennese cultural life and Jewish cultural life comingled. During their three-year sojourn in Vienna, the Steins participated in Jewish activities both religious and secular (Wineapple 1996, 15). While Daniel, Gertrude's father, returned to the US for the better part of a year on business, Milly, her mother, opted to stay with her children in the city, where they attended lectures, participated in Jewish women's intellectual salons, and stayed involved in the Hebrew Society (17). Thus, we see the depth of Stein's roots in Jewish women's activities and salons date at least from her mother's involvement during Gertrude's early youth in Europe. Following Vienna, the Steins briefly relocated to Paris before settling in Oakland in 1880, where they remained throughout Gertrude's high school years.

The Oakland Base

Stein's father, Daniel, advanced in his career, selling stocks and bonds before becoming the vice president of the California Bay Area Omnibus Cable Company (Wineapple 1996, 22). Such success for an Oakland Jew in this period is noteworthy; most of Daniel's Jewish contemporaries in the region were artisans or storekeepers (F. Rosenbaum 2009, 67). Just as Daniel had welcomed the cultural education that Vienna offered his children, he encouraged the children to partake in San Francisco's elite cultural events. In addition to receiving private instruction in music, the arts, and religion, the Stein children attended many of the main cultural events the city had to offer (Wineapple 1996, 22). The Steins also continued their Jewish activities in Oakland, which were inherently connected to this secular cultivation of the children's minds and vistas (37).

Although Oakland's Jewish population was increasing steadily in the 1880s, it remained below one thousand throughout the decade (F. Rosenbaum 2009, 67). Nonetheless, Daniel was an active member of the First Hebrew Congregation and a close friend to Rabbi Myer Sol Levy, and the Stein children attended the First Hebrew Congregation Sabbath school (Wineapple 1996, 22, 40). Also attending the Sabbath school during the 1880s was Judah Leib Magnes (1877 to 1948), who became a Reform rabbi, activist, and key proponent of the binational solution for Palestine (Brownfeld 2011), with which Hannah Arendt would also align herself. An ardent Zionist like Meir and Arendt, Magnes served as the first chancellor of the Hebrew University of Jerusalem and later as president.

While the Steins were residents, Jews experienced antisemitism in this context.[9] Still, Oakland also presented an unusual opportunity for cultural and economic growth for many Jews. Gertrude reflected that the Steins and their "rich right of living" were distinct from her peers in East Oakland (Wineapple 1996, 37). Indeed, the Oakland experience set Gertrude apart not only from her gentile friends in Oakland but also from her soon-to-be East Coast friends, who were virtual foreigners to the cosmopolitan, secular culture of the San Francisco Bay Area, in which Jews figured prominently. According to Fred Rosenbaum (2009, 68), Stein credited Oakland as "a special environment that brought forth a rare kind of fin de siècle Jew, one who knew no constraints."[10] Below, we will note Oakland's Jewish women's salons and what that rare kind of environment afforded a certain class of Jewish women in the area of the time. While Gertrude left Oakland as a teenager, this local culture continued to nurture other interesting Jewish women who would come (back) into Stein's life when she was an adult living in Paris.

Stein in Cambridge

After being raised abroad as well as in Oakland, Gertrude Stein attended the all-female Harvard Annex (Albright 1959). That Stein, a young Jewish woman hailing from outside of New England, managed to attend the Harvard Annex is remarkable. Founded by Elizabeth Cary Agassiz in 1879, the Harvard Annex offered courses to a mere two hundred women, primarily from the local area (Faust 2004, 453). Nevertheless, Stein began attending the Annex in 1893. She ultimately earned her undergraduate degree from Radcliffe College in 1898 (Albright 1959).

Fred Rosenbaum (2009, 82) describes Stein's group of Cambridge friends as "almost exclusively Jewish, and her closest companion was the brilliant Leon Solomons, from a noted San Francisco Sephardi family." In addition to her kinship with Solomons, Rosenbaum writes that Stein "felt almost tribal bonds of friendship with other Harvard Jews as well" (82).

While women were a minority at Harvard and subject to derision—reportedly taunted in the *Harvard Lampoon*, for example—the percentage of Jewish students was also small (Malkiel 2016; Wineapple 1996, 55). In 1908, the Jewish population at the university was 6 percent (S. Steinberg 1971). With their small numbers, Jewish students gravitated toward each other, and Stein and her brother, Leo, were no exception. The Stein siblings built lasting friendships, for example, with Adele and Ben Oppenheimer and Leo Victor Friedman (Wineapple 1996, 56).

Stein explicitly described her allegiance to fellow Jews in an essay she wrote while at Radcliffe: "The Modern Jew Who Has Given Up the Faith of His Fathers Can Reasonably and Consistently Believe in Isolation." In this early writing, Stein pointed to the need for Jews to be together, and reflected, "Wherever a Jew goes no matter into what strange lands and he meets another Jew, he has found a friend" (Stein and Feinstein 2001, 426). One of the few works in which Stein directly addresses the "Jewish problem," the essay portrays Jewishness as being both actualized by religious practice and inherited genetically. This rendering of Jews as a race echoed the prevailing racial science of the day (416). Interestingly, Stein argued that intermarriage between Jews (whether practicing or not) and gentiles "would be the death-blow of the race" (423). Working with Arendt's paradigms, we can understand Stein Jewishly and politically also. Often with Stein, we find the notion that a Jew who turns away from Jewish community will live an alienated existence. This is not generally the Stein discussed in academic studies or among more popular Stein aficionados.

In addition to ostracizing women, Harvard had a history of antisemitism. The Jewish population on campus steadily increased following Stein's era; it reached 20 percent by 1922 (S. Steinberg 1971). As a response to this influx, Harvard president Abbott Lawrence Lowell, in a now-infamous move, proposed establishing a quota to limit the Jewish student population. Such a measure would incrementally reduce the proportion of Jewish students to 15 percent. In a well-worn reversal of accountability, Lowell couched the Jewish quota as a means to curb the university's pernicious antisemitism (S. Steinberg 1971). For the most part, stakeholders rejected the original, explicit quota proposal. Instead, soon afterward, Harvard made changes in its entrance exam requirements, still effecting a decrease in its Jewish population to 15 percent by 1933, on the cusp of the Holocaust (Gladwell 2005).

Though Stein attended Radcliffe before the Jewish quota proposal, antisemitism flourished during her tenure there. In 1890, three years before Stein enrolled, a Harvard professor wrote in a questionnaire that "many Jews have personal and social qualities and habits that are unpleasant. . . . Most Jews are socially untrained, and their bodily habits are not good" (qtd. in S. Steinberg 1971). Harvard students also used what to them was a derogatory nickname for the campus dormitory where many Jewish students lived at the time: "Little Jerusalem" (S. Steinberg 1971).

Such prejudice was not uncommon among professors of the day. Indeed, it is still seen today and extends to other groups marginalized in US society. In recent years, Harvard has been undertaking some degree of reckoning with its past participation in, and benefit from, the US slave trade. Still, students at Harvard from non-elite backgrounds continue to face significant challenges, broadly within the university culture and specifically in practice. In 2024, for example, most of the country got to see a remaining anti-Jewish slice of Harvard culture during a tense period of the serious escalation of the Israel-Hamas war. Jewish, Muslim, and Palestinian students were subject to an increase in overt acts of hate. The Republican Party and other right-wing players exploited this situation to wage an explicit campaign against diversity initiatives on college campuses across the country. Among a spate of lawsuits and other attacks regarding the safety of Jewish and other minority students on campuses, women presidents (often the first women in such positions at these institutions) of three northeastern elite universities were called into congressional hearings. They were publicly grilled for hours about whether, and how, they were able to protect students in the minority—this, by publicly known antisemites and leaders of campaigns against progress on diversity issues. The first Black woman president at Harvard, Claudine Gay, faced the most intense scrutiny among those targeted. The sorts of problems faced by Stein and her Jewish cohort while at Harvard, as well as by students from numerous other groups over time, have not "been solved." Harkening back to Stein's days studying in the Ivy League, today's Jewish students' presence at such elite universities has fallen again to historic lows.

Johns Hopkins and Early Adult Life in Baltimore

After successfully graduating from Radcliffe, Stein entered Johns Hopkins University in 1897. Hopkins was by then considered a more progressive institution in extending education opportunities to women. Founded by a woman philanthropist in 1893, the Johns Hopkins School of Medicine is heralded as the first graduate-level medical school in the United States to admit both women and men (Sander 2002). In its first year of operation, roughly 16 percent of the students were women (Morgan 1986). This formal inclusion of women notwithstanding, female students often found themselves fodder for jokes and targets of taunting in the classroom and on campus, as at Harvard (Wineapple 1996, 124). Stein reportedly felt "snubbed [at Johns Hopkins] as a Jew and even more as a female" (J. Rosenbaum 2009, 82).

By the time Stein was in Baltimore for medical school, her German Jewish community had established itself. Already by the mid-1800s, some Jews had cultivated their own select place in Baltimore society. While the Baltimore Jewish community was considered relatively large for the US at the time, Jewish representation in the overall population of the city remained small. Approximately twenty-five thousand Jews inhabited Baltimore in 1902, constituting less than 5 percent of the total population (Barnett 1902, 62).[11] Stein still had family in Baltimore. When she and Leo relocated to the city together to pursue their education at Johns Hopkins following their time in Cambridge, they found themselves immediately welcomed into the exclusive high ranks of Baltimore's German Jewish society. The Stein siblings both relied on and resisted this cultural association. The Stein siblings maintained friendships from this period in Baltimore for decades. At the same time, Leo wrote scathing op-eds in the local Jewish newspaper, the *Jewish Comment*, in which he criticized the narrowmindedness and prejudice of the Baltimore German Jewish community in seeking to distance itself from the newer Russian Jewish immigrants so as to preserve their "respectability" (Wineapple 1996, 132). German Jews in the US had, as a group, assimilated enough to improve their class status, and they now looked down on the more recent eastern European Jewish immigrants as low class and uncivilized; in doing so, they were reproducing gentile antisemitic renderings of Jews in the West more generally.[12] Thus, Leo and Gertrude, who agreed with his criticism of the city's German Jewish elite as hiding behind "a complacent, assimilated gentility," found themselves on the outskirts of both the "old bourgeois Jews" and the general gentile society in Baltimore (Wineapple 1996, 132). Note, however, that Leo published this public condemnation in a Jewish newspaper. His was a critique made by a Jew, as a Jew, for Jews.

Not surprisingly, Jews were also a minority group at Johns Hopkins, and instances of antisemitism transpired there, as they had at Harvard. Gertrude's esteemed Hopkins professor John Whitridge Williams allegedly "couldn't stand her marked Hebrew looks, her sloppy work and her intolerance," according to her classmate Dorothy Reed Mendenhall (Wineapple 1996, 124). Just as Stein had sought out Jewish friends in Cambridge, she also befriended Jewish women at Johns Hopkins. Most notably, Stein befriended Claribel Cone, who was doing graduate research at Hopkins, and her sister Etta (Sander 2002). The parallels between Stein and the Cone sisters are unmistakable. The father of the Cone sisters was a German Jewish immigrant who had arrived in Tennessee in 1846. Also, similar to Stein, Claribel defied the expectations and limitations placed on women in the US in general as well as within their elite segment of the Jewish community regarding appearance, mannerisms, and aspiration (Wineapple 1996, 119). Avid art collectors, the Cones later frequented Stein's salons in Europe, and Stein wrote the 1910 prose portrait "Two Women" in honor of the sisters (see Rosenberg 2011).

Politics and the Jewish Reform Movement Context

While Stein is often portrayed as politically conservative,[13] it is helpful to put her politics into a Jewish context. Stein's life was anything but conservative, as references to her as an "unkept" woman, living publicly as a lesbian and a gender bender, make clear. Her life among artists, intellectuals, and freethinkers is also significant. Similarly, her work posed a radical political critique of oppressive presumptions of subjectivity. Still, Stein often spoke in national generalizations and hierarchies, and, as I discuss below, her political allegiance has been called into question because she managed to survive as a US Jew living in France during the Holocaust. At the same time, Stein's family's relationships within the Reform movement are also politically interesting.

US Jewish women of Stein's milieu were often leaders and otherwise active in various progressive causes both locally and nationally. These Jewish women of the late 1800s and early 1900s, many of them early feminists, chose a variety of venues for this work, including explicitly Jewish organizations, broader groups that were largely but not explicitly Jewish, and general US movements. In the era of Stein's youth and younger adult years, Jewish women were active in the US as feminists and specifically in movements for women's suffrage, contraception, peace, abolition, and the array of causes within what was called the "free speech" movement (for more elite Jewish women's roles in these movements, see Klapper 2013). Jewish women's activism in these issue areas crossed class lines as well as color and ethnicity ones. Those involved in these public political movements extended from poor, eastern European radicals like Golda Meir and Emma Goldman through to Stein's lighter-skinned, "genteel" German groups. Also, there were wealthy Sephardi women involved in most of the more elite Jewish women's groups. Some of the early politically active Jewish women's groups had both Ashkenazi and Sephardi wealthy women reformers who sought to assimilate their embarrassing eastern European cousins.

Middle-class US Jewish women of this era created and developed feminist groups still with us, such as the National Council of Jewish Women (NCJW), which worked on all of these matters.[14] NCJW comprised both upper-class Sephardi women, whose families had long been established in the US prior to the German Jewish emigration, and newly elite German Jewish women. Working-class Jewish women were often active on these and other social justice issues in their heavily Jewish anarchist, socialist, communist, and union groups. Jewish women, across class and Jewish ethnicity, were also involved in broader US groups, such as the League of Women Voters, suffragist organizations, contraception clinics, and the Women's International League for Peace and Freedom, as well as class-based organizations. The types of organizations, political analyses, and strategies developed among working-class Jewish women, such as Emma Goldman and Golda Meir, often differed from those favored by middle-class Jewish women. For example, Golda Meir's working-class, activist Russian-immigrant family also participated in socialist Zionism. Emma Goldman's working-class Russian-immigrant path was as a US and often universalism-centered anarchist. Working-class activists conducted their work largely in Yiddish, while those better off economically generally worked in English. Jewish women using English as their medium for activist work also tended to be somewhat more removed from their immigrant roots. Stein's family was associated with the more elite Jewish initiatives. But even among Stein's class, Jewish organizations and individuals, particularly Jewish women, especially feminists, were active in the public sphere. In particular, the Reform movement in the US, with which Stein's family was closely associated, was a leader in all of these areas.

The Reform movement, which prioritized progressive political causes, was a primary space for this sort of expression of Jewish political engagement and class assertions of identity in the US. Reform male rabbis and communal leaders mainstreamed progressive political priorities. Jewish abolitionists were usually associated with the Reform movement (Sokolow 2010). Women's efforts and voices were also prominent within the Reform movement, and Jewish women's engagement nurtured there often extended beyond the Jewish community. Many Jewish organizations and women's clubs, such as the salons that the women of Stein's family and their friends held and in which they participated, featured regular discussions and hosted speakers for education and action on these issues. Gertrude Stein's family, and particularly the women of her family, came from a community that was very public in its political activism as it worked to pursue progressive issues in a community context. During her time in Baltimore, Stein was called upon as a speaker for such women's groups.

Stein's Salons: A Jewish Women's Tradition

The Stein of the famed 27 Rue de Fleurs salon is of interest to many scholars and laypeople. Stein's hosting a salon seems to pique people's interest. This is rightly so; Stein ran a salon at her home that drew an array of trendsetters in the visual arts, literature, and ideas. The salon's feminist dimensions and grounding are significant and best understood in a Jewish context. Stein comes from a long line of women *salonnières*, and specifically a tradition of urban Jewish women *salonnières* across Europe and the US. The Parisian salon of Gertrude Stein did not emerge ex nihilo; Stein's salon belonged to a mode of being that had nurtured Stein throughout her life and that the mature Stein, in turn, chose to cultivate and carry forward. This was a distinctly independent Jewish woman's way of engaging actively with the world, and it was at once profoundly secular and deeply Jewish.[15]

Alice B. Toklas came from this Jewish women's tradition as well. For most of her early life, Toklas, who would become Stein's life partner, lived in San Francisco, not far from where Stein was raised. Toklas was connected to Stein through family relations such as Gertrude's sister-in-law Sarah. There were women's salons in Toklas's Jewish world. The wealthier Jewish women's salons in the Bay Area hosted meetings on a variety of topics, including the arts, but also on suffrage, birth control, peace, and other progressive political matters. Stein and Toklas did not meet until Toklas accompanied her neighbor to Stein's Rue de Fleurs apartment in 1907. This eventual crossing of paths in a foreign country illustrates the transnational interconnections among these Jewish women whose networks spanned the US from coast to coast and reached across the Atlantic.

Gertrude Stein was not the only Jewish woman connected to this Bay Area Jewish community to relocate from the US to Paris while maintaining deep connections to the US West Coast and her family's artistic and intellectual traditions. Within months of their arrival, Gertrude and Leo's brother Michael and his wife Sarah also moved to their neighborhood in Paris, where they remained until the 1940s (J. Rosenbaum 2009, 83). Together, these four formed an artistic Jewish enclave, which they dubbed the "Stein Corporation" (83). For a time, Sarah held her own salon, as a rival to Gertrude's, also on Saturday nights. The daughter of a Jewish lawyer, Sarah Stein also enabled several female Jewish artists and intellectuals from the Bay Area to move to their Parisian neighborhood and partake in the salons. Following the San Francisco earthquake of 1906, Michael and Sarah Stein's family returned to the Bay Area to assess their property and to showcase their newly acquired collection of works by Matisse (83). During their visit back to California, Sarah Stein made arrangements for Jewish sculptor and psychoanalyst Annette Rosenshine, a cousin and longtime friend of Alice B. Toklas, to work for the Stein family in Paris. Additionally, teenage pianist Theresa Ehrman (later Jelenko), whose father served as sexton at Temple Emanu-El, joined Michael and Sarah Stein's family in Paris to continue her studies in music and tutor the Steins' son in piano (83). Harriet Lane Levy, yet another Jewish woman and aspiring writer from this circle of Bay Area Jewish intellectual and arts-oriented women, also set out to join the Steins in Paris. Levy's next-door neighbor, Alice B. Toklas, who had been caring for her family in her grandfather's O'Farrell Street house, accompanied Harriet to visit the Steins and her cousin Annette (Levy 1996; Corn 2011). Upon arriving at the Stein apartment on the Rue de Fleurs, Toklas found Gertrude serving as Annette's psychoanalyst, while in return Annette typed Gertrude's manuscripts (Corn 2011).

In Stein's mature years, when she was running the salon in her Paris home, she continued to surround herself with Jews and particularly a set of Jewish women to whom she had closer ties. As noted, scholars on Stein usually situate her among a small group of non-Jewish male artists who achieved prestige and renown, in large part through Stein's activities on their behalf, such as Picasso and Hemingway. However, there are biographers, such as Linda Wagner-Martin (1995) and Brenda Wineapple (1996), who present detailed work on Stein's closest associates. While not the focus of their works, their examinations demonstrate that among the many frequent salon attendees, approximately half were women and a third were Jews. Among the Jewish regulars, the majority were women. Within this more intimate circle of Jews and women, Stein developed and maintained especially close ties with a few select Jewish women, such as Mina Loy and Natalie Barney

(Wagner 1995, 185). The mature Gertrude Stein who hosted the Parisian salon was forged from a long family and community line of Jewish artistic, bohemian, political, and intellectual trendsetters, and her salon continued to reflect this heritage.

Feminist historians have written reclaiming the significance of women's salons in Europe from the eighteenth to the twentieth century. Often, though not exclusively, hosted by elite women, salons provided a setting where women both literally and figuratively created a space for the leading discourse of their day. In these salons, women hosted, guided the tenor of conversations, selected and sometimes mentored the attendees, and selected the topics for discussion. Salons were also important places where women could participate in and lead semipublic gatherings among arts and intellectual leaders. In societies where women had few, if any, outlets for artistic, political, or cultural exchange and influence, the semiprivate nature of salon culture afforded certain women access to participate, and often lead, in forms of public discourse.[16]

The similar and distinct ways in which Jewish women developed and used salon culture have received less attention from feminist historians. While topics of theology or other matters of Jewish religious development might be discussed in Jewish women's salons on occasion, Jewish women more often created spaces for expertise outside the traditionally patriarchal zones of Jewish religious thought and learning. These secular Jewish spaces were part of a radical reformulation of Jewish possibility within and following the Enlightenment. The innovative salon context allowed Jews to transition from largely ghettoized religious communal structures to newer communal configurations that remained solidly Jewish while simultaneously permitting their members to feel at home in the world.[17] In this, we find close parallels for Stein with the aspirations and some successful practices of other women as different from each other as Kincaid, Meir, Arendt, Kahlo, and Goldman.

For example, prior to Stein, among the first European Jewish *salonnières* were Fanny von Arnstein and her sister Cäcilie von Eskeles, who hosted a salon in Vienna in the mid-1780s (Bilski, Braun, and Botstein 2005, 34–35). Berta Zuckerkandl-Szeps formed her early-twentieth-century salon in the tradition of Arnstein's (87). In Berlin, Henriette Herz and Rahel Levin Varnhagen were also hosting salons around the turn of the nineteenth century. Herz's literary salons brought together a collection of emancipated Prussian Jews, whereas Varnhagen's focused more on politics and philosophy (Bilski, Braun, and Botstein 2005, 27–28; Spiel and Wise 2013). Amalie

Beer's salon became Berlin's premier musical lounge during the 1820s, and Fanny Mendelssohn Hensel's musical salon similarly in 1830s Berlin (Bilski, Braun, and Botstein 2005, 38–42). Toward the end of the nineteenth century, Anna Kulisciofff's subversive political salon hosted journalists, socialist leaders, seamstresses, and rice pickers alike, providing a place of refuge for leftists of all walks of life to exchange ideas (76–78). Margherita Sarfatti's early-twentieth-century salon attracted Milan intellectuals and artists, and her Roman salon in the 1920s has been heralded as the most important salon of the era (99–103).

Therein, in large part, lay the attraction of Rahel Varnhagen and her salon for Hannah Arendt. In and through her salons, throughout the shifting course of her life, Varnhagen negotiated new terrain on how to be Jewish—particularly, a Jewish woman—and a full participant in her political and cultural milieu. Varnhagen's troubled navigations became a source of deep exploration for Arendt in her examination of justice and of how Jews can be Jews (avoiding both cultural and literal genocide) and full participants in modernity. (Arendt's work broke significantly from the young Stein's perspective on Jews keeping to their race as a way to be "in" the world.) For the next century after Varnhagen's salons in Berlin, Jewish women developed and adapted her creative, if tense, balance between Jewishness and full participation in the surrounding milieu. Gertrude Stein's family history and her own life choices situated her firmly within this secular Jewish feminist tradition.

A US Jew in Nazi-Occupied France

Questions regarding how Gertrude Stein could live through World War II as a Jew in France have interested scholars and Stein's fan base for a long time. In this section I present the contours of this conversation over time. In particular, this will then let us queer Ring's (1997) gender-based assessment of the Jewish "fall" of Hannah Arendt. Stein's out lesbian status and her genderqueer physicality enable us to note the heterosexual/queerly gendered aspect of hostility toward certain Jewish women for their not being "nice Jewish girls." I offer this reading of "famous" and extraordinary women such as Arendt and Stein to enable us to see that all Jewish women, feminists and allies, are potentially subject to such public enmity and "canceling."

Stein and Toklas were Jewish women and known lesbians who somehow managed to stay alive throughout the German occupation of France during World War II. Stein, moreover, was old enough at the time for deprivations to present additional challenges to her survival. Stein and Toklas left Paris and lived mainly in Bilignin and then Culoz during the war years. Bilignin is approximately fifty kilometers from the internment camp created at Fort Barraux. Culoz is approximately an hour from Gurs, where the German Jewish Hannah Arendt was in an internment camp and where if Frida Kahlo had Jewish women relatives in Baden-Baden they may well have been sent (before being sent to their deaths). Stein and Toklas were US citizens, unlike Arendt's and Kahlo's relatives, who had German citizenship until it was revoked by the Nazis, and unlike the countless other Jews taken from France. Stein (1945) writes about some of her experiences, anxiety, and their reasons for deciding to stay in France in the intense work *Wars I Have Seen*.[18]

Numerous sources (e.g., Sterling 2011) bring together the literature on Stein's situation during the Holocaust. In this section, I first note the general historical context and then review some of the most prominent works in English on the controversy of Stein's survival. In the end, I cannot stake a position in a binary argument on whether Stein was an evil collaborator and Jew hater or a Jewish victim. The parameters of this version of the debate yield little understanding of the travails of these lesbian Jewish US citizens living through World War II in Vichy France. This binary framing does, however, point to the ways that Jewish women are easily demonized for using their wits and survival strategies even in clearly complex and deadly circumstances.

As we note as of import for at least Meir, Arendt, Kahlo, and Goldman, France and Britain declared war on Germany following Germany's invasion of Poland in September 1939. On May 10, 1940, Germany invaded France and occupied the northern part of the country, including Paris, where Stein had been living. A new regime, referred to as Vichy, was established in the unoccupied southern portion of the country, south of what was termed the line of demarcation (as established by the Armistice of June 22, 1940). While technically governing a "free zone," Vichy leaders have long been criticized for collaborating with the Nazis. Conditions for those remaining in France during the war were very difficult. Even those in the south faced significant food and fuel shortages. Those in the north endured the stresses of living under direct German occupation. Those in the south had to contend with German directives to quarter soldiers, who were present throughout their territory. The Vichy government was suspended in late 1944, before the Allies liberated France.

Initially, the Nazis did not formally target US citizens living in northern France. However, informally, the Nazis made distinctions between white, Christian US citizens and Jewish and African American US citizens from the beginning of the occupation, and these widened as the war progressed. For example, even prior to the US entering the war, the Nazis required Black US citizens to report to the police with no protection from the US consulate. Additionally, Nazis sought to wipe out what they called "degenerate Jewish-Negro Jazz" (Glass 2010, 5) by detaining some African American jazz performers in Paris. Approximately two thousand US citizens remained in Paris after the US declared war following the bombing of Pearl Harbor in 1941. At that time, the Nazis ordered all US citizens to register with the nearest German *Kommandatur* and to report to local police stations weekly. Differential treatment continued in the north, where, for example, the Nazis arrested 340 American men under the age of sixty, a disproportionate ninety-five of whom were Jewish. Additionally, later in the war, Germans arbitrarily ceased to recognize the passports of US Jews (Glass 2010).

In the south, the situation for US citizens was a bit different from that in the north. Charles Glass notes that "American Jews, including Gertrude Stein and Alice B. Toklas, who had left Paris before the occupation, remained in the so-called Free Zone, where the Vichy government—to maintain cordial relations with Washington—did not discriminate against them as it did European Jews" (148). Additionally, Mitchell Bard (1996) writes of the lesser-known history of US citizens interned in Nazi camps, and the differential treatment of Jewish US citizens and soldiers. According to Glass, however, no (US) Americans were interned in Vichy. Still, the situation of US citizens likely became more precarious as the war continued and US-Vichy relations deteriorated. In 1942, Germany entered Vichy France and occupied the US embassy, leaving US citizens with no embassy to represent them.

For Jews in France in general, the war was catastrophic. On the eve of the Second World War, there were at least 300,000 Jews in France. About two thirds of these were immigrants from eastern Europe. Half of these immigrants arrived in France during the decade before World War II. Many of them had first emigrated from Poland to Germany, which they left for France after the Nazis rose to power. The majority of these immigrants did not receive French citizenship, even after years of living in France. In this crucial moment in France, those such as Arendt shared the same fate as the more recent immigrants from eastern Europe to Germany. The importance of this status became clearer during the primary years of deportation (1942 to 1944); "stateless" Jews such as Arendt were the first to be deported.

At the time of the German occupation of France, new anti-Jewish laws were passed and continued to be developed over time. Germans instituted anti-Jewish laws in the north. The statutes in the Vichy south aimed at depriving Jews of citizenship and the right to hold public office, generally designating Jews as a distinct and lower class and paving the way for deportation and extermination.[19] From the time of the German occupation of northern France, many Jews fled Paris and northern France. By October 1940, about 150,000 Jews had crossed the demarcation line to seek protection from the Vichy regime in the south, only to find they were subjected to fierce discrimination along lines similar to what was practiced under the formal German occupation in the north. Twenty-six internment camps were set up in the north, among which Drancy, near Paris, was the most central. The Vichy government established additional camps in the south. By the autumn of 1942, some 42,000 Jews had passed through the Drancy transit camp. Nearly one-third of these individuals came from unoccupied France. A significant percentage of these victims were foreign or stateless Jews, sacrificed by the Vichy government, supposedly in a vain attempt to spare France's Jewish citizens. Out of a total of 75,721 deportees from Vichy, fewer than 2,000 survived. Of the approximate 300,000 Jews total, about 25,000 French Jews and 50,000 foreign Jews were deported from France to extermination camps in Germany or eastern Europe. Including the Jews who died in concentration camps in France, historians note that 90,000 Jews from France were murdered; this constituted nearly one-quarter of the total French Jewish prewar population (Marrus and Paxton 1981).

Additionally, in 1935, the Nazis broadened the 1871 provision in the German criminal code outlawing same-sex sexual acts between men (East Germany only abolished the Nazi additions in 1950 and revoked the law itself in 1988. In West Germany, the law was not repealed until 1994.) The Nazis extended the law to include "lewd acts" that did not include physical contact. Those deemed homosexuals and others accused under this law were sent to concentration camps during the Holocaust. The Nazis murdered most of the approximately ten thousand people sent to the camps for the crime of homosexuality, whether their being gay was real or imagined.[20]

Now we return to the specificity of Stein's circumstances after she and Toklas fled Paris and took refuge in Belignin and then Culoz in the south of France. There is a litany of reasons for the critique against Stein, beginning with the very fact that she survived such deplorable conditions and avoided the fate of the many thousands of other Jews who were murdered. Critique aside, some applaud her luck and ingenuity. A 1934 *New York Times* interview notes that Stein said publicly that Hitler should be awarded the Nobel

Peace Prize.[21] She supposedly supported Franco and denounced Roosevelt. Stein translated works by Philippe Pétain into English and praised him in writing.[22] Above all, critics point to her troubling long-term relationship with Bernard Faÿ.

Faÿ (1893 to 1978) was a French historian who focused primarily on US culture. Faÿ was a gay man, a public antisemite, and an active opponent of the Freemasons. He became an official in the Vichy government. Stein and Faÿ had begun their friendship and collaboration long before World War II. Scholars question their alliance, and particularly note that Faÿ seems to have been instrumental in the complex web of tactics allowing Stein and Toklas to survive the war in France. After the war, Stein wrote a letter on Faÿ's behalf for use in his defense at his trial for Nazi collaboration.

Understandably, scholarship on Stein's life during the war presents a precarious situation. As early as 1974, James Mellow, in his *Charmed Circle*, questioned Stein's situation in Vichy France, although he did not conclude with an outright condemnation. In 1995, right-wing Jews circulated misinformation in the Jewish press about Stein "lobbying" the Nobel Peace Prize committee on behalf of Hitler (see Stendhal 2012; Dydo and Burns 1996, particularly the appendix). Literature on Stein continued to address the issue, but a full-scale Jewish outcry did not erupt until 2012, nearly seventy years after Stein's death. (For an overview, see Michael Lerner's [2012] tepid editor's introduction to Stendhal [2012].)

Much of the scholarship had long presented nuance. For example, in her 1995 *"Favored Strangers": Gertrude Stein and Her Family*, Linda Wagner-Martin gives a historical account of Gertrude and Alice's lives during World War II. Wagner-Martin (1995) argues that Stein used her friend Bernard Faÿ's position in the Vichy government for security. She notes that Stein translated Pétain's speeches because she, like many others, appreciated Pétain's early role in preventing a total German occupation of France, not because she sympathized with the Vichy government. I doubt that most any Jew who might have had prewar connections to a Nazi who could keep them alive would not seek to rely on those ties. Wagner-Martin argues that the war entailed many contradictions and the apparent cooperation of Stein with the Vichy government should not shock contemporary readers. In Stein's defense, Wagner-Martin also clarifies that Stein played a role in the resistance and claims that Stein harbored sympathizers to the resistance simultaneously with maintaining her friendship with Faÿ.

We can also take a comparative look at Josephine Baker's circumstances in this context. During her war years as a spy for the Allies, Baker could likely be described in much the same terms as Stein. One could note

Baker's exchanges with French and other elites during the war to present her as a Nazi collaborator. In fact, however, Baker developed these ties at great personal risk. She had been approached to be and took on the work of a spy for the Allies. Despite some Jewish critics who say that Stein and Toklas "lived it up" in war-torn France, Wagner-Martin portrays Stein's life under the occupation as unbearable, marked by deprivation, filled with fear and uncertainty. Stein and Toklas were obvious targets. Stein's work was on the French list of forbidden books by Jewish authors. Stein and Toklas lived with deprivations similar to those of others in the south of France; they endured scarcity of food, lack of fuel for heat and other needs, and, of course, the ever-present threat of war, as well as the requirement to quarter soldiers (Italian, German, and then US).

In a somewhat different vein, Janet Malcolm argues that Faÿ intervened with Pétain on behalf of Stein and Toklas to ensure their survival. To make this point, Malcolm (2007, 50) cites a letter written by Faÿ stating that Pétain had agreed to look after Stein and Toklas. Nonetheless, Malcolm accepts that cooperating with a Nazi collaborator (Faÿ) was complex for Stein. Here Malcom offers the example of Stein's testimony in front of the court that ultimately convicted Faÿ of Nazi collaboration. Stein's testimony stated that Faÿ saved her paintings, but Malcom notes that the friendship between Stein and Faÿ is apparent.

In an opposing view, Barbara Will (2011) also outlines the origins of the friendship with Bernard Faÿ and argues that this friendship contributed to Stein's cooperation with the Vichy government. In this work, Will accepts that the World War II period in France produces a gray area for evaluations of Stein's life. Nonetheless, Will argues that Stein exploited her friendship with Faÿ and collaborated with the Vichy government, as demonstrated, in her view, by Stein's translations of Pétain's speeches. Further, Will argues that Stein survived the German occupation of France because of her friendship with Faÿ and attributes their mutual survival to "the complex web of double dealing and backstage mechanisms within which both individuals were trapped" (148). I have yet to review an account of partisans, Jewish women couriers, resistance fighters, and ordinary people during Nazi reign who did not demonstrate this fraught and stressful complex web.

Will's work was at the center of a renewed, primarily right-wing, Jewish anti-Stein campaign in 2012. Think cancel culture is new and only possibly with online social media? Around that time, three important public exhibitions featured Stein. In 2011, the San Francisco Contemporary Jewish Museum developed an exhibit on Stein, which then moved to the Smithsonian's National Portrait Gallery in Washington, DC. Stein was originally included in a 2012 celebration of Jewish American Heritage Month at the White House, but she was quickly removed in response to protest. There was another exhibit on Stein at San Francisco's Museum of Modern Art. This exhibit then came to New York's Metropolitan Museum of Art. Some high-profile Jews[23] campaigned publicly and vehemently to include notice of Stein's activities in Vichy in the exhibition of her art collection at the Met.

In 2012, Charles Bernstein collected numerous documents that, taken together, present Stein's views and actions on this issue in a more positive light. He notes that those arguing that Stein was a collaborator tend to avoid numerous significant aspects of her record during these awful years. For example, Bernstein brings back into public view pertinent issues related to works Stein published in the years of the war. With this, he clarifies for ordinary readers that Stein worked with unusual publishers committed to intellectual freedom during these repressive years. In a related vein, the views of most Jewish feminists with whom I have spoken sound similar to arguments presented by Bernstein; they consider it obvious that Stein's comment about Hitler was meant ironically and any other interpretation shows lack of contextual understanding.[24] Also related to the content of Stein's work during this period, we find that Stein wrote her opera, *The Mother of Us All*, directly following the war. The opera is a clear celebration of US-style democracy.

We must put an examination of Stein in this manner into perspective: Stein was not the only Jew to survive under Vichy, nor the only Jewish US citizen to have made it through the war years in southern France. Many have shown some sympathy for Stein in trying to understand the extraordinary difficulty she faced as a US Jew in Vichy France. Most detractors do not examine the fact that in addition to being Jews, Stein and Toklas were quite public as lesbians prior to the war. The vitriolic nature of the attack on Stein for surviving, however, also requires some unpacking. Yes, she found fame, and being in the public eye tends to invite a level of scrutiny that the thousands of other less public queers, Jews, and US citizens like her managed to avoid. Because she was a public figure, we also know of at least some of the complex alliances that she forged and maintained to help protect herself and Toklas, as well as the resistance fighters they supported. Stein's long-standing, somewhat convoluted politics of conservatism, and in particular her belief in the "nature of races," at the very least complicates matters, as does her radicalism (in defying the confines of an empty modern subjectivity, itself exploited by the very fascists against whom she struggled to survive). The most helpful analysis of the venom underlying the "case against Stein," however, must come from a Jewish feminist queer context. To undertake this, let us turn to Jennifer Ring's analysis of the bitter tone of the Jewish castigation of Hannah Arendt for her work on the trial of Adolph Eichmann.

Arendt attended the Eichmann trial in Jerusalem, reported on it for the *New Yorker*, and later published these articles as the book *Eichmann in Jerusalem*. A well-known Jewish figure, prominent intellectual, and Holocaust survivor, Arendt had been associated with various Jewish and Zionist groups for most of her life. Numerous Jewish intellectuals and organizations, with some of whom she had long enjoyed good relations (such as Gershom Scholem), were vile and unforgiving in their response to Arendt's work on Eichmann. Ring (1997), however, notes how much Arendt's work actually borrowed from that of Raul Hilberg, itself quite problematic. Interestingly, Ring points out that Hilberg did not meet with the kind of scathing criticism reserved for Arendt. Hilberg is still seen as a prestigious Holocaust studies scholar. Ring's careful analysis argues that the difference in response to the two thinkers points to a gendered problem. Arendt was taken to task as a woman. Ring includes a queer-style analysis of the ways that antisemitism in the West has operated by "feminizing" Jewish men and "masculinizing" Jewish women. The public perception (not necessarily substantiated) of Arendt's critique of Jewish leadership during the Holocaust threatened the new heteronormative patriarchal strategy of standing up to much historic Western antisemitism by reclaiming a Western-style masculinity for Jewish men. As a prominent, independent, and outspoken thinker, Arendt ultimately faced policing for not being a patriarchal and heterosexist version of a good Jewish girl.

While Stein's survival in Vichy France has been treated as the subject of scholarly inquiry, the most vile and extreme critiques came from right-wing Jewish men picking up on Will's 2011 work. Ring's detailed analysis of the sexist and homophobic aspects of the vilification of Arendt is most helpful in assisting us with understanding the "controversy" regarding Stein and her purported Nazi collaboration. Stein was a well-known gender-bending, nonconformist Jewish lesbian.

As for me, I have no need to enter the debate to merely excoriate or defend Stein, and I would be surprised to find any simple story of heroism. The feminist methodology I employ throughout this work, treating the political as personal, comes from a move in feminism that requires us to allow our foremothers their complexity and lack of pristine ethical binaries.

Ring's assessment of the extreme nature of the attack on Arendt seems a fitting contribution to understanding the Jewish anti-Stein vitriol. Arendt and Stein are both complex thinkers and figures, defying easy categorization. They are also excellent examples of how public Jewish women can evoke patriarchal and anti-queer ire for not being "nice Jewish girls."[25] The Stein controversy, nearly seventy years after her death, erupted in a world in which Jewish feminist, lesbian, gender-bending, and queer activism had long been a norm. But decades of feminist, lesbian, gender-bending, and queer activism clearly do not mean that this struggle is over.

Conclusion

In this chapter I undertake a feminist Jew-ing of Gertrude Stein and her legacy. A complex figure, Stein has been the subject of much academic inquiry in literature studies, by feminists, and to some degree in Jewish studies. Similar to Kahlo, Stein is also an iconic feminist and lesbian pop-cultural figure. She would likely revel in her contemporary celebrity and be incessantly hurt by any criticisms made against her. In this examination, I do not pretend to understand some "true" Stein, or to "represent" her. I have used my training as a political theorist to bring together feminist, queer, class-based, antiracist, and de-colonial analytic frames through a Jewish lens. In doing so I find a rich example of a Jew living out some of the best opportunities available and the toughest situations presented to post-Emancipation Jews.

Racist, elitist, anti-woman, transphobic, heterosexist, and antisemitic views and systems were rife in the various contexts of Stein's life, spanning seven decades and numerous major urban centers across two continents. These views and systems, both similar and different to those contouring Stein's circumstances, are with us still today. Stein, clearly brilliant, also benefited from privileges of wealth, light-skin/European culture, and cosmopolitanism, making possible some of the opportunities available to her as a Jewish woman and lesbian of her time. She was a somewhat rootless cosmopolitan, wandering around in diaspora and making multiple homes, as did all the women in this study, from Kincaid in chapter one to Goldman in the next chapter.

At a historical moment when many think they have "figured out" Jews, or that European-heritage Jews are somehow now "fine" and proceed easily in the Christian-dominated West, we need new analyses of figures such as Stein even more. Jews have not figured out a simple mode of living full lives in societies where some aspects of historical Christian antisemitism are more underground (and too often still blatant). Anti-Jewish views and systems operate well beyond Christiandom. Pressures of assimilation and cultural genocide remain intense even in the US. Additionally, across the globe, Jews of every cultural group, nation-state, and skin pigmentation still seek to create vibrant lives as Jews and as humans—on their own, with Jews, and with many other "others."

The challenge of how to be a Jew and how to be a person remains before us. Stein's life and legacy show us that living rich lives as Jews, however we define that, is possible. This queer feminist Jew-ing of Gertrude Stein also shows us the many ways that we cannot expect such life paths to be easy in a world still wracked by insecurity, fear, and outrageous exploitation.

Chapter 7

Emma Goldman

Anarchist Feminism, a New Frame for Diasporic Longings and Jewish Studies?

I want freedom, the right to self-expression, everybody's right to beautiful, radiant things.

—Emma Goldman, *Living My Life*

Anarchism, then, really stands for the liberation of the human mind from the dominion of religion; the liberation of the human body from the dominion of property; liberation from the shackles and restraint of government. Anarchism stands for a social order based on the free grouping of individuals for the purpose of producing real social wealth; an order that will guarantee to every human being free access to the earth and full enjoyment of the necessities of life, according to individual desires, tastes, and inclinations.

—Emma Goldman, "Anarchism: What It Really Stands For"

My first class in graduate school was an introduction to political theory. The professor was the first WASP I ever really knew well, as straight, white, cis, male, US-born, and elite as they come. In his way, he unexpectedly showed me a path for my career doing Jewish feminist political theory. He was a self-identified radical Presbyterian, an elder in his church, an anarchist. He taught us to understand Marx in the Hebrew prophetic tradition, railing against injustice and calling us to our best collective responsibilities. He introduced us to Marx as a messianic figure (others call such revolutionaries "utopian"), a secular thinker and activist leading us on a journey of collective liberation. He ended the course, which surveyed thousands of years of Western political thought, with anarchism.

I had already begun studying Emma Goldman on my own at this time.[1] I read in Goldman's "Anarchism: What It Really Stands For," "Anarchism is the great liberator of man from the phantoms that have held him captive . . . Anarchism has declared war on the pernicious influences which have so far prevented the harmonious blending of individual and social instincts, the individual and society. Religion, the dominion of the human mind; Property, the dominion of human needs; and Government, the dominion of human conduct, represent the stronghold of man's enslavement and all the horrors it entails" (Goldman [1917] 1969, 52–53). The Jewish grounding that my professor had insisted on for Marx made sense for me in understanding both Goldman and anarchism, and this helped to solidify my interest.

Both in the US and internationally, Goldman earned a reputation as a prominent Jewish radical feminist.[2] Goldman's became a household name at a time when that was extremely rare for a woman, and particularly for Jewish women. As feminists today, we often do not know much about the history of the feminist movement or its vibrancy in the 1800s and early 1900s. Additionally, many today are not aware of the significant role that anarchism played in feminism and the Left more generally, nor of Goldman's leadership in this movement. We also have lost much of the anarchist roots of our Jewish history of thought and activism on the left. It is helpful to get a sense of the ways in which Emma Goldman, Jewish anarchist and feminist, inspired many in her day and ours. Readers: Don't get nervous. I will explain what I mean by anarchism. Despite scary renderings in the media, it's a legitimate political theory that is quite interesting.

While any biographical note on Goldman will mention that she was born to a Jewish family, most say little to nothing of explicit Jewish interest, despite the rich Jewish context for her life and work. Scholars often dismiss Goldman's Jewish grounding, either as part of a tendency to ignore Jewishness in general or because Goldman was so explicitly anti-religion. As addressed in this book, people often conflate the absence of Jewish religious observance with a lack of Jewish import for the individual. Like most Jews in the US even in her day, Goldman was secular and identifiably Jewish culturally.[3] She was concerned about the potential statism of Zionism, though, at the time, most Jews in the US and globally, of all political stripes, were similarly not Zionist. She also never hesitated to offer apt critiques of Jews whose politics differed from hers (Wexler 1989, 41).[4] In all of this, and using a Jewish feminist critical lens, we can see Goldman engaged with Jewish political issues of her day.

Emma Goldman and anarchism more generally are foundational to the US Jewish experience. As Paul Avrich (1988, 188) notes, for a period in the late 1800s central to Goldman's contribution, "Anarchism emerged as probably the largest and certainly the most dynamic movement among Jewish radicals in the United States . . . they played an important role in the social and cultural life of the Lower East Side and of ghettos in other cities, organizing clubs, cooperatives, and mutual-aid societies, sponsoring lectures, picnics, and concerts . . . creating a kind of alternative society, or counterculture." More broadly, in his three-part essay in *Tablet* magazine, Paul Berman (2019) assesses the Jewish immigrant and refugee anarchist tradition at the beginning of American Jewish culture.[5]

Emma Goldman's anarchism held a central commitment to the deep liberation needed for the internally linked combination of individual freedom and ending systemic exploitation. Our activism and lived lives require attending to the full worth of each, in their social context, through collective action. This has been central for feminism, the development of the concept that the personal is political, and more recently the articulation of intersectionality. This connecting of personal liberty within a community-based commitment to ending oppression as we see it on individual, group-based, and structural levels also formed a basis for the self-conscious political and cultural shift in queer liberation.

Identified as "the most dangerous anarchist in America" of her day and a "most dangerous woman,"[6] she was accused of terrorism for her political ideals and activism in a way that foreshadowed the ensuing century of US elites targeting justice workers by calling them terrorists. Emma Goldman is a key Jewish feminist political thinker worthy of our serious attention. Increased awareness of Emma Goldman and her tradition of anarchism would likely well serve Jewish feminists and their allies today. Goldman and her anarchist context are far more Jewishly inflected than most renditions of that history acknowledge or take seriously. Awareness of the principles of this political theory and Goldman's period of activism will help us ground our understanding of post-1960s US feminism and Jewish feminism in ways that we can mobilize concertedly today. More broadly, for Jews and Jewish studies, anarchist theory and what that meant for this historic Jewish feminist activist and thinker are among the best frames for understanding Jewish life without a central authority structure, and particularly in the diasporic context.

Despite common reference to anarchism as merely chaos and violence, anarchism is a robust political theory and historically a dynamic transnational political movement. What we can note in the process of taking Goldman seriously is that, empirically, Jewish life mainly operates within an anarchic field, as complicated as this is in actuality. Normatively, I thus also suggest that a more conscious grounding in anarchism, and particularly Goldman's nuanced and explicitly feminist formulation, is a helpful theoretical tool for Jewish life and studies, feminist and generally. Additionally, the complications of the empirical assessment are then best examined with anarchism's critical approach.

In this chapter, following a biographical overview of Goldman, I present a basic introduction to anarchism for those unfamiliar with the political theory as well as a groundwork for the anarchist base of most grassroots post-1960s feminism, which is especially resonant for contemporary US Jewish Left and Jewish feminist engagement. We will then turn specifically to exploring Goldman in her varying Jewish contexts and conclude by noting how Jewish studies and specifically Jewish attraction to radical diasporism will be much aided by a study of Goldman's anarchist contributions.

Biographical Note

Emma Goldman was born in 1869 into an Orthodox Jewish family living in what was then Kovno, part of the Russia Empire, and is now Kaunas Lithuania. Her mother had had two daughters from a previous marriage, and Emma was the first child (with three sons following) of her mother's (arranged) second marriage. The family moved a few times during her youth, including to Königsberg, a Prussian city within the German Empire of the time, and later back to Russia's St. Petersburg.

Goldman shares stories of her early personal history that demonstrate her experiences with the sorts of oppression she will devote her life to fighting. When writing about her experience in tsarist Russia, for example, Goldman portrayed her father as a violent tyrant. She also recounted stories of violence from her teachers. A smart girl and good student who passed the admissions exam, Goldman was furious that the gymnasium denied her entrance. Her father also thwarted her continuation of her formal education at home. During these early years in Europe, Goldman also experienced sexual violence, including rape. Like Golda Meir, Goldman was first exposed to radical politics at her home in Europe by her older sister.

At fifteen (in 1885), she emigrated with her sister Helena to Rochester, New York, where she lived with her sister Lena and Lena's husband. Their parents and brothers sought refuge in the US a year later, fleeing anti-Jewish violence. While still in St. Petersburg, Goldman worked a number of jobs. After immigration, Goldman was among the masses of New York's poor immigrants and refugees, including many young Jewish women, to work in a factory as a seamstress and at similar jobs. The 1886 Haymarket demonstrations and repercussions in Chicago became a turning point for her. Workers had staged a demonstration calling for an eight-hour workday. The police intervened with excessive violence and seven policemen were killed. Despite scant evidence, eight anarchists were held accountable and four eventually executed.

In 1887, Goldman married a man she met at work, Jacob Kershner, with whom she shared a love of books, of living life fully, and a hatred of factory work. Goldman and Kershner faced stress from living with Goldman's family, and later Goldman reported that Kershner was impotent. As Goldman confronted the pressures of family, sexuality, and worker oppression and explored anarchist writers, her mind and heart continued to grow more fiery. After much drama with Kershner and with her family, Goldman divorced her husband. Her shocked parents would not let her live with them.

In 1889 she left Rochester with her sewing machine and headed to New York City to join anarchists there. Right away she met Alexander Berkman and then also began working with the well-known anarchist Johann Most, from whom she later split. Goldman became a significant force among these activists and thinkers. Partnering with Berkman both personally and politically, she edited and published her own anarchist paper, *Mother Earth*, for more than ten years (1906 to 1917), during turbulent times and amid much censorship and harassment of radicals (Monk 1968; Ferguson 2011). Goldman also published numerous books, including her oft-studied memoir, *Living My Life* (1931), which she wrote while living in England, France, and Canada; *The Social Significance of the Modern Drama* (1914); and *Anarchism and Other Essays* (first published 1910), a book collection of a number of her key articles from *Mother Earth*.

Goldman's anarchism focused on oppressive structures of "power over": government, militarism, capitalism, patriarchy, prisons, and religion.

Explicitly a feminist, she was outspoken on the subjects of birth control, prostitution, free love, women's liberation, and homosexuality, along with more general free speech and labor issues. With Berkman, she planned to assassinate Henry Clay Frick, a financier and industrialist, in 1892, as part of her early conviction that the violence of capitalism required targeted violence to fight back. This has been noted as the first terrorist attack in the US (Avrich and Avrich 2012), though we might rightly situate this act within a history of enslaved peoples', Native Americans', and others' acts of resistance to tyranny. Frick survived the botched plan, and Berkman was sentenced to a prison term of twenty-two years. Following the ordeal, Goldman revised her anarchist grounding and moved away from supporting political violence.

For a time, Goldman worked as a nurse treating women and others, particularly the worst off. Her experience with real people living in dire circumstances further grounded her radical politics. She had begun studying medicine on her own following an encounter with a friendly doctor during a stint in the infirmary at Blackwell's Island Penitentiary in the mid-1890s. After her release from prison, she studied midwifery in Europe and earned two diplomas in Vienna (where Stein, a few years Goldman's junior, had lived briefly during her childhood). While in Europe during this period, she lectured widely, working closely with anarchist comrades in numerous cities and countries, and met with the leading European anarchists of her day.

Goldman was routinely arrested and detained in prison, so much so that she made a practice of always carrying a book in case of a lock-up. While imprisoned, she made common cause with the flood of fellow women prisoners. She led a pacifist campaign during World War I and spent two years in prison for opposing the draft (see Goldman 2017). In 1919, Goldman and Berkman were released from their prison sentences for their antidraft and pacifist agitation against World War I. The year 1919 witnessed the first major US Red Scare against leftists and immigrants as well as concerted Christian white supremacist attacks. The summer of 1919 is often referred to as Red Summer, a term coined by civil rights activist James Weldon Johnson, a focused period when white supremacists terrorized their Black neighbors and rioted in dozens of cities across the country. Also in 1919, J. Edgar Hoover, then head of the US Department of Justice's General Intelligence Division (which later became the FBI), partnered with Attorney General Palmer to raid anarchist, immigrant, and other leftist groups in dozens of cities spanning the country (this period is frequently referred to as that of the Palmer Raids). This was also Hoover's opportunity to deport Goldman and Berkman, with whom he had become obsessed. To do so, Hoover utilized the earlier, turn-of-the-century Anarchist Exclusion Act (part of the Immigration Act of 1903). The 1903 act relied on hundreds of years of anti-Jewish notions equating Jews with contagion and sexual perversion, creating a new set of exclusions from immigration for new classes of people, notably anarchists, the poor, people with certain health conditions, and "importers of prostitutes." While Goldman and Berkman were in prison, Hoover and his allies succeeded in expanding the provisions. By 1918 the US had given itself the legal justification to deport anarchists and revolutionaries, meaning an effective way to deport many Jews.

In 1919, Hoover deported Goldman with her longtime ally and dear friend Berkman, and hundreds of others, to Russia. While Berkman and Goldman were still in prison, Hoover had written that "Emma Goldman and Alexander Berkman are, beyond doubt, two of the most dangerous anarchists in this country and return to the community will result in undue harm" (cited in Drinnon 1961, 215). The two made arrangements with the newly formed Soviet government to travel across Russian territories in designated railway cars to collect materials intended for a museum. This project provided them with a measure of independence from government and party. Additionally, this project allowed them to travel and begin to appraise the Bolshevik revolution of 1917. Goldman refused to abandon her longstanding opposition to any form of state, even in the communist Soviet Union. Interestingly, one of many points of disagreement between Goldman and the Russian Communist Party leadership was the issue of free speech. Goldman had done much of her anarchist work in the US under the rubric of free speech. Appealing to this framework in the US enabled many progressives to support Goldman's radical political work. In Bolshevik-run Russia, free speech was considered bourgeois. At an in-person meeting with the revolutionary leader, Lenin told Goldman that free speech was not possible in a revolutionary period. While originally a hopeful supporter of the revolution, she and Berkman remained anarchists and became significant critics of what had emerged as a dictatorship in the new Soviet Union (Goldman 1923, 1924).[7] Particularly following the Soviet government's violent response to the Kronstadt Rebellion (a confrontation with and massacre of anarchist soldiers and sailors), their situation in Russia became increasingly untenable, and they left in 1921.

Goldman spent numerous peripatetic years in Europe, including early on in Latvia, Sweden, and a few years in Berlin. Goldman moved to London in 1924. While fiercely anti-marriage, in 1925 Goldman married a Welsh comrade in order to gain access to English citizenship. (Such marriages were not uncommon for political refugees at the time.) While still active with her writing, speaking, and activism, Goldman experienced these years as exilic and lonely. She travelled to anarchist Spain a number of times to work for women and more generally against fascism. She was allowed into Toronto in 1927, in the midst of the uproar about the expected executions of the Italian-born US anarchists Nicola Sacco and Bartolomeo Vanzetti in Boston. (Sacco and Vanzetti were originally arrested in 1920.) During these years in exile, Goldman did manage to have a relatively settled period in the south of France, supported by comrades while she drafted her memoir.[8]

With a one-time exception from the US government for a 1934 speaking tour (from February to May; Gertrude Stein's one time back in the US from her expatriate life in France to undertake a major speaking tour occurred later in that same year), Goldman secured this permission agreeing to only discuss her autobiography and her work on drama. She was never allowed back in the US again. While in London during the 1930s, Goldman worked for the anarchists in the Spanish Civil War (see Goldman 1983) and was first invited to Spain to work in the anarchist revolution there in 1936. While not known comrades with the other Jewish feminists we examine in this book, Goldman repeatedly crisscrossed Europe and the US with them during these years, often in the same cities at similar times. Goldman went on wildly popular speaking tours around the US when a young Golda Meir might have been in the audience,[9] and over the course of 1939 her life in Paris was contemporaneous with Kahlo, Stein, and Arendt and their circles. While most of these women were immigrant refugees to the US (Kahlo was Mexican although she lived on and off in the US,[10] and Stein was a first-generation US American), Goldman's citizenship status was among the most precarious (along with Arendt's as a German Jew during the Nazi period), and her US citizenship was revoked.

By 1939 Goldman returned to Canada, where she worked on raising funds for the Spanish Refugee Fund and also on a campaign on behalf of arrested Italian anarchist activist Arthur Bortolotti. She spoke to groups in Yiddish and English about the situation in Spain (Wexler 1989, 234). Goldman died in Canada from a series of strokes on May 14, 1940, when she was seventy years old. "Her coffin was wrapped in the flag of the International Anti-Fascist Solidarity organization for the Spanish anarchists" (Ferguson 2011, 292), an organization that Goldman had helped to build. Emma Goldman is buried in Chicago, close to Haymarket Square.

Introduction to Anarchism

To understand Emma Goldman and her life, work, and politics, we need to understand the basics of anarchism. Anarchism is a political philosophy that analyzes and rejects all forms of "power over" and authoritarianism. In the context of the contemporary US, it is helpful to understand anarchism as a form of radical democracy in which people make collective decisions on public matters. Goldman's anarchism seeks to engage people in exploring and defining their own ideals of human freedom and fulfillment, individually and collectively. To do so, it also works to prepare people, as communities and personally, to create structures and systems for decision-making to support and enhance the well-being of each and all with profound respect for our diversity.

In the prophetic tradition, Goldman sought to make the impossible possible, to combine a bold vision with a sober critique of current conditions so as to forge a concrete path forward. In "A New Declaration of Independence," she wrote, "Existing institutions prove inadequate to the needs of man. . . . They serve merely to enslave, rob, and oppress. . . . The history of the American kings of capital and authority is the history of repeated crimes, injustice, oppression, outrage, and abuse, all aiming at the suppression of individual liberties and the exploitation of the people" (quoted in Falk, Pateman, and Moran 2003, 450; see also Falk, Pateman, and Moran 2005). While Goldman doesn't use the term *colonialism*, her politics overlap significantly with those Kincaid would come to develop. Alternatively, in anarchism, Goldman pursues what she deems the most practical ideal, for "the scheme has vitality enough to leave the stagnant waters of the old, and build, as well as sustain, new life" (Goldman [1917] 1969, 49).

The English term *anarchism* comes from the ancient Greek word for "without a ruler"; in Western political theory it is often portrayed negatively as a charge of chaos. Western scholars often cite the British William Godwin, husband of eighteenth-century feminist political thinker Mary Wollstonecraft and father of Mary Wollstonecraft Shelley, as the first modern anarchist thinker. Proudhon ([1840] 1994) is credited with first using the term.[11] While Goldman's activist world was densely populated with women activists, speakers, and thinkers (many Jewish feminists among them, such as the younger Mollie Steimer), it is helpful to note the major male anarchist thinkers influencing Goldman.[12] Peter Kropotkin's work had a major influence on Goldman, despite some important differences between them, most notably on matters of sexuality. Additionally, Goldman favored the collectivist strain of anarchism of Mikhail Bakunin, despite his antisemitism. Nikolay Chernyshevsky's *What Is to Be Done?* (1863; see Tchernuishevsky 1986) also had a significant influence on Goldman's generation of Russian activists and intellectuals and specifically on Emma. With differences between them, we can also see a similar set of influences inspiring other well-known feminist anarchists of her day—for example, US-born Voltairine de Cleyre (1866 to 1912) and Jewish feminist anarchist Rose Pesotta (1896 to 1965), active also in the early twentieth century in the US.[13]

Goldman's early-nineteenth-century words still ring true for activists today: "the State is itself the greatest criminal, breaking every written and natural law, stealing in the form of taxes, killing in the form of war and capital punishment" ([1917] 1969, 59).We find anarchist activists central to many Jewish initiatives as well as contemporary mass mobilizations such as those at the World Trade Organization and G8 meetings in Seattle in 1999 and in Geneva in 2001, the Occupy Wall Street movement begun in 2011, a lot of climate justice and Black Lives Matter work over these decades, and the women's march movement (its first action on Trump's presidential inauguration day a march on Washington, in January 2017).[14]

Anarchism emerged alongside of and in critical dialogue with the work of Karl Marx (who died when Goldman was approximately fourteen). Both anarchism and Marxism are committed to the well-being of the working class and seek to end capitalism, alienation, and exploitation.[15] However, Marx criticized anarchism as insufficiently grounded in existing conditions, and anarchists critiqued Marxists for being too centralized.[16] While Marx actually says relatively little about how he imagined the organization of a postrevolutionary communist society, what he does say bears a keen resemblance to anarchist visions of self-governing groups of people in voluntary association, with no need for states as we know them. This orientation served as the basis for the revolutionary Russian concept of the "soviet." Tensions among anarchists, socialists, Jewish Bundists, and communists continued over time, while the Soviet experiment followed the path of extreme centralization, with deadly consequences for anarchists and countless others, and these tensions still continue. While the labor movement and large leftist movements for collective living in Israel self-identified primarily as socialist historically and for civil rights in more contemporary politics, Israeli forms of radical democracy and small-scale collective life closely resemble Goldman's form of collectivist anarchism, and many anarchists were active in the movement.[17]

Central to anarchism's eschewal of all forms of power over is its general anti-statism. It is true that today progressive activists seem to focus critique somewhat exclusively on the problems of statism found increasingly in Israel. This exclusive critique of Israel is a problem and also can obscure a unique aspect of anarchism with an important message for us all, in a world wracked not only by transnational forces of domination but also by states. At least as old as Hobbes's mid-sixteenth-century articulation at the foundation of the creation of the modern state, Westerners would come to rely on Max Weber's ([1919] 2004) formulation of the state as the form of society "that (successfully) lays claim to the *monopoly of legitimate physical violence*" (33). This dynamic of state violence relies upon its own legitimization, and most political philosophies provide this, albeit with variations on the terms of legitimization. In contrast, anarchism is the main political philosophy that interrupts the re-legitimation process. In her primary definition of anarchism, Goldman writes that anarchism is "the theory that all forms of government rest on violence, and are therefore wrong and harmful, as well as unnecessary" ([1917] 1969, 50). This has also led most anarchists to reject revolutionary efforts directed at reestablishing power within the confines of the state and utilizing party politics as a mechanism of activism. Such rejections are among the main fault lines between anarchism, much of Bundism, and most socialist and communist political organizing historically. Additionally, despite a good deal of anarchist engagement in the creation of a Jewish homeland in Palestine and work to secure the rights of refugees to settle there in the crisis of the Holocaust, this anti-statism became a central wedge between anarchists and Zionists, who became increasingly state-focused following World War II.[18]

While there exists a wide range of views among anarchist thinkers and organizers, Goldman's "beautiful ideal" sought beauty through human diversity and fulfillment on the spiritual, physical, and emotional planes. This led Goldman to write extensively on art and sexuality in addition to addressing the evils of capitalism and critiquing the multiple forms of coercive mass structures such as the state, marriage, prisons, religion, and the military. This aspect of Goldman's multifaceted approach to anarchism forms the basis for the popularized misquotation from her work: "If I can't dance, I don't want to be part of your revolution."[19]

Goldman was a proponent of radical individual freedom. As she frequently referred to freedom of speech in her defense when arrested, she often made common cause with those in the free speech movement (Cohen and Zelnik 2002). However, her anarchism differs from US-style libertarianism and some American Civil Liberties Union–style protections of personal freedom in two primary ways. US mainstream proponents of personal freedom, privacy, and First Amendment freedoms often focus on the individual. Goldman, however, engages in systemic critical analysis of structures of domination. Additionally, anarchism differs from US-style libertarianism (often used to support right-wing agendas by skewing interpretation of the US First Amendment to cover only individual rights, with no relation to a public good despite the adaption from the 1919 Supreme Court dictum in *Schneck v. United States*) foundationally in that anarchism maintains a commitment to pursuing freedom on a collective level, including interrupting structural oppression. As Goldman notes, "The individual and social instincts,—the one a most potent factor for individual endeavor, for growth, aspiration, self-realization; the other an equally potent factor for mutual helpfulness and social well-being" ([1917] 1969, 51).

A central strategy of anarchism is known as direct action: "the open defiance of, and resistance to, all laws and restrictions, economic, social, and moral" (Goldman [1917] 1969, 65). Anarchist thinkers engage in deep critical analysis of the problems and potential of existing conditions. Anarchist activists often undertake long-term organizing plans such as launching syndicated trade unions, establishing educational and social services, and developing grand-scale strategies to transform oppressive institutions. At the same time, anarchists also carry out actions that are both symbolic (demonstrations, arts, education) and aimed directly at interfering with business as usual or in direct support in the moment.

As Jews have been without a state apparatus or other central authoritative structure for most of the past two millennia, anarchism provides fertile theoretical frameworks for understanding Jewish collectivist navigations in history. Jewish diasporic efforts to exist as dynamic communities based on internal communal organizational modes, usually in defiance of larger systems, can be said to be anarchic, and a study of Goldman's anarchism can help those who seek to develop communities based increasingly on voluntary association. Similarly, Goldman's anarchism brings her to investigate and critique multiple forms of exploitative power dynamics within oppressive systems beyond the state. This capacity also can be helpful for Jews' and others' interest in challenging the problematic ways that power operates in our communities and across the vast systems Goldman critiqued, such as patriarchy, militarism, capitalism, and clericalism.

Jews have long needed to create and maintain communal life with some independence from, and often in opposition to, larger and often hostile cultural forms. Similarly, while anarchists generally promote full-scale social transformation, they also emphasize the need to build alternative structures within existing capitalist societies.[20] This was a significant tension between Marxists and anarchists, particularly in the nineteenth and twentieth centuries. The anarchist commitment is based largely on the concept of preparation. No form of revolution, no matter how grand its ideals, can simply create the multilayered capacities people need to live together in empowering ways not based on exploitation (see chapter 4, pp. 75–98 in Brettschneider 2016). Anarchists argue that we must prepare ourselves to live democratic lives. "Anarchism, the great leaven of thought, is today permeating every phase of human endeavor. Science, art, literature, drama, the effort for economic betterment, in fact every individual and social opposition to the existing disorder of things" (Goldman [1917] 1969, 67). We see this model used in the movement for Black lives and, earlier, in the 2010s Occupy Wall Street movement and its ancillaries. In the case of Occupy, activists created alternative and radically democratic mini-societies, usually established illegally on corporate-owned urban space. Critiquing capitalism and the vast inequality between the top one percent and the mass of the ninety-nine percent, Occupy activists did not advocate for waiting for a wholesale revolution to bring about more egalitarian human relationships. Instead, they engaged in analysis, critique, education, and direct action while creating communities aimed at meeting the existing material needs of participants. In this context, participants understood these needs to include everything from food, shelter, and medical care to education and art. Such has long been operative in Jewish communal experiments across the globe and in the US, such as with free loan societies, education, social services, *havurot*, and cultural endeavors. It is certainly the case that over the past two millennia, Jewish communities needed to organize their own systems as they were usually excluded from anti-Jewish endeavors for schools, hospitals, banks, sanitation, and so forth. In the process, Jewish communities across the globe developed an array of self-governing and collective-organizing practices that also have served them well even when they are allowed entrance to some educational, health, and other institutions.

Anarchism has often been associated with violence in popular culture. This is due in part to normative equations of noncoercive power with chaos, violence, and insecurity. There is only a fine line between the criminalizing structures of antisemitism Goldman and other Jewish refugees have experienced in the US and the characterization of anarchists as criminals and menaces to society. Grotesque characterizations in political cartoons can look quite similar. Goldman responds to this charge: "Destruction and violence! How is the ordinary man to know that the most violent element in society is ignorance; that its power of destruction is the very thing Anarchism is combating?" ([1917] 1969, 49–50).

A popular association of anarchism with chaos and violence also relates to an anarchist concept called "propaganda of the deed," or *attentât*. This principle centers anarchism's emphasis on praxis, a reciprocally productive relationship between theory and practice. Propaganda of the deed means a dramatic, attention-grabbing enaction of revolutionary principles; it does not always entail violence. As with some anticolonial and antiracist movements within the next century, particularly in the period of classical anarchism in the late nineteenth and early twentieth centuries, some anarchists sought to resist what they saw as the primary organizations of violence, the state and capitalism, with violent acts of protest. These activists sometimes intended such acts to disrupt actual structures of oppression (e.g., to disrupt the functioning of a factory) and sometimes intended to provide a symbolic demonstration of the gaps in the supposedly total power of a primary oppressive institution, such as the state. This tradition of propaganda of the deed inspired Goldman's action with Berkman against Frick.[21] While never a pacifist, after the Frick action, Goldman adjusted her politics, but she nonetheless continued to appreciate the strategic violence of some others.[22]

Jews and other subaltern groups and colonized populations are often seen as uncivilized, disorganized, messy, and ungovernable. Setting "others" up in this fashion has been used to justify elite violence, slavery, imperialism, surveillance, and mass incarceration of such populations. Mostly, subaltern populations live according to norms of social organization not always recognized, or not recognized as worthy, by elites. While anarchism is often mistakenly portrayed as opposed to organization or structure per se, anarchism actually opposes specifically those forms of organization that rely on unequal power relations based on exploitation.[23] Thus, anarchists have long engaged in creating and maintaining vast webs of organizations, often worker-led, as part of their activism. The early heyday of anarchism in the US spanned three decades, beginning in the 1880s, the period in which Goldman was active and became a leader. This period saw widespread collectivist experiments launched by anarchists who helped to found syndicated labor unions, cultural initiatives, schools, and health facilities. Along with most leftists of her day, Goldman would have known about the grand historic period of the Paris Commune (1871), which also inspired Marx.[24] In her lifetime, Goldman was also witness to mass-scale enactments of what she considered anarchism (though proponents of these initiatives may have used other terms, such as *communist* or *socialist*). Following World War I (similar to the Jewish, anarchist-inspired, smaller-scale Amalgamated Housing Cooperative movement in New York City during this period; Berman 2019), Austrian leftists established a transformative system via democratic elections in what has come to be called Red Vienna, a radical period in the city from 1918 to 1935.[25] People often speak of the critical period of anarchist organization in the Spanish Civil War (1936 to 1939) as the primary example of anarchism practiced on a large scale.[26] We can also note the collectivist Zionist experiment in the Yishuv, where Kropotkin's *Mutual Aid* circulated widely as among the first books to have been translated into modern Hebrew (Horrox 2009, 5).

The Spanish Civil War began in 1936, with anarchists playing a central role within the Republican side. This conflict is of particular import for understanding Goldman and the significance of her anarchist legacy for our time and was significant for other women studied in this book, such as communist-identified Kahlo. Goldman accepted an invitation and went to Spain during the early period of the struggle. Her invitation for firsthand engagement with this struggle had her highlighting the Spanish anarchist fight in additional to what she also critiqued as an increasing antisemitism operating in Europe during her exile.[27] While in Spain, Goldman was able to tour collectives spanning more geographical expanse than any critics had ever thought possible to run under anarchist principles. She also had the opportunity to live in such a community, where she told the resident workers, "Your revolution will destroy forever [the notion] that anarchism stands for chaos" (cited in Drinnon 1961, 303). While in some ways a heyday for Goldman and anarchism as practiced on a wide scale, it was also a very difficult and complicated situation. The Left had numerous factions engaged in fierce internal struggles. These struggles internal to the Spanish Left were compounded by the support and pressures of Soviet involvement as well as the imperative to fight against fascism and international capitalist forces. By mid-1937, communist groups had attacked anarchist areas and broken up the anarchist collectives. Goldman had left and then returned to Spain to work there in person, but the local anarchist groups were losing international support, and the fascist Nationalists took control before Goldman left Spain for the last time and returned to London.[28]

Anarcho-Feminism

While masses of women served among the rank-and-file activists in the fin de siècle progressive, trade unionist, socialist, communist, and anarchist movements, far fewer women reached the rank of leadership.[29] Emma Goldman, Rose Pesotta, and Voltairine de Cleyre were rare as women among anarchist leaders. Anarchism's consistent opposition to "power over," by standing "for the spirit of revolt, in whatever form, against everything that hinders human growth" (Goldman [1917] 1969, 63), lends itself to resisting patriarchy in the many ways it operates. However, as we see in many revolutionary movements, not all anarchists prioritize—or even attend to—efforts to end sexist, racist, and homophobic oppression. Some activists consider focusing on gender- and sexuality-based oppression as bourgeois folly, or on racism as a deflection from what they consider more core issues of class and economics. As was common on the Left, many leading anarchists also considered Goldman's feminist concerns a "digression" from the "real" revolutionary work (Ackelsberg 1991).

As Ferguson notes, "Jewish anarchist communities [were] far more likely to include activist women than were the Italians or the Spanish" (2011, 268). Fittingly, Goldman centered anti-patriarchy within her work against multiple tyrannical institutions, such as militarism, statism, capitalism, and clericalism (Lumsden 2007). Goldman's ire at myriad modes of gender-based and specifically women's subjugation informed her anarchism, as her anarchism fueled her capacity for profound feminist critique and engagement. During periods of despair over the revolutionary potential of the anarchist masses, particularly amid the growing precarity and mass immigrations of the 1930s, Goldman and Berkman also discussed the potential of anarchism to enliven other revolutionary movements (Wexler 1989, 166–67). In this vein, while anarchism's specific contributions are usually unnamed, Goldman's anarcho-feminism has proven foundational for US feminism for more than a century.

Goldman's Jewish experiences and the depth of her anarchism enabled her complex feminism and anticipated contemporary forms of feminism (such as intersectionality as well as de-colonial and transnational feminisms) that address global and local, multiple and mutually constitutive power dynamics, which both produce and reinforce co-constructed gender-based, sexual, racist, and other structures of domination. Here, we can see how Goldman's contributions are still vital for moving beyond the limits of liberal, rights-based progressivism. Goldman's anarchist philosophy and methodology, praxis (where theory and practice foundationally inform each other), foreshadowed the later feminist articulation of the personal as political and subsequent rejection of primary binaries within patriarchy. The decentralization of Goldman's anarchism, with her emphasis on collectives as the basis for organizing and on living radical democracy, makes her contributions significant for later feminist consciousness raising, co-ops, and experimentation, Jewish and generally. Her attention to beauty and the freedom of the human spirit provides a grounding for forms of feminism that celebrate aesthetics and the power of the arts, nature, the erotic, and the sublime. In these, Goldman shows feminists and all of us ways of attending to spiritual needs beyond the confines of clericalism, theism, and oppressive religious institutions.

While usually unacknowledged, Goldman's anarchism continues to be an important source for Jewish and wider feminist work seeking to articulate and resist multiple co-constructed systems of "power over," which simultaneously create various forms of gender-based, sexual, and other forms of domination. In a post-1960s US context, feminists seeking to leave behind identitarian forms of identity politics have been working in this mode (sometimes now referred to as intersectionality) in conjunction with resistance to numerous politically salient structures of oppression. These structures include racism, heterosexism, ableism, cisgender normativity, classism, colonialism, and, at times in the West, Christian hegemony.[30] Goldman's anarcho-feminism deepens this diversity-oriented analysis, as she says with her unusual "regard to individual and social variations and needs" ([1917] 1969, 61). Goldman's work inherently links identity-based political work with structures that the Left also generally addresses as complicit in oppression, such as militarism, capitalism, statism, colonialism, and religious fundamentalism. While intersectional feminists claim to resist the problems of "identity politics," it is still all too easy to remain stuck in this paradigm, or to engage comparatively limited analyses that attend to two modes of oppression instead of only one, rather than embracing a multifaceted approach. The structure of Goldman's approach helps activists and scholars maintain multiple commitments that are inherently related to each other. Additionally, Goldman's anarcho-feminism can keep us grounded in a framework focused on addressing broad institutional forms of power over. In the vital justice work continuing to this day in US intersectional and identity politics on race, gender, sex, class, disability, colonialism, and Indigeneity, Goldman's approach is central to addressing the dangers inherent in the hierarchies of capitalism, colonialism, mass incarceration, militarism, ecological devastation, statism, and clericalism (or, today, religious fundamentalism; Brettschneider 2016).

Goldman's anarchism was anti-statist, arguing that the state as we know it is a centrally coercive force. Thus, for Goldman, participation with the state will not yield revolutionary results. This put her and most anarchists at odds with socialist and communist activists and parties across the globe. We can also clearly see the significance of this insight and analysis in her critique of and alternative to women's suffrage. Goldman's position clarified the limitations of the rights-based and state-centered approach to social transformation that we have seen repeated all too often since her day, for example in the antiracism, feminism, and gay rights movements. Due to US and Western hegemony around the globe, the state-centered rights-based paradigm and its limitations continue to constrict freedom movements internationally. As a result, Goldman's anarchist analysis remains essential today for leftist activism both within the US and globally.

In this vein, the import of Goldman's opposition to the women's suffrage movement of her day remains crucial for us still. Movements for suffrage have been key in democracies. US Americans of African descent have been formally enfranchised in the US since the end of the Civil War. However, when Goldman was active, women (as a group) did not yet have the right to vote in the US. The Fifteenth Amendment to the Constitution's extension of the franchise did not extend to women, despite their "race, color, or previous condition of servitude." Women and allies organized a movement for suffrage. For the most part, elite white and sometimes xenophobic women are credited for leading this movement, which it is important to note nonetheless included women of all classes across race and ethnicity, for whom it entailed significant risks.[31] However, Goldman pointed out that women voting in the existent corrupt system would not effectively change the system or change the actual conditions of women's material and emotional oppression and exploitation. In addition to antisemitism, Goldman was deported because of the gender inequality that US women experienced: women's very citizenship depended on their husbands' status, and accordingly many women lost their citizenship if they married noncitizens. As we saw with Golda Meir, immigrant women also lost their citizenship and other basic protections following divorce or other changes in their relational status to specific men. This situation made refugees and immigrants, including Goldman, Meir, and thousands of others, far more vulnerable to deportation.[32]

Instead, Goldman's anarchist, anti-statist feminism sought to interrupt and transform the root causes of women's, people's, and various forms of gender-based subjugation. Similarly, Goldman's approach sought women's (and all people's) liberation not only in the formal sphere of electoral politics but also in the multiple power dynamics of familial and interpersonal relationships that curtail human desire and fulfillment. This tension between often well-meaning, progressive "civil rights" approaches and more radical ones persists among activists and scholars in many campaigns. For example, Black theorists and activists have taken a variety of approaches to ending racial discrimination and white supremacy; this diversity in perspective and tactics predates the "civil rights approach" that gained traction in the 1950s and continues today as antiracism work is growing, in large part through the movement for Black lives.[33] We saw such diversity in approach in the mid-twentieth century among feminists seeking to end sexist discrimination via an equal rights amendment to the US Constitution. There were similar tensions between the approaches of queer liberation versus a gay rights agenda, particularly the emergent 2000s focus on same-gender marriage (said to have "culminated" in the 2015 US Supreme Court *Obergefell v. Hodges* decision). As early as the late 1800s, Goldman formulated a critical analysis of a liberal-state-based focus on voting, civil rights, and reformist legislation and sparked an alternative activist movement. While the international Left often distanced itself from US-style identity-group-rights-based movements, belittling them as bourgeois, reactionary, and at best inadequate to address the material conditions of race, gender, capitalist, colonial, and sexual domination, Goldman's work demonstrates how to take such issues seriously within a broader leftist agenda. Critically analyzing and working against supremacy in the state, the limitations within religious authority structures, and in various movements and micro-publics, Goldman's approach holds promise for collective liberation work, specifically for Jewish feminists as well.

Goldman's praxis mode of anarchism is also thus important for understanding both her and our feminism, then and now. Recent feminist scholars have looked to Goldman and her complex of thinking, activism, and life story for insights to address the continued need to move beyond the compartmentalization of thought, grand political action, and the quotidian.[34] Western thought has favored binary approaches with hierarchically ordered categories as the foundation both of intellectual understandings and of social organization since the ancient Greek philosophers; Christianity continued and spread this approach. While Goldman used many dichotomies in her fiery oratory, we can also see her thought moving more deeply beyond the entrenched binaries in ways that are important for feminists today. In contrast to Platonic separations contrasting and prizing thinking over experience and mind over body, Goldman was among those anarchists who emphasized connecting theory and practice. Goldman's contributions here remain valuable for those seeking to undo the multiple, and inherently related, binaries of mind/body and, later, the spirit/body dichotomy that dominant forms of Christianity encoded. (For a contemporary Jewish context, see Plaskow 1991.) Today, cutting-edge work continues in these areas, and also with binary-gender deconstruction as we saw with Meir. This work builds on anarchism's groundbreaking achievements in insisting on the relationship between means and ends that has become essential for many feminist and other thinkers and activists. Espousing direct action, preparation, and emergent anti-violence, Goldman wrote ([1917] 1969, 50), "The new social order rests, of course, on the materialistic basis of life; but while all Anarchists agree that the main evil today is an economic one, they maintain that the solution of that evil can be brought about only through the consideration of *every phase* of life,—individual, as well as the collective; the internal, as well as the external phases." Later feminist work articulating the political nature of supposedly personal issues such as rape, sexual harassment, reproductive justice, and the broader women's and LGBTQ health movement draws heavily on Goldman's work shattering such binary thinking and the ways in which it influences our activist strategies.[35]

Important for feminists also is that Goldman emphasized not only the exploitation of most people as laborers but also the importance of people's bodily needs, which she insisted a revolutionary movement could not ignore. In part due to her experience working as a nurse, Goldman agitated for women's and all people's health. Of note is her early 1900s work for birth control and what today we would call reproductive justice (Price 2017; Klapper 2013; for US Jewish women's history on reproductive rights as well as reproductive justice in a Jewish context, see Brettschneider 2016). The movement for reproductive justice critiques a middle-class history of women's health activism that focused only on options for limiting births. Goldman was key to this history. In her radical agenda and work with women across classes, this Jewish anarcho-feminist's legacy was central to laying the groundwork for a contemporary reproductive justice movement that protects not only women who want to reproduce and also those who do not but also the well-being of the children and families created in the process.³⁶ As Goldman notes, "Real wealth consists in things of utility and beauty, in things that help to create strong, beautiful bodies and surroundings inspiring to live in" ([1917] 1969, 55).

From this historical vantage point, and as inheritors of a post-1960s feminist understanding of the personal as political, it may be difficult to appreciate the radicalness of Goldman's feminist anarchist agenda for human freedom. Goldman's writings on drama and the arts were also part of her work on the importance of aesthetics to liberation, and they remain key to the feminist commitment to culture and the arts. While an urban dweller, Goldman appreciated the need for nature and natural beauty that we can find important in the feminist climate, holistic health, and food security movements of the twenty-first century. Goldman advocated for what she called free love, which reemerged in the US of the 1960s. In an essay on "Marriage and Love" in *Anarchism and Other Essays*, Goldman ([1917] 1969, 236) wrote, "Love, the strongest and deepest element in all life, the harbinger of hope, of joy, of ecstasy; love the defier of all laws, of all conventions; love the freest, the most powerful moulder of human destiny." Goldman spoke regularly about the need to destigmatize and decriminalize prostitution. Remarkably for her time, Goldman included alternatives to heterosexuality and a binary gender in her calls for sexual liberation.³⁷ We can see elements of Goldman's work on the power of love and the need for sexual freedom in the work of Black lesbian feminists, such as Audre Lorde's (1984) classic articulation of the power of the erotic, the essential role of poetry in the political, and much of feminism's commitment to both the political and beautiful.³⁸

Goldman's anarcho-feminist work on free love led her to an anti-marriage stance, also as radically needed today as it was in her day. Committed philosophically to nonmonogamy as part of her free-love agenda, Goldman struggled with the question of how to live this out in her own life (see Marso 2006). Goldman connected her analysis of monogamy to her opposition to conventional motherhood and marriage, which she situated among the major oppressive power-over structures in our societies. Her work on monogamy and jealousy ranked them as oppressive forms of capitalist private property. Goldman wrote of free love and marriage, "How can such an all-compelling force be synonymous with that poor little State and Church-begotten weed, marriage?" ("Marriage and Love," Goldman [1917] 1969, 231). Goldman's feminist anti-marriage work contributed to feminist and queer critiques of the rise of a same-gender marriage movement as a predominant force in LGBTQ activism in the 2000s.³⁹ Her work remains sorely needed as queers and others committed to ending heteropatriarchy and cisgendered normativity seek to regroup in the political climate in the US and internationally following the 2015 *Obergefell v. Hodges* and 2022 *Dobbs v. Jackson Women's Health Organization* decisions and facing the success of right-wing public retrenchment of basic feminist, queer, antiracist dignities and rights.

Goldman's anarchism led her to explore the radical potential in lived decentralized and collective experiments as part of her revolutionary agenda. Goldman's anarchist methodology, "a living force in the affairs of our life, constantly creating new conditions" ([1917] 1969, 63), has been key to the creation of post-1960s feminist cooperatives.[40] Goldman insisted on the need to connect one's emotional and physical fulfilment with structural social transformation. She notes, "Economic and social rights for women alone are not enough to fill her life" (Wexler and Goldman 1981, 116). While Goldman, and Wollstonecraft before her, valued their close women friends and comrades, they did not have the opportunity to live in a time of a broad feminist movement committed to encouraging women and gender outlaws to speaking their truths. In this, Goldman left a legacy for twentieth- and twenty-first-century feminism to develop consciousness raising, feminist art initiatives, bookstores, food and health collectives, take back the night marches and movements, battered women's shelters, and rape and sexual assault crisis centers.[41]

Goldman, Anarchism, and Yiddish Traditions

We turn now to an exploration of the co-constitutive and more explicitly Jewish matters of interest in our study of Emma Goldman and her life, thinking, and activism. While Goldman was fluent in numerous languages, Yiddish was a base language and formed the culture of her young life and of her Jewish communities in the US, Canada, and Europe.[42] During Goldman's life, Yiddish was the primary Jewish language in both northern Europe and the US, and 80 to 90 percent of Jews murdered during the Holocaust were from Yiddish-speaking communities. Both Jewishly and in the Christian West, Yiddish has become coded as "feminized" and weak. In dominant narratives, *Jewish*, as Yiddish is sometimes called, is also forever foreign, backward, queer, and deviant. For some Jews, Yiddish became associated with the disempowerment of European diaspora Jewish life. In the US today, Yiddish is often associated with ultra-orthodox Jewish communities of northern European heritage. While this association has a basis in fact, there is also a clear politics in this association that is important for understanding Goldman. A fresh look at both Yiddish and Goldman's anarchism will help us reclaim legacies of feminist, queer, and leftist Jewish politics.[43] Casting Yiddish as foreign, insular, and religiously extreme serves the US status quo in its refusal to work productively with difference. In looking to Emma Goldman and her anarchism, we must look at some central features of Yiddish and also note the feminist and queer histories and reclamations of the language and its culture. In doing so, we will find that an analysis of Goldman's Jewish context and her specifically Yiddish anarchist politics also reveals an active world of resistance and a radical leftist revaluing of diaspora.

Unusually, Goldman was able to function across both Jewish culture and the broader Left. Due to a common antidiversity presumption that one who functions well in the dominant culture must have abandoned any deep connections to one's particular communities, Goldman's ability to work in English and with non-Jewish radical groups leads many to discount her Jewish connections. However, Goldman lived within Yiddish subcultures in the US and connected to them across Canada and Europe. She could be critical of Jewish groups, as she was of all groups. I'd like us to ask about the ways her grounding within transnational Yiddish communities might have mattered to her fulfillment, popular success, and survival throughout her lifetime.

As the contemporary punk and anarchist Yiddish band Koyt Far Dayn Fardakht ("the filth of your suspicion")[44] writes of their songs,

> we sing them in our language, the language they were written in, because our ashkenazi culture is alive and well, despite the best efforts of zionists, nazis, enlighteners, fundamentalists, assimilationists, necro-nostalgists. yiddish has never been the only language of ashkenaz, but for 1000 years it has been one of our cultural anchors—especially for women, for the proste folk, for the kultur-tuers, for the revolutsionistn. & as we add our own links to the goldene keyt, we embrace it as a mark of both our diasporism (one jewish language among many) and our indigeneity (one eastern european language among many). ("Koyt Far Dayn Fardakht," n.d.; lowercase in original)

Such contemporary critique and radical visioning bring forward Goldman's feminist anarchist legacy.

Yiddish was the main spoken language that developed among Ashkenazi Jews (those of a Jewish ethnicity that emerged around the turn of the first millennium among those living in the Roman Empire). The communities that would become Ashkenazi began developing distinct traditions as they moved north into Germany and France. They later also moved eastward within Europe over the course of centuries of expulsions and migration due to antisemitism. Mainly reserving Hebrew and Aramaic for study and prayer (primarily male spheres, culturally), these communities developed Yiddish as a language for daily use (meaning also a Jewish language accessible to women) that integrated Hebrew, Aramaic, and the languages of the host regions of northern Europe where Ashkenazi Jews were living. While in her later years Goldman would use more English (Ashbolt 2003, 2), she was part of the early wave of refugees from Yiddish-speaking eastern Europe. Goldman continued to lecture in Yiddish her entire life, including also on explicitly Jewish subjects, such as her lecture series on Yiddish playwrights later in life for a British Jewish literary society.[45]

Let us first take note of the role of the Yiddish anarchist press, important for understanding Goldman's Jewish context.[46] As a multilingual person, along with publications in English and other languages, Goldman studiously read the Yiddish press. In the US, the Yiddish press was largely associated with the Left: many Yiddish papers were explicitly socialist, communist, and anarchist. For example, the *Morgan Freiheit* (Morning Freedom) was a daily NYC-based, Yiddish-language communist paper.[47] The *Forverts*, or the *Jewish Daily Forward*, began publishing in 1897 and was originally associated with socialism.[48] The *Folkstsaytung* (the People's Paper, 1921 to 1939) was a European daily and the official publication of the General Jewish Labor Bund in Poland.[49] Of particular note for us here is the Yiddish-language anarchist newspaper *Freie Arbeiter Stimme* (Free Voice of Labor), published and distributed among the Jewish immigrant-refugee communities of the Lower East Side of New York City from 1890 to 1977. The *Freie Arbeiter Stimme* began as the weekly Yiddish anarchist paper *Varhayt* (Truth), published for a few years in the 1880s by the Jewish anarchist group Pioneers of Liberty, which organized to support those arrested in the Haymarket affair. Among the many Yiddish-language periodicals in Europe and the US, this anarchist paper is heralded as the oldest Yiddish newspaper. Signaling the strong connection between Jewish leftist politics and anarchism, the *Freie Arbeiter Stimme* is also noted as one of the longest-running anarchist publications and was the last anarchist paper published in a foreign language in the United States (Avrich 1988, 198). The paper published works by and about

Goldman, among other literary figures and international anarchist leaders. The intensity of the political alliances always contentious, the community split following Goldman and Berkman's assassination attempt against Frick.[50] Periodically, Goldman partnered (through her own English-language publication *Mother Earth*) with the *Freie Arbeiter Stimme* on joint campaigns.[51]

Feminist scholars have pointed out the ways in which Yiddish became gendered as female among Jews, particularly in connection with Hebrew becoming gendered male (Seidman 1997). In yeshiva (a Jewish house of study) and synagogue, Hebrew was the central textual language, combined with some Aramaic. Hebrew was associated with the lofty world of G-d and study, a world dominated by men, and Hebrew was correspondingly gendered masculine in the European diaspora. Yiddish, the quotidian language of a world in which Jewish women had considerably more power, was, on the contrary, feminized.[52] Historically, while illiteracy was common, Jewish women tended to be more literate than women of their surrounding areas. Their language skills, however, tended to be stronger in Yiddish and the local secular host languages than in Hebrew or Aramaic. Women remained barred from the valued masculinist Jewish spaces where Hebrew and Aramaic formed the primary linguistic landscape, such as the yeshiva. They also tended to be stronger in the national host languages and sometimes even Yiddish than were some Jewish men.

As Zionism emerged, major debates took place as to what language Jews from around the world should speak when resettled together in a Jewish homeland. While modern Zionism was a largely secular movement, eventually, proponents of Hebrew won out. Many Ashkenazi Zionists consciously associated Yiddish with an increasingly rejected life in the diaspora. They invested Hebrew and modern Israel with new ideas about valued Christian masculine qualities that differed significantly from traditional Jewish ideas about gender. Yiddish, the language of patriarchal Jewish life for centuries and still a vibrant language when this linguistic shift was beginning, became feminized generally and devalued as the language and cultural matrix of the diaspora.

Of course, most ordinary Yiddish speakers likely did not think about this question in their daily lives. Yiddish was the primary daily language of their community. When Goldman moved to the US, she added English to the array of languages she used. She became a passionate orator, and her writing was similarly passionate. While today people in the US remember Goldman mostly in the context of her English-language writings, in her lifetime Goldman also continued to function, and conduct her political work, in Yiddish. Throughout her lifetime, Goldman often gave two speeches at each stop on her wildly popular speaking tours: one in English, geared primarily for a range of immigrants and English speakers, and the other in Yiddish (Ferguson 2011, 81).

In Western Jewish communities of the eighteenth century, a Jewish form of "enlightenment," known as the Haskalah, developed. This included a secularization and a mode of assimilation of Jewish communities within European host countries. In western Europe, these communities began shifting away from Yiddish and instead using more German and Hebrew in their public and intellectual work. New western European Haskalah leaders cast Yiddish as a bastardized creole dialect. In doing so, they to gendered Yiddish as female and valued it less in comparison with Hebrew. In eastern Europe, however, many Haskalah leaders chose to continue to conduct their intellectual work in Yiddish. In the radical upheaval of the Soviet revolutions, Yiddish became, for a time, an official language in more than one of the new Soviet Socialist Republics.[53] Eastern European Yiddish cultures bequeathed a radical political legacy to the emergence of US Jewish culture. Contemporary leftist Yiddish communities embrace this radical legacy and the status Yiddish gained in much of eastern Europe. Similarly, radical feminist and queer Ashkenazi circles often explicitly revalue its feminized history.

At the same time, in US culture unfamiliar with and semi-to-overtly hostile to Jews, Yiddish is a marker of Jewish difference, negatively valenced. Yiddish can be used to delineate Jews as old-fashioned; parochial; oriented toward G-d rather than the world; clustered closely in a way that appears to reinscribe Christian antisemitic tropes of Jews as backward, a people burdened by rules and a vengeful god, as opposed to the open, merciful tradition of Jesus that supposedly superseded theirs. This became a secular set of antisemitic associations in the US as well, and it emerged in particular ways on the left—just as the Christianity of the colonial mindset developed tropes of its light over and against the darkness of domestic Jewish populations and the Indigenous peoples it found in imperialist ventures: bringing the torch of education, ending patriarchal oppression, and joyously ending the rule of superstition and racist, homophobic tyrants. As a result, many Jews seeking to move beyond both material discrimination and abject associations attached to Jewishness sought to distance themselves from Jewish identifications. Yiddish came to epitomize just such a Jewish marker, perhaps because it served as a Jewish grounding common to both secular and religious Jews. Jewish men have been at the forefront of this rejection of Yiddish, given the heterosexist and sexist devaluing of Jews as feminized (with its particular impact on Jewish Men). Despite the ways that Yiddish can be mobilized in antisemitic tropes, which many Jews have also internalized, Yiddish also has a grand place in the history of the Jewish Left and US anarchism, in Goldman's time and today.

Feminists, lesbians, and a range of queers have been central to the revitalization of Yiddish arts and culture and the development of an exciting Yiddish leftist and anarchist scene. Attention to Yiddish culture in the 1986 publication of *The Tribe of Dina* by Melanie Kaye/Kantrowitz and Irena Klepfisz reflects developments in Jewish feminism and various queer and leftist communities. Adrienne Cooper, who came out later in life, was a significant leader in the 1980s revival of Klezmer music. The founders of one of the most popular modern Klezmer bands, the Klezmatics (klezmatics.com), included out queer musicians, such as the well-known Jewish lesbian Alicia Svigals. The Klezmatics named their first album, *Shvaygn = Toyt* (1988), Yiddish for "silence = death," the slogan of the AIDS activist group ACT UP, and their logo reclaimed anti-Jewish Holocaust symbols. In 1998, Eve Sicular, leader in the band Metropolitan Klezmer since 1994, began giving presentations from her project "The Celluloid Closet in Yiddish Film" (Sicular 1999) and formed the explicitly lesbian band Isle of Klezbos (klezbos.com). Many lesbians and other queers were active in the US Klezcamp (klezkamp.org) and the still-operating Canadian KlezKanada (klezkanada.org). Lesbians and queers have been central to an array of Yiddish music and performance art.[54] Additionally, the activist Esther Kaplan and lesbian scholars and activists Alisa Solomon and Marilyn Neimark initiated the WBAI New York weekly radio show *Beyond the Pale*, which ran for nineteen years, until its demise in 2014. The program featured Jewish culture along with politics and analysis from a Jewish perspective (beyondthepale.org).[55] The history of Jewish anarchist collectives remains alive and well through various other Jewish Left, feminist, and queer experiments, such as the Linke Fligl—active during the time this book was prepared and disbanding in 2022—"a queer Jewish chicken farm & cultural organizing project that uses farming and gathering to grow a Jewish culture aligned with the values of disasporism, collective liberation and dreaming the world to come" (linkefligl.com).

Eclipsing Judeo-Spanish in the late 1800s,[56] Yiddish has been a primary "Jewish language" spoken in the US for more than a century. Hollywood and US popular culture continue to portray Yiddish as a "feminized" language, an embarrassment for Jews and a signifier of inherent queerness or suspect gender and sexuality. Tracing Goldman's anarchism, together with her feminist and proto-queer politics, to vibrant Yiddish traditions of anarchism and the Left places these radical traditions at the heart of the US Jewish experience. Understanding the significant connections both Goldman and anarchism have to Yiddish communities, their languages, and cultures helps to reveal an inspiring legacy of feminist, queer, and leftist Jewish politics in the West.

Goldman's Wider Jewish Grounding

Having grounded Goldman in a Yiddish context, clarifying the vivacity of Yiddish culture within the Jewish Left and among Jewish anarchists, we can now look to related aspects of Goldman's Jewish commitments. Despite the general silence among scholars and activists on Jewish matters of import with respect to Goldman, there is much here of interest. In this section we will address three particular arenas of note: (1) not uncommon in her day or ours, Goldman often used biblical, spiritual, and Jewish references in her oratory (including reference to the thought of Jewish anarchist Gustav Landauer); (2) Goldman's meetings with and writings on the Jewish situation in Ukraine were singular and affected her interest in being able to consider Jewish concerns not only within a wider revolutionary movement but also in their specificity; and (3) throughout her life, Goldman maintained ties to a wide array of Jewish comrades and Jewish anarchist groups. These transnational ties were central to her popular success and often also to her well-being and even survival.

While a fierce critic of organized religion and theism, her ire was reserved mostly for Christianity (for example, see Goldman 1916). She was intensely spiritual, as are many Jewish feminists and radicals today.[57] In her insistence on beauty and spiritual freedom, Goldman often referred to the spiritual in her political oratory, especially in the way she waxed eloquent about a love of liberty, the desire for beauty in art, or spiritual deprivation under capitalism (especially in the US). While biblical references are not uncommon for leftist revolutionaries, it is instructive to note some of Goldman's particular use. It can be helpful to resituate what is often referred to as the "utopianism" of revolutionaries such as Goldman within Jewish messianic traditions, inspiring and organizing communities (as a secular version, not waiting on any divine presence) to usher in an age of harmony and freedom. As an example, Goldman relied heavily on metaphors of the promised land to refer to the US when she was young and finding her way as a refugee and immigrant from the Russian Empire; she later used the same metaphors for Russia after the revolutions there had begun (Ashbolt 2003). Additionally, Goldman consistently leaned on the Hebrew prophetic tradition in railing against injustice.

As young people, Goldman and Berkman both left a Europe teeming with violent antisemitism. But their departure predated the worst decades of the pre–World War II pogroms. As pogroms throughout the Russian Empire increased and as the Bolshevik (communist) party grew following the 1917 revolution, many Jews became pro-communist because they saw the Bolsheviks as the primary force opposing the pogroms and the czarist regime that countenanced them. Berman (2019) notes that as pogroms in eastern Europe increased and refugee resettlement in the US soared, Jewish leftist movements, and particularly radical ideologies such as anarchism, simultaneously gained more ground in their new country. Like Meir later and many others in this period, Goldman, too, arrived as a Russian Jewish refugee and became a leader in these burgeoning movements. The blossoming of the Jewish Left within the context of an adaptive Jewish and Yiddish culture in the US had a profound influence on her as she became an instigator and draw for millions.

While in exile from the US back in Russian and Ukraine, Goldman met with Jews of all political affiliations—anarchists, Zionists, communists, Bundists—as well as individuals in the intelligentsia and bourgeoisie generally. While a small minority within each of their political groupings and in the country, approximately two million Jews were active in the various political movements in Ukraine at that time. Goldman noted the virulent antisemitism of many Christian peasants and others whom she met in Ukraine (Wexler 1989, 40). In the years of Goldman's later period there, after the US deported her to Russia in 1919, the czarist forces carried out even more lethal pogroms killing approximately sixty thousand Jews (39). From inside Russia and Ukraine, both Goldman and Berkman wrote on Jewish matters, along with anarchist issues, from their firsthand experience while there.[58] Alice Wexler notes, "As few Western visitors had access either to the Russian anarchists or to the Ukraine at the height of the civil war, Goldman's account was valuable as one of the earliest to present a first-hand report of these relatively unknown sides of Russia" (74–75).

Goldman's Jewish experience contributed to her struggle with a central tension for many political theorists and activists. Across the political gamut, most theorists, from the right to mainstream liberalism to the left, have tended to eschew particularism. Despite their differing aims, most Western political theories and movements consider attention to diversity a threat to overall goals, whether those goals be nationalism, a well-ordered state under the rule of law, or an international workers' revolution. While Goldman was always in close connection with Jewish communities, she did not always integrate a concern with Jewish specificity deeply into her larger revolutionary agenda. In contrast, attention to cultural specificity has become key to post-1960s feminism, and to queer and intersectional leftist movements more broadly, and Goldman's grappling with Jewish experience makes her an interesting forerunner of this shift on the left.

With her firsthand experience, visiting with Jews and speaking on an array of issues including antisemitism and the growing pogroms, Goldman adjusted her stance about the need to take a distinctive position on explicitly Jewish matters. She wrote, "When I was in America I did not believe in the Jewish question removed from the whole social question. But since we visited some of the pogrom regions I have come to see that there is a Jewish question, especially in the Ukraine."[59] While increasingly vocal in opposing the Soviet revolution's centralization of power and aware that many communists were also antisemitic, Goldman still acknowledged the central role the Soviet government played in challenging such widespread and destructive antisemitism. She also encouraged the US Jewish community to press at least for the US to establish diplomatic relations with Russia (a matter of great contention in the West).

Lastly for this section, in Goldman's early years in the US, and particularly in her later years of exile, her Jewish ties continued to be a main grounding for her. When Goldman's Jewish ties flagged, her isolation and desolation grew.[60] Certainly, there were numerous contributing factors to Goldman's sense of isolation while in exile in Europe after her time in Russia. She was then over fifty and her financial support had grown spotty. Her outspoken criticism of the Soviet Union caused significant rifts between her and many on the left (including long-term comrades). At the same time, due to antisemitism, this period marked significant Jewish refugee resettlement outside of Europe, and the European Jewish Left was therefore in precipitous decline. This decline of the Jewish Left in many European capitals in this period decimated the communities in which Goldman usually found her emotional support. For example, by the time Goldman moved to London in the fall of 1924, the radical and anarchist Jewish immigrant and refugee communities of the East End (akin to New York City's Lower East Side) had largely dispersed (Wexler 1989, 93). Wexler (1989) notes that Goldman expected to find a strong base for her work with remaining Jewish anarchists there, but unfortunately that turned out not to be her best option, as the anarchist groups and press there were no longer hotbeds of activity.[61]

Throughout her life, and particularly during her later years in exile, connecting to Jewish communities continued to be central for Goldman's survival and success. To see this in operation, we can look to Goldman's next period in Canada. While Goldman was received well by many comrades in London, she was not able to find sufficient grounding for herself there at that time. In 1925, she organized to get to Canada, primarily because she had ties in the Jewish immigrant and refugee anarchist and leftist Yiddish communities there, with whom she had stayed in touch over time and from whom she received a generous welcome. Once there, Goldman was also able to organize among English-speaking anarchists as well. Her disillusionment with the Canadian Jewish anarchist movement was connected to her larger difficulty working with any anarchist groups at that historical moment, for she wrote to Berkman that she was not used to working in groups and found group meetings tiresome (Wexler 1989, 120–22).[62]

As she continued to move often into and throughout the 1930s, Goldman's ties to Jewish communities helped revive her presence in the news and her reputation as a dynamic speaker. Goldman became very popular again in the US during the 1930s, despite the frequent vilification she had previously experienced here from both the mainstream and even much of the Left. Her autobiography was very popular, reviving her celebrity. Wexler (1989, 163) also notes that by the 1930s and heading into what would become World War II, Goldman "had become a symbol of a world situation in which growing numbers of people had become refugees from political persecution by fascist regimes," central for Jews and so many.[63]

Goldman worked actively during the rise of fascism in the years leading up to World War II.[64] On the eve of the war, though not a pacifist, Goldman recommitted to her anti-war position. While she hated Hitler, Franco, and Mussolini, she still assessed the Western democracies that she knew as "fascist in disguise," criticized England and France for not doing enough to prevent fascist victories, and warned that the new war would bring about "a new form of madness in the world" (Wexler 1989, 236). These remain important critiques given the facile ways propaganda in places such as the US distanced the Allied powers from Nazism to aid the war effort, who nonetheless practiced—then and now—many despicable policies. Like Arendt, she also criticized German and French Jewish leadership of the time for not standing up sufficiently to rising antisemitism (Wexler 1989, 237–38). However, even as late as the end of 1939, despite maintaining close ties to Jewish friends and comrades internationally (235), Goldman likely severely underestimated the antisemitism of the German Nazi program. This did not mean that she abandoned her Jewishly related work. She continued to speak out loudly against Hitler and other fascist leaders and movements and to agitate for Jewish refugees as well (238).[65] We cannot know if her analysis would have shifted or how she might have centered antisemitism (as she did in seeing the catastrophe of eastern European pogroms firsthand) and Nazism had she lived through the ensuing war years.

Goldman and Contemporary Jewish Political Theory: Anarchism and Radical Diasporism

In addition to her own important Jewish context in her time, Goldman also remains an important figure for those seeking Jewish collective solutions as part of their revolutionary struggles. The turn into modernity in the West opened some new options for ending centuries of antisemitism (Avineri 1981). There were new narrow, yet interesting, opportunities for Jews to participate in revolutionary movements, such as Liberalism's emphasis on the potential radical equality of individual citizenship (in the stead of seeing people mainly as groups in conflict-ridden ethno-tribes); the creation of new nation-states in western Europe sometimes appeared to have positive prospects for ending Jewish otherness; and socialism of the 1800s promised liberation of all workers and all peoples from exploitation. As Jews in parts of Europe were slowly allowed beyond historically segregated ghetto walls, some Jews opted for individual assimilation into their host countries. Many other Jews invested in Liberal and national revolutions. Jews also joined socialist movements in droves and participated actively in the Bolshevik revolutions in Russia. With this, some Jews also sought explicitly Jewish collective avenues against antisemitism and toward revolution.

Jewish autonomous movements also developed in many forms.[66] Some Jews created Jewish sections of socialist parties. Others advocated for semiautonomous Jewish regions in Europe. Often referred to as "the Bund," the socialist General Jewish Labor Bund emerged throughout the late 1800s across Lithuania, Poland, and Russia. One could argue that the Bund became the driving force of Polish Jewry moving into World War II, when most of its members were murdered in the Holocaust, along with the larger decimation of Polish Jewry.[67]

Zionism, with its many strains from binationalism, to cultural autonomy, to statist paradigms, developed in these years also as a significant Jewish collective response to the problem of antisemitism and as a Jewishly specific aspect of international revolutionary and anticolonial movements. Zionism was not widely embraced by Jews as a movement or political theory.[68] Even since the founding of the modern state of Israel, most Jews continue to live across the globe instead of within this Jewish homeland. Jewish debates between Zionists, non-Zionists, and anti-Zionists on the best avenues to combat antisemitism and how to engage Jewish specificity in larger revolutionary struggles have long been vibrant and often fierce. Intense divisions existed (and exist) also among Zionists. As not all strands of Zionism were (or are today) statist, there were also Jewish anarchists who engaged with Zionism and developments in Palestine. In a telling glimpse into the intricacies of this period, despite her criticism of Zionists, in 1937, Goldman wrote in a letter to a friend that she might go to Palestine if she would not be able to obtain a visa back into the US (Ferguson 2011, 279).

Consider Goldman's articulation of this vision of anarchism: "economic arrangements must consist of voluntary productive and distributive associations, gradually developing into free communism, as the best means of producing with the least waste of human energy. Anarchism, however, also recognizes the right of the individual, or numbers of individuals, to arrange at all times for other forms of work, in harmony with their tastes and desires" ([1917] 1969, 56).[69] The collectivist orientation, what some consider small communitarian socialist experiments if they have not seriously studied anarchism, of the kibbutz and moshav movements was inspiring for many anarchists.[70] Additionally, some activists worked to keep anarchist principles engaged in the strong labor movement developing in the Yishuv and later Israel.[71] There remains a small but active anarchist movement in Israel today.

Another aspect that some on the radical left today might find surprising, given an all-too-often superficial critique of Zionism at its foundation as a simple instantiation of settler colonialism, is that, particularly since the Holocaust period, many Jews and others across the political spectrum supported Jewish emigration to Palestine, even if non- and anti-Zionist.[72] Many anarchists, including Goldman, were among these politically active Jews seeking solutions to the extreme refugee crisis created up to and during the Holocaust and believing Jews deserved access to the human right to settle and form individual and collective lives in safety. Many anarchists, including Goldman (Wexler 1989, 238), remaining fiercely anticolonial, anti-statist, anti-militarist, and anti-organized religion, worked hard to end barriers to Jewish refugees to then-British-occupied Palestine. In praxis, real-life circumstances, and theory, these are not contradictory positions.

The diverse organizations within the Zionist movement have long been a home for numerous politically active Jews. Still, many Jews today are inspired when learning of the Bund tradition. Masses of engaged Jews long affiliated outside the rather small infrastructure of Zionist organizations in the diaspora. Particularly with extreme right-wing leadership developing in the 1970s in Israel and extending decade after decade, many Jews actively seek alternatives to the Zionist paradigm as an example of a Jewish collective option for ending antisemitism and participating in social justice movements. Goldman's legacy can be of great help in this current moment on these questions as well.

Despite the rich Jewish history of Western anarchism, not enough is generally known today about anarchism as a political theory and activist movement. However, a study of Goldman's feminist anarchism can help us do the work needed today in making sense of the Jewish condition and imagining Jewishly grounded vistas for justice, particularly in a diasporic context. Not only does anarchism critique statist paradigms of sovereignty, but, in their experiments of direct action and propaganda by the deed, activists also live out and test collective alternatives to statist structures. While there was a diaspora even during the period of the ancient biblical Jewish kingdoms in the land of Israel, for the past two millennia, Jewish life has existed in an anarchic field outside the parameters of states or premodern politically sovereign entities.

While local understandings and practices of Jewish law have been important for Jewish communities for centuries of diasporic life, Jews have no single authority structure even in religious, non-statist terms. Thus, it can be helpful to note that, empirically, Jewish life has mostly operated within an anarchist field. This does not mean that there are no power structures within Jewish communities or modes of power any subgroups or individuals experience as oppressive. But Jewish communal diasporic organizational configurations as a whole are anarchic, without a structure such as the church or pope functioning the way that they have historically for Christians, or any governing structures within statist paradigms.

Like anarchists and anarchist collectivist experiments in the past century or so, for the past two thousand years Jewish communities have existed within states and empires, often requiring interaction with states that create much of the contours of their vistas of possibility. At times, these empires or states have granted Jewish bodies governance rights over their populations, in fraught relation with the larger states within which they are situated. In these various incarnations of Jewish grappling with power and communal self-organization transnationally and across centuries, anarchists have much to learn from Jewish life over time and place in history. Similarly, Jews, in all of our diversity, have much to learn from anarchism.

Many Jews today explore options to embrace and revalue the antisemitic characterization of Jews as rootless cosmopolitans. Goldman's and larger anarchist traditions of transnationalism are helpful here. In this vein, it is also not surprising that there is a renewed Jewish interest in the Bund. Jews seek to envision new forms of radical diasporism.[73] In addition to self-identified contemporary non- and anti-Zionists, any number of Jews (both within and outside of Israel) seek to explore options for vibrant Jewish communal life in the places that Jews live around the globe. Looking to articulate and live out experiments for positively valenced diasporic Jewish life, many Jews explore options outside of various Zionists paradigms developed over time.

Appealing to many today, Yiddishist Bundism promulgated a theory of *doikayt*, or "hereness," looking for solutions for Jewish and other problems and paths for vibrant lives lived with meaning in the places Jews make their homes.[74] This has made much sense in the US context of the twenty-first century, with both rising antisemitism and still relatively open conceptual and actual spaces for Jewish ingenuity and collective experimentation. While the Bund was historically associated as socialist and communist, many of these ideas are central anarchist contributions.

Bundists were proudly Jewish and generally secularist. They sought to center Jewishness in their activities, analyses, and political work. They created explicitly Jewish organizations to work on distinctly Jewish issues as also part of their wider revolutionary agendas.[75] While any particular Bundists historically may have come from religiously knowledgeable and/or observant families and continued as such in their own lives, the Jewishness put forward publicly was expressly secular. This secularism, and secular engagements with Jewish history (from which one cannot separate Jewish law, mysticism, theology, holidays, ancient texts, etc.), is also appealing to many Jews. As we saw with Kahlo, and in some ways all of the subjects with whom we have been thinking in these pages, it is helpful to clarify understandings of Jewishness as beyond a largely Protestant imperialist creation as a religion. An attraction for Jewish communal options developed in secular, or not exclusively religious, modes is particularly important in a country such as the US where many Jews are not affiliated Jewishly as a religious category. Similarly, the overwhelming majority of US Jews affiliate Jewishly outside of orthodoxy and other halachic structures to contour their Jewish aspirations, while religiously observant and orthodox-affiliated Jews often still find these culturally informed Jewish engagements exciting as well.[76]

Conclusion

Emma Goldman was a notable figure in her lifetime, notorious to some, inspiring to many. Goldman's life and legacy remain important for us today. Goldman's ideas, activism, networks, and organizing, as well as her publications, were provocative, keeping the radical edge of the Left fresh and a force with which to be reckoned. Her strain of anarchism provided a foundation for 1960s-style US grassroots political movements by feminists, antiracists, post-McCarthy democratic socialists, queers, anticolonialists, and climate justice activists within which we still operate in many ways. Her insistence on grassroots democracy and collective experiments, on taking seriously relations between the personal and political, on women's conditions in their diversity, on sexual and gender liberation, on beauty and art, on facing the powers that be, on standing up to statist, capitalist, militaristic, and religious imperialism as individuals and groups continue to be lessons for us today.

Anarchism is both a political theory and a robust activist movement. It has had a long history that has critically examined and tested on the ground many facets at the heart of what is most attractive to many contemporary Jews about Bundism and other left Jewish historical movements. These crossovers between contemporary Jewish interest and Goldman's "beautiful ideal" include the anarchist core concepts critiquing the "power over" modes of exploitation key to statism, militarism, patriarchy, religious fundamentalism, capitalism, and the more expressly articulated homophobic, transphobic, racist, and anti-colonial struggles of her time and ours.

Finally, I remind us that Jewish life, in culturally diverse settings and over time, has functioned empirically largely in an anarchist field. Given the vibrancy of Goldman's contributions and anarchism more broadly, it behooves us to attend to the conflicts within anarchism and its insights as a frame for Jewish studies, and particularly Jewish feminist and queer politics, thinking, and world making. In this way I argue that anarchism is both empirically (about what is) and normatively (about what might be) of central interest in Jewish life and Jewish studies today.

Notes

Chapter 1

1. I owe a deep gratitude to Lori Marso in many ways and for the methodology she employed and developed in her *Feminist Thinkers and the Demands of Femininity* (Marso 2006). That book (an early publication in Marso's productive career) and method helped me early on to envision how to approach this project.

2. I would rerun my searches for new material every so often over the years. Of course, I am sure that I missed too much good work. For example, I thank Evi Beck for introducing me to Amy Feinstein's (2022) work on Stein and Jewish modernism as I was prepping the volume for production. Academic works can take an awfully long time to get out into the world.

3. There are excellent resources for those in search of other Jewish women to think with. Also, to move beyond my anglophone limitations, see, for example, *The Shalvi/Hyman Encyclopedia of Jewish Women* (https://jwa.org/encyclopedia) and the Jewish Women's Archive database in general (jwa.org); Khazzoom (2022); Sartori and Cottenet-Hage (2006).

4. See pivotal collections such as Honig (1996) on Arendt and an example of the flourishing of multiple modes of Arendt scholarship since such as Jones (2013).

5. In the Kahlo chapter, I clarify where this question regarding Kahlo's Jewish identity comes from and some relevant aspects of her self-presentation (and Rivera's self-presentation). Before we get to Kahlo, readers will learn with me that Arendt identified four character types for her category of a pariah. Arendt chooses Charlie Chaplin to represent one of these. Chaplin was not Jewish. But people often thought he was. Looking at Chaplin worked for Arendt because of what he stood for. Whatever Kahlo's Jewish status is, I find her inspiring in helping me learn that one of many ways we might be Jewish is to live in dense transnational networks of connection with many Jews.

6. The term comes from Higginbotham (1993).

7. *Parvenu* is the traditional spelling of this term, from the French. The word with the *u* ending is masculine. Some write *parvenu.e* to note masculine

and feminine in the singular and *parvenu.e.s* plural. Moving still beyond a gender binary but honoring new language developments among French speakers, I use a question mark, hence *parvenu?e* and *parvenu?e.s*, to continue to query the gender binary in language exploration.

Chapter 2

1. After working in the register of home and away for this chapter, I also explored Kincaid's way of weaving together multiple places of home and away.

2. Kincaid does not often directly address each of these themes in a Jewish context. In a rare joining of Jewish, African, and Caribbean critical tropes, in her novel *Mr. Potter*, Kincaid writes of a Czech Jewish refugee, Dr. Weizenger, and Kincaid's biological father, Mr. Potter, who is of African and European descent: "And Dr. Weizenger was thinking how beautiful light of any kind was, light that did not come from a furnace, a real furnace fed by the fuel of coal or human bodies; light, real light, with its opposite being darkness, not a metaphor for the darkness from which Mr. Potter and his ancestors had come" (2002, 16). On Holocaust imagery in Kincaid, see Phillips-Casteel (2013), where Black and Jewish are seen as separate entities needing an encounter.

3. In one example, Thomas (2019) analyzes Kincaid in the context of faith and politics in a diaspora-studies context but places her only within a Christian frame. This absence in the scholarly literature on Kincaid continues even since the publication of her most explicitly Jewish work, her 2013 *See Now Then*.

4. A small body of work in this field begins with Memmi (1967) and more recently includes examples such as Cheyette (2014), Slabodsky (2014), Brettschneider (2015, 2019), Abbasi (2017), Levins-Morales (2019), and Kałczewiak (2019). On the Jewish Levinas in this context, see, for example, Maldonado-Torres (2007) and P. Anderson (2017).

5. Some scholars have discussed the role of diaspora in Kincaid's work, and in relation to colonialism (Soto-Crespo 2002).

6. Note this self-reflection in *At the Bottom of the River*: "But I swim in a shaft of light, upside down, and I can see myself clearly, through and through, from every angle. Perhaps I stand on the brink of a great discovery, and perhaps after I have made my great discovery I will be sent home in chains" (Kincaid 1983b, 21).

7. Kincaid (1997) wrote in *My Brother*, "I could not have become a writer while living among the people I knew best, I could not have become myself while living among the people I knew best—and I only knew them best because I was from them, of them, and so often felt I was them—and they were—are—the people who ought to have loved me best in the whole world, the people who should have made me feel that the love of people other than them was suspect" (162). For a queer-studies analysis of *My Brother*, see Walcott (2011).

8. Or in *The Autobiography of My Mother*: "This picture was nothing but a field full of grass and flowers on a sunny day, but it had an atmosphere of secret abundance, happiness, and tranquility; underneath it was written in gold letters the one word HEAVEN. Of course it was not a picture of heaven at all; it was a picture of the English countryside idealized" (Kincaid 1996, 9). For a de-colonial critique of this text, see Adair (2019).

9. Only years later, in a news interview, does Kincaid make any comparison with the Western Wall in Jerusalem in the Jewish tradition (Schwartz 2019). In Brettschneider (2016) I argue that Kincaid's frame for exile is more the biblical Garden of Eden than the Jewish dispersion from Jerusalem. See also Kincaid's (2020) "The Disturbances of the Garden," written more recently, on this point.

10. See Gordon (2016). Kincaid's text with the most explicit Jewish references is *See Now Then*. Even here, the Jewish references are not always as direct as those regarding African heritage: "What is the essence of Love? But that was a question for Mr. Sweet, for he grew up in the atmosphere of questions of life and death: the murder of millions of people in a short period of time who lived continents away from each other; on the other hand hovering over Mrs. Sweet, though she had been made to understand it as if it were a style of a skirt, or the style of the shape of a blouse, a collar, a sleeve, was a monstrosity, a distortion of human relationships: The Atlantic Slave Trade" (Kincaid 2013, 12).

11. Previous eminent winners include Gwendolyn Brooks, James Baldwin, Maya Angelou, Toni Morrison, Octavia Butler, Zadie Smith, and Rita Dove.

12. "What I am really interested in is balance of power and the abuse of power and the collecting of power—this is the only thing that matters. In the end, it doesn't matter who has the power" (Lev-Ari 2004). See also Aldrich (2012).

13. In *Lucy*, "Mariah says, 'I have Indian blood in me,' and underneath everything I could swear she says it as if she were announcing her possession of a trophy. How do you get to be the sort of victor who can claim to be the vanquished also?" (Kincaid 1990, 40–41). See also Brettschneider (2002); Gregg (1999).

14. From *Autobiography of My Mother*: "I ask, What makes the world turn against me and all who look like me? I own nothing, I survey nothing, when I ask this question; the luxury of an answer that will fill volumes does not stretch out before me. When I ask this question, my voice is filled with despair" (Kincaid 1996, 132). Kincaid also states,

> *Mr. Potter* describes the world of blacks living in a state of perpetual humiliation, a world without human emotion, even without despair. A world in which people learn to hate themselves and cannot help but hate everything around them. Can a human being exist in a wilderness, a world so empty of human feeling: love and justice; a world in which love, and even that, justice, only exist from time to time and in small quantities, or unexpectedly, like a wild seedling of some necessary and

common food (rice would do, or corn would do, or grain of any kind)? The answer is yes and yes again and the answer is no, not really, not so at all. (Lev-Ari 2004)

15. Speaking of her brother in a corresponding text, Kincaid (1997) writes:

> He was obsessed with the great thieves who inhabited his part of the world, the great hero-thieves of English maritime history. . . . He thought that the thing called history was an account of significant triumphs over significant defeats recorded by significant people who had benefited from the significant triumphs; he thought (as do I) that this history of ours was primarily an account of theft and murder ("Dem tief, dem a dam tief"), but presented it in such a way as to make the account seem inevitable and even fun: he liked the costumes of it, he liked the endings, the outcomes; he liked the people who won, even though he was among the things that had been won." (94, 95)

Or see *At the Bottom of the River* (Kincaid 1983b, 48–49).

16. See a parallel dynamic also in *Lucy*: "Early that morning, Mariah left her own compartment to come and tell me that we were passing through some of those freshly plowed fields she loved so much. She drew up my blind, and when I saw mile after mile of turned up earth, I said, a cruel tone to my voice, 'Well, thank god I didn't have to do that.' I don't know if she understood what I meant, for in that one statement I meant many different things" (Kincaid 1990, 33).

17. From *A Small Place*: "We, for as long as we have known you, *were* capital, like bales of cotton and sacks of sugar. . . . You will have to accept that this is mostly your fault. Let me just show you how you looked at us. You came. You took things that were not yours, and you did not even, for appearances' sake, ask first. . . . You murdered people. You imprisoned people. You robbed people" (Kincaid 1988, 34–37).

18. Selengut (2006) writes of Kincaid:

> She traced the history of her own culture back to that crucial moment of other-defined identity—the arrival of Columbus in the Bahamas in 1492. As a Spanish-speaker landing in an unfamiliar locale, the explorer attempted to "feel at home" by giving Spanish names to the places he saw, as well as by writing descriptions of the natives, whom he described as "serviceable" in his journals. For Kincaid, the very act of writing, employed by Columbus at that time and still used by many today, constitutes a power act. To describe a group of people, how they look and act, is to own their identity, she suggested. This is even truer, she added, when the individuals described are illiterate and thus have no literary voice with which to respond.

19. Kincaid (1988) describes, with respect to tourists visiting Antigua,

> You have brought your own books with you, and among them is one of those new books about economic history, one of those books explaining how the West (meaning Europe and North America after its conquest and settlements by Europeans) got rich: the West got rich not from the free (free—in this case meaning got-for-nothing) and then undervalued labour, for generations, of the people like me you see walking around you in Antigua but from the ingenuity of small shopkeepers in Sheffield and Yorkshire and Lancashire, or wherever . . . (isn't that the last straw; for not only did we have to suffer the unspeakableness of slavery, but the satisfaction to be had from "We made you bastards rich" is taken away, too), and so you needn't let that slightly funny feeling you have from time to time about exploitation, oppression, domination develop into full-fledged unease, discomfort; you could ruin your holiday. (9–10)

20. Kincaid (2013) relays her character's child's Global Northern critique: "The fucking stupid little island on which she was born, full of stupid people whom history would be happy to forget but she has to keep reminding everybody about that place and those people and no one cares and she can't stand it" (129).

21. See Plaskow (1991) for a critical reckoning of this concept. Kincaid's point in this interview is of note: "You think: Here's the thing about human beings and bad things—we do it again, but in a somewhat different form. The same thing doesn't happen twice. The same thing happens, but differently. Everyone would like to be the only victim. We don't make room for the fact that the other people are capable of narratives, that they are people" (Sela 2010).

22. From *Mr. Potter*:

> And I hold in my hand a document that certifies the day of my own birth (the twenty-fifth of May, nineteen hundred and forty-nine), the name given to me at my own birth (Elaine Cynthia), the name of my mother (Annie Richardson) . . . and there is an empty space with a line drawn through it where the name of my father, Roderick Nathaniel Potter, ought to be, for Mr. Potter was my father; my father's name was Roderick Nathaniel Potter. And this line that runs through Mr. Potter and that he then gave to me, I have not given to anyone, I have not ceded to anyone, I have brought it to an end, I have made it stop with me, for I can read and I can write and I now say, in writing that this line drawn through the space where the name of the father ought to be has come to an end, and that from Mr. Potter to me, no one after shall have a line drawn through the space where the name of their father ought to be. (Kincaid 2002, 100–101)

23. Of note: the text known to many Jews as "the bible" is also not necessarily known in the same form to Jewish communities across the globe or specifically to Jews in Africa and the African diaspora, and many of these colonized and diasporic communities are pre- or non-Talmudic (Brettschneider 2015).

24. From *A Small Place*:

> What I see is the millions of people, of whom I am just one, made orphans: no motherland, no fatherland, no gods, no mounds of earth for holy ground, no excess of love which might lead to the things that an excess of love sometimes brings, and worst and most painful of all, no tongue. For isn't it odd that the only language I have in which to speak of this crime is the language of the criminal who committed the crime? And what can that really mean? For the language of the criminal can contain only the goodness of the criminal's deed. The language of the criminal can explain and express the deed only from the criminal's point of view. It cannot contain the horror of the deed, the injustice of the deed, the agony, the humiliation inflicted on me. (Kincaid 1988, 31–32)

25. Kincaid's character Lucy writes about having a pen pal on a neighboring island colonized by France, "The stamps on her letter were always canceled with the French words for liberty, equality, and fraternity; on mine there were no such words, only the image of a stony-face, sour-mouth woman. I understand the situation better now; I understand that, in spite of those words, my pen pal and I were in the same boat; but still I think those words have a better ring to them than the image of a stony-face, sour-mouth woman" (1990, 136).

26. In a *Missouri Review* interview, Kincaid reflects on how being raised under British colonialism is present within her work:

> When I read it out loud, I become aware of the influence of the things I read as a child—images from Christian mythology and Paradise Lost . . . I was brought up to understand that English traditions were right and mine were wrong. Within the life of an English person there was always clarity, and within an English culture there was always clarity, but within my life and culture was ambiguity. A person who is dead in England is dead. A person where I come from who is dead might not be dead. I was taught to think of ambiguity as magic, a shadiness and an illegitimacy, not the real thing of Western civilization. (Bonetti 2002)

27. Kincaid's (1983b) character is questioned about how life in Antigua is different from the colonizer's daily life:

"But things are so funny here."
"But where? But how?"
"We are going to the May fair, but it's July. They are dancing a May dance around a Maypole, but it's July. They are crowning a May queen, but it's July. At Christmas, just before our big dinner, we take a long swim in the warm seawater. After that, we do not bathe, and in the heat the salt dries on our bodies in little rings."
"Aren't things funny here?"
"Yes, things are funny here." (34)

28. Note how Kincaid (1997) offers this portrayal: "I once did not see my mother for twenty years, even though I thought of her first thing in the morning and last thing at night" (154). For more on Kincaid's complex politics presented in the tangle of mother-daughter relations, see Dance (2015) and Morris (2014).

29. Kincaid (1997) muses, "On the whole, every scene, every memory remained itself, just itself, and sometimes a certain color might make memory more vivid and sometimes again, not so at all, just not so at all; sometimes a memory is without color, a dream is often like that, without color, but the absence of color does not mean an absence of truth, or truth in a way that one could understand as not falsehood" (170).

30. In exile now from the Caribbean, Kincaid (2013) employs this trope from Hebrew prayers (always and forever ever, Amen): "Inside now, it was as if the children, her own children did not exist, only herself as a child did exist, and she now entered the temple, the sacred heart of her own life: See, Now, Then, and so it went on and on, these visitations, a holy journey into her past, around and around that room in which she sat and examined her life as it had been, as it was, and as it would be, for it was all the same, always just as it ever was and always just as it always would be" (166).

31. In *Mr. Potter*: "The mind's eye is the land of the almost, the geography of the mind's eye is the almost, it's atmosphere is made of the elements, the almost, the as if, the like, the in the vicinity of, the almost, its reality: the almost!" (Kincaid 2002, 107). Or see in *My Brother*:

> My mother gathered up all the books I owned and put them on her stone heap, sprinkling them with kerosene and setting them alight; I cannot remember the titles of these books, I cannot remember what they were about . . . but it would not be strange if I spent the rest of my life trying to bring these books back to my life by writing them again and again until they were perfect, unscathed by fire of any kind . . . the source of the books has not died, it only comes alive again and again in different forms and other segments. (Kincaid 1997, 197–98)

32. In *Lucy:*

> While the weather sorted itself out in various degrees of coldness, I walked around with letters from my family and friends scorching my breasts. I had placed these letters inside my brassiere, and carried them around with me wherever I went. It was not from feelings of love and longing that I did this; quite the contrary. It was from a feeling of hatred. There was nothing so strange about this, for isn't it so that love and hate exist side by side? Each letter was a letter from someone I had loved at one time without reservation. (Kincaid 1990, 21)

33. Note this rumination in *At the Bottom of the River*:

> What is my nature, then? For in isolation I am all purpose and industry and determination and prudence, as if I were the single survivor of a species whose evolutionary history can be traced to the most ancient of ancients; in isolation I ruthlessly plow the deep silences, seeking my opportunities like a miner seeking veins of treasure. In what shallow glimmering space shall I find what glimmering glory? The stark, stony mountainous surface is turned to green, rolling meadow, and a spring of clear water, its origins of mystery, its purpose of beauty constant, draws all manner of troubled existence seeking solace. And again and again . . . (Kincaid 1983b, 48)

34. "Luxury being absent from my existence unless I saw an illustration of what might be on a tin cheap powder imported from England, and this picture of luxury only demonstrated what it might look like if one did not have to work at all, and so luxury was presented as contempt for working and any association with the dullness of the everyday" (Kincaid 1997, 132–33).

35. Kincaid (1996) writes, "I was taught the principles involved in writing an ordinary letter. . . . It was well known that a person in the position that I was expected to occupy—the position of a woman and a poor one—would have no need whatsoever to write a letter, but the sense of satisfaction it gave everyone connected with teaching me this, writing a letter, must have been immense" (18–19).

36. "The earth spins on its axis, the axis is imaginary" (Kincaid 1983b, 39).

37. However, this image from Kincaid's youth as a colonial subject in Antigua could serve as a diaspora text as well: "We began our meetings with the whole troop standing in the yard of the Methodist church, forming a circle around the flagpole, our eyes following the Union Jack as it was raised up; then we swore allegiance to our country, by which was meant England. For an hour and a half, we did all sorts of Brownie things; then we gathered again around the flagpole to lower the flag and swear allegiance" (1983a, 115). Barnwell (1994) explores power dynamics of homelands and other lands via a concept of motherlands.

38. Kincaid conjures this image in *Mr. Potter*: "A perfection, like a glass figurine from somewhere far away and completely unfamiliar, somewhere he [Mr. Shepherd] had read of in a book, and the mere reading of it came to be a personal experience (that would be London)" (2002, 92–93).

39. Kincaid is clear on this: "The England we were told about . . . the England we could never be from, the England that was so far away, the England that not even a boat could take us to, the England that, no matter what we did, we could never be of" (1988, 30).

40. Similar to the comments in "On Seeing England," Kincaid notes, "On the wall behind the wooden table and chair was a map; at the top of the map were the three words 'THE BRITISH EMPIRE.' These were the first words I learned to read" (1996, 14).

41. From *A Small Place*:

> Antigua is too beautiful. Sometimes the beauty of it seems unreal. Sometimes the beauty of it seems as if it were stage sets for a play, for no real sunset could look like that; no real seawater could strike that many shades of blue at once; no real sky could be that shade of blue—another shade of blue, completely different from the shades of blue seen in the sea—and no real cloud could be that white and float just that way in that blue sky; no real day could be that sort of sunny and bright, making everything seem transparent and shallow; and no real night could be that sort of black, making everything seem thick and deep and bottomless. (Kincaid 1988, 77)

42. "Everything about us is held in doubt and we the defeated define all that is unreal, all that is not human, all that is without love, all that is without mercy. Our experience cannot be interpreted by us; we do not know the truth of it. Our God was not the correct one, our understanding of heaven and hell was not a respectable one" (Kincaid 1996, 37). See also Diallo and Kincaid (2017) for Kincaid's further reflections on victimizers' truths standing in over and against narratives told by the conquered.

43. "I was so happy so reach my home, that is, the home I have now made for myself, the home of my adult life" (Kincaid 1997, 98).

44. "Whatever I was told to hate I loved and loved the most. . . . Whatever about me caused offense, whatever was native to me, whatever I could not help and was not a moral failing—those things about me I loved with the fervor of the devoted" (Kincaid 1996, 33).

45. "Hugh said, 'Isn't it the most blissful thing in the world to be away from everything you have ever known—to be so far away that you don't even know yourself anymore and you're not sure you ever want to come back to all the things you're a part of?' I knew so well just what he meant, and it made me sigh and press myself against him as if he were the last thing in the world" (Kincaid 1990, 66).

46. Exemplifying the obstacles and limitations to marginalized groups forming alliances with other marginalized groups,

> Mr. Potter said, "Me name Potter, Potter me name," and the sound of Mr. Potter's voice, so full of all that had gone wrong in the world for almost five hundred years that it could break the heart of an ordinary stone, meant not a thing to Dr. Weizenger, for he had been only recently inhabiting the world as if it were composed only of extinction, as if it were devoted to his very own extinction . . . Dr. Weizenger was of the mammal species . . . so used to observing, not being observed, and so used to acting, not being acted upon. And his own extinction had almost succeeded and how surprised he was by this, and surprised he would remain for the rest of his life, as if such a thing had never happened before, as if groups of people, one day intact and building civilization and dominating heaven and earth, had not the next found themselves erased and not even been remembered in a prayer or in a joke by the rest of humanity; as if groups of people had not been erased from the beginning of life and human memory. (Kincaid 2002, 23)

47. "I also knew the history of an array of people I would never meet. That in itself should not have kept me from knowing them; it was only that this history of people that I would never meet—Romans, Gauls, Saxons, Britons, the British people—had behind it a malicious intent: to make me feel humiliated, humbled, small" (Kincaid 1996, 59).

48. Kincaid remains insistent at times: "Her wanting to wear jodhpurs made of denim, uniform of workmen in some faraway country, to parents' night at his [Heracles's] school so all the other parents could see that she wasn't at all like them" (2013, 161).

49. Once in diaspora also from Antigua, Kincaid acerbically writes in the voice of Persephone to Mrs. Sweet, "You think you are with us, you think we think you are with us, but we know that you are really inside your own head and only what's there is real to you and you live in that little room with the big desk and we mean nothing to you, only your childhood with all its pain" (2013, 140).

50. As a younger woman sent to live in diaspora from Antigua, Kincaid writes, "I went to stare out the front window. . . . Everything I could see looked unreal to me; everything I could see made me feel I would never be part of it, never penetrate to the inside, never be taken in" (1990, 154).

51. See Kincaid's metaphor regarding the hole in *At the Bottom of the River* (1983, 41–42).

52. "I became eligible to partake of Holy Communion, and I remember feeling already disappointed and already defeated, already hopeless, thinking and feeling that I was standing on a fragile edge and at any moment I might fall off

into a narrow black hole that would amount to my entire earthly existence" (*My Brother* 1997, 140–141).

53. In Kincaid's interview with Vorda (1991, 8), she clarifies that under colonialism Blackness was the norm, not needing to be explained, as opposed to the US diasporic situation of a comment from Henry Louis Gates Jr. on her work, wherein African-heritage peoples may presume it is the minority Black experience that would need explanation.

54. Kincaid (1996) writes on this experience:

A human being, a person, many people, a people, will say that their surroundings, their physical surroundings, form their consciousness, their very being; they will get up every morning and look at green hills, white cliffs, silver mountains, fields of golden grain, rivers of blue-glinting water, and in the beauty of this—and it is beautiful, they cannot help but find it beautiful—they invisibly, magically, conquer the distance that is between them and the beauty they are beholding, and they feel themselves become one with it, they draw strength from it, they are inspired by it to sing songs, to compose verse; they invent themselves and reinvent themselves and they are inspired (again), but this time to commit small actions, small deeds. And eventually large actions, large deeds, and each success brings a validation of the original idea, the original feeling, the meeting of people and place, you and the place you are from are not a chance encounter; it is something beyond destiny, it is something so meant to be that it is beyond words. (191)

55. In an interview, Kincaid responds to a query:

AR: In your new book, you have this substitution of mythology for your own biography. And so, when you started reading "Paradise Lost" tonight, it was striking to me that you would substitute a great myth for your own work.

JK: Yes. The thing about invoking myths in everyday life, as we call it—that's how you really are thinking. You are not you, but—in your mind's eye, something bigger than you is going on. And I wanted to allude to that, to allude to the fact that things are bigger than—we are bigger than the thing we see. We stand still, and then we are bigger, and move around much more. I wanted to say that. (Loh 2013)

56. In a pointed link between colonialism and Christian missionizing, Kincaid writes,

The population of Roseau, that is, the ones who looked like me, had long ago been reduced to shadows; the forever foreign, the margins, had long ago lost any connection to wholeness, to an inner life of our own invention, and since it was Sunday, some of them now were walking in a trance, no longer in their right minds, toward a church or away from a church. This activity—going to church, coming from church—had about it the atmosphere of a decree. It also signified defeat yet again, for what would the outcome have been of all the lives of the conquered if they had not come to believe in the gods of the people who had conquered them?" (1996, 132–33)

57. See Lorde (1984). An alternative view is offered by Patel (2007, 78).

58. In a personalized version of this complex dynamic, Kincaid explains, "I accepted the love she gave me without a thought to her and took it for my own right to live in just the way that would please me; and then my mother became angry at me because I did not love her in return and then she became even more angry that I did not love her at all because I would not become her, I had an idea that I should become myself; it made her angry that I should have a self, a separate being that could never be known to her" (2013, 29).

59. Kincaid describes in her novel *Lucy* being made to memorize and recite a poem while attending Queen Victoria's Girls' School: "I was then at the height of my two-facedness: that is, outside I seemed one way, inside I was another; outside false, inside true. And so I made pleasant little noises that showed both modesty and appreciation, but inside I was making a vow to erase from my mind, line by line, every word of that poem" (1990, 18).

60. Kincaid's character Lucy reflects on her upbringing in school, standing up in choir practice and saying "that I did not wish to sing 'Rule, Britannia! Britannia, rule the waves; Britons never, never shall be slaves,' that I was not a Briton and that until not too long ago I would have been a slave. My action did not create scandal; instead my choir mistress only wondered if all their efforts to civilize me over the years would come to nothing in the end" (1990, 135).

61. "And see him [Mr. Potter] now round a corner, not yet in possession of the knowledge of his own misery, never to be in possession of the knowledge that the world has rained down on him injustice upon injustice, cruelty upon cruelty, never to be in possession of the knowledge that though his very being was holy, his existence was a triumph of evil" (Kincaid 2002, 80).

62. Of this complex dynamic, Kincaid notes, "Mrs. Sweet had buried her past—in the cement that composes memory, even though she knew quite well that cement deteriorates, falls apart, and reveals eventually whatever it was meant to conceal" (2013, 93).

63. This resonates in a novel as well: "my father, was named after Alfred the Great, the English king, a personage my father should have despised, for he came to know this Alfred not through the language of the poet, which would have been

the language of compassion, but through the language of the conqueror. My father was not responsible for his own name, but he was responsible for the name of his son. His son's name was Alfred. My father perhaps imagined a dynasty" (Kincaid 1996, 109–10).

64. In *A Small Place*, Kincaid (1988) clarifies: "We were taught the names of the Kings of England. In Antigua, the twenty-fourth of May was a holiday—Queen Victoria's official birthday. We didn't say to ourselves, Hasn't this extremely unappealing person been dead for years and years? Instead, we were glad for the Holiday" (30).

65. Heard again here: "Wherever you went you made sure to build a school, a library (yes, and in both of these places you distorted or erased my history and glorified your own)" (1988, 36).

66. Expressed as vanity: "I became fascinated with this expression of vanity: the perfume of your own name and your own deeds is intoxicating, and it never causes you to feel weary or exhausted; it is its own inspiration, it is its own renewal" (Kincaid 1996, 59–60).

67. On a similar note, Kincaid's character Lucy, after reading a letter from her mother updating her on life on the Caribbean island of Antigua, states, "The object of my life now was to put as much distance between myself and the events mentioned in her letter as I could manage. For I felt that if I could put enough miles between me and the place from which that letter came, and if I could put enough events between me and the events mentioned in the letter, would I not be free to take everything just as it came and not see hundreds of years in every gesture, every word spoken, every face?" (1990, 31). See also Kincaid's unyielding view in *At the Bottom of the River* (1983b, 19).

68. Kincaid's character thinks with despair: "The natives, had become bogged down in issues of justice and injustice, and they had become attached to claims of ancestral heritage, and the indignities by which they had come to these islands, as if they mattered, really mattered" (1996, 117).

69. Kincaid's *My Brother* has her narrator state, "We are not instinctively empathetic people; a circle of friends who love and support each other is not something I can recall from my childhood" (1997, 42).

70. As Kincaid (1996) writes,

> You cannot trust these people, my father would say to me, the very words the other children's parents were saying to them, perhaps even at the same time. That 'these people' were ourselves, that this insistence on mistrust of others—that people who looked so very much like each other, who shared a common history of suffering and humiliation and enslavement, should be taught to mistrust each other, even as children, is no longer a mystery to me. The people we should naturally have mistrusted were beyond our influence completely; what we needed to defeat them, to rid ourselves of them, was something far more powerful than mistrust. (47–48)

71. Kincaid's character describes people inside of a church, "They were singing a hymn. The words were: 'O Jesus, I have promised / To serve Thee to the end: / Be Thou for ever near me, / My Master and my friend.' . . . I wanted to say, Let me tell you something: This Master and friend business, it is not possible; a master is one thing and a friend is something else altogether, something completely different; a master cannot be a friend" (1996, 134).

72. See examples in *Annie John* (1983a, 96), *At the Bottom of the River* (1983b, 7), and *A Small Place* (1988, 63–65).

73. Kincaid clarifies such between her characters as an example here:

> Mrs. Sweet's eyes were not impenetrable at all to anyone else and everyone she met wished they were so; for behind her eyes lay scenes of turbulence, upheavals, murders, betrayals, on foot, on land, and on the seas where horde upon horde of people were transported to places on the earth's surface that they had never heard of or even imagined, and the murderer and murdered, betrayer and betrayed, the source of the turbulence, the instigator of the upheavals, were all mixed up, and the sorting out of the true, true truth and the rendering of judgments, or the acceptance of wrongs, and to accept that, to accept and lay still with being wronged will wear you down to nothing so that eventually you are not more than the substance that makes up the Imperial Sand Dunes in the Imperial Valley California, or the pink beaches surrounding the rising shelf of landmass that is now, just now, the island of Barbuda, or the lawn of a house in Montclair, New Jersey. (2013, 19)

74. In *My Brother*, Kincaid (1997, 186) states pointedly, "To see someone suffer in a moment when you are not suffering can inspire such a feeling, superiority, in a place like Antigua, with its history of subjugation, leaving in its wake humiliation and inferiority; to see someone in straits worse than your own is to feel at first pity for them and soon better than them."

Chapter 3

1. She is also sometimes addressed in a small cluster of women heads of state such as Indira Gandhi and Benazir Bhutto. See Steinberg (2008) and Genovese (1993). Cottin Pogrebin (1991) does this as well. Gandhi is one of the few other women in Fallaci's (1976) collection of interviews.

2. See, for example, Eisenhower (1977); Burkett (2008); M. Cooper (2018); Katav (2020); and even Slater (1981).

3. Cottin Pogrebin's (1991) moving chapters on Meir make somewhat similar arguments. As one example of how this type of feminist critique of Meir works,

note how Cottin Pogrebin called Meir, among the four women heads of state of her time, a "female impersonator" (153) and noted the "untenable pressures and contradictions that plague virtually all achieving women" (152). Cottin Pogrebin's assessment in 1991, carried through with her encyclopedia entries on Meir (Cottin Pogrebin 1997, 2009), was that "although she [Meir] was the most elevated Jewish female figure in the world, ultimately she was not a worthy role model" (153). Role model—need to rethink that. I intend to extend and reconfigure analyses such as this. In this work I deepen the assessment of the contradictions and pressures through the kinds of critique and compassion we have learned as feminists in the past few decades and in transnational studies, as well as queering the notion of gender impersonators.

4. Gratitude to Penina Weinberg and those gathered at the first Jewish queer Ruach Hayam for taking time to explore this with me.

5. She was one of three women in the series, along with Gertrude Stein and Sandra Bernhardt (Warhol 1980).

6. In the foreword to a book of Meir's papers, Eleanor Roosevelt described Meir as "a woman one cannot help but deeply respect and deeply love" (1962, xiv). A few examples of the "age of Golda" are as follows: In 1972 Golda was elected deputy chairperson of the worldwide Socialist International, an honor, had I known about it at the time, I would have considered very impressive. In 1971 Meir became only the second woman from outside the US to be at the top of the list of the most admired women in (US) America compiled by Gallup, and she repeated this achievement in 1973 and 1974. In 1973 she was named the most admired woman in England. Her 1975 autobiography, *My Life*, was an international bestseller. While my friends and I were all reading the works of Italian feminist journalist Oriana Fallaci, I never knew about Fallaci's 1972 interview with Meir. An anti-Zionist, Fallaci wrote, "Even if one is not at all in agreement with her, with her politics, her ideology, one cannot help but respect her, admire her, even love her" (88).

7. See Tsoref (2018).

8. See Christman (1962) as a good source for finding many of Meir's speeches and other materials in one place.

9. Meir's time as prime minister motivates most biographies and even newer works, however scholarly (or sometimes not so much). See, for example, Schmidt (2004); Weitz (2011); Lipstadt (2023).

10. Interestingly, this was long before the Hamas attack in Israel on October 7, 2023. The date of the 2023 attack was planned to commemorate fifty years after the attack on October 6, 1973, which formally began the fighting in the Yom Kippur / Ramadan War. Meir had long been criticized for her leadership as prime minister of Israel at the time. Further, Israelis tend to think of the tragic loss of (at least Israeli) life from this armed conflict and associate what they consider Israel's failure with Meir. The 2023 Hamas attack was likely intended to capitalize on this depressive national memory. Also interestingly, after many decades of assumed

consensus regarding the assessment of the 1973 war, not long before October 7, 2023, a new narrative began to circulate. New research demonstrated that Meir was not as catastrophically at fault as she had earlier been made out to be. Initial comparisons between Netanyahu's disastrous response to the 2023 attack and Meir's role in the 1973 war quickly dissipated. What became obvious very quickly was that one did not have to even consider Meir positively in any way to note that Netanyahu's role in 2023 was cataclysmic.

11. Later in her life, Golda's sister Sheyna would publish her memoirs. These have important information on many subjects and include interesting material on Golda as well. See Korngold (1968).

12. While Morris supported Meir's activism, he was likely not much of a Zionist. Klagsbrun (2017, 59) notes that Morris was more of an internationalist and a pacifist, and we might find his politics somewhat more aligned with Emma Goldman's anarchism.

13. Much has been made of Golda as a mother, of both the children she raised and the nation of Israel. See, for example, Klagsbrun (2017, 73); Greenwald and Lehman-Wilzig (2019).

14. Note that in socialist organizations, "secretary" is usually the designation for the head position.

15. During that time she was also Minister of Internal Affairs for a brief period.

16. This is not an uncommon way for some to try to make sense of and even compliment women operating in patriarchal systems. See, for example, Margalit Stern (2009). Interestingly, in the first full biography on Meir, Martin (1988) took the time to characterize her physically and described her as both beautiful and irresistible to men.

17. Cottin Pogrebin (1997) notes that Meir replied to this, amused that "this was the greatest possible compliment that could be paid to a woman. I very much doubt that any man would have been flattered if I had said about him that he was the best woman in the government!" (909).

18. Interestingly, one of Meir's early and oft-reprinted articles was for a women's organization about the challenges of the working woman and mother (G. Meir 1982).

19. Israeli feminist Marie Syrkin did consider Meir in her life's work. Important for her own work, she was also daughter of the renowned Zionist thinker Nachman Syrkin. Marie Syrkin wrote on and with Meir in her desire to present this woman to the world (Syrkin 1963, 1969; G. Meir 1973a, 1973b). See Kessner (2009) for a brief biography of Syrkin. See Antler (1997) and also specifically Triger (2014), Lahav (2018, 2021), and Lipstadt (2023) for more current analyses.

20. Interestingly, Emma Goldman was able to rouse crowds in both English and Yiddish. Meir was capable in Yiddish but is said to have never learned Hebrew with the same comfort level. In Klagsbrun's (2017, 64) descriptions of Meir's public speaking during her younger days organizing candidates from Milwaukee to the then-new American Jewish Congress, Meir sounds very much like Emma Goldman.

21. See Ferguson (2011) and its companion website (https://www2.hawaii.edu/~kferguso/).

22. The US government's efforts to deport Goldman were ultimately realized by noting the same standing of women, citizenship, and marriage that Meir faced.

23. The Cable Act was passed in 1922, just following Meir's departure to Palestine, overturning the 1907 law so that women no longer automatically were considered to have the nationality of their husbands (Watt 2011).

24. Interestingly, Emma Goldman's feminist credentials are not challenged today even as she critiques the women's suffrage movement of her time for missing the central aim of ending the oppression of women. For Meir's situation, women's suffrage was granted in Israel when the state was founded in 1948 (not without a history of political activity), and a woman's citizenship in Israel was never contingent on her marital status to a man. Needless to say, people in same-gender marriages still continue to respond to the vagaries of their status via marriage, as do any of us when a partner undertakes a gender transition.

25. Tronto (1993) can be read as a raced, classed corrective to Carol Gilligan's (1982) work.

26. At a large J Street conference plenary session in 2013, a group of esteemed women political actors including Israeli Knesset members Ruth Calderon and Merav Michaeli discussed this issue at a panel entitled "The Changing Face of Politics in Israel: Will Women Lead the Way?" Michaeli noted that she created a women's caucus in the Knesset because "the Knesset is a boys' club, just like the media and other institutions. True, there are more women than ever before in the current parliament, but they still only hold 27 out of 120 seats." The women discussed various issues and challenges to the notion of women's solidarity, noting the quandary of when a "women's rights issue conflicts with party politics" along with "another question likely to plague feminists in the Knesset: What do you do when a women's rights issue conflicts with other liberal causes, like fighting the occupation?" (Samuel 2013).

27. Aside from feminist and pacifist critics, there are also voices such as Medzini (2008), who argues that Meir had little influence beyond that of a fundraiser and in her relation to the US. Yet this critique itself supports the unusual relationship Meir had and successfully mobilized with the US and its Jewish community throughout her life.

28. The historical record demonstrates many such examples. For instance, after retiring as prime minister, Meir was called back from a trip abroad to be in Jerusalem for Egyptian president Anwar Sadat's historic visit. Later, Sadat said he preferred to deal with Meir. In his words, "The old lady. She has guts, really" (*TIME* 1978). Another nasty gendered example is the language used by Leibowitz in his critique: "The transformation of Israel into a colonial power didn't start with Meir Kahane, or even Menachem Begin. It started with Golda Meir, an evil, old woman who ruled the state of Israel for five years" (Leibowitz and Egan 1986, 106).

29. Meir met with Abdullah at least twice, in 1947 and 1948, traveling by car through territory that was considered hostile to Jews in yet another form of drag to keep her safe and help secure the clandestine Israeli national mission. For more information, see Karsh (1999) and "Golda Meir" (n.d.).

30. It is worth reading her son's 1983 biography of Meir. In the context of smashing gender expectations, Menahem publishes that work under the last name Meir, not Meyerson. When Golda became foreign minister (the second-highest-ranking government post), Ben-Gurion demanded a name change to one that sounded more Hebrew (Meir) than a product of the diaspora (Meyerson). Golda had taken Morris's last name when they married in the US. As an Israeli government official, Golda Meyerson became Golda Meir.

31. In Brown's (1992) article on the role of the US in Meir's biography, he notes the shift from anti-Americanism in Israeli Zionist circles so that by 1928 a Yishuv leader noted, "It has become accepted in the Zionist world that the yishuv can be built [only] with the help of the Diaspora; and the Histadruth Campaign in American is one of the ways [of mobilizing that help]" (43). Still, the binary idea lives on in many ways. For some pushing back, see Boyarin and Boyarin (1993, 2002); Biale (1986, 2002); Aviv and Shneer (2005); Kaye/Kantrowitz (2007).

32. Though, supposedly, Meir had already relinquished it in Naples on her way to Palestine in the 1920s (Brown 1992, 38).

33. Taking into account the language politics here can be quite interesting for challenging the home/away binary. Work has been done on the Hebrew-Yiddish language politics of modern western Zionism. Integrating de-colonial theorizing will have us complicate this binary with the role of English as the US was becoming a world power (even as the British Empire was in decline). We might also productively further trouble a Hebrew-Yiddish dualism with this case study of Meir in Russia, as the Russian language was also being mobilized as an emergent imperial force. Despite intense antisemitism in the Bolshevik revolution, for a time, Yiddish was recognized as an accepted language, whereas Soviet policy deemed Hebrew explicitly threatening. Meir sorted through four language options and likely shifted the choices she wielded with different audiences during her brief trip.

34. The US had just recognized Israel's de facto independence.

35. See also Kostyrchenko (2004).

36. For Meir and for Russian Jews in this context, her attendance at synagogue was clearly a political, cultural assertion of Jewish independence and not only a religious one.

37. See Shindler (2009) also on the impact of Soviet influence on internal Zionist politics in moving the Zionist Left, such as Hashomer Hatzair, to abandon its position for a binational state and to support partition.

38. See Brettschneider (1996). There is much work that can be done complicating binaries in Meir's case study given the Christian grounding of interest in Jews and Israel in religious terms in the US, which claims to be a secular democracy, and Meir's secular Zionist project.

39. I look forward to future work using Meir's experience here also as a case study—in this example of complicating the diaspora binary, how Meir's ties to the US at the historical moment it emerges as a global power and with the largest diasporic Jewish population make possible this highly developed Jewish homeland project.

40. Both activists responded publicly to the rise in pogroms around 1919, Meir when she was still young in Milwaukee (Klagsbrun 2017, 76), and Goldman as an older woman from her experiences back in Russia when deported from the US.

41. For future work, a more pointed analysis of the queer gendered aspects of Meir's Israel-US experiences, focusing particularly on the co-construction of raced Christian and Western Jewish gender norms, will also press the limits of a home/away binary construct.

42. Klagsbrun (2017, 47) does make specific mention, at the very least, that as the young Meir continued to be politicized while living with her sister in Denver, she learned about both anarchism and Emma Goldman.

43. In 1960 when Argentina complained to the UN Security Council that Israel violated its sovereignty in capturing Adolph Eichmann on its territory and bringing him to Israel for trial, Meir addressed the council as the Israeli foreign minister with a powerful speech on the Holocaust. The council decided that an expression of regret by Israel was sufficient and endorsed the idea of bringing the wanted Nazi to trial. Meir's success as a stateswoman at that time set in motion the Eichmann trial in Jerusalem, which Hannah Arendt covered for the *New Yorker* and which eventually caused irrevocable strains between Arendt and many US Jews and Jewish power brokers. Arendt supposedly met Meir at a party in Israel during her time there covering the Eichmann trial. Not surprisingly, Arendt considered Meir a superficial ideologue.

Chapter 4

1. See Benhabib's (1988, 1995) important essays on Arendt in a Jewish feminist context.

2. On Arendt's ongoing resistance to publishing the project, Karl Jaspers writes to Arendt in 1952, "This work still seems to me to be your own working through of the basic question of Jewish existence, and in it you use Rahel's reality as a guide to help you achieve clarity and liberation for yourself" (qtd. in Ring 1997, 3).

3. Interestingly, Edith Stein, born to an observant German Jewish family in 1891, also studied philosophy. She earned her PhD in 1916 from the University of Göttingen, having worked with the phenomenologist Edmund Husserl, who was born Jewish and converted to Lutheranism. She converted to Catholicism in 1922 and became a Carmelite nun. After her death in the gas chambers of Auschwitz, she was canonized as a saint.

4. Bernstein (1996, 73) quotes Arendt describing her escape from the internment camp: "A few weeks after our arrival in the camp . . . France was defeated and all communications broke down. In the resulting chaos we succeeded in getting hold of liberation papers with which we were able to leave the camp."

5. For example, Kohn (2007) notes that while Arendt's later and most abstract works appear to be "ageless, sexless, without qualities, and without a life story" (xi), Arendt "probably wrote more about Jewish affairs in general than about any other topic" (xiv). Additionally, Kohn argues that all of Arendt's work, even the more abstract philosophical projects and those that do not much mention things Jewish, "cannot be fully grasped without recognizing its poignancy as originating in Arendt's experience as a Jew living in the twentieth century" (x).

6. Ring (1997, 2) chooses not to focus on Varnhagen, expressing her "disinterest" in the text and that she does not find it particularly "compelling." This characterization is interesting given Ring's acknowledgment that the text is Arendt's working out of central issues for herself and that Ring includes the pariah-parvenu?e paradigm as core throughout her work.

7. As Arendt ([1974] 1997) assesses Rahel's situation and the terrain of her choices:

> The bourgeoisie did not accept them [Jews], and the nobility drew away from them. This new rejection was becoming evident before and during the war of 1813–14; after 1815 it was manifested quite openly. Not until social isolation was a fait accompli did the Jewish intelligentsia ally itself with revolutionary movements. In Rahel's present situation such solidarity was out of the question. Now she had no choice but to consider the possibility of her finding an individual way out. Abandoned and disillusioned, aware that everything had changed for the worse, she was fundamentally unable to comprehend the altered climate of the times. The only way out was Varnhagen. (223)

8. Frequent visitors to Rahel's first salon in Berlin were Alexander and Wilhelm von Humboldt; Friedrich Schlegel; Schelling; Friedrich von Gentz; Schleiermacher; Prince Louis Ferdinand of Prussia and his mistress, Pauline Wiesel; Friedrich August Wolf; Jean Paul; Franz Brentano; and the Tieck brothers. Frequent visitors to her second salon (Berlin, 1821 to 1832), which she hosted with her then husband, were Bettina von Arnim, Heinrich Heine, Prince Pückler-Muskau, Hegel, Ranke, and Eduard Gans.

9. See Weissberg (2000).

10. Arendt notes an interesting set of ways to understand Rahel's form of "homelessness." Given the times, she needed to live without foundations: "She believed neither in the god of her ancestors nor the god of Christianity, believed least of all in the 'new-fashioned' religiosity which was characterized by a bigotry she hated—as did every thinker of the Enlightenment. She needed neither 'found-

ers' nor 'proofs'; in respect to religion she was just as traditionless, just as blind to tradition, as she was in everything else" (Arendt [1974] 1997, 145).

11. "There remained for her, therefore, only social assimilation through marriage—a course very frequently adopted in those days. Rahel's engagement to Finckenstein was, in the beginning, hardly anything but just such an attempt" (Arendt [1974] 1997, 109).

12. "The salon which had brought together people of all classes, in which a person could participate without having any social status at all, which had offered a haven for those who fitted in nowhere socially, had fallen victim to the disaster of 1806. The age of Frederick the Second, in which Jews could live, which gave 'room for every plant in his sun-welcoming land,' was over. Only now, in a time of breakdown, did Rahel realize that her life also was subject to general political conditions" (Arendt [1974] 1997, 176–77).

13. "Frau von Grotthus and Frau von Eybenberg, Dorothea Schlegel and Henriette Herz, her sister Rose and Rebecca Friedlander—all of them, all of them had married. If Germans, their husbands had usually been noblemen; if Jews, rich businessmen who had a vital part to play in the world and hence were assured a place in it, even if that place was often challenged" (219).

14. One way that Arendt ([1974] 1997) describes this in Rahel's situation is as follows: "Being a Jew could develop from a politic-social circumstance into a personal, individual problem. . . . As a personal problem the Jewish question was insoluble, and for that reason everything Rahel undertook always ended in the 'madness of gloom, fright and despair winding up like snakes for all eternity—despair over my position, my situation'"(254).

15. As Arendt ([1974] 1997) notes, "Freedom and equality were not going to be conjured into existence by individuals' capturing them by fraud as privileges for themselves" (258).

16. In Arendt's words in historical context:

> Prussia tolerated only fairly prosperous Jews, only businessmen and no workmen. The State punished bankruptcy by deportation, prevented overpopulation by a marriage tax and forced emigration, made the Jewish communities responsible as a body for the tax debts of every individual member. By all these measures, the State created an atmosphere of collective responsibility—its allies against the poor immigrant members of their own people. The Jewish question was, in Berlin and in all of Prussia, the problem of the rich Jews, and assimilation was the solution this propertied class hoped for. They seemed, indeed, predestined to merge with the prosperous middle-class stratum of society. ([1974] 1997, 222)

17. Arendt describes the quotidian ways Rahel participated in this new status as female citizen: "For the Prussian Jews, who had just been made citizens of the

state by the edict of 1812, the war was the first opportunity to prove that they belonged, and that they had a legitimate right to be called citizens. Rahel began to do what all the women in her sphere were doing: organize help, collect money and clothing for the wounded, and so on" ([1974] 1997, 232).

18. "The nobility still set the tone in society. Hence, the bourgeois as well as the Jews who became parvenus . . . all went to enormous trouble to reach the position already held by the few who had it by birth; they had, as a body, a mania for acquiring titles and nobility" (Arendt [1974] 1997, 240).

19. If allowing a connection between themselves and other Jews or the Jewish people, Arendt ([1974] 1997, 106) notes the tendency of "the privileged wealthy Jews [to] appeal . . . to the sublimities of the Hebrew prophets in order to prove that they were indeed the descendants of an especially exalted people." Or in a case where a Jew actually does rise to an objectively powerful position, such as Disraeli, she notes he "sought to validate their people by endowing it with some extraordinary, mystic power." We find these examples today especially in the Reform tradition based on the prophets, even as this has enabled the Reform movement to most successfully pursue social justice as a *Jewish* movement in the contemporary US.

20. By writing in German but including occasional Jewish themes, characters, and words, "Heine is the only German Jew who could truthfully describe himself as both a German and a Jew. He is the only outstanding example of a really happy assimilation in the entire history of that process" (Arendt 1944, 106).

21. Arendt (1944, 101n1) writes, "Chaplin has recently declared that he is of Irish and Gypsy descent, but he has been selected for discussion because, even if not himself a Jew, he has epitomized in an artistic form a character born of the Jewish pariah mentality."

22. One way we can see this demonstrated in Arendt's assessment of Varnhagen's critical thinking is her concept: "She had realized that the 'diseased matter' which had to 'get out of us' was not contained in the Jews alone, that the pox only broke out on the Jews, infecting them by contagion; that everything she herself had undertaken to fight it, all her life, was nothing but a 'cosmetic' which did not 'help, even if it were slapped on with housepainter's brushes'" (Arendt [1974] 1997, 258).

23. An aspect of what became a controversial work reporting on the Eichmann trial was Arendt's assessment that Eichmann failed to think what he was doing. Thank you to Pat Moynagh for having me rethink that.

24. "If one wishes to be a normal person precisely like everybody else, there is scarcely any alternative to exchanging old prejudices for new ones . . . if one really assimilates, taking all the consequences of denial of one's own origin and cutting oneself off from those who have not or have not yet done it, one becomes a scoundrel" (Arendt [1974] 1997, 256).

25. "'We have been created to live the truth in this world. . . . We are alongside of human society. For us no place, no office, no empty title exists! All lies have some place; eternal truth, proper living and feeling . . . has no place! And thus we are excluded from society. You because you offended it . . . I because I cannot

sin and lie along with it.' One had to pay for becoming a parvenu by abandoning truth, and this Rahel was not prepared to do" (Arendt [1974] 1997, 242).

26. As Arendt explains of Rahel's situation, "to enter society all alone, marked with the blemish and condemned to be one of the last, was far worse than waiting outside and hoping for better conditions. Always having to represent oneself as something special, and having to do it all alone, in order to justify her bare existence, was so strenuous that it nearly consumed all her strength." Arendt quotes Rahel's writing and notes, "'How loathsome it is always having to establish one's identity first. That alone is enough to make it so repulsive to be a Jew.' Legitimation, moreover, was not even possible most of the time; only in rare, isolated situations did the kindness of the others give her a chance, leave a crack through which she could put her head and proclaim her uniqueness. In all ordinary converse, at all ordinary times and in every unexpected encounter with people, that was ruled out; as a Jew the world attributed to her what it considered to be the Jewish qualities" (Arendt [1974] 1997, 252).

27. Arendt learns this over and over, unfortunately, not only in the study of Rahel and her experiences in the Holocaust but again in her new home. Once in the US, Arendt lived through the McCarthy period. This period of red-baiting showed again that individuals are "safe" and political freedom operative in Liberal democracy only as long as they fit paradigms acceptable to elites. Not surprisingly, Jews (and other marginalized minorities) were disproportionately targeted in the Red Scare.

28. As Arendt ([1974] 1997, 257) notes about Rahel's time, "It became apparent that the fate of the Jews was not so accidental and out of the way, that on the contrary it precisely limned the state of society, outlined the ugly reality of the gaps in the social structure."

Chapter 5

1. For example, Herrera (1983); Lindauer (1999). The one significant exception to the lack of Jewish insight into Kahlo's work (Ankori) will be discussed below. Additionally, there has been work published stating that Guillermo Kahlo may not actually have been Jewish (Franger and Huhle 2005, 247), and this has led many people to say that Kahlo was not Jewish. Actually, there is no evidence that Kahlo's paternal grandmother, Henriette Kaufmann, was not Jewish or did not have Jewish roots. If she was Jewish, then, according to Jewish law, Guillermo Kahlo was Jewish. There is also evidence that Frida Kahlo knew this and was not misrepresenting herself. Among the photos that inform *My Grandparents, My Parents, and I*, the two of her paternal grandparents bear relevant inscriptions from Kahlo. On the back of the photo of her paternal grandfather, Kahlo wrote, "My father's father (Hungarian)." On the back of the photo of her paternal grandmother, Kahlo wrote, "My father's mother (A German Jew)" (Ankori 2013, 39). She explicitly notes that her paternal grandmother was Jewish, in contrast to her note about her paternal grandfather.

2. See, for example, Witzling (1991). In 1983, Kahlo and Tina Modetti's works were shown together in New York City, despite the differences between their art, likely because both were women. See the Glueck (1983) *New York Times* review, which praises Kahlo and is not as favorable to Modetti.

3. Biographies of Kahlo abound. In addition to the biographies identified below, see also Grimberg and Herrera (2008); Morrison (2003); Kettenmann (2000); Wilcox and Henestrosa (2018); Souter (2011).

4. Reviving Kahlo as an inspiring figure for the disabilities movement in various ways, as with much attention to Kahlo, runs from activist and informal groups to the realm of academic scholarship. For example, see "Disability History Month Trailblazers" (2013); Appelbaum (2019); Daunton (2015); Crosby (2014); Malti-Douglas (2013).

5. Photos of Kahlo's paintings are accessible online. There are also various books with vibrant photos of her work. Dexter and Barson (2005) is a particularly lovely one.

6. A typical example looks like this review of an exhibit on surrealist art, where the author notes, "While few Jewish women Surrealists directly addressed their ethnicity, much of their work responded to themes coming from their 'Jewishness,' such as alienation, identity and displacement" (Loren 2012). This would also explain motivations in Kahlo's work, but in speaking of the exhibit explicitly, the article plays down Kahlo's Jewishness in contrast to that of other artists: "Highlighting Surrealism in the United States and Mexico, it showcases heavyweights like Frida Kahlo and Helen Lundberg, but it also includes many female Jewish Surrealists, such as Rose Mandel, Kati Horna, Ruth Bernhard and others who used Surrealist art to explore spirituality, psychology and trauma." In this chapter, I argue that we need to blur the lines that have separated Kahlo from explorations of Jewish import.

7. The following resources were also used to prepare this section: Mays (2013); "Mexico Virtual Jewish History Tour" (n.d.); "Christian-Jewish Relations" (n.d.); Moskowitz (1939); Goldberg (2013); Cánovas (2009).

8. They estimate that the other half million participated in Ashkenazi Jewish practices. This perspective omits Jews from other regions, such as the Middle East, China, India, and Africa. However, I include the reference to suggest what clearly points to the historic vivacity and centrality of the Sephardi community.

9. See, for example, Meyerson and English (1999); Mays (2013); Aron-Beller (2010).

10. See, for example, material in the Southwest Jewish Archives at the University of Arizona: https://swja.library.arizona.edu/content/crypto-jews.

11. During World War II, Mexico, like many other countries that were part of the former Spanish Empire in this region, closed its doors to Jewish immigration. Individual efforts to save Jews persisted nonetheless. For example, Gilberto Bosques Saldívar, who had been a leftist active in the Mexican Revolution that deposed Porfirio Díaz, took advantage of his position as a consul in Marseille to issue approximately forty thousand visas to targeted European Jews and exiles from

the Spanish Republic. Knowing that these Jews would not be admitted to Mexico under the new antisemitic immigration restrictions, he issued them visas for the sole purpose of helping Jews flee German-occupied territory. He chartered ships and assisted many Jews in their escape to northern Africa. See also Lillian Lieberman's 2010 documentary, *Visa al paraíso*. For a first-person testimony from Jews saved by Bosques, see Kantorowicz (1941).

12. Numerous Jewish institutions were built in Mexico City during the course of Guillermo and Frida Kahlo's lives. The oldest surviving Jewish institution in Mexico is the Orthodox La Sociedad de Beneficencia Alianza Monte Sinai. Immigrants from the same wave that brought Guillermo Kahlo to Mexico established it in 1912. This beneficent society now boasts 2,300 families, with a preponderance of Jews originating from Damascus and Lebanon. In 1922, the Consejo Comunitario Ashkenazi was created, an Orthodox institution made up of about 2,500 families today. Jews from Aleppo, Syria, established the Orthodox Comunidad Maguén David in 1937; today it comprises an estimated 2,800 families. In 1941 Jews from Turkey, Greece, and the Balkans created the Comunidad Sefaradí. Another Orthodox institution, today it boasts 1,100 families. In Frida's lifetime, the Jewish Sport Center was established, in 1950. Today this sports, social, and cultural center has 280,000 members from all local Jewish communities, both Sephardi and Ashkenazi. Jewish institutions and synagogues in Mexico City continued to grow after Frida Kahlo's death. Today in Mexico there are about thirty synagogues, some of which require additional meeting space during the Jewish High Holy Days. When I last visited in the 2010s, synagogues in Mexico City had significant security protocols, long before such became more common to US Jewish organizations. Reform and Reconstructionist Jewish institutions are mainly not found in Mexico to date ("Communities: Mexico," n.d.). However, the wave of Mexicans discovering their converso/a history has led many to seek formal recognition from Jewish institutions and some to seek conversion within contemporary expectations. This is leading to a shift in religious affiliation for new synagogues and Jewish organizations across Latin America as the region experiences a parallel shift from nearly exclusive Catholic affiliation to Christian evangelical (as is occurring on most continents in these decades).

13. In biblical stories, descent is patrilineal. Communities not exposed to the rabbinic revolution and those that rejected this development continued the tradition of patrilineal descent, as in sub-Saharan Africa (Brettschneider 2015). A future area of research might be on how Jewish communities constituted themselves in a daily, cultural way in early 1900s Mexico. Historically, there are examples of Jews resettling across the globe who did not abide by the halachic (Jewish legal) practice of matrilineal descent. For example, some Portuguese men fleeing the Inquisition set up Jewish communities in western Africa, where they married local non-Jewish women and counted their offspring as Jews (Schorsch 2004). Additionally today, Reconstructionist and Reform communities also permit patrilineal descent.

14. Mordecai Kaplan (1980) is best known for articulating a highly developed concept of Jewishness as a civilization.

15. In a pattern that will become familiar in this chapter, Marx's father converted from Judaism to Protestantism. Marx's grandfathers on both sides were rabbis; on his father's side he came from a line of rabbis dating from the early 1700s. With his conversion, Marx's father sought to protect the family from the formal antisemitism widespread in Germany in their day.

16. The Jewish press and many opinion leaders in Jewish communal circles excoriated Arendt for challenging the emerging norms of Holocaust theory of her day. Like Deutscher, the Jewish feminist and anarchist Emma Goldman eventually had to leave the Soviet Union because of the ways in which she would not align with the Communist Party line. Both Kahlo and Rivera would have similar problems with the Communist Party.

17. While Kahlo was steeped in Jewish history and cultural relations, she was not a scholar of ancient Jewish texts, as Deutscher was, and her mother was not Jewish. Until recently, the study of ancient Jewish texts was primarily the domain of men.

18. Thanks to Eric Cohen for his conversations with me on this subject and for introducing me to Batnitzky.

19. Weber ([1930] 1985), in particular, was a primary thinker making such connections between Liberalism, capitalism, and Protestantism.

20. At the time, Ankori was lecturer in the Department of Art History at the Hebrew University of Jerusalem. See also Ankori (2002). It was not until more than a decade later and having drafted this chapter that I saw the portrait myself. Thank you to Carol Conaway for making sure that she took me to see this work in an exhibit at the Museum of Fine Arts in Boston.

21. In 1936, Kahlo was closely entwined with both Rivera and Bertram Wolfe. Wolfe, the son of a German Jewish immigrant to the US, was politically active in Mexico City at that time and became one of Rivera's most important biographers. In addition to some joint projects with Wolfe, Rivera was also then illustrating Isaac Berliner's book of Yiddish poetry, *City of Palaces*.

22. I am grateful to Rosie Pegueros for introducing me to a history of alternative Mexican styles of delineating families' mixed-race heritages. See Katzew (2004) for pictorial renderings and a historical analysis.

23. Chagall is often credited for achieving in art what Mendelsohn is said to have accomplished in philosophy in the eighteenth century. Chagall managed to gain acceptance as both a Jewish artist and a modernist (a humanist, not specifically a Jewish category). Chagall was also living in Paris at the start of World War II and received help in his escape from the same initiatives led by Julien Levy, Hiram Bingham, Varian Fry, and others who assisted André Breton, Arendt, and nearly two thousand others. Arendt is usually the only woman named among those assisted, but many of the wives of the famous men on this list were saved in the effort, and likely many other interesting women who do not get named in this history. I am certain that there were also many women involved in organizing and carrying out these rescues.

24. See also Mays (2013).
25. See also Kantorowicz (1941).
26. See also, for example, Drucker (1991); Maso (2002); Ankori (2003).
27. New options to research a foundation of many communist activists in antifascism opened in the post-Soviet era. For many, especially many Jews, this was further grounded in their anti-Nazism and their resistance to its antisemitism. Unfortunately, much of this history will likely remain lost to us, as so many Jewish and other communists were murdered during the Holocaust. Post-Holocaust, the Soviet turn valorized antifascism and anti-Nazi resistance. It did so while expressly suppressing the Jewish inspirations for many who engaged this struggle. See also Heckman (2018) for other examples of additional international, non-Western, Jewish communist commitments grounded in antifascist and anti-Nazi imperatives.
28. As we now know, Kahlo might have been targeted for additional reasons as well: She was disabled, politically leftist, bisexual, and often gender bending (for discussions of Kahlo's "androgyny," see Tibol 1993; B. Cruz 1996; Ankori 2002).
29. Herrera (1983, 20, 64, 85); B. Cruz (1996, 13, 15); Kettenmann (2000, 10–11, 18).
30. Prior to 2005, many biographers noted Kahlo's father's Jewish ties, including Herrera (1983); Zamora (1990); Tibol (1993); B. Cruz (1996); Kettenmann (2000).
31. Rivera's notation is quoted frequently. A couple of examples are Jewish sources such as Lipman (2010) and Bush (2015).
32. I often hear of this binding through Jewish marginality anecdotally in my multiracial Jewish communities. A contemporary example may be found in the publicity regarding the pairing of Lenny Kravitz and Lisa Bonet. The two married in 1987 and had a child before divorcing in 1993. They are both Black entertainers, and Bonet's mother is Jewish, as is Kravitz's father. Bonet told reporters, "It was interesting when we were first finding out about each other, that our backgrounds were so similar. When I first told him my mom was Jewish, and he said 'So's my dad,' I thought that was both unusual and enchanting. I felt like, 'Okay, here's someone who really knows how it is.' And I think I trusted him a little more with my feelings and let him inside a little more than I ordinarily would have" (C. Cooper 1990).
33. For example, the president of MoMA, Anson Conger Goodyear, commissioned Frida to paint a self-portrait, while *Vanity Fair*'s managing editor, Clare Boothe Luce, requested a portrait of Dorothy Hale for Hale's mother (Mahon 2011). Both *Vogue* and the *Time* magazine wrote about Frida's show at the Julien Levy Gallery.
34. In September 1939, after Germany invaded Poland, the Seligmanns left Paris. Kurt was supposedly the first of the European surrealists to get to New York. Officially, the Seligmanns left Europe to attend an exhibit of his work, but many speculate that it was their way to get out of Europe ("Kurt Seligmann," n.d. [*Weinstein Gallery*]). Seligmann then became active in getting out other French artists targeted by the Nazis, including Breton and Lamba ("Kurt Seligmann," n.d. [*Jewish Virtual Library*]). In 1943, the Seligmanns were able to visit with Wolfgang Paalen

and Kahlo in Mexico. After the war, Paalen lived for a time in Kurt Seligmann's atelier building in Paris.

35. Earlier in Paris, Lamba's close friend, the photographer Dora Maar (née Henriette Theodora Markovitch), had introduced Lamba to surrealists and the artists' circle that met at the Café de la Place Blanche, where Lamba first met Breton. Maar was born to a Croation architect rumored to be Jewish, which she denied. Maar later had a significant relationship with Picasso (a close friend of Gertrude Stein's and also a good friend of Rivera's since 1914). While in Paris, Frida also has an affair with Josephine Baker. We will think again about Baker when taking on judgments of Stein's time in Vichy France. Based in Paris and married to a Jewish man at the time, Baker had been working as an Ally spy since September 1939 (United States Holocaust Memorial Museum 2021).

36. Paalen's father, Gustav Robert, was a part-Ashkenazi, part-Sephardi Jew who converted to Protestantism and changed his name from Pollak to Paalen in 1900. With his conversion, Pollak/Paalen was able to cross the real yet invisible border dividing the Jewish upper-class intelligentsia (to which Stein's family belonged while they lived in Vienna) from the more distinguished Viennese Protestant upper class. In May 1939, Paalen left France and soon found himself in exile in Mexico, where he connected with Kahlo and Rivera. Following Trotsky's assassination, Paalen disassociated from Kahlo and Rivera for political reasons. During this period in Mexico City, Paalen continued his artistic work and, together with Julien Levy, organized immigration visas for Jews, artists, and political refugees from Vichy France.

37. That year, Frida's art was also included in the exhibition *Modern Mexican Painters* at the Institute of Contemporary Art in Boston. In 1942 Kahlo's *Self-Portrait with Braid* was included in the exhibition *20th Century Portraits* at MoMA. During the same period, another of Kahlo's paintings was included in the *First Papers of Surrealism*, sponsored by the Coordinating Council of French Relief Societies. In 1943, Peggy Guggenheim's Art of This Century gallery in New York included Kahlo's work in its *Exhibition by 31 Women*.

38. In addition to Lina Boytler, many of Kahlo's close women friends are often known today through their husbands, as in the case with Ella Wolfe and Elise Haas; Mary Sklar is known primarily through her brother.

39. In 1949 Kahlo also began to keep a diary. She continued this practice until her death, and it has become a significant part of her legacy. In June 1951, Fernando Benitez wrote an important tribute to the life and art of Kahlo in the newspaper *Novedades*. In 1952, Frida helped collect a list of signatures supporting the peace movement. Rivera immortalized her actions in his murals. She produced thirteen still lifes over the next two years despite excruciating pain and frequent periods in which she was confined to bed.

40. The Guerilla Girls is a group of radical feminist activist artists who use primarily political graffiti art and performance art (see guerrillagirls.com). The group formed in the mid-1980s. Its members remain anonymous so that artists can come in and out of the group without note and so as to keep the focus on political issues,

not on the personalities of members of the group. The members use pseudonyms for their work with the collective, and they usually take their pseudonyms from the names of women artists from the past. "Frida Kahlo" is among the pseudonyms.

41. Kahlo is also referred to as Jewish in that entry. See also the entry on Sabina Berman (Weingarten 2021).

Chapter 6

1. As demonstrated by Edmund Wilson's devoting a chapter to her in his 1931 *Axel's Castle*. Wilson's work was a major study of modern literature that included chapters on Yeats, Proust, and Joyce; Stein was both the only woman and the only Jew with a chapter in the volume. In the US Jewish community of the time, Stein was mentioned numerous times in the press. For example, see Barnes (2000), with notices on and talks by Blanche London on Stein's influence (London 1930, 2000a, 2000b) and "American Jewish Historical Society" (1930).

2. For some interesting exploration, see Zafar (2013); Vester (2015).

3. I am taken by Truong's analysis. There is also likely interesting linguistic study to be done in Jewish frames. For example, Sartori and Cottenet-Hage (2006, xxv) discuss how multilingual Jewish women writing in French were creating new language patterns. They also invite us to consider Cixous's well-known language innovations in this Jewish diasporic setting, grounded in colonial context (148).

4. Truong responds to an interview question:

Q) Is there really a manuscript by Stein entitled "The Book of Salt"?

A) No, I made that up. In the novel, Bính claims that Stein's "The Book of Salt" is about him. Stein has written about cooks and servants. In *Portraits and Prayers*, for instance, there is a piece called "B. B. or the Birthplace of Bonnes" about all the women from Brittany who had worked in the Stein and Toklas household. Also, two of the "lives" in Stein's *Three Lives* were servants'. So, it does not seem improbable to me that Stein could have devoted a few words to a cook like Bính. (Houghton Mifflin Harcourt, n.d.).

The scholarly literature on Truong's novel is quite rich. See, for example, Cohler (2008); Edwards (2012); Xu (2008); D. Cruz (2013).

5. A database search on the scholarship provides weight to this claim. In April 2017, the University of New Hampshire Discovery Service database—comprising 125 academic research databases such as the *MLA International Bibliography*, *JSTOR*, and *Project MUSE*—indicated that while over 2,500 works are classified as discussing Gertrude Stein as a subject, a mere twenty-nine (less than 2 percent) are classified as discussing both Stein and Jewishness as subjects. Even fewer works

actually engage Stein and Jewish figures or Jewish-related topics. Database searches for more general results show that the proportion of these works engaging Stein in any Jewish way to the overall breadth of scholarship on Stein is miniscule. As a counterpoint, see Damon (1996).

6. Antler's (1997) work in general, and her chapter segment on Stein in particular for this case, are rare examples of Jewish feminist analysis of historical figures such as Stein.

7. The Jewish Emancipation repealed legal restrictions, such as quotas, and finally granted Jews citizenship rights (Aberbach 2013, 77).

8. Although later than the period when Stein's family lived in Vienna, the impacts of World War I and World War II on the Viennese Jewish population cannot be understated. In WWI, more than 300,000 Jews fought for the Dual Monarchy of Austria-Hungary (Woolf 2014). While many Jews left the city to join the army, the war also increased Jewish immigration to Vienna. In 1914 and 1915, the Russian army displaced some 400,000 Jews from the region of Galicia, and many sought refuge in Prague and Vienna (Woolf 2014). Later, World War II left the Jewish population of Vienna in ruins. In 1938, the city was home to as many as 200,000 Jews (including some who had converted out of Judaism). By 1942, however, only 8,000 Jews remained in all of Austria ("Vienna," n.d.). Many of these Jews emigrated, but those who remained were deported to forced labor and extermination camps ("Vienna," n.d.). Of the 65,000 Viennese Jews who were deported, it is estimated that only 2,000 survived ("Vienna, Austria," n.d.).

9. Some examples mentioned in the literature include anti-Jewish racial slurs such as "sheeney" (a term for Jew that became a rude slur after the 1870s). Wineapple (1996, 37) also notes the anecdote that a classmate of Leo's, believing Leo to be out of earshot, once commented, "Oh, those damned Jews always get ahead of us."

10. Stein famously wrote of her Oakland childhood in her memoir *Everybody's Autobiography*: "what was the use of my having come from Oakland it was not natural to have come from there yes write about it if I like or anything if I like but not there, there is no there there" ([1937] 1993, 298). This excerpt is commonly misconstrued as Stein excoriating Oakland (for example, see this *Frommer's* article characterizing Stein as "Oakland's ungrateful daughter": "Oakland after Gertrude Stein," *Frommer's*, http://www.frommers.com/trip-ideas/road-trip/oakland-after-gertrude-stein). However, others interpret this as Stein's painful acknowledgment that the once-bucolic and beloved Oakland of her childhood had become unrecognizable to her as an adult due to rampant urbanization (Werner 2012; F. Rosenbaum 2009, 87).

11. By comparison, the total Jewish population in the United States in 1899 was 1,043,800 ("Jewish Statistics" 1899, 284). Jews represented 1.37 percent of the overall US population, an estimated 76,094,000 in 1900 (United States Census Bureau 2000).

12. "No one was more disturbed by the revelations of Jewish crime in the downtown ghetto than uptown German Jews. Distressed by the political radicalism and religious Orthodoxy of eastern Europeans and repelled by their 'strange ways and speech,' German Jews saw their immorality and vice as a great threat to themselves. 'If there should grow up in our midst a class of people abnormal and objectionable to our fellow citizens,' read the proceedings of the Nineteenth Annual Convention of the Union of American Hebrew Congregations, 'all of us will suffer . . . the question is largely one of self-preservation.' Spurred by this insecurity, German Jewish leaders sponsored a series of programs to remake their coreligionists" (Sorin 1992, 86).

13. Dupee (1962) states, "Gertrude Stein felt no deep identification with the oppressed; life was a struggle that she could very probably win."

14. NCJW (ncjw.org) remains an active and vibrant Jewish feminist network.

15. Thanks to Penina Weinberg for her contributions to this section on Jewish *salonnières*.

16. On women *salonnières*, see Balducci and Jensen (2014) and their chapter on Stein; Goodman (1994); Kale (2006); Landes (1996).

17. See Bilski, Braun, and Botstein (2005); Hertz (2005); Shapiro (2002); *Power of Conversation* (2005) and its web resources at https://mcmullenmuseum.bc.edu/exhibitions/salons/ (accessed February 12, 2018).

18. Banks (2011) makes a play on the title for his article "Wars They Have Seen," with the subtitle "How an Unlikely Friendship with a Vichy Collaborator Complicates Our Understanding of Gertrude Stein," in his contribution to the debates discussed here.

19. The denaturalization law was enacted on July 16, 1940. The first Jewish status laws, dated October 3, 1940, excluded Jews from the army, the press, commercial and industrial activities, and the civil service. The second status law (July 1941) required the registration of Jewish businesses and excluded Jews from any profession, commercial or industrial. A further law on "Aliens of Jewish Race" (October 4, 1940), promulgated simultaneously with the Jewish status laws, allowed for the immediate internment of foreign Jews (those who did not hold French citizenship). By July 1941, the Laval government instituted an extensive program of "Aryanization," appropriating Jewish-owned property for the French state. Aryanization left most Jews in France destitute; the effect of this was particularly severe on foreign Jews.

20. See Blasius and Phelan (1997, 134). For a story about women's experience, one Jewish, see Fischer (1995).

21. The quotation in the interview is "I say that Hitler ought to have the peace prize . . . because he is removing all elements of contest and struggle from Germany. By driving out the Jews and the democratic and Left elements, he is driving out everything that conduces to activity. That means peace" (Warren 1934).

Those not part of the campaign against Stein note that she made these comments ironically, as part of her hatred of patriarchy, fascism, and overbearing father figures.

22. Pétain was an avowed antisemite and a high official in the Vichy government. As early as 1970, Richard Bridgman discussed Stein's work on Pétain in his biography of Stein. In 1996, Van Dusen published Stein's introduction to the Pétain translations, including Stein's laudatory comments on Pétain. Stendhal (2012) writes on this: "Did Stein approve of Pétain's evolving reactionary and antisemitic politics, or blindly give him carte blanche for his past merits? Nobody knows. What we know for sure is that at the same time Stein worked on her translation project, she also wrote a whole satirical novel about Hitler and Stalin, *Mrs. Reynolds* (1940–1943), which she unsuccessfully tried to publish in the States."

23. For example, New York State assemblyman Dov Hikind, Manhattan borough president Scott Stringer, and commentator Alan Dershowitz.

24. Joan Retallack in the Bernstein (2012) dossier and Stendhal (2012) in the Jewish intellectual journal *Tikkun* both share this opinion.

25. The history of an oppressive expectation of Jewish women being "nice Jewish girls" inspired the title of Evelyn Torton Beck's 1982 groundbreaking *Nice Jewish Girls: A Lesbian Anthology*.

Chapter 7

1. Typically, Goldman was not among the anarchist theorists assigned in graduate political theory courses. I had to explore Goldman's work on my own. Likely, my professor followed a common current that did not appreciate Goldman, fiery activist and orator, as worthy of study in political philosophy. Zinn's (1986) play did much to revive popular interest in Goldman in the 1980s. Overall, biographies tend to focus on her personal life, which they separate from her thinking and politics (for example, see Drinnon [1961]; Wexler [1984b]; Morton [1992]; Frankel [1996]; Chalberg [2008]; Gornick [2011]). In popular culture, most attention to Goldman either demonizes her or puts her on a pedestal. We do have some works that undertake some level of analysis. (Falk [1990]; Haaland [1993]; Drinnon [1961]; and Solomon [1987] are somewhat typical in offering no serious analysis of Goldman's ideas.) In the 2000s, new work on Goldman (such as the essays Weiss and Kensinger [2007] brought together) emerged that shifted this tendency. Marso (2006) and Ferguson (2011) are rare feminist political theorists who take Goldman seriously as a thinker. While Morton's (1992) and Ferguson's (2011) works note some aspects of Jewish import (see also Goldman's entry in the Jewish Women's Archive [n.d.] and, more broadly, Kessler-Harris [1976]; Antler [1997]; Kosak [2009]), most work does not situate Goldman in a centrally Jewish context.

2. Ashbolt (2003, 2) calls Goldman "a remarkable instance of a European Jewish woman coming to radical prominence in America." (See J. Rosenbaum's [2009] questioning of this.) This reception is similar to that of Meir, known mostly

within the US Jewish community until her rise to the top ranks of the Yishuv and then the Israeli establishment.

3. By the late nineteen-teens, when Jewish immigration had caused a major increase in the size of the US Jewish community, Michels (2005) notes that only a small number, about 12 percent, even belonged to a synagogue.

4. While scholars such as Wexler (1989, 41) note that Goldman "counted many of her warmest supporters among them [immigrant Jews in the US]," Wexler also states that Goldman stayed away from the "Yiddish-speaking Jewish immigrant anarchists in America." This simplistic characterization does not help us develop our understanding of the important Jewish grounding for Goldman or the importance of Goldman, her anarchism, and her anarcho-feminism for Jewish politics.

5. Berman (2019) writes, "And—this was their achievement—they succeeded in imposing a spirit of those ideas on a visible portion of the mass immigration: not every twist of the doctrine, but the spirit as a whole, such that Jewish trade unionism on the Lower East Side and in similar neighborhoods came to reflect the basic concepts, not just as a passing fad. Here, then, was a beginning of American Jewish culture—not the only beginning, and not a fully worked out beginning, but, even so, a starting point for a substantial number of people." Berman's publication was paired with the 2019 Yiddish Anarchism: New Scholarship on a Forgotten Tradition conference; some of the papers from that conference are also referenced below.

6. As in the title of Moritz's 2001 work. Weiss and Kensinger (2007) write about the connections between Goldman's time and theirs in their introductory essay to a book of feminist interpretations of Emma Goldman. They write, "Many of us learned from Goldman as we, like Goldman herself, discovered feminism, labored against internal tyrants, and worked for social change in hostile times. Globally, issues essential to Goldman's work continue to be at the center of political debate: patriotism and political violence, birth control and governmental control, artistic expression and freedom of speech, personal relationships and revolution, corporate greed and global imperialism, rights and liberation" (6). Writing the bulk of this chapter during Trump's time in office, there is nothing necessarily that I could delete from this list of pressing current issues. We can add colonialism, racism, homophobia and transphobia, antisemitism, Islamophobia, and immigration.

7. Berkman also wrote on his emerging critical analysis of the Bolshevik revolution, following his early enthusiasm. See for example his critique in the form of a diary from 1920 to 1922 (Berkman [1925] 1989).

8. Among these supporters was the wealthy, unconventional Jewish Peggy Guggenheim (see Dearborn 2004), who is another interesting nodal point between the otherwise unlikely trio of Goldman, Stein, and Kahlo.

9. Goldman spoke widely across the Midwest and also specifically to socialist Zionist groups in the US and Canada (Wexler 1989, 120).

10. Goldman was older than Kahlo and worked closely with anarchist comrades active in the Mexican Revolution, which formed a core of Kahlo's lifelong political commitments.

11. See Goldman's essay on Wollstonecraft (Wexler and Goldman 1981). For major historical works on anarchism, see Bakunin (1990); Berkman (1929); Godwin (1793); Goldman ([1917] 1969); Kropotkin and Avrich (1972); Proudhon ([1840] 1994). For a portrait of the period of the Spanish Civil War, see Orwell ([1938] 1969). For a more contemporary overview, see Marshall (2010).

12. For a brief review of Steimer in a Jewish feminist context, see Goldstein (2009). More broadly, see Ferguson's (2011, 277–312) detailed work on Goldman's women's habitus (and on the book's companion website at http://www2.hawaii.edu/~kferguso/).

13. For works on Cleyre and Pesotta, see Avrich (1978); Cleyre (2005); Leeder (1993); Pesotta (1944, 1958).

14. Berman (2019) also notes in the US activity of a group in 2010, the Alexander Berkman Social Club, and activity of another in 2017, the Friends of Aron Baron, named after a Chicago-based Jewish anarchist who went to Russia (first his wife, Fanya, and later he was shot there during the early Bolshevik period). While of course there have been shifts and developments among anarchist activists and thinkers, some also see a good deal of continuity from Goldman's time to our own. See for example Cornell (2016) and Goyens (2014) for a helpful overview across time in New York City.

15. See, for example, Goldstene (2014).

16. For a brief overview of this position, see section 3 (pp. 114–18) on "Critical-Utopian Socialism and Communism" in Marx and Engels's (1967) *Communist Manifesto*.

17. See Horrox (2009); Oved (2000). Additionally, it has not been uncommon to find a slippage in usage between the terms *anarchist* and *socialist*, contributing to a loss of historical awareness of the role of anarchism historically. As an example, Jewish anarchist Gustav Landauer titled one of his major anarchist works *On Socialism* (Landauer 2010; see also Mendes-Flohr, Mali, and Delf von Wolzogen 2016).

18. See Shumsky (2018) for the non-statist history of Zionist efforts to create a homeland for Jews.

19. See Shulman (n.d.) for this popular culture legend. It likely emerged from Goldman's insistence on her enthusiasm at movement dances, where she writes that she "was one of the most untiring and gayest," and where she affirms her commitment to "life and joy."

20. See Ackelsberg and Addelson (2007).

21. We can see this legacy, with continued debates regarding strategic violence, in Antifa (an abbreviation for antifascist), a loose network of activists with mixed political commitments across the Left, including anarchists (for example, see Bray 2017). Began as an antifascist group in Italy during Mussolini's rise to power, Antifa has seen moments of revival, particularly in the US since the 2016 election of Trump and across Europe with fascism on the rise. Antifa groups rely on some basic aspects of anarchism such as decentralization, mutual aid, direct action, and

anti-statism. In the US, the anti-statism is also specifically anti-police and focused on disrupting white supremacy. As in the classical anarchist period of fin-de-siècle, Antifa activists have a range of interpretations of the most effective forms of direct action, from confrontational to physical violence. As anarchists have historically been opposed to private property, one can also find some Antifa activists distinguishing between destruction of property and violence against people.

22. Goldman's dogged anti-militarism and growing eschewal of violence as a selected strategy brought her closer to the Russian pacifist anarchist tradition of Tolstoy in the same period. One of the earlier anarchist journals was created in this Tolstoyan frame and titled *The Peaceful Revolutionist*.

23. A classic text confusing anarchist ideas of radical democracy with lack of organization is Engels's (1978) essay "On Authority."

24. The people of Paris managed to set up a revolutionary socialist ruling system in the city from March 18 to May 28, 1871. It was a secular and democratic system that put in place major social services for the people. Marx saw in the Paris Commune a working example of his concept of "the dictatorship of the proletariat."

25. Just before Goldman's deportation from the US, a communist movement by Austria's Social Democratic Workers Party (SDAP) established in the capital city what they saw as an alternative to Bolshevism, by forming a coalition between parliamentary-style socialism and what was considered a more radical communist front. They were anticlerical and enacted a sweeping worker-initiated transformation of the life of the city, intellectually and culturally, and in terms of public housing, economic safety nets, social services, health care, education, and infrastructure. Even with and after Nazi devastation, Vienna remains the most affordable city in Europe, and the majority of residents live in municipally supported or nonprofit co-ops.

26. This occurred in the lead-up to and at the forefront of the Spanish Civil War. Also, anticlerical, anarchist peasants and workers succeeded in collectivizing both industry and land, localizing democratic decision-making, and establishing pro-worker policies and social supports. While the Soviet Union backed the Republican side generally during the civil war, and many socialist and communist parties participated, the Soviet Union opposed the anarchist movement and its programs.

27. Even with her clear statements about rising antisemitism in France, where she was living in the mid-1930s, and on Kristallnacht in Germany in 1938 (Ferguson 2011, 239–40).

28. For one of the most theoretically sophisticated and detailed accounts of this period, see Jewish anarcho-feminist Ackelsberg's (1991) work on feminist activism in this Spanish context. For Spanish anarchist activists' impact beyond Spain, see Ackelsberg (2016).

29. For a helpful overview of European-heritage Jewish women's activism in this era, see Shepherd (1993).

30. Numerous feminist scholars and masses of activists have been developing this mode of feminism for a long time (for a political-theory background, see

Hancock 2016). Critical legal scholar Kimberlé Crenshaw (1989) is credited for introducing the term that has become a popular identifier of this mode.

31. On some of the Jewish participation in this movement, see Klapper (2013).

32. At this time, US women had citizenship through their husbands. Hoover and Palmer succeeded in deporting Goldman because they were able to revoke her citizenship, making her fair game for action under the Anarchist Exclusion Act, which made it possible to deport anarchists who were not US citizens. Goldman's ex-husband Kershner had had his citizenship revoked following a conviction. The government charged that with Kershner's citizenship revoked, so was Goldman's, despite their divorce and this being years later (Hollis 2016).

33. See the Black Panther movement, the works of Derrick Bell (for example, Bell 1992), and Black feminists such as Audre Lorde (for example, Lorde 1984).

34. Marso's (2006) work is central here, in particular on how Goldman looked to Mary Wollstonecraft in this regard: her writing as a feminist political theorist, her concrete work for women, and her lived struggles with intimacy, desire, and motherhood. In this book, I argue with Marso the importance of this mode, as when Arendt took up the genre with Varnhagen.

35. See Antler's (1997) work for examples of Jewish feminist engagement with this.

36. It was Jewish anarchist Ezra Heywood who was first arrested for activism on birth control. Margaret Sanger began to do work for Goldman's *Mother Earth* and went on to focus on birth control, whereas for Goldman it remained part of a web of issues for women and all people's freedom (Wehling 2007, 33). In 1916, Goldman was arrested for her public lecture on how to use contraception. During these years, Goldman collaborated with Margaret Sanger, who focused on access to contraception and is credited for coining the term "birth control." Both Goldman and Sanger were arrested under the then intensive Comstock Act (aimed at "Suppression of Trade in, and Circulation of, Obscene Literature and Articles of Immoral Use" including using the US postal services for delivering such materials on what it deemed "lewd, or lascivious" subjects. These laws are being revived in the 2020s to use against feminist, antiracist, disabilities, and LGBTQ activism). In addition to abortion and birth control, Goldman the activist and nurse also worked for women's capacities to birth children, especially for the poorest women, and to link motherhood to a movement to protect and free all people young and old. (On Goldman's strategic use of the rhetoric of motherhood, see Ostman 2009.)

37. In part, Goldman's views on same-gender sexuality were part of her overall anarchist feminist analysis that constraints on bodies and sexualities were part of broad structures operating to discipline the masses. She was a fierce campaigner for free love and freeing up human sexual diversity. She lectured widely on the subject of same-sex love and sexuality in the US particularly until her deportation (Goldman [1931] 1970, 555). Gay men and lesbians often came to thank her personally following her public lectures on homosexuality. Goldman often pleaded publicly on behalf of the well-known British writer Oscar Wilde when he was imprisoned

for "gross indecency" (for example, see Goldman [1931] 1970, 269). She also had numerous close friends and comrades who were gay and lesbian (531). Goldman's friends Margaret Anderson and Harriet Dean, lovers, published *The Little Review*, which not only included anarchism among its topics but addressed anarchism in positive ways. Biographers often comment on Goldman's close relationship with Almeda Sperry and Sperry's passionate letters to Goldman. On Goldman and homosexuality, see Wiesen Cook (1977, 56); Katz (1992, 523); Falk (1990); and Goldman's *Living My Life*. See also Haaland (1993); Wexler (1984a). For how Goldman included attention to lesbians and gay men in ways that were not at all current as yet, on the left or among anarchists, see Katz (1992, 376–80).

38. As an example, Wexler (1989, 166) notes that Goldman wrote to Rose Pesotta, "If people do not even long for beauty and the things of the spirit, how can they be expected to fight for it?"

39. For Jewish feminist work on this matter, see Brettschneider (2006) and Ackelsberg and Plaskow's response (2004, 107–12).

40. For a Jewish context, see Ackelsberg (1986); Prell (1989). For Goldman and more broadly, see also Goyens (2007); Ferguson (2011).

41. On the centrality of mid-twentieth-century Jewish women to these aspects of the feminist movement, see Antler (2018).

42. For an excellent resource, see the *Guide to the YIVO Archives* (yivoarchives.org).

43. For some work on Yiddish and Jewish anarchism, see Avrich (1978, 1988); Avrich and Avrich (2012); Berman (2019); Ehrlich (2019); Horrox (2009); Howard (2017); Michels (2005, 2012); J. Rosenbaum (2009); Torres (2016); Türk and Cohn (2018); Zimmer (2015, 2017); Torres and Zimmer (2022).

44. Self-described as a band that plays "Yiddish anarchist and bundist songs (and some other Yiddish radical tunes)—the soundtrack to strikes, uprisings, assassinations, and revolutionary movements from Odessa and Vilna to New York and Galveston to Buenos Aires and Havana" ("Koyt Far Dayn Fardakht," n.d.).

45. Note Ferguson (2011, 184); Falk (2002, 21).

46. See Ferguson's (2011, 99–116) work on Goldman's textual counterpublics and important work on anarchist presses (Ferguson 2014).

47. The paper was formally affiliated with the Communist Party USA from 1922 to 1988. Srebrnik (2010) notes that for a time it was the leading (among the nine) daily CPUSA newspapers in the United States, although it was kicked out of the party for its post–World War II so-called pro-Israel politics. On political conflicts within the leftist Yiddish press, see M. Hoffman (2010).

48. The *Forward* published leading Yiddish writers, such as Isaac Bashevis Singer, and other well-known Jewish socialists and communists, such as Leon Trotsky (whom Kahlo hosted and had an affair with when he was in Mexico). Some shorter-lived US Yiddish-language socialist papers included *Di Arbeter Tsaytung* (the Workman's Paper) and *Dos Abend Blatt* (the Evening Paper). Other politically related Yiddish publications included short-lived ventures such as *Der Morgenshtern* (the

Morning Star) and *Di Fraye Gezelshaft*. See Avrich (1988) on these initiatives. See also Rubenstein (1980) and Buhle (1998), and on anarchist presses see Ferguson (2011, 2014).

49. See Gurianova (2019) for a study of a paper in the context of anarchist organizing in Moscow.

50. The paper also published Berkman's writings, and portions of his *The ABC of Anarchism* were originally printed there.

51. For example, in 1912 Goldman, through *Mother Earth*, partnered with the *Freie Arbeiter Stimme* on a celebration at Carnegie Hall for Kropotkin's seventieth birthday.

52. Two interesting developments in the Hebrew-Yiddish language wars today: Haredi girls in Israel will have less exposure to Yiddish than to Hebrew, as Yiddish remains the language of instruction in yeshivot, which are populated by males. Haredi leaders today often emphasize the need to preserve Yiddish, calling Hebrew the "mongrelized invention of secularization" (Rabinowitz 2017, 2).

While Yiddish is experiencing a reconstituting moment, enrollment in Hebrew language courses in US universities was down during the writing of this book (Kushner 2019).

53. Whereas Hebrew, though a part of these intense language politics internationally, was later made illegal in Soviet Union.

54. For more on KlezKamp, see Living Traditions' archived website: https://web.archive.org/web/20020330081924/http://klezkamp.org/. Of special note are Jennifer Miller and other lesbians such as Jenny Romain, who spearheaded Circus Amok (circusamok.org); performance artist Sara Felder; the musicians Natalia Zukerman (nataliazukerman.com) and Jewlia Eisenberg (charminghostess.com); and Jill Sobule's conceptualization of a more trans approach to Isaac Bashevis Singer's *Yentl* (jillsobule.com/yenta).

55. Special thanks to Eve Sicular for her extensive knowledge and her support with this section. Many of these people and activities had ties with JFREJ (Jews for Racial and Economic Justice) over the years. Outside the US, Hinde Burstin is an example of a lesbian in Australia with a Yiddish and bundist background who activated the Jewish lesbians of Melbourne (Burstin 2018). Joanna Britton is doing similar activist work in Belgium. For more on queer Yiddishkeit in this vein, see *In Geveb: A Journal of Yiddish Studies* (ingeveb.org); Shandler (2006a, 2006b); Freedman (2008); Nepon (2014); Pellegrini (2007); Mallet (2004); W. Hoffman (2009); Weiman-Kelman (2018); and the Mayrent Institute for Yiddish Culture (mayrent.wisc.edu).

56. Spanish as a language in Jewish communities in the US began flourishing a century later, around 1980.

57. For example, see the works of secular Jewish lesbian feminists and leftist activists Kaye/Kantrowitz and Klepfisz (1986).

58. Berman (2019): "Berkman produced a pamphlet or two, which were even earlier, followed by *The Bolshevik Myth*, in 1925, which was, I think, the most brilliantly written of the American ex-pat books, with extraordinary and horrifying pages devoted to the pogroms in the Ukraine and the sufferings of the Jews."

59. As Avrich (1988, 188) notes, "As many Jewish anarchists had revisited their rejection of attending to Jewish specificity following the Kishinev and other pogroms between 1903 and 1906." Michels in Ehrlich (2019) further clarifies:

The big turning point was the Kishinev pogrom in 1903. That was shocking to anarchists who had stressed universalism and who did not invest importance in Jewishness for the most part. After Kishinev, there was a pretty intensive reassessment of universalism (they used the word 'internationalism'). It was at that point that a good number of the pioneers of anarchism in America started to think about the importance of the specificity of Jewishness, and even work towards a synthesis of Jewish nationalism and anarchism. That's something admirable in anarchists, that they looked at the world around them and saw that ideas needed to be reassessed, and then struggled seriously with them. They worked hard to keep this universalistic impulse alive and also deal with the specific plight of Jews that demanded attention, and couldn't be subsumed or ignored.

60. While some celebrate an anarchist anti-statism that supposes that anarchists can therefore feel at home anywhere, such celebrations on Goldman's behalf are likely overstated (Ashbolt 2003, 9).

61. Ashbolt (2003, 6) notes that Goldman's appreciation of the US grew again during her later exile from, and disillusionment with, Russia as her ties on the left dwindled in response to her criticism of the Russian revolution. Her sense of rootlessness contributed to a sense of despair.

62. As another example, Goldman's ties with the Jewish Anarchist Federation in New York helped her keep her promise to Berkman to help support his partner Emmy after his death in 1936. In addition to supporting Emmy herself, Goldman enlisted various comrades to contribute to her support and arranged for the Jewish Anarchist Federation to pledge ten dollars monthly for Emmy (Wexler 1989, 196).

63. Resonating with us still today, in her written statement prepared for her deportation hearing on October 27, 1919, Goldman wrote, "Today so-called aliens are deported. Tomorrow native Americans will be banished" (*New York Times* 1919).

64. Goldman crisscrossed with most of the other women studied in this book including as she traveled and spoke extensively around Europe in the early 1930s, especially following the 1931 publication of her autobiography. In Paris, she tended to avoid general anarchist groups, but she still spoke to Jewish refugee anarchist groups, whom she addressed in Yiddish (Wexler 1989, 157), and was back in Paris (likely meeting with them again) as late as 1939 (234). Her plans to return to Germany at this time were thwarted by Hitler's 1933 rise to power (15).

65. Despite Goldman's desire to deliver a series of lectures on Hitler and "Dictatorships, Right and Left" while in the US in 1933, she was refused (Wexler 1989, 158). She was also characteristically critical of ordinary people and leftists who she thought were not doing enough to resist fascism, including the European Jewish middle class. This led to tensions with comrades across political affiliation. Figures such as Arendt were similarly lambasted for holding ordinary people accountable for a failure to turn back fascism. At the same time, after Goldman's death, this form of critique became a more mainstream self-criticism among many.

66. On Jewish autonomous movements, see Rabinovitch (2012); Pianko (2010); Shumsky (2011); Srebrnik (2010).

67. See the essays in Jacobs (2001).

68. Berman (2019) notes that Zimmer's research shows that for the Yiddish-language anarchist *Freie Arbeiter Stimme*, "By 1914, circulation was up to 30,000, which, according to Zimmer, was more than double the size of the combined memberships of all the Zionist organizations of America, in clear demonstration that labor anarchism was still a going concern; and Zionism, not yet."

69. For example, in Ehrlich (2019) Anna Elena Torres discusses Yankev-Meyer Zalkind, an anarchist Talmudic scholar, referred to as "*der go'en anarkhist*, the anarchist sage." Zalkind was educated at the Volozhin yeshiva,

> where his chavrusa [study partner] was the poet Hayyim Bialik. Then he moved to London and became a radical anti-militarist, surveilled by Scotland Yard; the police records describe how Jewish mutual aid groups were organizing against the war. Zalkind published a few tractates from the Talmud in Yiddish in the 1920s and continued translating it for years, preparing an accessible version for workers. He remained an orthodox rabbi and a fiery anarchist throughout his life.

He wanted to create an anarchist society in mandate Palestine, to overthrow the British and cultivate the land, to build Haifa into a refugium, in Agamben's term—a space of refuge for the world's refugees. . . . Zalkind's life can tell us a lot about these convergences of religiosity, Zionism, and anarchism. From ads in Yiddish newspapers, we know he gave public lectures framing the Talmud as a proto-anarchist ethical tradition with no state power behind it. He represents a strain of Yiddish anarchism rooted in textual tradition, in defiance of antisemitism and Christian hegemony.

70. As noted, Linke Fligl was a contemporary Jewish anarchist experiment in this vein, active over the years of research on this book, from their self-description (https://linkefligl.com/our-story). Linke Fligl was located on occupied Schaghticoke territory tended by WILDSEED, and emerging Black- and Brown-led, feminine-centered, queer-loving, earth-based international community, organic farm, healing sanctuary, and political and creative home on 181 acres in Millerton, NY.

Linke Fligl paid a 10 percent land tax to the Schaghticoke First Nations on all sales and event donations. Linke Fligl envisions a deep, de-assimilating, diasporist, and songful Jewish culture that uplifts the multiplicity of Jewish identities. This culture seeks to find belonging through reclaiming intrinsic connection to land and ancestry while also being accountable to the reality that many of us are settlers on this land. Through growing food, participating in reparations, being in prayer, and connecting to land and tradition, they shifted and reimagined diasporic Jewish life.

71. See more on Rose Pesotta as an example of a Jewish feminist anarchist active at the time who also participated according to her anarchist principles in Yishuv and Israeli-related institutions, such as the American Trade Union Council for the Histadrut, which was the primary labor organization in Israel. As a later example, Noam Chomsky's commitments can also be seen in this context. See Schivone (2011) and, on the US Left at the time more generally, Howard (2017).

72. On anarchism and anticolonialism, see B. Anderson (2005); Knight (2012).

73. I first learned of this tradition from Irena Klepfisz starting in the 1980s and then Melanie Kaye/Kantrowitz, who also wrote on it specifically in 2007. See also Linfield (2019); Arkush (2009); Slucki (2010).

74. Many Goldman scholars note her profound experience of exile. Learning from Goldman's experience, we can explore creative possibilities for radical diasporism, without glorifying the condition of exile. On Goldman, for example, see Hollis (2016); Ashbolt (2003); Morton (1992). For broader Jewish discussion on diaspora in US and Europe, see Rabinovitch (2012).

75. Rarely addressed in the recent revival of leftist Jewish interest in Bundism, anarchists would not have created the sort of electoral and party organizations developed by Bundists historically because they rejected statist strategies. As most Jews who are excited by learning about and reclaiming Bundist traditions also do not aim to create Jewish political parties or Jewish corporate representation in electoral forums, anarchism provides a likely more promising treasure trove of historical inspiration.

76. See, for example, Torres (2016); Türk and Cohn (2018).

References

Abbasi, Alexander. 2017. "Let the Semites End the World! On Decolonial Resistance, Solidarity, and Pluriversal Struggle." In *On Antisemitism: Solidarity and the Struggle for Justice*, edited by Jewish Voice for Peace, 105–9. Chicago: Haymarket Books.

Aberbach, David. 2013. *The European Jews, Patriotism and the Liberal State, 1789–1939: A Study of Literature and Social Psychology*. Abingdon, UK: Routledge.

Ackelsberg, Martha. 1986. "Spirituality, Community, and Politics: B'not Esh and the Feminist Reconstruction of Judaism." *Journal of Feminist Studies in Religion* 2 (2): 109–20.

———. 1991. *Free Women of Spain: Anarchism and the Struggle for the Emancipation of Women*. Bloomington: Indiana University Press.

———. 2016. "It Takes More Than a Village! Transnational Travels of Spanish Anarchism in Argentina and Cuba." *International Journal of Iberian Studies* 29 (3): 205–23.

Ackelsberg, Martha, and Kathryn Pyne Addelson. 2007. "Anarchist Alternatives to Competition." In Weiss and Kensinger 2007, 285–300.

Ackelsberg, Martha, and Judith Plaskow. 2004. "Response." In "Roundtable Discussion: Same-Sex Marriage," by Mary E. Hunt et al., *Journal of Feminist Studies in Religion* 20 (2), 107–12.

Adair, Gigi. 2019. "Postcolonial Sabotage and Ethnographic Recovery in Jamaica Kincaid's *The Autobiography of My Mother*." In *Kinship across the Black Atlantic: Writing Diasporic Relations*, by Gigi Adair, 35–58. Liverpool, UK: Liverpool University Press.

Albright, Alice P. 1959. "Gertrude Stein at Radcliffe: Most Brilliant Women Student." *Harvard Crimson*, February 18, 1959. http://www.thecrimson.com/article/1959/2/18/gertrude-stein-at-radcliffe-most-brilliant/.

Aldrich, Marcia. 2012. "Kincaid's Bite." *Fourth Genre: Explorations in Nonfiction* 14 (1): 165–71.

Alt Miller, Yvette. 2015. "Surprising Facts about the Jews of Mexico." *Aish.com*, April 25, 2015. http://www.aish.com/jw/s/Surprising-Facts-about-the-Jews-of-Mexico.html.

"American Jewish Historical Society Concludes Sessions." 1930. *Jewish Daily Bulletin*, June 13, 1930, p. 2.

Anderson, Benedict. 2005. *Under Three Flags: Anarchism and the Anti-Colonial Imagination*. London: Verso Books.

Anderson, Patrick. 2017. "Levinas and the Anticolonial." *Journal of French and Francophone Philosophy* 25 (1): 150–81.

Ankori, Gannit. 2002. *Imaging Her Selves: Frida Kahlo's Poetics of Identity and Fragmentation*. Westport, CT: Greenwood Press.

———. 2003. *Frida Kahlo's Intimate Family Portrait*. New York: Jewish Museum, presented September 5, 2003–January 4, 2004. Exhibition webpage accessed May 20, 2019. https://thejewishmuseum.org/exhibitions/frida-kahlos-intimate-family-portrait.

———. 2013. *Frida Kahlo*. London: Reaktion Books.

Antler, Joyce. 1997. *The Journey Home: Jewish Women and the American Century*. New York: Simon and Schuster.

———. 2018. *Jewish Radical Feminism: Voices from the Women's Liberation Movement*. New York: New York University Press.

Appelbaum, Lauren. 2019. "Frida Kahlo, Role Model for Artists, People with Disabilities and Bisexual Women." *RespectAbility*, March 7, 2019. https://www.respectability.org/2019/03/women-disabilities-frida-kahlo/.

Arendt, Hannah. (1929) 1996. *Love and Saint Augustine*. Translated and edited by Joanna Vecchiarelli Scott and Judith Chelius Stark. Chicago: University of Chicago Press. Originally published as *Der Liebesbergriff bei Augustin* (Berlin: Julius Springer Verlag, 1929).

———. 1944. "The Jew as Pariah: A Hidden Tradition." *Jewish Social Studies* 6 (2): 99–122.

———. (1951) 1973. *The Origins of Totalitarianism*. Third edition with new prefaces. New York: Harcourt Brace Jovanovich.

———. 1958. *The Human Condition*. Third edition with new prefaces. Chicago: University of Chicago Press.

———. 1961. *Between Past and Future*. New York: Viking Press.

———. 1963. *On Revolution*. New York: Viking Press.

———. 1965. *Eichmann in Jerusalem: A Report on the Banality of Evil*. Revised and enlarged edition. New York: Viking Press.

———. 1968. *Men in Dark Times*. New York: Harcourt Brace Jovanovich.

———. 1972. *Crises of the Republic*. New York: Harcourt Brace Jovanovich.

———. (1974) 1997. *Rahel Varnhagen: The Life of a Jewess*. First complete edition, edited by Liliane Weissberg, translated by Richard Winston and Clara Winston. Baltimore: Johns Hopkins University Press.

Arkush, Allan. 2009. "Diaspora Nationalism to Radical Diasporism." *Modern Judaism* 29 (3): 326–50.

Aron-Beller, Katherine. 2010. "Disciplining Jews: The Papal Inquisition of Modena, 1598–1630." *Sixteenth Century Journal* 41 (3): 713–29.
Ashbolt, Anthony. 2003. "Love and Hate in European Eyes: Emma Goldman and Alexander Berkman on America." *Australasian Journal of American Studies* 22 (1): 1–14.
Avineri, Shlomo. 1981. *The Making of Modern Zionism: Intellectual Origins of the Jewish State*. New York: Basic Books.
Aviv, Caryn, and David Shneer. 2005. *New Jews: The End of the Jewish Diaspora*. New York: New York University Press.
Avrich, Paul. 1978. *An American Anarchist: The Life of Voltairine de Cleyre*. Princeton, NJ: Princeton University Press.
———. 1988. "Jewish Anarchism in the United States." In *Anarchist Portraits*, 176–99. Princeton, NJ: Princeton University Press.
Avrich, Paul, and Karen Avrich. 2012. *Sasha and Emma: The Anarchist Odyssey of Alexander Berkman and Emma Goldman*. Cambridge, MA: Harvard University Press.
Bakunin, Mikhail. 1990. *Statism and Anarchy*. Translated and edited by Marshall Shatz. Cambridge: Cambridge University Press.
Balducci, Temma, and Heather Belnap Jensen, editors. 2014. *Women, Femininity and Public Space in European Visual Culture, 1789–1914*. Farnham, UK: Routledge.
Banks, Eric. 2011. "Wars They Have Seen: How an Unlikely Friendship with a Vichy Collaborator Complicates Our Understanding of Gertrude Stein." *Chronicle of Higher Education*, October 23, 2011. https://web.archive.org/web/20120811121059/http://chronicle.com/article/Wars-They-Have-Seen/129465/
Bard, Mitchell G. 1996. *Forgotten Victims: The Abandonment of Americans in Hitler's Camps*. Oxford: Westview Press.
Barkai, Avraham. 1985. "German-Jewish Migrations in the Nineteenth Century, 1830–1910." *The Leo Baeck Institute Yearbook* 30 (1): 301–18.
Barnes, Djuna. 2000. "Matron's Primer." In Curnutt 2000, 136–38. First published in *Contemporary Jewish Record*, 1945.
Barnett, Geo. E. 1902. "The Jewish Population of Maryland." In *The American Jewish Year Book: 5663*, vol. 4, edited by Cyrus Adler, 46–62. Philadelphia: Jewish Publication Society of America.
Barnwell, Kattian. 1994. "Motherlands and Other Lands: Home and Exile in Jamaica Kincaid's *Lucy* and Paule Marshall's *Praisesong for the Widow*." *Caribbean Studies* 27 (3/4): 451–54.
Batnitzky, Leora. 2011. *How Judaism Became a Religion: An Introduction to Modern Jewish Thought*. Princeton, NJ: Princeton University Press.
Beck, Evelyn Torton. 1982. *Nice Jewish Girls: A Lesbian Anthology*. Berkeley, CA: Crossing Press.

Bell, Derrick. 1992. *Faces at the Bottom of the Well: The Permanence of Racism*. New York: Basic Books.
Benhabib, Seyla. 1988. "Arendt, Politics, and the Self." *Political Theory* 16 (1): 29–98.
———. 1995. "The Pariah and Her Shadow: Hannah Arendt's Biography of Rahel Varnhagen." *Political Theory* 23 (1): 5–24.
Berkman, Alexander. (1925) 1989. *The Bolshevik Myth (Diary 1920–1922)*. London: Pluto Press.
———. 1929. *Now and After: The ABC of Communist Anarchism*. New York: Vanguard Press.
Berliner, Isaac, and Diego Rivera. 1996. *City of Palaces*. Translated by Mindy Rinkewich. Basking Ridge, NJ: Jacoby Press.
Berman, Paul. 2019. "The Anarchists and the Jews." *Tablet*, June 11–13, 2019. Three installments. https://www.tabletmag.com/sections/news/articles/anarchism-jewish-working-class-left-1.
Bernstein, Charles, editor. 2012. "Gertrude Stein's War Years: Setting the Record Straight." *Jacket2*, May 9, 2012. http://jacket2.org/feature/gertrude-steins-war-years-setting-record-straight.
Bernstein, Richard J. 1996. *Hannah Arendt and the Jewish Question*. Cambridge, MA: MIT Press.
Biale, David. 1986. *Power & Powerlessness in Jewish History*. New York: Schocken Books.
———, editor. 2002. *Cultures of the Jews: A New History*. New York: Schocken Books.
Bilski, Emily D., Emily Braun, and Leon Botstein. 2005. *Jewish Women and Their Salons: The Power of Conversation*. New Haven, CT: Yale University Press.
Blashfield, Jean. 2010. *Golda Meir*. New York: Benchmark Books.
Blasius, Mark, and Shane Phelan. 1997. *We Are Everywhere: A Historical Sourcebook of Gay and Lesbian Politics*. New York: Routledge.
Bonetti, Kay. 2002. "Interview with Jamaica Kincaid." *Missouri Review* 25 (2), June 1, 2002. http://www.missourireview.com/archives/bbarticle/interview-with-jamaica-kincaid/.
Botticini, Maristella, and Zvi Eckstein. 2012. *The Chosen Few: How Education Shaped Jewish History, 70–1492*. Princeton, NJ: Princeton University Press.
Boyarin, Daniel, and Jonathan Boyarin. 1993. "Diaspora: Generation and the Ground of Jewish Identity." *Critical Inquiry* 19 (4): 693–725.
———. 2002. *Powers of Diaspora: Two Essays on the Relevance of Jewish Culture*. Minneapolis: University of Minnesota Press.
Bray, Mark. 2017. *Antifa: The Anti-Fascist Handbook*. Brooklyn, NY: Melville House Publishing.
Brettschneider, Marla. 1996. *Cornerstones of Peace: Jewish Identity Politics and Democratic Theory*. New Brunswick, NJ: Rutgers University Press.
———. 2002. *Democratic Theorizing from the Margins*. Philadelphia, PA: Temple University Press.

———. 2006. *The Family Flamboyant: Race Politics, Queer Families, Jewish Lives.* Albany: State University of New York Press.

———. 2015. *The Jewish Phenomenon in Sub-Saharan Africa: The Politics of Contradictory Discourses.* Lewiston, NY: Edwin Mellen Press.

———. 2016. *Jewish Feminism and Intersectionality.* Albany: State University of New York Press.

———. 2019. "Jewish Women's Anti-colonialism in Madagascar." In *Africana Jewish Journeys*, edited by Marla Brettschneider, Edith Bruder, and Magdel Le Roux, 64–77. Newcastle upon Tyne, UK: Cambridge Scholars Publishing.

Bridgman, Richard. 1970. *Gertrude Stein in Pieces.* New York: Oxford University Press.

Brown, Michael. 1992. "The American Element in the Rise of Golda Meir: 1906–1929." *Jewish History* 6 (1/2): 35–50.

Brownfeld, Allan C. 2011. "Judah Magnes: Seeking to Keep Judaism's Highest Ideals Alive in an Age of Nationalism." *Issues of the American Council for Judaism*, Spring–Summer 2011. http://www.acjna.org/acjna/articles_detail.aspx?id=569.

Buhle, Paul. 1998. "Freie Arbeter Shtimme." In *Encyclopedia of the American Left*, edited by Mari Jo Buhle, Paul Buhle, and Dan Georgakas, 245–46. New York: Garland Publishing.

Bureau of Jewish Social Research. 1921. "Statistics of Jews." In *The American Jewish Year Book: 5681*, vol. 22, edited by Harry Schneiderman, 361–83. Philadelphia: American Jewish Committee.

Burkett, Elinor. 2008. *Golda Meir: The Iron Lady of the Middle East.* London: Gibson Square.

Burstin, Hinde Ena. 2018. "Jewish Lesbian Group of Victoria (JLGV)." In *Living and Loving in Diversity: An Anthology of Australian Multicultural Queer Adventures*, edited by Maria Pallotta-Chiarolli, 308–10. Mile End, South Australia: Wakefield Press.

Bush, Lawrence. 2015. "August 21: Diego Rivera and Frida Kahlo." *Jewish Currents*, August 19, 2015. http://jewishcurrents.org/august-21-diego-rivera-and-frida-kahlo/.

Butler, Judith. 1990. *Gender Trouble: Feminism and the Subversion of Identity.* New York: Routledge.

Butt, Gerald. 1998. "Golda Meir." *BBC News*, April 21, 1998. http://news.bbc.co.uk/2/hi/events/israel_at_50/profiles/81288.stm.

Cánovas, Rodrigo. 2009. "Los relatos del origen: Judíos en México." *Nueva Revista de Filología Hispánica* 51 (1): 157–97.

Chalberg, John. (1991) 2008. *Emma Goldman: American Individualist.* New York: Pearson Longman.

Cheyette, Bryan. 2014. *Diasporas of the Mind: Jewish and Postcolonial Writing and the Nightmare of History.* New Haven, CT: Yale University Press.

"Christian-Jewish Relations: The Inquisition." n.d. *Jewish Virtual Library*, American-Israeli Cooperative Enterprise. Accessed March 20, 2017. https://www.jewishvirtuallibrary.org/the-inquisition.

Christman, Henry, editor. 1962. *This Is Our Strength: Selected Papers of Golda Meir*. New York: Macmillan.
Cohen, Robert, and Reginald Zelnik, editors. 2002. *The Free Speech Movement: Reflections on Berkeley in the 1960s*. Berkeley: University of California Press.
Cohler, Deborah. 2008. "Teaching Transnationally: Queer Studies and Imperialist Legacies in Monique Truong's *The Book of Salt*." *Radical Teacher*, no. 82, 25–31.
"Communities: Mexico." n.d. World Jewish Congress (website). Accessed March 21, 2017. http://www.worldjewishcongress.org/en/about/communities/MX.
Conte, Carolyn. 2020. "Six Jewish Facts about Actress Natasha Lyonne." *Baltimore Jewish Times*, September 17, 2020. https://www.jewishtimes.com/six-jewish-facts-about-actress-natasha-lyonne/.
Cooper, Carol. 1990. "Let Love Rule—Lisa Bonet and Husband Lenny Kravitz." *Essence* 20 (10): 54–57. http://web.archive.org/web/20070214130023/http://www.findarticles.com/p/articles/mi_m1264/is_n10_v20/ai_8320587.
Cooper, Marilyn. 2018. "The Lioness Roars Again: Golda Meir at 120." *Moment* 43 (1): 74–77.
Corn, Wanda M. 2011. *Seeing Gertrude Stein: Five Stories*. San Francisco: University of California Press.
Cornell, Andrew. 2016. *Unruly Equality: U.S. Anarchism in the Twentieth Century*. Oakland: University of California Press.
Cottin Pogrebin, Letty. 1991. *Deborah, Golda, and Me: Being Female and Jewish in America*. New York: Crown Publishers.
———. 1997. "Golda Meir." In *Jewish Women in America: An Historical Encyclopedia*, vol. 2, edited by Paula E. Hyman and Deborah Dash Moore, 903–9. New York: Routledge.
———. 2009. "Golda Meir." In *The Shalvi/Hyman Encyclopedia of Jewish Women*. Jewish Women's Archive. http://jwa.org/encyclopedia/article/meir-golda.
Crenshaw, Kimberle. 1989. "Demarginalizing the Intersection of Race and Sex: A Black Feminist Critique of Antidiscrimination Doctrine, Feminist Theory and Antiracist Politics." *University of Chicago Legal Forum* 1989 (1): 139–67.
Crosby, Margaret. 2014. "Frida Kahlo's Illustrated Autopathography: A Voice of Disability." *A/B: Auto/Biography Studies*, 21 (2): 161–75.
Cruz, Bárbara. 1996. *Frida Kahlo: Portrait of a Mexican Painter*. Springfield, NJ: Enslow Publishers.
Cruz, Denise. 2013. "'Love Is Not a Bowl of Quinces': Food, Desire, and the Queer Asian Body in Monique Truong's *The Book of Salt*." In *Eating Asian America: A Food Studies Reader*, edited by Robert Ji-Song Ku, Martin F. Manalansan IV, and Anita Mannur, 354–70. New York: New York University Press.
Cudjoe, Selwyn R. 1989. "Jamaica Kincaid and the Modernist Project: An Interview." *Callaloo*, no. 39, 396–411.
Curnutt, Kirk, editor. 2000. *The Critical Response to Gertrude Stein*. Westport, CT: Greenwood Press.

Damon, Maria. 1996. "Gertrude Stein's Jewishness, Jewish Social Scientists, and the 'Jewish Question.'" *Modern Fiction Studies* 42 (3): 489–507.
Dance, Daryl Cumber. 2015. "'I Married My Mother': Jamaica Kincaid's *See Now Then*." *Journal of West Indian Literature* 23 (1–2): 8–18.
Daunton, Nichola. 2015. "Disabled Icons: Painter Frida Kahlo and Pushing Boundaries." *Disability Horizons*, December 17, 2015. https://disabilityhorizons.com/2015/12/disabled-icons-painter-frida-kahlo-and-pushing-boundaries/.
Declaration of Israel's Independence. 1948. May 14, 1948, Tel Aviv.
De Cleyre, Voltairine. 2005. *Exquisite Rebel: The Essays of Voltairine de Cleyre—Anarchist, Feminist, Genius*. Edited by Sharon Presley and Crispin Sartwell. Albany: State University of New York Press.
Dearborn, Mary. 2004. *Mistress of Modernism: The Life of Peggy Guggenheim*. Boston, MA: Houghton Mifflin.
Deutscher, Isaac. 1968. "Who Is a Jew?" In *The Non-Jewish Jew*, by Isaac Deutscher, edited by Tamara Deutscher, 42–59. New York: Verso Books.
Dexter, Emma, and Tanya Barson, editors. 2005. *Frida Kahlo*. London: Tate Publishing.
Diallo, Nafissatou, and Jamaica Kincaid. 2017. "Tainted Witness in Law and Literature: Nafissatou Diallo and Jamaica Kincaid." In *Tainted Witness: Why We Doubt What Women Say about Their Lives*, by Leigh Gilmore, 133–56. New York: Columbia University Press.
Diner, Hasia R. 1999. "German Immigrant Period in the United States." In *The Shalvi/Hyman Encyclopedia of Jewish Women*, Jewish Women's Archive, December 31, 1999. https://jwa.org/encyclopedia/article/german-immigrant-period-in-united-states.
"Disability History Month Trailblazers: Frida Kahlo." 2013. National Union of Students. https://www.nus.org.uk/en/news/disability-history-month-trailblazers-frida-kahlo/.
Drinnon, Richard. 1961. *Rebel in Paradise: A Biography of Emma Goldman*. Boston, MA: Beacon Press.
Drucker, Malka. 1991. *Frida Kahlo: Torment and Triumph*. New York: Delacorte Books.
Du Bois, W. E. B. 1961. *The Souls of Black Folk*. New York: Dodd, Mead.
Dupee, F. W. 1962. "Gertrude Stein," *Commentary*, June 1, 1962. https://www.commentarymagazine.com/articles/gertrude-stein/.
Dydo, Ulla E., and Edward M. Burns, editors. 1996. *The Letters of Gertrude Stein and Thornton Wilder*. With William Rice. New Haven, CT: Yale University Press.
Edwards, Naomi. 2012. "Melancholic Ghosts in Monique Truong's *The Book of Salt*." *Women's Studies Quarterly* 40 (3/4): 167–86.
Ehrlich, Claire. 2019. "The Lost World of Yiddish Anarchists." *Jewish Currents*, January 15, 2019. https://jewishcurrents.org/the-lost-world-of-yiddish-anarchists.
Eisenhower, Julie. 1977. "Golda Meir: An Unforgettable Interview with the Lioness in Winter." *Ladies Home Journal* 94 (3): 8.

Engels, Friedrich. 1978. "On Authority." In *The Marx-Engels Reader*, edited by Robert C. Tucker, 305–8. New York: Norton.
Falk, Candace. 1990. *Love, Anarchy, and Emma Goldman*. Revised edition. New Brunswick, NJ: Rutgers University Press.
———. 2002. "Emma Goldman: Passion, Politics, and the Theatrics of Free Expression." *Women's History Review* 11 (1): 11–26.
Falk, Candace, Barry Pateman, and Jessica Moran, editors. 2003. *Emma Goldman: A Documentary History of the American Years: Made for America, 1890–1901*. Vol. 1. Berkeley: University of California Press.
———, editors. 2005. *Emma Goldman: A Documentary History of the American Years: Making Free Speech, 1902–1909*. Vol. 2. Berkeley: University of California Press.
Fallaci, Oriana. 1976. *Interview with History*. Translated by John Shepley. Boston, MA: Houghton Mifflin.
Fanon, Franz. 2004. *The Wretched of the Earth*. Trans. Richard Philcox. New York: Grove Atlantic.
Faust, Drew Gilpin. 2004. "Mingling Promiscuously: A History of Women and Men at Harvard." In *Yards and Gates: Gender in Harvard and Radcliffe History*, edited by Laurel Ulrich, 317–28. New York: Palgrave Macmillan.
Feinstein, Amy. 2022. *Gertrude Stein and the Making of Jewish Modernism*. Gainesville: University Press of Florida.
Ferguson, Kathy. 2011. *Emma Goldman: Political Thinking in the Streets*. Lanham, MD: Rowman and Littlefield.
———. 2014. "Anarchist Printers and Presses: Material Circuits of Politics." *Political Theory* 42 (4): 391–414.
Ferry, Barbara, and Debbie Nathan. 2000. "Mistaken Identity? The Case of New Mexico's 'Hidden Jews.'" *The Atlantic*, December 2000. https://www.theatlantic.com/magazine/archive/2000/12/mistaken-identity-the-case-of-new-mexicos-hidden-jews/378454/.
Fischer, Erica. 1995. *Aimée & Jaguar: A Love Story, Berlin 1943*. New York: Harper Collins.
Franger, Gaby, and Rainer Huhle. 2005. *Fridas Vater: Der Fotograf Guillermo Kahlo*. Munich: Schirmer Mosel.
Frankel, Oz. 1996. "What Ever Happened to 'Red Emma'? Emma Goldman, from Alien Rebel to American Icon." *Journal of American History* 83 (3): 903–42.
Freedman, Jonathan. 2008. *Klezmer America: Jewishness, Ethnicity, Modernity*. New York: Columbia University Press.
Frydberg, Tracy. 2014. "Jewish Mexico: The Land of Chile and Honey." *Moment Magazine*, August 4, 2014. http://www.momentmag.com/jewish-mexico-land-chile-honey/.
Garner, Dwight. 1996. "Jamaica Kincaid." *Salon*, January 13, 1996. http://www.salon.com/1996/01/13/kincaid_2/.

Genovese, Michael. 1993. *Women as National Leaders.* Newbury Park, CA: Sage Publications.

"German Immigration." 2004. In *U.S. Immigration and Migration Reference Library: Almanac,* edited by Lawrence W. Baker, Sonia Benson, James L. Outman, Rebecca Valentine, and Roger Matuz, 1:221–46. Detroit: UXL. *U.S. History in Context.* http://link.galegroup.com/apps/doc/CX3436800018/UHIC?u=gray02935&xid=efaf4636.

Gilligan, Carol. 1982. *In a Different Voice: Psychological Theory and Women's Development.* Cambridge, MA: Harvard University Press.

Gitlitz, David M. 1996. *Secrecy and Deceit: The Religion of the Crypto-Jews.* Lincoln: University of Nebraska Press.

Gladwell, Malcolm. 2005. "Getting In: The Social Logic of Ivy League Admissions." *New Yorker,* October 10, 2005. http://www.newyorker.com/magazine/2005/10/10/getting-in.

Glass, Charles. 2010. *Americans in Paris: Life and Death under Nazi Occupation.* New York: Penguin Books.

Gleizer, Daniela. 2013. *Unwelcome Exiles: Mexico and the Jewish Refugees from Nazism, 1933–1945.* Leiden, the Netherlands: Brill Publishers.

Glueck, Grace. 1983. "Art: 2 Unusual Women." *New York Times,* March 4, 1983. https://www.nytimes.com/1983/03/04/arts/art-2-unusual-women.html.

Godwin, William. 1793. *An Enquiry Concerning Political Justice, and Its Influence on General Virtue and Happiness.* London: G. G. J. and J. Robinson.

"Golda Meir." n.d. *Jewish Virtual Library,* American-Israeli Cooperative Enterprise. Accessed July 16, 2024. http://www.jewishvirtuallibrary.org/jsource/biography/meir.html.

Goldberg, Mel. 2013. "A Brief History of the Jews in Mexico." *MexConnect,* February 8, 2013. http://www.mexconnect.com/articles/3966-a-brief-history-of-the-jews-in-mexico.

Goldman, Emma. 1914. *The Social Significance of the Modern Drama.* Boston, MA: R. G. Badger.

———. 1916. *Philosophy of Atheism and The Failure of Christianity: Two Lectures.* New York: Mother Earth Publishing Association.

———. (1917) 1969. *Anarchism and Other Essays.* With an introduction by Richard Drinnon. New York: Dover Publications.

———. 1923. *My Disillusionment with Russia.* Garden City, NY: Doubleday.

———. 1924. *My Further Disillusionment with Russia.* Garden City, NY: Doubleday.

———. (1931) 1970. *Living My Life.* New York: Dover Publications.

———. 1983. *Vision on Fire: Emma Goldman on the Spanish Revolution.* Edited by David Porter. New Paltz, NY: Commonground Press.

———. 2017. " 'The War Antithesis': New York, December 1915—Emma Goldman: Preparedness, the Road to Universal Slaughter." In *World War I and America:*

Told by the Americans Who Lived It, edited by A. Scott Berg, 217–25. New York: Library of America. Originally published in 1915.

Goldstein, Eric L. 2009. "Mollie Steimer, 1897–1980." In *The Shalvi/Hyman Encyclopedia of Jewish Women*. Jewish Women's Archive. https://jwa.org/encyclopedia/article/steimer-mollie.

Goldstene, Claire. 2014. *The Struggle for America's Promise: Equal Opportunity at the Dawn of Corporate Capital*. Jackson: University Press of Mississippi.

Goodman, Dena. 1994. *The Republic of Letters: A Cultural History of the French Enlightenment*. Ithaca, NY: Cornell University Press.

Gordon, Lewis. 2016. "Rarely Kosher: Studying Jews of Color in North America." *American Jewish History* 100 (1): 105–16.

Gornick, Vivian. 2011. *Emma Goldman: Revolution as a Way of Life*. New Haven, CT: Yale University Press.

Gorsky, Jeffrey. 2015. *Exiles in Sepharad: The Jewish Millennium in Spain*. Philadelphia: Jewish Publication Society.

Goyens, Tom. 2007. *Beer and Revolution: The German Anarchist Movement in New York City, 1880–1914*. Urbana: University of Illinois Press.

———, editor. 2014. *Radical Gotham: Anarchism in New York City from Schwab's Saloon to Occupy Wall Street*. Urbana: University of Illinois Press.

Greenwald, Gilad, and Sam Lehman-Wilzig. 2019. "Is She Still 'the Legendary Jewish Mother'? A Comparative Look at Golda Meir's and Tzipi Livni's Election Campaign Coverage in the Israeli Press." *Israel Affairs* 25 (1): 42–64.

Gregg, Veronica. 1999. "'What a History You Have': The Mistress and the Servant in Jamaica Kincaid's *Lucy*." *Journal of West Indian Literature* 8 (2): 38–49.

Grimberg, Salomon, and Hayden Herrera. 2008. *Frida Kahlo: Song of Herself*. London: Merrell.

Gurianova, Nina. 2019. "Moscow Anarchists: The Brothers Gordin and the Newspaper *Anarkhia*, 1917–1918." Paper presented at Yiddish Anarchism: New Scholarship on a Forgotten Tradition, YIVO Institute for Jewish Research, New York, January 20, 2019.

Haaland, Bonnie. 1993. *Emma Goldman: Sexuality and the Impurity of the State*. Montreal: Black Rose Books.

Hancock, Ange-Marie. 2016. *Intersectionality: An Intellectual History*. New York: Oxford University Press.

Heckman, Alma. 2018. "Jewish Radicals of Morocco: Case Study for a New Historiography." *Jewish Social Studies* 23 (3): 67–100.

Herrera, Hayden. 1983. *Frida: A Biography of Frida Kahlo*. New York: Harper and Row.

Hertz, Deborah. 2005. *Jewish High Society in Old Regime Berlin*. Syracuse, NY: Syracuse University Press.

Higginbotham, Evelyn Brooks. 1993. *Righteous Discontent: The Women's Movement in the Black Baptist Church, 1880–1920*. Cambridge, MA: Harvard University Press.

Hobhouse, Janet. 1975. *Everybody Who Was Anybody: A Biography of Gertrude Stein.* New York: Putnam.

Hoffman, Matthew. 2010. "The Red Divide: The Conflict between Communists and Their Opponents in the American Yiddish Press." *American Jewish History* 96 (1): 1–31.

Hoffman, Warren. 2009. *The Passing Game: Queering Jewish American Culture.* Syracuse, NY: Syracuse University Press.

Hollis, Catherine. 2016. "The World Is My Country: Emma Goldman among the Avant-Garde." In *Virginia Woolf and Her Female Contemporaries: Selected Papers from the 25th Annual International Conference on Virginia Woolf,* edited by Julie Vandivere and Megan Hicks, 15–21. Clemson, SC: Clemson University Press.

Honig, Bonnie. 1996. *Feminist Interpretations of Hannah Arendt.* University Park: Pennsylvania State University Press.

Horrox, James. 2009. *A Living Revolution: Anarchism in the Kibbutz Movement.* Oakland, CA: AK Press.

Houghton Mifflin Harcourt. n.d. "A Reader's Guide: *The Book of Salt.*" Houghton Mifflin Harcourt (website). Accessed November 17, 2017. http://www.houghtonmifflinbooks.com/readers_guides/truong_salt.shtml.

Howard, Adam. 2017. *Sewing the Fabric of Statehood: Garment Unions, American Labor, and the Establishment of the State of Israel.* Champaign: University of Illinois Press.

Hyman, Paula, and Dalia Ofer, editors. 2006. *Jewish Women: A Comprehensive Historical Encyclopedia.* Jerusalem: Shalvi Publishing. CD-ROM.

Immigration Act of 1903. Pub. L. No. 57-161, 32 Stat. 1213 (1903).

Jacobs, Jack, editor. 2001. *Jewish Politics in Eastern Europe: The Bund at 100.* New York: New York University Press.

"Jewish Statistics." 1899. In *The American Jewish Year Book: 5660,* vol. 1, edited by Cyrus Adler, 283–85. Philadelphia: Jewish Publication Society of America.

Jewish Women's Archive. n.d. "Emma Goldman." *Women of Valor.* Accessed on August 4, 2020. https://jwa.org/womenofvalor/goldman.

Jones, Kathleen B. 2013. *Diving for Pearls: A Thinking Journey with Hannah Arendt.* San Diego, CA: Thinking Women Books.

Kafka, Franz. 1958. *Description of a Struggle.* New York: Schocken Books.

———. 1992. *The Castle.* New York: Knopf.

Kahn, Ava Fran. 2002. *Jewish Voices of the California Gold Rush: A Documentary History, 1848–1880.* Detroit, MI: Wayne State University Press.

Kale, Steven D. 2006. *French Salons: High Society and Political Sociability from the Old Regime to the Revolution of 1848.* Baltimore: Johns Hopkins University Press.

Kałczewiak, Mariusz. 2019. "Anticolonial Orientalism: Perets Hirshbeyn's Indian Travelogue." *In geveb,* July 8, 2019. https://ingeveb.org/articles/anticolonial-orientalism.

Kaminer, Michael. 2015. "Frida Kahlo's Jewish Lover." *Forward,* August 19, 2015. https://forward.com/culture/318988/frida-kahlos-jewish-lover/.

Kantorowicz, Alfred. 1941. Letter to Gilberto Bosques. March 23, 1941. "Testimonials," International Raoul Wallenberg Foundation. http://www.raoulwallenberg.net/category/saviors/diplomats/bosques/testimonia/.

Kaplan, Mordecai M. 1980. *Judaism as a Civilization: Toward a Reconstruction of American-Jewish Life*. Dulles, VA: Jewish Publication Society.

Karsh, Efriam. 1999. "The Collusion That Never Was: King Abdallah, the Jewish Agency and the Partition of Palestine." *Journal of Contemporary History* 34 (4): 569–85.

Katav, Orit Miller. 2020. "Golda Meir: The Israeli Iron Lady." In *Global Perspectives on Women's Leadership and Gender (In)Equality*, edited by Elena V. Shabliy, Dmitry Kurochkin, and Gloria Y. A. Ayee. London: Palgrave Macmillan.

Katz, Jonathan. 1992. *Gay American History: Lesbians and Gay Men in the U.S.A*. New York: Penguin Books.

Katzew, Ilona. 2004. *Casta Painting: Images of Race in Eighteenth-Century Mexico*. New Haven, CT: Yale University Press.

Kaye/Kantrowitz, Melanie. 1992. *The Issue Is Power: Essays on Women, Jews, Violence, and Resistance*. San Francisco: Aunt Lute Books.

———. 2007. *The Colors of Jews: Racial Politics and Radical Diasporism*. Bloomington: Indiana University Press.

Kaye/Kantrowitz, Melanie, and Irena Klepfisz, editors. 1986. *The Tribe of Dina: A Jewish Women's Anthology*. Sinister Wisdom 29/30. Special issue.

Kessler, Carole. 2009. "Marie Syrkin." In *The Shalvi/Hyman Encyclopedia of Jewish Women*. Jewish Women's Archive. http://jwa.org/encyclopedia/article/syrkin-marie.

Kessler-Harris, Alice. 1976. "Organizing the Unorganizable: Three Jewish Women and Their Union." *Labor History* 17 (1): 5–23.

Kettenmann, Andrea. 2000. *Frida Kahlo, 1907–1954: Pain and Passion*. Los Angeles: Taschen.

Khazzoom, Loolwa, editor. 2022. *The Flying Camel: Essays on Identity by Women of North African and Middle Eastern Jewish Heritage*. New York: Seal Press. Originally published in 2003.

Kincaid, Jamaica. 1983a. *Annie John*. New York: Farrar, Straus and Giroux.

———. 1983b. *At the Bottom of the River*. New York: Plume.

———. 1988. *A Small Place*. New York: Farrar, Straus and Giroux.

———. 1990. *Lucy*. New York: Farrar, Straus and Giroux.

———. 1991. "On Seeing England for the First Time." *Transition*, no. 51, 32–40.

———. 1996. *The Autobiography of My Mother*. New York: Plume.

———. 1997. *My Brother*. New York: Farrar, Straus and Giroux.

———. 2002. *Mr. Potter*. New York: Farrar, Straus and Giroux.

———. 2013. *See Now Then*. New York: Farrar, Straus and Giroux.

———. 2020. "The Disturbances of the Garden." *New Yorker*, September 7, 2020. https://www.newyorker.com/magazine/2020/09/07/the-disturbances-of-the-garden.

Klagsbrun, Francine. 2017. *Lioness: Golda Meir and the Nation of Israel*. New York: Schocken Books.

Klapper, Melissa R. 2013. *Ballots, Babies, and Banners of Peace: American Jewish Women's Activism, 1890–1940*. New York: New York University Press.

Knight, Ryan Allen. 2012. "Anti-colonial Anarchism, or Anarchistic Anti-colonialism: The Similarities in the Revolutionary Theories of Frantz Fanon and Mikhail Bakunin." *Theory in Action* 5 (40): 82–92.

Kohn, Jerome. 2007. Preface. In *The Jewish Writings*, by Hannah Arendt, edited by Jerome Kohn and Ron Feldman, ix–xxxii. New York: Schocken Books.

Korn, Bertram Wallace. 1951. *American Jewry and the Civil War*. Philadelphia: Jewish Publication Society.

Korngold, Sheyna. 1968. *Memoirs*. Tel Aviv: Ferlag Idpress.

Kosak, Hadassa. 2009. "Anarchists, American Jewish Women." In *The Shalvi/Hyman Encyclopedia of Jewish Women*, February 27, 2009. Jewish Women's Archive. https://jwa.org/encyclopedia/article/anarchists-american-jewish-women.

Kostyrchenko, Gennadii. 2004. "Golda at the Metropol Hotel." *Russian Studies in History* 43 (2): 77–84.

"Koyt Far Dayn Fardakht." n.d. Facebook profile. https://www.facebook.com/koytfilthband/about_details.

Kropotkin, Peter, and Paul Avrich. 1972. *Mutual Aid: A Factor of Evolution*. London: Allen Lane.

"Kurt Seligmann." n.d. *Jewish Virtual Library*, American-Israeli Cooperative Enterprise. Accessed July 17, 2024. https://www.jewishvirtuallibrary.org/seligmann-kurt.

"Kurt Seligmann." n.d. *Weinstein Gallery*. Accessed July 17, 2024. http://www.weinstein.com/artists/kurt-seligmann/.

Kushner, Aviya. 2019. "No One's Studying Hebrew Anymore—That's a Big Problem." *Forward*, July 11, 2019. https://forward.com/culture/427477/no-ones-studying-hebrew-anymore-thats-a-big-problem/.

Lahav, Pnina. 2018. "'A Great Episode in the History of Jewish Womanhood': Golda Meir, the Women Workers' Council, Pioneer Women, and the Struggle for Gender." *Equality Israel Studies* 2 (1): 1–25.

———. 2022. *The Only Woman in the Room: Golda Meir and Her Path to Power*. Princeton, NJ: Princeton University Press.

Landauer, Gustav. 2010. *Revolution and Other Writings: A Political Reader*. Translated and edited by Gabriel Kuhn. Oakland, CA: PM Press.

Landes, Joan B. 1996. *Women and the Public Sphere in the Age of the French Revolution*. Ithaca, NY: Cornell University Press.

Leeder, Elaine. 1993. *The Gentle General: Rose Pesotta, Anarchist and Labor Organizer*. Albany: State University of New York Press.

Leibowitz, Yeshayahu, and John P. Egan. 1986. "Yeshayahu Leibowitz: Liberating Israel from the Occupied Territories." *Journal of Palestine Studies* 15 (2): 102–8.

Lerner, Michael. 2012. "Editor's Note on 'Why the Witch-Hunt Against Gertrude Stein?'" *Tikkun*, June 4, 2012. https://www.tikkun.org/nextgen/editors-note-on-why-the-witch-hunt-against-gertrude-stein-by-renate-stendhal.

Lev-Ari, Shiri. 2004. "She Doesn't See in Black and White." *Haaretz*, January 22, 2004. http://www.haaretz.com/culture/arts-leisure/she-doesn-t-see-in-black-and-white-1.111699.

Levins-Morales, Aurora. 2019. "Puerto Ricans and Jews." In *Medicine Stories: Essays for Radicals*, by Aurora Levins-Morales, 157–72. Durham, NC: Duke University Press.

Levitt, Laura. 1997. *Jews and Feminism: The Ambivalent Search for Home*. New York: Routledge.

Levy, Harriet Lane. 1996. *920 O'Farrell Street: A Jewish Girlhood in Old San Francisco*. Berkeley, CA: Heyday Books.

Lieberman, Lillian, director. 2010. *Visa al paraíso*. Mexico City: Fondo Para la Producción Cinematográfica de Calidad.

Lindauer, Margaret. 1999. *Devouring Frida: The Art History and Popular Celebrity of Frida Kahlo*. Hanover, NH: University Press of New England.

Linfield, Susie. 2019. *The Lion's Den: Zionism and the Left from Hannah Arendt to Noam Chomsky*. New Haven, CT: Yale University Press.

Lipman, Jennifer. 2010. "On This Day: Diego Rivera Dies." *The JC*, November 24, 2010. https://www.thejc.com/on-this-day-diego-rivera-dies-1.19579.

Lipstadt, Deborah. 2023. *Golda Meir: Israel's Matriarch*. New Haven, CT: Yale University Press.

Loh, Alyssa. 2013. "A Conversation with Jamaica Kincaid." *American Reader*. http://theamericanreader.com/a-conversation-with-jamaica-kincaid/.

London, Blanche. 1930. "Gertrude Stein, Modernist: Her Career and Influence." Lecture at the American Jewish Historical Society, Boston, MA, June 12, 1930.

———. 2000a. "The Career of a Modernist: Gertrude Stein Is Famous for Her Influence on Current Literature." In Curnutt 2000, 200–202. First published in *New York Jewish Tribune*, March 6, 1931.

———. 2000b. "Gertrude Stein." In Curnutt 2000, 191–94. First published in *New Palestine*, April 5, 1929.

Lorde, Audre. 1984. *Sister Outsider: Essays and Speeches*. Trumansburg, NY: Crossing Press.

Loren, Sammy. 2012. "Jewish Surrealist Art on Display at U.S. Exhibition." *Haaretz*, February 21, 2012. https://www.haaretz.com/jewish/1.5188240.

Lowenstein, Steven M. 1981. "Voluntary and Involuntary Limitation of Fertility in Nineteenth Century Bavarian Jewry." In *Modern Jewish Fertility*, edited by Paul Ritterband, 94–111. Leiden, Netherlands: E. J. Brill.

Lumsden, Linda L. 2007. "Anarchy Meets Feminism: A Gendered Analysis of Goldman's *Mother Earth*, 1906–1917." *American Journalism* 24 (3): 31–54.

Mahon, Alyce. 2011. "The Lost Secret: Frida Kahlo and the Surrealist Imaginary." *Journal of Surrealism and the Americas* 5 (1): 33–54.
Malcolm, Janet. 2007. *Two Lives: Gertrude and Alice*. New Haven, CT: Yale University Press.
Maldonado-Torres, Nelson. 2007. "On the Coloniality of Being: Contributions to the Development of a Concept." *Journal of Cultural Studies* 21 (2–3): 240–70.
Malkiel, Nancy Weiss. 2016. *"Keep the Damned Women Out": The Struggle for Coeducation*. Princeton, NJ: Princeton University Press.
Mallet, Eleanor. 2004. *Tevye's Grandchildren: Rediscovering a Jewish Identity*. Eugene, OR: Pilgrim Press.
Malti-Douglas, Fedwa. 2013. "Beauty between Disability and Gender: Frida Kahlo in Paper Dolls." In *Beauty Unlimited*, edited by Peg Zeglin Brand, 243–55. Bloomington: Indiana University Press.
Margalit Stern, Bat-Sheva. 2009. " 'She's Got a Man's Head on Her Shoulders': Ada Fishman (Maimon) as a Test Case for Private, Public and Gendered Aspects of Women's Political Activity." *Nashim: A Journal of Jewish Women's Studies and Gender Issues*, no. 17, 141–75.
Marrus, Michael, and Robert Paxton. 1981. *Vichy France and the Jews*. New York: Basic Books.
Marshall, Peter. 2010. *Demanding the Impossible: A History of Anarchism*. Oakland, CA: PM Press.
Marso, Lori. 2006. *Feminist Thinkers and the Demands of Femininity: The Lives and Work of Intellectual Women*. New York: Routledge.
Martin, Ralph. 1988. *Golda Meir: The Romantic Years*. New York: Random House.
Marx, Edward. 2013. *Leonie Gilmour: When East Weds West*. Santa Barbara, CA: Botchan Books.
Marx, Karl, and Friedrich Engels. 1967. *The Communist Manifesto*. New York: Penguin.
Maso, Carole. 2002. *Beauty Is Convulsive*. Berkeley, CA: Counterpoint.
Matsui, Hisako, director. 2010. *Leonie*. Sherman Oaks, CA: Hyde Park Entertainment.
Mays, Devi. 2013. "Transplanting Cosmopolitans: The Migrations of Sephardic Jews to Mexico, 1900–1934." PhD dissertation, Indiana University.
Medzini, Meron. 2008. "Israel's Midwife: Golda Meir in the Closing Years of the British Mandate." *Israel Affairs* 14 (3): 374–97.
Meir, Golda. 1973a. *Golda Meir Speaks Out*. Edited by Marie Syrkin. London: Weidenfeld and Nicolson.
———. 1973b. *A Land of Our Own: An Oral Autobiography*. Edited by Marie Syrkin. New York: Putnam.
———. 1975. *My Life*. New York: G. P. Putnam's Sons.
———. 1982. "Working Mothers." *Pediatrics* 70 (3): 436–16.
Meir, Menahem. 1983. *My Mother Golda Meir: A Son's Evocation of Life with Golda Meir*. New York: Arbor House.

Mellow, James. 1974. *Charmed Circle: Gertrude Stein and Company.* New York: Praeger.
Memmi, Albert. 1967. *The Colonizer and the Colonized.* Boston, MA: Beacon Press.
Mendelssohn, Moses. 2013. *Jerusalem; or, On Religious Power and Judaism.* Translated by Allan Arkush. Waltham, MA: Brandeis University Press.
Mendes-Flohr, Paul, Anya Mali, and Hanna Delf von Wolzogen, editors. 2016. *Gustav Landauer: Anarchist and Jew.* Berlin: De Gruyter Oldenbourg.
"Mexico Virtual Jewish History Tour." n.d. *Jewish Virtual Library*, American-Israeli Cooperative Enterprise. Accessed May 25, 2017. https://www.jewishvirtuallibrary.org/mexico-virtual-jewish-history-tour.
Meyerson, Mark D., and Edward D. English, editors. 1999. *Christians, Muslims, and Jews in Medieval and Early Modern Spain: Interaction and Cultural Change.* Notre Dame, IN: University of Notre Dame Press.
Michels, Tony. 2005. *A Fire in Their Hearts: Yiddish Socialism in New York.* Cambridge, MA: Harvard University Press.
———. 2012. *Jewish Radicals: A Documentary History.* New York: New York University Press.
Monk, Craig. 1968. "Emma Goldman, *Mother Earth*, and the Little Magazine Impulse in Modern America." In *The Only Efficient Instrument: American Women Writers and the Periodical*, edited by Aleta Feinsod Cane and Susan Alves, 113–25. Iowa City: University of Iowa Press.
Morgan, Julia. 1986. *Women at the Johns Hopkins University: A History.* Baltimore: Johns Hopkins University Press.
Moritz, Theresa. 2001. *The World's Most Dangerous Woman: A New Biography of Emma Goldman.* Vancouver, BC: Subway Books.
Morris, Susana M. 2014. "Sins of the Mother? Ambivalence, Agency, and the Family Romance in Jamaica Kincaid's *Annie John.*" In *Close Kin and Distant Relatives: The Paradox of Respectability in Black Women's Literature*, by Susana M. Morris, 45–73. Charlottesville: University of Virginia Press.
Morrison, John. 2003. *Frida Kahlo.* New York: Chelsea House.
Morton, Marian. 1992. *Emma Goldman and the American Left: Nowhere at Home.* Boston, MA: Twayne Publishers.
Moskowitz, Moses. 1939. "Mexico." In *The American Jewish Year Book: 5700*, vol. 41, edited by Harry Schneiderman, 356–60. Philadelphia: American Jewish Committee.
Nepon, Ezra Berkley. 2014. "Zamlers, Tricksters, and Queers: Re-Mixing Histories in Yiddishland and Faerieland." In *Transformative Language Arts in Action*, edited by Ruth Farmer and Carryn Mirriam-Goldberg, 79–93. Lanham, MD: Rowman & Littlefield.
New York Times. 1919. "Will Fight Deportation: Emma Goldman and Berkman Hailed as Martyrs in Chicago." December 1, 1919.
Orwell, George. (1938) 1969. *Homage to Catalonia.* San Diego, CA: Harvest Books.

Ostman, Heather. 2009. "The Most Dangerous Woman in America: Emma Goldman and the Rhetoric of Motherhood in *Living My Life*." *Prose Studies* 31 (1): 55–73.
Oved, Iacov. 2000. "Anarchism in the Kibbutz Movement." *Kibbutz Trends*, no. 38, 45–50.
Patel, Eboo. 2007. *Acts of Faith: The Story of an American Muslim, the Struggle for the Soul of a Generation*. Boston, MA: Beacon Press.
Pellegrini, Anne. 2007. "After Sontag: Future Notes on Camp." In *A Companion to Lesbian, Gay, Bisexual, Transgender, and Queer Studies*, edited by George E. Haggerty and Molly McGarry, 168–93. Hoboken, NJ: Blackwell Publishing.
Pesotta, Rose. 1944. *Bread upon the Waters*. New York: Dodd, Mead.
———. 1958. *Days of Our Lives*. Boston, MA: Excelsior Publishers.
Phillips-Casteel, Sarah. 2013. "Calypso Jews: Holocaust Refugees in the Caribbean Literary Imagination." *Holocaust Studies* 19 (2): 1–26.
Pianko, Noam. 2010. *Zionism and the Roads Not Taken*. Bloomington: Indiana University Press.
Plaskow, Judith. 1991. *Standing Again at Sinai: Judaism from a Feminist Perspective*. San Francisco, CA: HarperCollins.
The Power of Conversation: Jewish Women and Their Salons. 2005. Exhibition by New Center for Arts and Culture, at McMullen Museum, Boston, MA, August 22–December 4, 2005.
Prell, Riv-Ellen. 1989. *Prayer and Community: The Havurah in American Judaism*. Detroit, MI: Wayne State University Press.
Price, Kimala. 2017. "Queering Reproductive Justice: Toward a Theory and Practice for Building Intersectional Political Alliances." In *LGBTQ Politics*, edited by Marla Brettschneider, Susan Burgess, and Christine Keating, 72–88. New York: New York University Press.
Proudhon, Pierre-Joseph. (1840) 1994. *What Is Property?* Edited by Donald Kelley and Bonnie Smith. Cambridge: Cambridge University Press.
Rabinovitch, Simon, editor. 2012. *Jews and Diaspora Nationalism: Writings on Jewish Peoplehood in Europe and the United States*. Waltham, MA: Brandeis University Press.
Rabinowitz, Aaron. 2017. "War on Hebrew: For Some Ultra-Orthodox, There Can Be Only One Language." *Haaretz*, September 23, 2017. https://www.haaretz.com/israel-news/.premium.magazine-for-some-ultra-orthodox-there-can-be-only-one-language-1.5452371.
Ring, Jennifer. 1997. *The Political Consequences of Thinking: Gender and Judaism in the Work of Hannah Arendt*. Albany: State University of New York Press.
Roosevelt, Eleanor. 1962. Foreword. In Christman 1962, ix–xiv.
Rosen, Robert. 2000. *The Jewish Confederates*. Columbia: University of South Carolina Press.

Rosenbaum, Fred. 2009. *Cosmopolitans: A Social and Cultural History of the Jews of the San Francisco Bay Area*. Berkeley: University of California Press.

Rosenbaum, Judith. 2009. "Rubber Workers, Anarchists, and Little Jewish Ladies." *Jewish Women, Amplified*, February 26, 2009. https://jwa.org/blog/Rose_Emma.

Rosenberg, Karen. 2011. "What They Loved and What They Bought." *New York Times*, May 5, 2011. http://www.nytimes.com/2011/05/06/arts/design/collecting-matisse-at-jewish-museum-review.html.

Rosengarten, Dale, and Theodore Rosengarten, editors. 2002. *A Portion of the People: Three Hundred Years of Southern Jewish Life*. Columbia: University of South Carolina Press.

Roth Pierpont, Claudia. 2000. *Passionate Minds: Women Rewriting the World*. New York: Knopf.

Rozenblit, Marsha L. 1984. *Jews of Vienna, 1867–1914: Assimilation and Identity*. Albany: State University of New York Press. SUNY series in Modern Jewish Literature and Culture.

Rubenstein, Lenny. 1980. "Free Voice of Labor: The Jewish Anarchists." *Cineaste* 10 (3): 49.

Samuel, Sigal. 2013. "Sparring over Feminism at J Street." *Daily Beast*, September 30, 2013. https://www.thedailybeast.com/sparring-over-feminism-at-j-street.

Sander, Kathleen Waters. 2002. "The Unknown Gertrude." *Hopkins Medical News*, Spring/Summer. http://www.hopkinsmedicine.org/hmn/s02/annals.html.

Sartori, Eva Martin, and Madeleine Cottenet-Hage. 2006. *Daughters of Sarah: Anthology of Jewish Women Writing in French*. Teaneck, NJ: Holmes and Meier.

Schivone, Gabriel Matthew. 2011. "A Portrait of Chomsky as a Young Zionist." *New Voices*, November 7, 2011. https://chomsky.info/20111107/.

Schmidt, Sarah. 2004. "Hagiography in the Diaspora: Golda Meir and Her Biographers." *American Jewish History* 92 (2): 157–88.

Schorsch, Jonathan. 2004. *Jews and Blacks in the Early Modern World*. New York: Cambridge University Press.

Schwartz, Yaakov. 2019. "Jamaica Kincaid Is Black and Jewish—but She's Through Talking about Identity." *Times of Israel*, March 31, 2019. https://www.timesofisrael.com/jamaica-kincaid-is-black-and-jewish-but-shes-through-talking-about-identity/.

Sedgwick, Eve Kosofsky. 1990. *Epistemology of the Closet*. Berkeley: University of California Press.

Seidman, Naomi. 1997. *A Marriage Made in Heaven: The Sexual Politics of Hebrew and Yiddish*. Berkeley: University of California Press.

Sela, Maya. 2010. "An Improbable Story, My Life." *Haaretz*, June 16, 2010. http://www.haaretz.com/weekend/week-s-end/an-improbable-story-my-life-1.296968.

Selengut, Suzanne. 2006. "Reluctantly Labeled." *Jerusalem Post*, May 17, 2006. http://www.jpost.com/ArtsAndCulture/Books/Article.aspx?id=22042.

Shandler, Jefferey. 2006a. *Adventures in Yiddishland: Postvernacular Language and Culture*. Berkeley: University of California Press.

———. 2006b. "Queer Yiddishkeit: Practice and Theory." *Shofar: An Interdisciplinary Journal of Jewish Studies* 25 (1): 90–113.

Shapiro, Malkah. 2002. *The Rebbe's Daughter: Memoir of a Hasidic Childhood*. Translated by Nehemia Polen. Revised edition. Philadelphia: Jewish Publication Society.

Shepherd, Naomi. 1993. *A Price below Rubies: Jewish Women as Rebels and Radicals*. Cambridge, MA: Harvard University Press.

Shindler, Colin. 2009. "Opposing Partition: The Zionist Predicaments after the Shoah." *Israel Studies* 14 (2): 88–104.

Shulman, Alix Kates. n.d. "Dances with Feminists." *The Emma Goldman Papers*. Accessed June 3, 2019. http://www.lib.berkeley.edu/goldman/Features/danceswithfeminists.html. Originally published in *Women's Review of Books* 9, no. 3 (December 1991).

Shumsky, Dimitry. 2011. "Brith Shalom's Uniqueness Reconsidered: Hans Kohn and Autonomist Zionism." *Jewish History* 25 (3/4): 339–53

———. 2018. *Beyond the Nation-State: The Zionist Political Imagination from Pinsker to Ben-Gurion*. New Haven, CT: Yale University Press.

Sicular, Eve. 1999. "The Celluloid Closet of Yiddish Film." In *When Joseph Met Molly: A Reader on Yiddish Film*, edited by Sylvia Paskin, 231–44. Nottingham, UK: Five Leaves Publications.

Slabodsky, Santiago. 2014. *Decolonial Judaism: Triumphal Failures of Barbaric Thinking*. New York: Palgrave Macmillan.

Slater, Robert. 1981. *Golda, the Uncrowned Queen of Israel: A Pictorial Biography*. New York: J. David.

Slucki, David. 2010. "Here-Ness, There-Ness, and Everywhere-Ness: The Jewish Labour Bund and the Question of Israel, 1944–1955." *Journal of Modern Jewish Studies* 9 (3): 349–68.

Sokolow, Jayme A. 2010. "Revolution and Reform: The Antebellum Jewish Abolitionists." In *Jews and the Civil War: A Reader*, edited by Jonathan D. Sarna and Adam Mendelsohn. New York: New York University Press.

Solomon, Martha. 1987. *Emma Goldman*. Boston, MA: Twayne.

Sontag, Susan. 2018. *Notes on "Camp."* London: Penguin Classics. Originally published in 1964.

Sorin, Gerald. 1992. *A Time for Building: The Third Migration, 1880–1920*. Vol. 3 of *The Jewish People in America*. Baltimore: Johns Hopkins University Press.

Soto-Crespo, Ramon. 2002. "Death and the Diaspora Writer: Hybridity and Mourning in the Work of Jamaica Kincaid." *Contemporary Literature* 43 (2): 342–76.

Souter, Gerry. 2011. *Frida Kahlo: Beneath the Mirror*. New York: Parkstone International.

Spiel, Hilde, and Michael Z. Wise. 2013. *Fanny von Arnstein: A Daughter of the Enlightenment, 1758–1818*. Translated by Christine Shuttleworth. New York: New Vessel Press.

Srebrnik, Henry Felix. 2010. *Dreams of Nationhood: American Jewish Communists and the Soviet Birobidzhan Project, 1924–1951*. Brighton, MA: Academic Studies Press.

Stechler, Amy, director. 2005. *The Life and Times of Frida Kahlo*. Daylight Films / WETA / Latino Public Broadcasting. Aired on PBS, March 23, 2005, in conjunction with publication on PBS website, March 2005. https://www.pbs.org/weta/fridakahlo/life/people.html.

Stein, Gertrude. 1934. *Portraits and Prayers*. New York: Random House.

———. (1937) 1993. *Everybody's Autobiography*. Cambridge, MA: Exact Change.

———. 1945. *Wars I Have Seen*. New York: Random House.

Stein, Gertrude, and Amy Feinstein. 2001. "The Modern Jew Who Has Given Up the Faith of His Fathers Can Reasonably and Consistently Believe in Isolation." *PMLA* 116 (2): 416–28.

Steinberg, Blema. 2008. *Women in Power: The Personalities and Leadership Styles of Indira Gandhi, Golda Meir, and Margaret Thatcher*. Montreal: McGill-Queen's University Press.

Steinberg, Stephen. 1971. "How Jewish Quotas Began." *Commentary*, September 1, 1971. https://www.commentarymagazine.com/articles/how-jewish-quotas-began/.

Stendhal, Renate. 2012. "Why the Witch-Hunt against Gertrude Stein?" *Tikkun*, June 4, 2012. https://www.tikkun.org/nextgen/why-the-witch-hunt-against-gertrude-stein.

Sterling, Michael. 2011. "Gertrude Stein and Bernard Faÿ." *Habitus: A Diaspora Journal*, November 1, 2011. https://web.archive.org/web/20120814073029/http://habitusmag.com/2011/11/5494/gertrude-stein-bernard-fay/.

Syrkin, Marie. 1963. *Golda Meir: Woman with a Cause*. New York: Putnam.

———. 1969. *Golda Meir: Israel's Leader*. New York: Putnam.

Tchernuishevsky [Chernyshevsky], Nikolaï Gavrilovich. 1986. *A Vital Question; or, What Is to Be Done?* Translated by Nathan Haskell Dole and S. S. Skidelsky. Ann Arbor, MI: Ardis.

"This Week in History: Artist Frida Kahlo Born." n.d. *Jewish Women's Archive*. Accessed July 17, 2024. https://jwa.org/thisweek/jul/06/1907/frida-kahlo.

Thomas, Reena. 2019. "Cultural Hybridity: Freedom and Faith in Diaspora Literature." In *Diaspora Christianities: Global Scattering and Gathering of South Asian Christians*, edited by Sam George and Andrew Walls, 253–66. Minneapolis, MN: 1517 Media.

Tibol, Raquel. 1993. *Frida Kahlo: An Open Life*. Albuquerque: University of New Mexico Press.

TIME. 1978. "Man of the Year: Anatomy of a Bold Action." Interview of Anwar Sadat. January 2, 1978. https://time.com/archive/6849609/man-of-the-year-anatomy-of-a-bold-action/.

Toklas, Alice B. (1954) 2010. *The Alice B. Toklas Cook Book*. New York: Perennial.
Toro, Alfonso. 1944. *La familia Carvajal*. Mexico City: Editorial Patria S.A.
Torres, Anna Elena. 2016. "'Any Minute Now the World's Overflowing Its Border': Anarchist Modernism and Yiddish Literature." PhD dissertation, University of California, Berkeley.
Torres, Anna Elena, and Kenyon Zimmer, editors. 2022. *Freedom's Fullness: Histories of Jewish Anarchism*. Champaign: University of Illinois Press.
Triger, Zvi. 2014. "Golda Meir's Reluctant Feminism: The Pre-State Years." *Israel Studies* 19 (3): 108–33.
Tronto, Joan. 1993. *Moral Boundaries: A Political Argument for an Ethic of Care*. New York: Routledge.
Truong, Monique. 2003. *The Book of Salt: A Novel*. Boston, MA: Houghton Mifflin.
Tsoref, Hagai. 2018. "Golda Meir's Leadership in the Yom Kippur War." *Israel Studies* 23 (1): 50–72.
Türk, Lilian, and Jesse Cohn. 2018. "Yiddish Radicalism, Jewish Religion: Controversies in the *Freie Arbeiter Stimme*, 1937–1945." In *Essays in Anarchism and Religion*, vol. 2, edited by Alexandre Christoyannopoulos and Matthew Adams, 20–57. Stockholm: Stockholm University Press.
United States Census Bureau, Population Division, Population Estimates Program. 2000. "Historical National Population Estimates: July 1, 1900 to July 1, 1999." https://www2.census.gov/programs-surveys/popest/tables/1900-1980/national/totals/popclockest.txt.
United States Holocaust Memorial Museum. 2021. "The Double Life of Josephine Baker." *Memory & Action*, February 3, 2021. https://medium.com/memory-action/the-double-life-of-josephine-baker-ad35134af8dd.
Van Dusen, Wanda. 1996. "Portrait of a National Fetish: Gertrude Stein's 'Introduction to the Speeches of Maréchal Pétain' (1942)." *Modernism/modernity* 3 (3): 69–92.
Vester, Katharina. 2015. "The Difference Is Spreading: Recipes for Lesbian Living." In *A Taste of Power: Food and American Identities*, by Katharina Vester, 137–95. Oakland: University of California Press.
"Vienna." n.d. *Holocaust Encyclopedia*, United States Holocaust Memorial Museum. Accessed April 7, 2022. https://www.ushmm.org/wlc/en/article.php?ModuleId=10005452.
"Vienna, Austria." n.d. *Jewish Virtual Library*, American-Israeli Cooperative Enterprise. Accessed April 7, 2022. http://www.jewishvirtuallibrary.org/vienna-austria-jewish-history-tour.
Vorda, Allan, and Jamaica Kincaid. 1991. "An Interview with Jamaica Kincaid." *Mississippi Review* 20 (1/2): 7–26.
Wagner-Martin, Linda. 1995. *"Favored Strangers": Gertrude Stein and Her Family*. New Brunswick, NJ: Rutgers University Press.
Walcott, Rinaldo. 2011. "Against the Rules of Blackness: Hilton Als's *The Women* and Jamaica Kincaid's *My Brother* (Or How to Raise Black Queer Kids)."

In *Sex and the Citizen: Interrogating the Caribbean*, edited by Faith Smith, 75–86. Charlottesville: University of Virginia Press.

Warhol, Andy. 1980. "Golda Meir." Screenprint in *Ten Portraits of Jews of the Twentieth Century*, fig. 233, by Andy Warhol. New York / Tel Aviv: Ronald Feldman Fine Arts / Jonathan Editions.

Warren, Lansing. 1934. "Gertrude Stein Views Life and Politics." *New York Times*, May 6, 1934. http://www.nytimes.com/books/98/05/03/specials/stein-views.html.

Watt, Donald A. 2011. "Cable Act of 1922." *Immigration to United States*, August 24, 2011. https://immigrationtounitedstates.org/397-cable-act-of-1922.html.

Weber, Max. (1919) 2004. *The Vocation Lectures: "Science as a Vocation"—"Politics as a Vocation."* Edited by David Owen and Tracy B. Strong, translated by Rodney Livingstone. Indianapolis: Hackett Publishing.

———. (1930) 1985. *The Protestant Ethic and the Spirit of Capitalism*. Translated by Talcott Parsons. London: Unwin.

Wehling, Jason. 2007. "Anarchy in Interpretation: The Life of Emma Goldman." In Weiss and Kensinger 2007, 19–37.

Weiman-Kelman, Zohar. 2018. *Queer Expectations: A Genealogy of Jewish Women's Poetry*. Albany, NY: State University of New York Press.

Weingarten, Laura. 2021. "Sabina Berman." In *Shalvi/Hyman Encyclopedia of Jewish Women*, updated by Jewish Women's Archive staff July 23, 2021. Jewish Women's Archive. https://jwa.org/encyclopedia/article/berman-sabina.

Weiss, Penny A., and Loretta Kensinger, editors. 2007. *Feminist Interpretations of Emma Goldman*. University Park: Pennsylvania State University Press.

Weissberg, Liliane. 2000. *Rahel Varnhagen: The Life of a Jewess*. Baltimore, MD: Johns Hopkins University Press.

Weitz, Yechiam. 2011. "Golda Meir, Israel's Fourth Prime Minister (1969–74)." *Middle Eastern Studies* 47 (1): 43–61.

Werner, Matt. 2012. "Gertrude Stein's Oakland." *Huffington Post*, July 30, 2012. http://www.huffingtonpost.com/matt-werner/oakland-in-popular-memory_b_1560227.html.

Wexler, Alice. 1984a. *Emma Goldman: An Intimate Life*. New York: Pantheon Books.

———. 1984b. *Emma Goldman in America*. Boston, MA: Beacon Press.

———. 1989. *Emma Goldman in Exile: From the Russian Revolution to the Spanish Civil War*. Boston, MA: Beacon Press.

Wexler, Alice, and Emma Goldman. 1981. "Emma Goldman on Mary Wollstonecraft." *Feminist Studies* 7 (1): 113–33.

Wiesen Cook, Blanche. 1977. "Female Support Networks and Political Activism: Lillian Wald, Crystal Eastman, Emma Goldman." *Chrysalis* 3 (Autumn).

Wilcox, Claire, and Circe Henestrosa. 2018. *Frida Kahlo: Making Her Self Up*. London: V&A Publishing.

Will, Barbara. 2011. *Unlikely Collaboration: Gertrude Stein, Bernard Faÿ, and the Vichy Dilemma*. New York: Columbia University Press.

Wilson, Edmund. 1931. *Axel's Castle: A Study of the Imaginative Literature of 1870–1930*. New York: Charles Scribner's Sons.

Wineapple, Brenda. 1996. *Sister Brother: Gertrude and Leo Stein*. New York: G. P. Putnam's Sons.

Witzling, Mara, editor. 1991. *Voicing Our Visions: Writings by Women Artists*. New York: Universe.

Wiznitzer, Arnold. 1962. "Crypto-Jews in Mexico during the Sixteenth Century." *American Jewish Historical Quarterly* 51 (3): 168–214.

Woolf, Avi. 2014. "The Jewish Holy War in Galicia, 1914–1916." *Mida*, August 28, 2014. http://mida.org.il/2014/08/28/jewish-holy-war-galicia-1914-1916/.

Xu, Wenying. 2008. "Sexuality, Colonialism, and Ethnicity in Monique Truong's *The Book of Salt* and Mei Ng's *Eating Chinese Food Naked*." In *Eating Identities: Reading Food in Asian American Literature*, by Wenying Xu, 127–61. Honolulu: University of Hawai'i Press.

Young-Bruehl, Elisabeth. 1982. *Hannah Arendt: For Love of the World*. Binghamton, NY: Vail-Ballou Press.

Zafar, Rafia. 2013. "Elegy and Remembrance in the Cookbooks of Alice B. Toklas and Edna Lewis." *MELUS* 38 (4): 32–51.

Zamora, Martha. 1990. *Frida Kahlo: The Brush of Anguish*. San Francisco: Chronicle Books.

Zimmer, Kenyon. 2015. *Immigrants against the State: Yiddish and Italian Anarchism in America*. Urbana: University of Illinois Press.

———. 2017. "Saul Yanovsky and Yiddish Anarchism on the Lower East Side." In *Radical Gotham: Anarchism in New York City from Schwab's Saloon to Occupy Wall Street*, edited by Tom Goyens, 33–53. Urbana: University of Illinois Press.

Zinn, Howard. 1986. *Emma: A Play in Two Acts about Emma Goldman, American Anarchist*. Cambridge, MA: South End Press.

Zola, Émile. 1992. *Emile Zola's J'accuse!* Translated by Mark K. Jensen. Soquel, CA: Bay Side Press.

Zollman, Joellyn. n.d. "Jewish Immigration to America: Three Waves." *My Jewish Learning*. Accessed March 6, 2017. http://www.myjewishlearning.com/article/jewish-immigration-to-america-three-waves/.

Index

Abdullah, King, 74, 228n29
abject groups, 26, 44, 91, 103, 106, 108, 111–13, 200
abolitionists, 160, 161
Ackelsberg, Martha, ix, 2, 10
Africa, 21, 44, 55–61 passim, 152, 216n23; North, 50, 121, 122
African Americans, 38, 153, 167, 192, 221n53
African diaspora. *See* diaspora: African
African-heritage Jews, x, 19, 27–31 passim, 38, 44, 46, 55, 56, 61, 122, 152, 212n2, 216n23, 234n8
Alhambra decree, 119
alienation, 234n6
alterity, 25
American Jewish Congress, 71, 226n20
anarchism, 6, 8, 13, 15–16, 21, 24, 25, 49, 57, 62, 84, 107, 110, 161, 169, 175–210 passim, 226n12, 229n42, 242–51nn passim; within capitalism, 187; collectivist, 186; and direct action, 186; compared to Marxism, 184; political philosophy of, 183–84; prominent thinkers, 183–84; in US activism, 184–88; and violence, 187–88
Anarchist Exclusion Act, 181
anarcho-feminism, 190–96

Ankori, Gannit, xi, 14, 115, 118, 121, 130–36 passim, 143, 236n20
antiassimilationism, 89
anticlericalism, 128, 245nn25–26
anticolonialism, 1, 21, 30, 36, 41, 60, 188, 208, 210, 251n72; and Zionism, 21, 50, 54, 57, 60, 87, 207
antifascism, 117, 133, 134, 237n27, 244n21
antifeminist attitudes, 12, 72
Antigua, 4, 28, 30, 40, 215n19, 216n27, 220nn49–50, 223n64, 223n67, 224n74
antiracism work, 193
antisemitism, 1, 16, 24, 61, 79, 115, 144, 147, 173–74; and Mikhail Bakunin, 184; and Bernard Faÿ, 151, 169; against Charlie Chaplin, 108–9, 211n5; and criminalization, 187; in the US, 55, 76, 134, 156, 158, 174, 200, 209, 243n5; Christian, 200; defiance against, 250; and Dreyfus, 108; in eastern Europe, 4, 6, 47, 78, 84, 94, 179; in England, 58; European, 107, 123, 129, 189, 154–55, 198, 203, 206, 236n15; gendered, 76, 172; German, 93, 103, 136, 198; at

277

antisemitism *(continued)*
  Harvard, 157–58; and Henry Ford,
  133; internalized against eastern
  European Jews, 93, 159; massacres,
  121, 139; in Mexico, 118, 120,
  123, 235n11; Nazi, 5, 24, 56, 90,
  95, 119–39 passim, 206, 237n27;
  racially based, 102, 124; Russian
  and Soviet, 56, 80–81, 137, 203,
  204; slurs, 240n9; and the Spanish
  Inquisition, 119, 131; and symbols,
  201; systemic, 106, 187; tropes
  of, 41, 55, 144, 181, 200, 209;
  in Ukraine, 203; under the Vichy
  regime, 168, 242n22; in Vienna,
  154–55; and violence, 4, 6, 47, 121,
  124, 179, 203; and Yiddish, 201;
  and Zionism, 207, 208
anti-statism, 176, 185, 190–93, 207,
  208, 210, 245n21, 249n60, 251n75
anti-Zionists, 14, 48, 57, 207, 209,
  225n6
anusim/anusot. See conversas/os
Aramaic, 198–99
Arendt, Hannah, 12, 89–113, 156,
  157, 167; and alienation, 22, 45,
  89, 91, 92, 97, 98, 110, 112; and
  antisemitism, 21, 90, 93, 94, 102,
  103, 106, 109, 117; arrest of, 5, 95;
  attacks on, 100, 173; biography of,
  93–96; and Chaplin, 108–9, 211n5,
  232n21; diaspora theorizing, 92; and
  Gurs internment camp, 95, 99, 140,
  166; and Heidegger, 94, 147; and
  Heinrich Heine, 107; and Holocaust,
  14, 99, 148, 236n16; and justice, 8,
  12, 22, 90, 92, 97, 101, 105, 112,
  165; and Kafka, 91, 106, 109–11;
  and Bernard Lazare, 107–8; and
  pariahs, 22, 89–92 passim, 106–13,
  136, 211n5, 230n6, 232n21;
  university affiliations of, 94, 95–96;
  and Zionism, 5, 14, 16, 22, 95,
  111, 156, 172
Arnstein, Fanny von, 164
Ashkenazis: critiquing Meir, 53; culture
  of, 197; German vs. "eastern," 93,
  159; hegemony of, 53, 72; and
  history, 23; and identity, 40, 130,
  238n36, 143; as immigrants, 72,
  120; language of, 197, 198; mass
  murder of, 55, 122; in Mexico, 118,
  120, 122, 234n8, 235n12; origins
  of, 198; in Palestine and Israel, 55;
  radical feminist and LBGTQ, 200;
  as reformers, 161; as Zionists, 199
Ashkenormativity, 9, 72
assimilation, 22, 92, 104, 110, 123,
  197, 231n11, 231n16
asylum seekers, 22, 92
attentat, 188
Atlantic slave trade. See slave trade,
  Atlantic
Auschwitz, 140, 229n3
Avrich, Paul, 177, 249n59
awe, 39, 41

Baden, 116, 140
Baden-Baden, 131, 166
Baker, Josephine, 169–70, 238n35
Bakunin, Mikhail, 184
Baltimore, 149, 153–54, 158–59, 162
Batnitzky, Leora, 126, 129, 130
beauty, 6, 16, 26, 33, 75, 107, 109,
  185, 191, 195, 202, 210, 218n33,
  219n41, 221n54, 247n38
Beck, Evelyn ("Evi"), xi, 13, 126,
  211n2
Ben-Gurion, David, 65, 72, 74, 85,
  228n30
Benhabib, Seyla, 6, 229n1
Berkman, Alexander, 179–81 passim
Berlin, 79, 97–98, 164–65, 181,
  230n8, 231n16

Berliner, Isaac, 132, 137
Bernstein, Charles, 171
binary thinking, 21, 50, 51, 62, 76, 87, 166, 193, 194; on gender, 8, 21, 50, 65, 66, 87, 194, 195, 212n7 (chap. 1)
binationalism, 207
Bính, 146, 239n4
bisexuality, 5; *see also under* Kahlo, Frida; *see also* LGBTQ+ identities
Black lesbian feminists, 195
Black lives, movement for, 187
Black Panthers, 53, 246n33
Black theorists and activists, 193
Bolsheviks, 203, 206
boundary smashing, 12, 15, 47
Brenner, Anna, 138
Breton, André, 138–40, 236n23, 237n34, 238n35
British Mandate of Palestine, 63, 64, 250n69
Bundism, 184, 185, 203, 206–9 passim

capitalism: critiques of, 6, 127, 179–80, 184–88, 190, 191, 202, 210; and Protestantism, 116, 123, 126, 127, 143–44, 236n19; rise of, 123
Caribbean diaspora. *See* diaspora: Caribbean
caste, 102
Chaplin, Charlie, 108–9, 211n5, 232n21
Christian antisemitism, 82–83, 99, 101, 120, 129, 137, 155, 173–74, 200, 203; *see also* Spanish Inquisition
Christian cultural imperialism, 13, 17, 18, 99, 120–30 passim, 144, 173–74, 194, 216, 221–21n56
Christian evangelical Zionism, 82–83
Christian gender understandings, 66, 67, 193, 196, 199, 229n41

Christian hegemony, 66, 101, 129, 173–74, 191, 250n69
Christian missionizing, 60, 119, 129, 221–22n56
Christian white supremacy, 124, 160
chronological clustering, 9–10
cisgendered normativity, 191, 196
cis/heteropatriarchy, 44, 66
citizenship and gender, US 70, 192, 227n22, 246n32
civil rights approaches, 193
Civil War, US, 153, 192
class-based theory, x, 3, 7, 11, 25, 48, 51, 73, 161, 173
class, socioeconomic, 161
Clinton, Hillary, 73
co-construction. *See* mutual constitutive theory and phenomena.
Cold War, 56, 76, 77, 80, 82, 85, 149
colonialism: and Arendt, 22; in binary stereotypes, 56, 62, 200; and cultural genocide, 103, 144; and diaspora, 1, 8, 10, 20, 22, 27–46 passim, 50, 51; and England, 4, 27–46 passim, 59, 216n26; European, 56, 60; and European state carving, 58, 59; and genocide, 10, 21, 23, 24, 26, 51, 64, 90, 103, 116, 134, 138; and Goldman, 183; and Israel, 4, 54, 72, 227n28; and Kahlo, 116; and Kincaid, 20, 27–46 passim, 76, 216n26, 218n37; and Latin America, 127; and Meir, 50, 51, 54, 72; among oppressive structures, 191, 193, 243n6; and Russia, 50; and Stein, 148; struggles against, 72; and Truong, 146, 239n3; *see also* settler colonialism; anticolonialism; de-colonial theory
communism, 5, 80, 95, 117–18, 125, 133, 134–35, 142, 181, 184, 185,

communism *(continued)*
189, 190, 192, 198, 203, 207, 209, 236n16, 237n27, 245nn24–25
community, transnational, 8, 10, 14, 21, 23, 25, 49, 85, 127, 162, 197, 202, 209
Cone, Claribel and Etta, 160
conquest, 33, 39–46 passim, 102, 103, 119, 120, 127, 215n19, 219n41, 221–22n56, 222–23n63
conversa/os, 119, 120, 137, 235n12
conversion, 18, 123, 235n12, 236n13, 238n36
cosmopolitans, rootless, 41, 173, 209
Cottin Pogrebin, Letty, 67, 224–25n3, 226n17
critical race theory, 3, 7, 11, 25, 48, 76, 90, 92; feminist, 92; Jewish, 9
crypto-Jews. *See* conversa/os
cultural fluency, 42
cultural imperialism, 17, 29, 42, 210; Protestant, 17, 23, 25, 116, 123, 126–29, 130, 143, 209

decentering, 152
de-colonial theory and action, x, 3, 7, 8, 11, 20–29 passim, 48–51 passim, 73, 76, 85, 86, 90, 173, 190, 228n33
democracy, 58, 59, 60, 89, 90, 93, 101, 104, 112, 113, 171, 183, 184, 187, 189, 191, 192, 205, 210, 233n27; *see also* liberal democratic theory
deportation, 49, 84, 138, 167–68, 180–81, 192, 227n22, 231n16, 240n8, 246n32, 249n63
Deutscher, Isaac, 16, 124–26, 136, 137
diaspora: African, 19, 28, 29, 33, 38, 44, 46, 212n2, 213n10, 216n23; and alienation, 22, 45, 91, 92, 112; binary model of, 21, 28, 50, 77, 78, 79, 84, 86, 87, 228n31, 228n33, 229n39, 229n41; Caribbean, 4, 40, 46; and colonialism, 4, 26, 27–46 passim, 51; home/away dichotomy: 33, 36, 38, 46, 50, 51, 71, 77, 78, 79, 99, 209, 228n33, 229n39; Jewish, 21, 22, 24, 25, 38, 41, 50, 51, 77, 86, 100, 102, 105, 178, 186, 208, 209, 215n23
diaspora theory, 8, 10, 20, 21, 28, 30, 34, 50, 51, 76, 77, 78, 79, 86, 87, 90, 91, 92, 112
diasporism, 178, 206
direct action, 186
disability rights, 5, 111, 191, 234n4, 237n28, 246n36
disassociation, 92
disenfranchisement, 33, 41
displacement, 22, 29, 57, 60, 90, 234n6, 240n8; literary, 151
diversity, 72, 183, 185, 193, 210; on campus, 158; among colonized people, 38; Jewish, 1, 19, 25, 26, 116, 124, 134, 144, 209; sexual, 246n37; as threat, 204
diversity theorizing, 7, 11, 191
Dobbs v. Jackson Women's Health Organization, 196
doikayt, 209
domination, 38, 76, 185, 191, 197; and Arendt, 92, 103, 105–6, 112; Christian, 125, 127, 130, 173; and colonialism/diaspora, 42, 43, 45; and Goldman, 186, 190, 193; and Kincaid, 32, 37, 215n19; male, 199
double consciousness, 42
double standards, 19, 72
Drancy concentration camp, 140, 168
Dreyfus, Alfred, 108
Drumont, Édouard, 107

East End, 204

education, US, 58–59
eastern Europe 40, 58, 62, 78, 130, 138, 167, 168, 198, 200, 203; *see also* Ashkenazis; European-heritage Jews
Eichmann trial, 14, 22, 96, 147, 172, 229n43, 232n23
Eloesser, Leo, 141
emancipation of Jews in Europe, 20, 91, 92, 100, 102, 105, 128, 148, 152, 154, 173, 206, 240n7; as a diaspora, 102, 104; and gender, 102; as genocidal, 103; through Zionism, 111
empire. *See* colonialism; England; Russian Empire; Soviet Union
England, 4, 14, 57, 58, 59, 60, 64, 71, 80, 125, 128, 166, 198, 205, 208; Kincaid on, 20, 27–46 passim, 216n26, 218n34; 218n37, 219nn39–40, 222n60, 223n64
enfranchisement, 192; *see also* disenfranchisement
equality: Arendt on, 22, 91, 92, 101, 103, 113; radical, 206
erasure, 19, 26, 39, 44, 92, 144, 220n46, 223n65
Eshkol, Levi, 65
European-heritage Jews, 151, 173, 197; *see also* Ashkenazis
exile, 35, 38, 40, 43, 46, 60, 102, 137, 234n11, 238n36; and Arendt, 22, 100, 102, 139; and Goldman, 6, 16, 24, 182, 189, 203, 204, 205, 249n61, 251n74; Jewish, 34, 59, 60, 61, 101, 102, 119; and Kincaid, 29, 44, 213n9, 217n30; Muslim, 119

fascism, 6, 139, 151, 171, 189, 205; opposition to, 5, 23, 115, 117, 133–35, 182, 189, 206, 237n27, 242n21, 244n21, 250n65

Faÿ, Bernard, 168–69
feminist bona fides, 12, 73, 74, 147
feminist theory, 1–30 passim, 50, 55, 69, 70, 73, 76, 79, 86, 90, 133, 143–47, 152, 164, 172, 177, 178, 199, 240n6, 246n34
Ferguson, Kathy, xi, 25, 190, 207
Fifteenth Amendment, 192
foreignness, 40, 46, 168, 241n19
forgetting, politics of, 43
Fort Barraux, 166
France, 5, 6, 22, 24, 59, 79, 91, 92, 94, 95, 107, 120, 139–40, 148–50, 160, 165–72 passim, 179, 182, 198, 205, 216n25, 230n4, 241n19, 245n27
franchise, 33, 41, 127, 192
French Revolution (1789), 102, 127, 128
freedom, 39, 42, 59, 70, 231n15; and Goldman, 6, 175, 183, 185, 191, 195, 202, 243n6; intellectual, 171; lack of, 89; and Liberalism/rights-based paradigm, 22, 91, 92–93 103–5, 112, 113, 192, 233n27, 246n36; and US, 85, 113, 152, 186
Freie Arbeiter Stimme, 198–99, 250n68
Freund, Gisèle, 142
Fry, Varian, 95, 236n23

gatekeeping, 15, 19, 23
Gay, Claudine, 158
Gaza, 17, 55, 56
gender: bending, 24, 68, 146, 147, 160, 172–73; binary, 8, 21, 50, 65, 66, 87, 194, 195, 212; identity, 65, 191; inequality, 192; and language, 198–200, 201; malleability of, 74; orientation, 2
genocidal phenomena: cultural, 8, 22, 29, 40, 42, 45, 91, 103, 105, 144, 165, 174; ideologies, 20; Nazi, 21,

genocidal phenomena *(continued)* 24, 56, 64, 81, 90, 104, 134, 136, 140, 148; settler colonialism, 1, 10, 20, 21, 22, 23, 24, 26, 51, 56, 64, 90, 116, 134, 136, 165
Germany, 5–6, 22, 79, 91, 93–95, 97–100, 102, 107, 116–17, 128–30, 138–39, 154, 166–68, 198, 236n15
German occupation of France, 139, 168
Godwin, William, 183
Goldman, Emma, 6, 12, 16, 24–25, 49, 62–63, 72, 84, 175–210; "Anarchism: What It Really Stands For," 175, 176; anarcho-feminism, 6, 190–96, 208; and anti-marriage work, 181, 185, 195; and anti-patriarchy, 6, 179, 186, 190, 210; and anti-statism, 176, 185, 190–93, 208, 210; arrests of, 180, 185, 246n36; and assassination attempt by, 180, 199; biography of, 178–82; in Canada, 179, 182, 196, 197, 205, 243n9; death of, 182; on capitalism, 6, 179, 180, 185, 186, 190, 191, 202, 210; deportation of, 70, 180–81, 192, 203, 227n22, 246n32; exiles of, 6, 16, 24, 182, 189, 203, 204, 205, 249n61, 251n74; as a feminist, 6, 24, 176, 177, 180, 190–96, 202, 208, 227n22; and free love, 180, 195, 247n37; and Henry Clay Frick, 180, 188, 199; influences on, 183–84, 203; and the "Jewish question," 204; marriages of, 63, 179, 181–82; and medical studies, 180; *Mother Earth*, 179, 199, 246n36; and mutual constitution focus, 190, 191, 193, 196; as nurse, 180, 194, 246n36; as an orator, 25, 85, 194, 199, 202, 226n20, 242n1; and Palestine, 16, 207; as proto-queer, 202; and reproductive justice, 194; and sexuality, 180, 195, 246–47n37; shattering binaries, 191, 194, 195; and Soviet Union, 84, 181, 204, 236n16; and suffrage, 72, 192, 227n24; and violence, 6, 62, 178–79, 180, 187–88, 194, 245n22; and wealth, 175, 195; and World War I, 180; and World War II, 205–6; and Yiddish, 85, 182, 196, 197, 198–200, 205, 226n20, 249n64
Gurs internment camp, 95, 99, 139–40, 166

Ha'am, Ahad, 107
Haganah, 49
Hamas, 56, 64, 158, 225n10
Harris, Kamala, 73
Haskalah, 200
Harvard Annex, 149, 156; *see also* Radcliffe
Harvard University, 31, 156; and antisemitism, 156–57; and racism, 158; and sexism, 157, 159; *see also* Radcliffe
Haymarket demonstrations of 1886, 179, 198
Hashomer Hatzair, 52
Havurot, 187
Hebrew, 69, 85, 110, 119, 198–99, 200, 217n30, 228n33, 248n52
hegemony, 42, 54, 116, 125; Ashkenazi, 53, 72; binary, 86; Christian, 66, 191, 250n69; colonial, 43; Jewish, 17; Protestant, 25; Western, 192, US, 192
Heidegger, Martin, 94, 147, 229n3
Heinrich Heine, 106, 107, 230n8
Herz, Henriette, 164, 231n13
heteronormativity, 6, 172

heteropatriarchy, 44, 50, 54, 66, 196
heterosexism, 76, 165, 172, 173, 191, 200
hierarchy, 8, 35, 66, 193; Arendt on, 89, 91, 104, 113; Goldman on, 191; Kincaid on, 44; and Stein, 160
Histadrut, 63, 64, 71, 228n31, 251n71; Council for Women Workers, 63
Hitler, Adolf, 94, 100, 131, 139, 205–6, 249n64, 250n65; Stein on, 171, 168–69, 241–42n21, 242n22
Holocaust, 60; and anarchists, 185; and Arendt, 14, 99, 136, 148, 233, 236n16; and the Bund, 206–7; and communists, 237n27; and Eichmann, 229; and gay men, 168; Israeli response to, 64; Jewish leadership during, 172; and Kafka, 110; and Kahlo, 13; and Kincaid, 212; and Meir, 50, 126, 229; refugees from, 57, 185; Sephardi Jews targeted in, 122; start of, 134, 139; and Stein, 24, 148, 160, 166; survivors of, 52, 142; symbols of, 201; and Yiddish, 196; and Zionism, 14, 126
home place, 36–40, 43, 218n37; *see also* "over there"
homophobia, 58, 172, 190, 200, 210, 243n6; against Jewish women, 145, 165; Nazi, 168
Hoover, J. Edgar, 180–81
Hovevei Tsiyon, 107

identity politics, 15, 125, 191
immigrants/immigration: to France, 167; German vs. eastern European Jewish, 84, 153, 159; to Israel/ Palestine, 49, 64, 71, 72–73; leftist, 62; to Mexico, 127, 138, 235n12; to US, 77, 92, 128, 151, 152–53, 179, 180, 192, 200; to Vienna, 154–55; *see also* migrants; refugees
Immigration Act of 1903, 181
imperialism, 29, 42, 80, 85, 119, 127, 200; cultural, 17, 18, 23, 29, 42, 86, 91, 116, 123, 126, 128, 143, 209, 210; *see also* colonialism
indigenous peoples: Antiguan, 31; and Christianity, 200; Jews as, 197; Mexican, 5, 116, 136; Palestinian, 126; in US 59, 191
inequality, 91, 109, 187, 192
injustice, 92, 101, 109, 112, 176, 183, 203, 216n24, 223n68
Inquisition. *See* Spanish Inquisition
insider/outsider status/perspective, 7, 126; *see also* outsiders
International Society for the Study of African Jewry (ISSAJ), ix, 27
intersectionality. *See* mutual constitution theory
invisibility, 17, 39; *see also* erasure
Iran, 56, 82
Islamophobia, 58, 158, 243n6
Israel, 14, 31, 46, 47–87 passim, 121, 130, 207, 209; collectivism in, 184; critiques of, 126, 184; Declaration of Independence, 59; and de-colonization, 21, 60, 77; and gender, 199; history of, 47–87 passim, 208; languages in, 59, 69, 85, 199, 248n52; leadership of, 4, 20–21, 208; as legitimizing Jewishness, 19; radical democracy in, 184; relationships with Global South, 21, 50, 55, 57, 60, 61; relationship with Iran, 56; relationship with Palestinians, 14, 48, 49, 53–54, 57, 60, 72, 126; relationship with the Soviet Union, 56, 79–82; relationship with US,

284 | Index

Israel *(continued)*
  56, 58, 82–83, 86; as secular, 57–58, statist critique of, 185
Israel-Hamas War of 2023–24, 17, 56, 64, 158, 225–26n10

Jaspers, Karl, 94, 229n2
jazz performers, 167
Jew-ing, 145–74
Jewish Agency, 54, 71
Jewish/Arab collaboration, 57
Jewish autonomous movements, 206, 250n66; *see also* Zionism
Jewish communal life, 16, 18, 41, 103, 104, 164, 186, 187; as anarchic, 208–9; and Arendt, 5, 95; and identity, 124; and Stein, 15
Jewish critical race theory, 9, 22
Jewish diaspora. *See* diaspora: Jewish
Jewish emancipation. *See* emancipation of Jews in Europe
Jewish feminist political theory, 2, 3, 6, 7, 13, 22, 175
Jewish gatekeeping/marginality, 15, 237n32
"Jewish lobby," 82
"Jewish question," 102, 112, 113, 157, 204, 231n14
Jewish refugees, 49, 57, 64, 71, 73, 187, 206, 208
Jewish theory, 3, 22, 25, 28, 30, 77, 206–10
Jewish women's groups, 161
Jews and Judaism in Black Africa and its Diasporas Conference, 27
Jews, Ashkenazi and racial identity in America, 154
Jews for Racial and Economic Justice (JFREJ), 125, 248n55
Jews, Ladino-speaking, 57, 122
Johns Hopkins, 158–60
justice, 1, 3, 4, 7, 8, 10, 12, 16, 22, 26, 32, 38, 41, 46, 48, 49, 54, 65,
  90, 92, 97, 101, 105, 109, 111–23, 125, 161, 165, 175–76, 183, 191, 208, 210, 213n14, 222n61, 223n68, 232n19

Kafka, Franz, 91, 106, 109–11
Kahlo, Frida, 5, 12, 13, 14, 23, 115–44, 182; affairs of, 117, 137–38, 238n35, 247n48; and antifascism, 5, 23, 115, 133, 134, 135; and antisemitism, 5, 115, 123, 133, 134, 135, 144; biography of, 116–18; and la Casa Azul, 116, 136, 137, 141, 143; and communism, 5, 117, 118, 133, 134, 135, 142, 189, 236n16; death of, 116, 143; and Diego Rivera, 12, 117, 118, 133, 134, 137, 138, 141, 142, 236n16, 236n21, 238n36, 238n39; and disability, 5, 117, 132, 138, 140–41, 134n4, 237n28; exhibits of, 15, 115, 130, 133, 134, 136, 138–43 passim, 234n2, 234n6, 136n20, 238n37; financial struggles, 117; and Holocaust, 166; Jewish aspects of, 13, 14, 16, 17, 23, 115–16, 118, 121–25, 128, 130–44, 209, 211, 233n1, 234n6; library, 133–36; and *Mexicanidad*, 5, 23, 116, 117, 136; *Moses*, 133, 142; *My Grandparents, My Parents, and I,* 130, 131, 132, 137, 138, 233n1; sexuality of, 5, 237n28; *What the Water Gave Me,* 138; *Without Hope,* 132–33
Kahlo, Guillermo/Wilhelm, 116, 118, 121, 127, 128, 130, 132, 136, 143, 233n1, 235n12
Kaunas/Kovno, 6, 178
Kaye/Kantrowitz, Melanie, 77–78, 125, 126, 201, 251n73
Kibbutz movement, 207
Kibbutz Merhavia, 52, 63, 74
Kibbutz Revivim, 63

Kincaid, Jamaica, 8, 10, 20, 27–46, 76, 79, 98; and anticapitalism, 31; and awe, 39, 41; biography of, 30–31; *At the Bottom of the River*, 31, 212n6, 218n33; and co-construction, 28, 51; and colonization, 20, 27–46 passim, 78; and diasporas, 20, 27–46 passim, 78; and England, 27–45 passim, 219nn39–40, 223n64; as a Jew, 4, 18–19, 29, 31, 37, 41, 212n2, 213n10, 217n29; and Langston Hughes Medal, 31; marriage, 31; methodology, 32–33; *Mr. Potter*, 212n2, 213–14n14, 215n22, 217n31, 218–19n38, 220n46, 222n61; "On Seeing England for the First Time," 20, 27, 28, 32, 34, 38, 39, 41, 43, 45, 46; *A Small Place*, 31, 214n17, 216n24, 219n39, 219n41, 223n64
Klezmer music, 201
Kristallnacht, 139
Kronstadt Rebellion, 181
Kropotkin, Peter, 183–84
Kyiv, 4, 61

Labor Party (Israeli), 48, 52, 65
laborers, 32–33, 43, 194, 215
labor issues, 72, 73, 180, 215
labor movement, 4, 16, 61–62, 69, 188, 198, 206
labor Zionist movement, 4, 61, 63, 69, 184, 207, 251
Labour Party (British), 48
Lamba, Jacqueline, 138, 139, 140, 238n35
Lazare, Bernard, 106, 107–8
Levy, Julien, 138–39, 236n23, 237n33, 238n36
LGBTQ activism, 194, 195, 246n36
LGBTQ identities, 76, 168
liberal democracy, 89, 91, 101, 112–13, 190, 193, 208, 233n27; theory, 102

Liberalism, 17, 18, 90, 91, 101, 103–4, 105, 126–27, 129, 204, 206, 208, 227n26, 236n19
liberals, 57, 101
liberation, 4, 39, 41, 92, 103, 109, 112, 166, 175, 176, 177, 180, 193, 195, 201, 206, 210, 229n2
Lithuania, 6, 178, 206
Linke Fligl, 201
Lorde, Audre, 195, 246n33
Lyonne, Natasha, 47, 51, 75

Magnes, Judah Leib, 156
Malcolm, Janet, 170
Mapai, 65
Mapam, 52
marginalization, 15, 18, 32, 33, 38, 45, 67, 73, 76, 89, 101, 103, 105–6, 118, 136–37, 147, 158, 220n46, 221–22n56, 233n27; normativized, 11
marriage: critiques of, 181, 185, 195; same-gender, 193
Marso, Lori, 25, 97, 195, 211n1, 242n1, 246n34
Marx, 175–76, 184
Marxism, 125, 184, 187
Meir, Golda, 4, 16, 21, 47–88, 161; approval ratings of, 51; as ambassador, 64, 76, 79–82, 85; as anticolonial, 21, 50, 54, 60, 87; attitudes toward Mizrahis, 48, 53, 55, 73; biography of, 61–65, 68–69; compared to Emma Goldman, 21, 49, 62, 63, 84, 85, 161, 192, 203; compared to Margaret Thatcher, 48, 49, 54; death of, 65; feminist gatekeeping of, 12, 21, 48–49, 67, 71, 73, 86, 225n3; as foreign minister, 4, 60, 65, 85, 228n30, 229n43; and gender, 4, 47, 49, 50, 51, 52, 54, 63, 65, 66, 67, 68, 70, 72, 74, 75, 76, 78, 80, 86, 87, 90,

Meir, Golda *(continued)*
192, 225n3, 226n17, 229n41; and Histadrut, 63, 64, 71; and housing work, 72–73; as inspiration, 47, 51, 53, 54, 71, 75; and kibbutzim, 4, 52, 63, 67, 74; and languages, 4, 64, 69, 79, 85, 226n20, 228n33; and linguistic inclusiveness, 73; marriage of, 62, 63, 67, 70, 74, 75, 86, 226n12; meeting with Abdullah, 74, 228n29; memories about, 52–53, 54; as minister of labor, 4, 65, 72, 74; motherhood, 63, 67, 74, 75, 83, 86; and 1973 war, 225n10, 226n10; and Palestinians, 48, 49, 53, 54; and Poalei Zion, 60, 70, 83; and poverty work, 73; as prime minister, 4, 20–21, 47, 48, 51, 65, 66; racism of, 49, 53, 54, 73; and refugees, 49, 64, 71, 73; sexuality of, 63, 67, 74, 75, 86; shattering binaries, 8, 47, 50, 51, 65, 68, 72, 79, 86, 87; shoes of, 53, 67; as socialist, 72, 73, 161; as speaker, 4, 64, 69, 85; US ties of, 64, 71, 82–86; and women, 68, 71, 73, 75; and worthiness debate, 48–49, 71, 225n3
Mendelssohn Hensel, Fanny, 165
Mendelssoh, Moses, 129, 236n23
Merhavia *See* Kibbutz Merhavia
methodology, 2, 21, 32, 172, 191, 196
Mexicanidad, 5, 23, 116, 117, 136
Mexico, 13, 116–44 passim; antisemitism in, 119, 122, 132, 234–35n11; as Catholic, 123, 124, 127; history of, 120; and immigration, 116, 120–22, 127, 130, 132, 138, 234–35n11; Jewish community in, 118, 123, 127, 130, 135; Jewish history in, 119, 120–22, 234–35n11, 234n12; settler-colonial history, 58
Mexico City, 5, 120, 122, 123, 127, 130, 131–32, 135, 136, 234n12
Middle Ages, 101
migrants, 92; *see also* immigrants; refugees
militarism: Goldman's opposition to, 6, 179, 186, 190, 191, 208, 210, 245n22; Kafka's opposition to, 110; and Meir, 54
Misrachi, Alberto, 136
Mizrahis, 9, 48, 49, 55, 57, 72, 73
Modernism, 9, 132, 147, 152, 236n23
Modetti, Tina, 117, 234n2
Moscow, 80–81, 82, 85
multi-disciplinary work, 7
Munich Olympics massacre, 47
mutual constitutive theory and phenomena, 3, 7, 10, 11, 25, 28, 50, 65, 72, 127, 148, 190, 191, 204, 229n41; and oppression, 45, 65, 112, 148

National Council of Jewish Women (NCJW), 161
nationalism, 80, 102, 121, 125, 189, 204
Nazi Party, 94, 95, 132, 134
Nazis and Nazism: among Allies, 205; and Arendt, 5, 22, 79, 93, 95, 98–99, 102, 103, 104, 148; and Goldman, 206; and Heidegger, 94; and Kahlo, 13, 23, 115, 123, 133–35; and Kristallnacht, 139; and Ladino culture, 57, 122; and Meir, 49; in Mexico, 121, 122, 131–32; and Palestine politics, 57; resistance to, 237n27; settler-colonialism of, 56, 104; and Stalinism, 125; and Stein, 5, 148–52 passim, 165,

169–70, 172; targeting Black US citizens, 167; targeting gay men, 168; targeting Jews, 13, 60, 94, 98–99, 104, 119, 122, 124, 129, 131, 134, 139, 140, 166, 167, 197; trials, 14, 229; and US citizens, 167; and Vichy, 166; and Yiddish, 57
New York City, 5, 6, 31, 40, 61, 63, 78, 96, 117, 130, 141, 179, 189, 198, 204
1973 war, 47, 48, 51, 53, 225–26n10
normalizing, 11, 12
normativization, 6, 45, 66, 171, 178, 187, 191, 196, 210; Ashkenazi, 9; see also Ashkenormativity

Oakland CA, 155–56
Obergefell v. Hodges, 193
Occupy Wall Street, 184, 187
October 7, 2023, 14, 16, 56, 60, 63, 225–26n10
oppression: from binary thinking, 87; colonial, 40, 41, 44, 45, 46, 215n19; of diaspora, 41, 43, 50, 64, 86; gender-based, 190, 192, 227n24; homophobic, 190; see also homophobia; of Jews, 4, 35, 55, 64, 78, 79, 108, 111, 120, 122, 132, 208; justifications given for, 40, 42; of Mizrahis, 53; mutually constitutive, 45, 112, 177–78; of pariahs, 108, 111; patriarchal, 200; political, 109; racist, 190; and Russian Empire, 77, 78; of subjectivity, 160; structural/systemic, 6, 65, 179, 188, 191, 195; in US, 183; see also abject groups; antisemitism; Nazis and Nazism; subjection and subjugation; racism
organizations: anarchist, 188; Jewish, 14, 16, 55, 95, 118, 123, 155, 161, 162, 172, 208, 209, 235n12; Jewish women's, 67, 71, 72; political, 95, 155, 161, 209, 226n14, 251n75; women's, 70, 74, 161, 162; Zionist, 14, 16, 55, 67, 95, 208, 250n68
orthodoxy, 6, 23, 116, 123, 151, 178, 210; Eastern, 130
Ostjuden, 93–94
Ottoman Empire, 4, 23, 55, 57, 120–21, 127, 130
outsiders, 7, 89, 92, 106, 136
"over there" place, 36–40, 42, 46; see also home place

pacifism, 180, 226n12, 245n22
Palestine: and Arendt, 5, 95, 156; and anarchists, 185, 207, 250; British Mandate of, 63, 64; conflict with Israel, 54, 56; and Goldman, 16; Jewish life in, 55, 77, 120, 121; and Jewish refugees, 57, 64, 71, 75, 95, 208; and Kafka, 110; and Meir, 4, 55, 64, 77, 227; Partition Plan for, 80; pre-1948, 4, 120, 121, 207; post-1948, 54, 56; see also Yishuv
Palestinians: and Arendt, 14, 22, 156; and binational solution, 156; casualties in 1973, 48; criticism of Israeli/Zionist response to, 22, 126; critiques of Jewish women's organizations, 72; and Meir, 47, 48, 49, 53, 54; refugee crisis of, 60; subject to hate, 158; supporting Jewish refugee settlement, 57
pariahs, 22, 89–92 passim, 106–13, 136, 211n5, 230n6, 232n21
Paris, 5–6, 13, 22, 95, 98, 99–100, 107, 117, 139–40, 146, 149–51, 155–56, 162–63, 166–68, 182
Paris Commune, 189, 245n24
particularism, 204

partition plan, 14, 80
parvenu?e.s, 21–22, 89–92 passim, 102, 105–6, 109–13, 136, 211–12n7, 230n6, 233n25
patriarchy: in binary pairings, 62; in England, 58; heteropatriarchy, 44, 50, 66, 172, 173; Jewish, 17, 18, 164, 172, 173, 199; in language, 145; opposition to, 6, 179, 186, 190, 196, 200, 210, 242n21; as perspective, 25, 48, 86, 191; systems, 48, 226n16; in traditional cultures, 17, 18, 58, 74, 164, 199; white supremacist, 44
personal-as-political methodology, 2
Pioneer Women, 71, 75, 83
Poalei Zion, 60, 70, 83
Pogrebin, Letty Cottin. *See* Cottin Pogrebin, Letty
pogroms, 56, 78, 139, 203, 204, 206, 229n40, 249nn58–59
political-as-personal methodology, 21, 101, 195
Portuguese Inquisition, 120, 235n13
postcolonialism, 4, 28, 30, 34, 60
poverty, 30, 61, 63, 73, 77; *see also* abject groups
power dynamics, 30, 33, 36, 37, 40, 46, 54, 72, 101, 109, 110, 119, 179, 186, 187, 191, 208, 229
power over, 8, 37, 76, 109, 179, 183, 185, 190, 191, 195, 208, 210, 213n12
praxis, 125, 188, 191, 193, 208
propaganda of the deed, 188, 208
Protestant cultural colonization. *See* cultural imperialism: Protestant
Protestantism, 25, 123, 129; conversions to, 98, 236n15, 238n36
Protestant political ideas, 127, 128, 130, 236n19
Protestant Reformation, 126

Protestants, 152

queer gender theory, 50, 74
queer theory, 3, 7, 21, 25, 48, 74, 76
quotas, 71, 157

rabbis, 17, 55, 124, 161
racism, 50, 53, 54, 58, 73, 121, 173, 190, 191, 200, 210, 243n6
Radcliffe, 149, 156–58
Red Vienna, 189
Reform Movement (Judaism), 160
refugees: in Israel/Palestine, 49, 57, 71, 73, 95, 207, 208, 250n69; Jewish, 16, 47, 50, 57, 62, 71, 77, 95, 99, 124, 138, 182, 187, 198, 203, 204, 205, 206, 207–8, 238n36; and marriage, 95, 182; in Mexico, 124; Palestinian, 60; in US, 47, 50, 77, 92, 170, 179, 182, 187, 192, 198, 203, 204; from World War II, 57, 71, 95, 138, 207, 238n36
Reiss, Lionel, 134
religious tolerance, decree of, 120, 127
resistance, 29, 32, 46, 133, 144, 186, 189, 191, 197; anti-Nazi, 133, 134, 169, 170, 171, 237n27
rights-based paradigm, 190, 192, 193
Ring, Jennifer, 6, 64, 96, 172, 230n6
Rivera, Diego, 12, 117–18, 119, 126, 128, 133, 134, 137, 138, 141, 142
Rochester, NY, 6, 179
Rosenshine, Annette, 163
rootless cosmopolitans, 41, 173, 209
Russian Empire, 6, 62, 68, 77, 78, 81–82, 85, 93, 178, 240n8; antisemitism in, 47, 56, 57, 70, 77, 78, 79, 203, 229n40; as colonial, 50; revolution in, 84, 206

Sacco, Nicola and Bartolomeo Vanzetti, 182

Salonnières, 8, 22, 98, 149, 151, 162
salons, 2, 5, 10, 24, 98–99, 129, 146, 149, 150, 151, 155, 156, 160, 162–65, 230n8, 231n12
sameness paradigm, 11, 91, 103
segregation, 28, 59, 153, 206
self-determination, 14, 22, 42, 58, 111, 128
Sephardis: as "aristocrats," 153; in Holocaust, 57; in Israel, 55; in Mexico, 23, 118, 120, 121, 122, 130, 136, 235n12; notable, 135, 156; origins, 118; thinking with, 9; women, 161; in the US, 152; and Zionism, 55, 62
settler colonialism, 54, 58, 103; genocidal: 1, 10, 20, 21, 22, 23, 24, 26, 51, 56, 64, 90, 116, 134, 136, 165; and Zionism, 54, 207
sexual freedom, 6, 180, 185, 190, 191, 193, 195, 210, 246n36
sexuality. *See under* Goldman, Emma; Kahlo, Frida; Meir, Golda; Stein, Gertrude; *See also* LGBTQ+ identities
slavery, 17, 59, 183, 188, 215n19, 222n60, 223n70
slave trade, Atlantic, 27, 59–60, 119, 152, 153, 158, 213n10
smallness, as feeling, 41
social transformation, 4, 46, 91, 187, 192, 196, 245n25
solidarity, 1, 22, 142, 182; Jewish, 71, 81, 125, 134; multicountry, 72; women's, 227n26
Soviet Union: antisemitism in, 56, 80–81, 137, 203, 204, 248n52; anarchists in, 84, 184; centralization in, 84, 184, 204; Goldman in, 84, 181, 204, 236n16; and Israel, 56, 64, 79–82, 85; Jews in, 80–83, 200, 228n33, 237n27; and Kahlo, 134; and Spanish Civil War, 189, 245n26; and Trotsky, 137
Spanish Civil War, 141, 182, 189, 245n26
Spanish Inquisition, 23, 30, 60, 118–19, 120, 124, 131, 133, 135, 142, 152
spirit/body dichotomy, 194
Stalin, Joseph, 79–80, 82, 84, 134, 242n22
Stein, Gertrude, 5–6, 15, 23–24, 129, 140, 145–74, 180; biography of, 149–51; and antisemitism, 151, 156, 157, 159, 173, 174, 242n22; cancellation campaign against, 165, 170–71; and collaboration debate, 149, 166, 169–72; education of, 149, 154, 155, 158–59; and Faÿ, 150, 169–70; as gender bender, 24, 146, 147, 148, 152, 160, 165, 172, 173; as lesbian, 6, 24, 145, 146, 147, 148, 149, 160, 165, 166, 171, 172, 173; and linguistic innovation, 145, 146, 150; "Miss Furr and Miss Skeene," 145; *The Mother of Us All,* 150, 171; in Nazi-occupied France, 165–73; as psychoanalyst, 163; relationship to Vichy regime, 6, 24, 148, 150, 166, 167, 169–72, 238n35, 242n22; salons of, 24, 142, 146, 150, 151, 160, 162–64; *Wars I Have Seen,* 150, 166
Stein, Leo, 149, 150, 151, 153, 157, 159, 163
Stein, Sarah, 162, 163
subjectivity, 151, 160 171
subjection/subjugation: of colonized subjects, 27–46 passim, 146, 224n74, 218n37; gender-based, 157, 165, 190, 193; of Jews, 99, 105, 125, 165, 168; *see also* abject groups; colonial experience, Nazis

subjection/subjugation *(continued)* and Nazism; oppression; segregation; settler colonialism; slave trade, Atlantic; Spanish Inquisition; Vichy regime
suffrage, 72, 160, 161, 162, 192, 227n24
suspect status, 7, 67, 70, 108–9, 147, 201, 212n7
syncretism, 42

texts as cultural signifiers, 29, 41, 46
theorizing/theory. *See* class-based theory, critical race theory, de-colonial theory, Jewish theory
thinking with, 1–24 passim, 28, 53, 58, 60, 61, 90, 92, 112, 125, 209, 211n3; defined, 2
Thrace massacre, 121
Tikkun Olam, 50
Toklas, Alice B., 5–6, 24, 140, 145, 146, 147, 149–71 passim, 239n4
Toro, Alfonso, 132–33
Toronto, 6, 182
trans identities and approaches, 9, 17, 54, 67, 76, 248n54
transnationalism, 209
transphobia, 76, 173, 210, 243n6
Tronto, Joan, 71, 73, 227n25
Trotsky, Leon, 137, 138, 141
troubling of categories, 3, 11, 13, 15, 21, 228n33
Truong, Monique, 146–47, 239n3
2023–2024 Israel-Hamas war, 17, 56. *See also* October 7, 2023

upper class, 104, 161, 238n36
USSR See Soviet Union

Varnhagen, Rahel, 8, 22, 90, 92, 96–105, 107, 113, 123, 128, 129, 136, 137, 149, 164, 165, 230nn7–8, 230–31n10, 231nn11–12, 231n14, 232n22
Versailles, Treaty of 1919, 58
Vichy regime, 6, 24, 139, 148, 150, 166–72, 238n36, 242n22
Vienna, 98, 149, 154–55, 164, 180, 238n36, 240n8, 245n25; Red, 189

Wagner-Martin, Linda, 169–70
Weber, Max, 113, 185, 236n19
white supremacy, 44, 55, 180, 193, 245n21
Will, Barbara, 170
women's leadership, 64, 67, 86, 176, 190
women's organizations, 70, 74, 161, 162; Jewish, 67, 71, 72, 161
working class Jewish women, 161
World War II, 6, 13, 81, 110, 122, 134, 139, 149, 150, 154, 165–71, 204, 240n8; and Zionism, 126, 185
World Zionist Organization, 64

xenophobia, 192

Yiddish, 69, 79, 85, 137, 161, 182, 196–202, 203, 205, 226n20, 228n33, 247nn43–48 passim, 248n52, 248n55, 249n64, 250n69; as victim of Nazis, 57
Yishuv: anarchists in, 189, 207, 251n71; labor movement in, 207; Meir's leadership of, 4, 47, 71, 242–43n2; strategies compared to present, 64
Yom Kippur / Ramadan War (1973 war), 47, 48, 51, 53, 225–26n10
Youth Aliyah, 5, 95

Zalkind, Yankev-Meyer, 250n69
Zion/diaspora dichotomy, 38, 51, 77, 209

Index | 291

Zionism: alternatives to, 128, 207, 209; and anarchists, 185, 189, 207, 250n68; as anticolonial, 57, 60, 207; and Arendt, 5, 11, 14–15, 16, 22, 95, 172; Christian, 83; and colonialism, 62; and diasporic "over there," 38; diversity within, 4, 55, 207, 208, 209; and *doikayt*, 209; and Goldman, 16, 176, 203; and Holocaust changing views towards, 126, 185; and Holocaust refugees, 52, 57; and Hovevei Tsyion, 107; and Israeli Declaration of Independence, 59; and Kafka, 110; and Kahlo, 126; Labor Zionism 4, 48, 61, 69; and language, 197, 199, 228n31; and Lazare, 108; and Magnes, 156; and Meir, 4, 12, 16, 47–48, 50, 51, 61, 67, 68, 69, 73, 77, 78, 79, 83, 86, 161, 228n38; non-(ethno-)statist, 14, 156, 207, 244n18; organizations for, 14, 16, 55, 67, 95, 208, 250n68; and the Ottoman Empire, 121; as revolutionary, 60, 73; as self-determination for Jews, 128; Sephardi and Mizrachi involvement in, 55, 62; and settler-colonialism, 207; socialist, 16, 52, 68, 77, 85, 161, 243n9; and the Soviet Union, 56, 80, 85, 228n37; Western Jewish elite opposition to, 55–56, 84

www.ingramcontent.com/pod-product-compliance
Ingram Content Group UK Ltd.
Pitfield, Milton Keynes, MK11 3LW, UK
UKHW041926140426
5217IPUK00014B/336